ROSE IS A ROSE IS

T0383292

GERTRUDE STEIN

by the same author

SQUARE HAUNTING:
FIVE WOMEN, FREEDOM AND LONDON BETWEEN THE WARS

GERTRUDE STEIN

AN AFTERLIFE

FRANCESCA WADE

faber

First published in 2025
by Faber & Faber Ltd
The Bindery, 51 Hatton Garden
London ECIN 8HN

Typeset by Sam Matthews

Printed and bound using 100 per cent renewable energy
by CPI Group (UK) Ltd, Croydon CRO 4YY

A CIP record for this book
is available from the British Library

ISBN 978–0–571–36931–7

Printed and bound in the UK on FSC® certified paper in line with our continuing
commitment to ethical business practices, sustainability and the environment.
For further information see faber.co.uk/environmental-policy

Our authorised representative in the EU for product safety is
Easy Access System Europe, Mustamäe tee 50, 10621 Tallinn, Estonia
gpsr.requests@easproject.com

2 4 6 8 10 9 7 5 3 1

Be is for biography.

Gertrude Stein,
The Geographical History of America

CONTENTS

CONTROVERSIAL FIGURE

ECCENTRIC AUTHORESS

Gertrude Stein Now Puzzling God

THE MAMA OF DADA

HIGH PRIESTESS OF THE CULT
OF UNINTELLIGIBILITY

Remarkable Egotist

Sibyl of Montparnasse

LITERARY FREAK

IS GOING GAGA

TYPHOID MARY OF PROSE STYLE .

L'ogresse de la rue de Fleurus

PROLOGUE PROLOGUE PROLOGUE PROLOGUE PROLOGUE PROLOGUE PROLOGUE PROLOGUE PROLOGUE PROLOGUE

*S*he came to Paris, she said, to kill the nineteenth century. Her weapons were a pencil and a supply of softcover notebooks, her targets dullness and cliché. She chopped off her long coils of hair and dispensed with punctuation; she spent her mornings asleep and her nights writing furiously, tossing loose scraps of paper to the floor as she went. She rubbed her head with both hands when she was excited, and sat with her knees planted far apart, taking up as much space as possible. She loved driving fast cars, especially through tunnels, and stepped out into roads without looking, long skirts flapping in the breeze. She was a hoarder, of papers, of words, of Catholic ornaments and antique figurines of kittens. Her favourite sound was a hooting owl, her favourite flowers were pansies and her favourite colour was salmon-pink. Her laugh, someone remembered, was 'like a beefsteak'. Stretched on a divan underneath her own Picasso portrait, Gertrude Stein was a myth and a monument, a larger-than-life figure whom friends and detractors viewed by turns with amusement, affection and alarm. She was at once a celebrity and an enigma: everyone knew she was famous, but no one was quite sure why.

'I have been the creative literary mind of the century,' she insisted, urging the reading public to 'think of the Bible and Homer think of Shakespeare and think of me'. Her work, spurred by her scientific background, asked questions that pushed language beyond its limits. How does perception work? How do words make meaning? What if writing set out not to describe the world, but to embody the very essence of people, places, objects, existence? But even as Stein gradually became a household name in her native America, her reputation was plagued by uncertainty. As her friend Thornton Wilder diplomatically put it, Stein pursued her aims 'with such conviction and intensity that occasionally she forgot that the results could be difficult to others'. Her writing, full of wordplay, non-sequitur and extended passages of repetition, confounded publishers, critics and readers. Bafflement soon became suspicion. Was Stein a genius, revolutionising a sterile literary tradition, or a self-important charlatan? A true experimenter who freed language from its formal constraints, or a pretender who knew nothing about the modern art she supposedly championed? An outcast, or the ultimate insider?

//

I came to Stein, first, through her legend. Like many, I'd absorbed the romantic nostalgia for the Golden Age of Twenties Paris. As a teenager my bedroom walls were adorned with posters for Montmartre cabarets; I'd seen Woody Allen's terrible film *Midnight in Paris*, in which Kathy Bates plays a matronly Stein cheerfully offering writing advice to a time-travelling screenwriter. And I'd read and loved *The Autobiography of Alice B. Toklas* – Stein's own contribution to that sepia-toned mythology. Written, with a wink, in the voice of her adoring partner, Stein's memoir tells the captivating story of her immersion in the city's bohemian world as the magnetic host of a starry salon, buying cheap canvases by Matisse and Picasso, befriending Ernest Hemingway and F. Scott Fitzgerald. Toklas, the book's ostensible narrator, watches on lovingly as Stein throws out witticisms that dazzle everyone around her, and triumphantly produces a succession of handwritten masterpieces. It's a deliciously intimate, teasing and very funny book, deservedly acclaimed as a classic – but I didn't yet know the circumstances under which it had been written. Because Stein had devised the book with an ulterior motive. In 1932, fed up with decades of mockery and poor sales of her avant-garde texts, Stein had crafted a self-portrait designed to draw in doubting readers and make the case for her 'real' work's importance – and, crucially, its pleasure. It was only half successful. The *Autobiography*'s popularity catapulted Stein (and Toklas) to international celebrity – yet threatened to submerge her in the very fictions she had created. Readers did go mad for Stein, just as she hoped, but the *Autobiography* cemented her public image as a personality rather than an artist; not a bold innovator, but a collector of other talents.

But one idea gave Stein hope. She had long believed that public recognition lags fifty years behind; that a truly radical artist could not expect to be appreciated in their own time. Those at the forefront of modern art, she wrote in 1926, 'are naturally only of importance when they are dead . . . the creator of the new composition in the arts is an outlaw until he is a classic'. In the last decade of her life, Stein began to set her sights on her posthumous legacy. 'I am working for what will endure, not for a public,' she wrote, adding that 'early setbacks aid the eventual greatness. Quick success is killing.' She began to send her papers – tranches of suitcases brimming with manuscripts, letters and notebooks – to the Yale University Library, to ensure that her final epitaph would be her work. She died, aged seventy-two, in July 1946, her status uncertain; the bulk of her writing was unpublished, and her popular image lingered as that of a sort of eccentric oracle, not a serious literary figure. But the Gertrude Stein Collection formed one of the most comprehensive archives in Yale's impressive holdings. Within months of its opening, a trail of scholars and biographers arrived to sift through this trove of clues and red herrings, seeking to unravel the enduring mysteries about the woman who remained, as one obituary put it, 'one of the least read and most widely publicised writers of her day'.

The more I learned about Stein, the more I was intrigued – and confounded – by her contradictions. I liked her indefatigable self-mythologising, her wry probing of genre and gender. Above all, I was drawn to her work – even if, at first, I didn't know what to make of it. Her monumental epic *The Making of Americans* – a family saga which morphs, over its thousand pages, into a history of 'everyone who ever was or is or will be living' – has acquired a dubious cult status; it's often rumoured to be 'unreadable'. It took me a long time to take the plunge and open it – but as soon as I did, I was hooked by its rhythms, eager to follow Stein's restless sentences as they quest towards conclusion. 'The business of an artist', she wrote, 'is to be exciting.' Stein renders words physical, sometimes beautiful ('What is a noun. A noun is grown with petals'), sometimes violent ('Prepositions are like burning paint'), always surprising, fresh and full of possibility.

Stein always believed she could win over even her fiercest critics. 'My sentences do get under their skin,' she chuckled – and I found that she was right. Stein's work defies traditional ways of reading. It's impossible, for one thing, to say what her texts are about. Her writing often starts from concrete source material – objects in her sightline, snippets of conversation, the people around her – and Stein evokes that material so deftly you can almost taste the Spanish cuttlefish, or luxuriate in the Majorcan breeze, or feel the whoosh of Isadora Duncan's whirling skirt. But her texts aren't so much *about* that ostensible subject matter: rather, they engage with the way words work together on the page, recasting everyday experiences and perceptions in surreal mutations of language. Stein left few clues to her work: she didn't keep a diary, and rarely discussed her writing in letters. 'I write to write,' she explained, impatiently – a statement, like many of Stein's, whose apparent flippancy masks a deep truth. Stein is less a writer in the conventional sense than a philosopher of language. Words were both her medium and her subject. To think with Stein as she interrogates their power and potential through cascades of rhythmic prose, I found, can be an intoxicating experience. Often, her texts start slowly, as if Stein is turning over thoughts in her mind, then gain momentum as she focuses in on a word or image, testing and stretching it with puns and soundplay before exploding it into a fresh direction. Her work is always about the conditions of its own creation: the process, to her, was more important than the finished text. She wanted each piece to preserve 'the intensity of the fight' that went into its making. The way to read Stein is to trust her: perhaps to say her words aloud, to savour the oddities of her phrasing and to resist the urge to explain what her writing means. But to read Stein's work like a code to be deciphered, I learned, is to set oneself up for serious frustration – and to miss the pleasures her work can offer.

//

Stein and Toklas at the rue de Fleurus, *c.*1922:
the cover image for the *Autobiography* (photo: Man Ray)

I first visited her archive – now held in the subterranean vaults of Yale's Beinecke Library – in the autumn of 2019. I wanted to pierce some of the myths: to see who Stein was when nobody was watching. As a public persona, she could be brash, capricious, arrogant, reactionary. 'There's good in her and there is downright evil,' wrote the novelist Richard Wright, who met her shortly before her death. 'I'm not used to seeing such things lying side by side in the same person.' But in the archive, the scraps and fragments of a storied life reveal a more vulnerable, contemplative Stein. Within the pages of the French children's exercise books in which she wrote, scrawling across the paper in pencil with just a few words to a line, drafts intermingle with shopping lists, doodles, addresses and telephone numbers, as well as loving dedications to Alice B. Toklas, silently excised from the typed versions of each text. Threaded through the archive – notes in the margins of manuscripts, punning lines dropped deep within poems ('I love my love with a b because she is peculiar') – is a complex love story, concealed even to those who knew Stein and Toklas as a couple. 'The private life is the life for me,' wrote Stein in 1912, five years after meeting Toklas, a fellow American transplant to Paris. These papers are the material remnants of forty years of shared domesticity: the vestiges of an intimacy Stein guarded as fiercely as she sought publicity for her writing.

They made an odd pair in those early days, walking around Paris: Toklas lithe in black silk, a cigarette nestled between her fingers, with high heels and a gold-tipped cane; Stein squat in her habitual brown corduroy gown, a rope round her middle and a stout staff clasped in her fist. Toklas had trained as a professional pianist, Stein cheerfully tapped out popular tunes on the white keys only. Toklas was a refined gourmand, while Stein was partial to hearty American classics until health problems ordained a diet of low-sodium gruel. Both grew up in California, both had lost their mothers at a young age, and both were utterly committed to the work of Gertrude Stein. It's impossible now to imagine either one without the other: even more impossible to conceive of Stein's enormous literary output without Toklas's almost fanatical devotion to her care.

Their image, as a couple, was one of Stein's most enduring creations. During Stein's lifetime, Toklas protected her from disturbance with a zeal some friends considered excessive: showing the door to visitors deemed to have overstayed their welcome, ending long-standing friendships on Stein's behalf. Toklas typed Stein's work, she proofread it, she set up her own publishing house to print it when no one else would touch it. And in the twenty-one years she lived on after Stein's death, Toklas dedicated her remaining energies to preserving her partner's legacy: to fighting dissenters like Stein's brother Leo, who derided his sister as a 'fake intellectual', and to cementing a narrative in which Stein was a saint, an angel, a genius. Between 1946 and her own death in 1967, Toklas received a stream of visitors, from young writers hoping to capture any lingering magic of the celebrated salon, to researchers fresh from stints in the Yale library, primed to disturb her memories with discoveries and discrepancies their time on the Stein trail had dislodged. The first Stein biographers were faced not only with a formidable wealth of documents but a moral minefield: they had to negotiate Stein's careful attempts to hide elements of her past she hoped to keep private, as well as their own anxieties about whether they had any right to defy her – and, more pressingly, Toklas's – wishes.

One particular visitor sparked my attention. I'd learned about Leon Katz from Janet Malcolm's 2007 book *Two Lives*, which told a story already famous in academic circles. In 1948, as a young doctoral student working among Stein's papers two years after her death, Katz had come across a cache of notebooks containing Stein's raw, unfiltered writings from her first decade in Paris, including early drafts of *The Making of Americans*, detailed character analyses of everyone in her orbit, and diary-like reflections on art, life and the 'struggle' – an oft-repeated word for Stein – of becoming a writer. Katz was convinced these notebooks held the keys to understanding a text that had perplexed readers for decades, and offered entirely fresh insights into Stein's mind during these formative years. Toklas, who had never seen these notebooks, agreed to an unprecedented collaboration. Over the freezing winter of 1952–3, Katz spent four months interviewing Toklas about her life with Stein, pressing her to untangle Stein's complicated web of reference and memory, and to embellish the notebooks' anecdotes with recollections of her own. Katz left Paris with material he claimed was dynamite – but never published the book he had planned. Fifty years later, Malcolm's attempts to meet him were thwarted, and the story she told was one of scholarly secrecy. 'Katz's notes of his interviews with Toklas in Paris', Malcolm concluded, 'remain locked in his possession – no scholar has ever seen them.'

Leon Katz died in 2017, and his papers were sold to the Beinecke Library, where they sit alongside Stein's own voluminous archive. I was the first researcher to examine them. As I sifted through the folders, overwhelmed by the accumulation of knowledge, I was looking, of course, for signs of the material Malcolm had been denied. Gold came in the form of a leather-covered notebook, into which Katz had scrawled during his sessions with Toklas, in the frantic handwriting of one struggling to keep up with the outpourings of spoken memories and hushed indiscretions. It became clear at once that this notebook contained a story – several stories – to be told. When Stein wrote *The Autobiography of Alice B. Toklas*, she smoothly elided years of self-doubt, erasing once-meaningful friendships from the record. But here was a counterpoint – an underside – to the official narrative. Though she was keen to forget it, the period of despair and self-questioning charted in her early notebooks sheds significant light on the swerve away from nineteenth-century realism which produced Stein's most distinctive and revolutionary writing. And Toklas's frank comments not only offer a further document of her absolute commitment to Stein and her work, but reveal a woman with her own private past, negotiating her position in a life devoted to another.

From that single leather notebook, my project soon expanded into a far larger enquiry – into the life and legend of Gertrude Stein, but also into the nature of biography, and the way literary history is made. I soon began to think of Stein's biography as a story in two parts. The first is the narrative she crafted carefully in her autobiographies, lectures and interviews, where her long struggle to find readers leads triumphantly to success, bolstered by the support of devoted and discerning champions who saw, as she did, the genius in her work. The second, filling in some of the first version's deliberate gaps, is a story that could only be told posthumously, taking account of the archive's secrets: the unpublished texts, the private jottings, the people – mostly women – Stein purported to have forgotten. These two stories mirror and complement one another: one cannot be told without the other.

Stein loved detective stories: during some stretches of her life she read at least one a day. She once referred to her readers as 'the witnesses of my autobiography', as if her book were a crime scene and her life a puzzle to be solved. 'Witnesses corroborate,' she wrote. They also contradict. As more and more voices enter Stein's narrative, she comes to seem less like the blank-faced figure Picasso painted, and more like a Cubist portrait: distorted, many-angled, brightly coloured, complex and human. The longer I worked on it, the more this project began to feel something akin to detective work. Biography, like detective fiction, tends to begin with a corpse – but Stein well knew that a writer's life does not end at death, if their work has the power to survive them. The first half of this book follows Stein from her childhood in Oakland to her death in Paris, as she created the work she fervently hoped would be recognised as a signature achievement of modern literature. The second half tells the story of her afterlife: the years in which her posthumous legacy was constructed, celebrated and contested, by all with a stake in the evolving legend – chief among them, Alice B. Toklas.

PART 1 LIFE

1 : OUT OF THE OLD WORLD

The run-down former piano factory at 13 rue Ravignan was an incongruous site for the birth of modern art and literature. Most days, over the winter of 1905–6, Gertrude Stein crossed Paris on the horse-drawn omnibus, then trudged up Montmartre hill to the small cobbled square. An unassuming entrance tucked in one corner led to a labyrinthine wooden building, where every slam of a door or clatter of a dropped bucket in the single shared toilet bled through the thin walls and resounded into the corridors. Inside Picasso's studio, both light and heat were drawn from a rusty cast-iron stove placed opposite the single bed. A stench of paint mingled with the distinctive scent of his dog, Gat; canvases were stacked deep against the wall, while the floor was scattered with pinched tubes of paint, fraying brushes and jerrycans oozing petrol.

In *The Autobiography of Alice B. Toklas*, Stein recalled posing for hours in a broken armchair while Picasso sat opposite her on a small kitchen chair, his forehead inches from his easel, brown and grey swirled on his palette. While he painted, she 'meditated and made sentences' in her mind. As the months passed, she watched Picasso's mounting frustration as he redid and scrubbed out her features, before reaching total impasse, painting out the entire head in anger, and vanishing to Spain. The next time they met, six months later, he silently presented Stein with the completed portrait. In the interval, Picasso's style had transformed. The original, naturalistic features were gone, and the face now resembled a sculptured mask, its features starkly outlined. She looks ageless, androgynous, out of time – and utterly assured in herself. When Stein protested that it didn't look at all like her – if anything, it bore a closer resemblance to the artist himself – he calmly replied, 'It will.'

When, in later life, Gertrude Stein was asked how her portrait came to be painted by the relatively unknown, twenty-four-year-old Pablo Picasso, she simply claimed that neither of them could remember. But – as was clear to visitors to her home, where she held court from a chair placed directly beneath her likeness – the painting became central to her sense of identity: 'For me,' she wrote in 1938, 'it is I, and it is the only reproduction of me which is always I, for me.' The aura of mystery around the sittings – which Stein, implausibly, numbered at eighty or ninety – turned the portrait, from its conception, into a myth. For Stein, it provided an origin story which would come to define her image, linking herself and Picasso indelibly as the two supreme geniuses of the twentieth century, in literature and in art. While Picasso was deep in the 'long struggle' of her portrait – inventing Cubism in the process – Stein was immersed in writing *Three Lives*, a trio of stories which she considered 'the first definite step away from the nineteenth century and into the twentieth'. There was, of course, another reason to foreground the connection. By the time Stein wrote the *Autobiography*, in 1932, Picasso's work was growing fast in stature, while hers languished in comparative obscurity. By representing their beginnings as intertwined, Stein was making a plea for their futures, too, to be equal.

//

Stein's tombstone proclaims that she was born, on 3 February 1874, in 'Allfghany': it's somehow fitting that this lifelong expatriate should have been laid to rest with the name of her hometown (Allegheny, Pennsylvania) doubly misspelled for perpetuity. Her uncle, Meyer Stein, was the first of his German Jewish family to leave their homestead in Weickersgrüben, a tiny farming village in northern Bavaria, and sail to Baltimore, landing in 1841. His parents and four of his eight siblings soon followed on a ship enticingly named the *Pioneer*, bringing the family – as Gertrude later put it – 'out of the old world into the new one'. Baltimore's Jewish population more than trebled in the Steins' first decade there; Meyer soon found commercial prosperity with a men's clothing shop, Stein Brothers – one of the first to sell clothes 'off the rack' – where Gertrude's father Daniel worked the shop floor as a teenager. Daniel met Amelia Keyser – like him, the child of German immigrants – through the local synagogue; they married on 23 March 1864, and their son Michael was born the next year. The couple planned to have five children, but after giving birth to Simon and Bertha, Amelia suffered two miscarriages. Thus the youngest Steins – Leo and Gertrude – grew up with the uneasy knowledge that their existence was contingent on the deaths of their elder siblings: an early brush with mortality, which haunted Gertrude all her life.

Before she was born, Gertrude's father and his brother Solomon left Baltimore for Allegheny, where they set up a second branch of the family clothing business, and built twin houses side by side. When Gertrude was a few months old, the partnership dissolved: the two sisters-in-law were no longer on speaking terms, tired of mediating bitter rivalries between their respective sets of young children and, especially, their husbands, whose contrasting temperaments made them totally incompatible as a business duo. Solomon, destined for a career in banking, moved his family to New York, while Daniel took his to Vienna, vaunting the benefits of a European education. Gertrude's memories of her earliest years were hazy: an impressive statue in the Schönbrunn Palace gardens, a taste of Austrian beer on her third birthday, a knowledge that as the adorable youngest, a 'round little pudding' known simply as Baby (a name she used throughout her life), her status in the family was elevated and secure. After four years in Vienna and one in Paris, they returned to Baltimore, where Uncle Meyer had now established a prominent banking house and was president of the local synagogue. But Daniel, an irascible figure prone to sudden changes of mind, was restless: he wanted distance from his and Amelia's large and overbearing families, and was eager to exploit the business opportunities he had heard were rife in California. The Steins settled in Oakland in 1879, when Michael was fourteen and Gertrude was five: the children enrolled in weekend Hebrew school, while Daniel began to invest in the city's fast-growing network of cable cars and street trolleys.

'It is better if you are the youngest girl in a family to have a brother two years older,' wrote Stein later, 'you go everywhere and do everything while he does it all for and with you.' As they grew up, Gertrude and Leo formed an inseparable unit, distinct from their elder siblings:

Michael too busy with his own hobbies to pay them much attention, Simon and Bertha scornful of their bookish interests. Gertrude was a dreamy child, much exercised at this time by the discovery that entire civilisations had once existed and vanished. Leo, painfully shy with outsiders but dominant at home, found his sister a willing disciple. They pored over the same books and magazines, skipped school to go to the cinema, and tramped miles through the hills – often camping out overnight – dissecting the characters of family and acquaintances and discussing literature (by age twelve, Gertrude later claimed, she had read all of Shakespeare's plays). But in 1884, her mother began to experience abdominal pain and exhaustion. Over the next four years, Amelia retreated more and more from family life. She died of cancer in July 1888, when Gertrude was fourteen. Gertrude – who loved psychologising others, but not herself – rarely discussed how she might have been affected by her mother's long illness and death, except for remembering the family was already used to doing without her by the time she died. But sixty years later, she recalled her life between age twelve and seventeen as 'the dark and dreadful days of adolescence, in which predominated the fear of death'. She had learned, at a formative age, that 'nothing is clear and nothing is sure, and nothing is safe'.

Both Gertrude and Leo remembered their mother as meek and self-sacrificing, ineffective at combating their father's aggression. Daniel Stein was a stern disciplinarian, harshly critical of his children's academic progress, table manners and future prospects. 'They never knew then', wrote Stein of a tempestuous father in her novel *The Making of Americans*, which she later described as a portrait of her own family, 'how the anger in him might drive him . . . when it might change in him to an outburst and then they never knew how far this burst would carry him'. The household collapsed into chaos after Amelia's death. Michael, who worked with his father at the Omnibus Railroad and Cable Company, was rarely around to defend his siblings, while Simon took odd jobs on local construction sites to avoid his father's wrath. Up to her mother's death, Gertrude had done well at school – an 1887 article in the *San Francisco Examiner* picked her out as an 'accomplished young miss' who was 'remarkably proficient' in all her classes, noting that the thirteen-year-old was 'the pet of her own household, and the favourite with her school companions'. But Gertrude's high school burned down in 1890, at which point she seems to have given up on formal education. Instead, she spent her days at the Mechanics' Institute Library and the Mercantile Library Association near the Golden Gate Park, reading through all the eighteenth-century literature she could find, and her evenings stalking the streets of East Oakland with Leo or a schoolfriend. Family mealtimes were abandoned when Bertha, who had followed her mother as manager of the home, gave up cooking, despondent at her father's criticism of her bungled efforts. Instead, Gertrude and Leo took to wandering through the city towards Michael's office, stopping at bookshops along the way, safe in the knowledge that he would stand them dinner if they had spent all their money by the time they reached him. Their father, who often stayed in his room for days, barely noticed they were gone. But one morning, three years after Amelia's death, Daniel didn't turn up to breakfast. His bedroom door was locked. Leo, aged nineteen, climbed through the window and found their father dead from a sudden stroke. 'Our life without a father began', recalled Gertrude forty years later, 'a very pleasant one.'

Michael, now the siblings' default guardian, set to assessing their father's accounts. As he gloomily unearthed more and more evidence of unpaid debts, he remembered hearing Daniel – who was full of brilliant plans but lacked the tenacity to carry them through – talk about a way to combine the separate lines of the San Francisco street railways into one consolidated business. Michael drew up a blueprint and took it to the railway magnate Collis P. Huntington, explaining frankly that none of his siblings seemed likely to earn money in the future, and he needed to find a way to support them all. Huntington, tickled and impressed, bought the idea and the franchise, effected the consolidation, and hired Michael as division superintendent. Michael used the significant profits from his sale to commission a local architect to build a block of duplexes in an up-and-coming part of San Francisco: soon, the rental income and the interest on Michael's stocks provided enough to afford each Stein an allowance of around $150 a month, meaning they could live – albeit modestly – without needing to earn money. Gertrude was grateful to her brother – a deeply reluctant but inspired businessman – for the rest of her life. He had shown 'extraordinary sympathy' for his sister's needs, Toklas later recalled, 'though he hadn't the faintest idea why her needs were such as they were'.

//

While Michael continued to work at the railway, and found employment for Simon there too, Gertrude, Leo and Bertha moved east in the spring of 1892. Gertrude and Bertha had been invited to live with their mother's sisters in Baltimore, and Leo was on his way to Harvard. Amelia's close-knit family were warm and welcoming: Gertrude found it strange moving from the 'internal and solitary and concentrated life' she had led in California to 'the cheerful life of all her aunts and uncles'. But even as she settled into their cosy home, Gertrude was looking to escape it. She saw her future aligned not with Bertha – whom she found uninteresting – but with Leo. Bertha had been willing to drop school and take care of the household, leaving Gertrude free to read and study just as Leo did. Only now, with their aunts eagerly matchmaking, did Gertrude face the fact that there was a gulf between the paths her life and her brother's were expected to follow. While Bertha was soon engaged to a local paper manufacturer, and preparing for a life of domestic duty, eighteen-year-old Gertrude began to research higher education establishments for women.

The Harvard Annex had been formed in 1879 by a committee of reformers determined – in the face of significant opposition within and beyond the university – to allow women access to education on equal terms with men. In 1894, the year after Gertrude enrolled, the Annex was officially chartered as Radcliffe College; female students were taught by Harvard faculty, and socialised freely alongside their male peers.

Gertrude lodged in a boarding house with a group of other women, and discovered – perhaps for the first time – how much she enjoyed conversation. Up to this point, her primary companions besides Leo had been characters in the novels she devoured in the corner of the San Francisco libraries. Now, she discovered that her peers were drawn to her, attracted by her infectious chuckle, her frequent exclamations of 'Great Jehoshaphat!', her bizarre hats and cheerful disregard for corsets, and her genuine curiosity about other people – if sometimes masked by her desire to prove herself always right.

Her aptitude for intellectual enquiry, meanwhile, was noticed by one of Harvard's most eminent professors, William James. Impressed by her performance in his junior philosophy class, James personally invited Stein – a watchful nineteen-year-old with an imperious manner – to join his seminar at the Harvard Psychological Laboratory. Psychology was a relatively new but fast-expanding field of study, and James was one of its leading theoreticians: his recent study *The Principles of Psychology* had been praised by Sigmund Freud. So a decade before she climbed the hill to Picasso's studio, Gertrude Stein spent her days in a very different

Gertrude and Leo Stein, *c.*1897

ferment of activity, where the walls were lined not with painted canvases but with glass specimen cases filled with wax models of the brain. Sessions in the laboratory were collaborative, with students encouraged to try out theories and use one another as guinea pigs. Under the supervision of James and his protégé Hugo Münsterberg, Stein began to conduct experiments designed to expand knowledge of the workings of the human mind.

'Her first real influence was William James,' wrote Toklas, many years later, to a student who had enquired after the origins of Stein's writing. 'He formed her mind, directed her path, before she was twenty, but left her free.' Stein's first experiments, made in partnership with a dashing graduate student named Leon Solomons, explored the ways in which perception of colour can be subjective. Next, Stein and Solomons turned to the question of how the brain pays attention; they devised a series of tests to study 'the process by which a reaction becomes automatic', and to prove the hypothesis that many of the actions and movements people make consciously might also be carried out involuntarily. In one experiment, Stein tried to absorb herself in a novel while Solomons spoke random words aloud at intervals for her to write down. At first, he reported in a précis of their findings published in the *Psychological Review*, she could focus only on either reading or listening. But before long, she was able to write his words without breaking her concentration; to carry out one activity (reading) in full consciousness, while simultaneously doing something else without registering the effort at all. To Solomons, their work suggested fascinating correlations between action and memory, implying that consciousness might be 'entirely superfluous' in people's ability to carry out habitual tasks. Despite this modified triumph, Stein remained sceptical of their conclusions: she considered her work with Solomons fatally flawed by the fact that she – as subject – was too self-conscious and aware of her surroundings to let her mind wander. Stein came to find the artificiality of the laboratory setting stifling, rather than enabling. When a fellow student whipped a cloth off a table to reveal a gun underneath, hoping to startle his peers into an involuntary reaction, she remained impassive, and explained to her disappointed colleague that she could not induce herself to feel fear when she knew perfectly well that the weapon was not going to be used. Such efforts to simulate situations and emotions, she felt, could never truly mirror reality: try as she might, she could not trick her brain to accept falsehood as truth.

Stein soon tired of acting as Solomons' medium: she wanted to direct her own experiments. William James and Leon Solomons shared an interest in Spiritualism, and were eager to pursue the possibilities of this kind of automatic writing for psychical research. But Stein's interest lay exclusively with the living. While the men pored over Ouija boards, discussing seances and hypnotism, she decided to make a comparison of men's and women's responses to various tests of attention, and see whether subjects' state of fatigue affected their suggestibility. Stein invited tired students to visit the laboratory immediately after an examination; she placed their hands on a glass plate mounted on metal balls, and set the plate moving in a circle or figure of eight. She would chat to them until they were sufficiently distracted, then release the plate to see if they came to a standstill or continued the movement automatically. 'I was supposed to be interested in their reactions,' Stein wrote later, 'but soon I found that I was not.' Instead, what fascinated Stein was her subjects' characters. She enjoyed talking to the students while they settled, asking about their sleep and study habits, their fears, motivations and superstitions; even without having read Freud (whose work was not yet translated into English), she was interested in drilling down, through conversation, to her subjects' inner lives. She wrote up her findings in an 1898 paper titled *Cultivated Motor Automatism*, an idiosyncratic document which reads more like notes for a novel than an academic treatise. 'It is very interesting to read,' she wrote three decades later, 'because the method of writing to be afterwards developed in *Three Lives* and *The Making of Americans* already shows itself.'

//

Composition classes were compulsory for Radcliffe students, so Stein wrote several essays and short stories during her undergraduate years, introspective pieces drawing on her own experiences and expressing a sense of loneliness and sexual longing. In one clearly autobiographical piece, a girl tells a friend about her 'bitter and often tyrannical' father; in another, she tosses and turns in bed, her mind racing with fears induced by the books she has been reading, while her sister sleeps peacefully beside her. Haltingly composed, and often trailing off before the end, the stories and essays reveal an avid reader – references range from George Meredith's *The Tragic Comedians* to Walter Pater's *Marius the Epicurean* – deeply engaged with fiction and philosophy, with German opera (particularly Wagner) and old Norse legends. Some pieces demonstrate Stein's hearty enjoyment of her studies: one fragment remarks on the 'fiendish yells, and explosive laughter' to be heard in a psychological laboratory, while another is a paean to William James, 'a scientist of force and originality embodying all that is strongest and worthiest in the scientific spirit'. Others depict a young woman lost in 'intense emotions': finding herself paralysed as a man rubs against her in a crowd, oddly intrigued that the sensation is not unpleasant; pondering her future as she sits in the college library, convinced that 'some change must come into her life' before her 'wild moods' overwhelm her altogether.

Stein completed her course at Radcliffe in 1897, and spent the summer studying advanced vertebrate embryology at the Woods Hole Marine Biological Laboratory on Cape Cod. That autumn, on James's recommendation, the twenty-three-year-old Stein enrolled at Johns Hopkins Medical School back in Baltimore, which had just become the first such institute in the country to welcome women. James had impressed on her that medical training was a prerequisite for a career in psychology; above all, she wanted to keep studying human behaviour, and hoped the course would expose her to practical experiences beyond the theoretical abstractions of the Radcliffe lab. She shared a house with Leo, who had enrolled – somewhat half-heartedly – in a graduate programme in zoology at the same university, unsure what else to do with himself. After finishing at Harvard, he had spent a year travelling around the world with his cousin Fred, falling in love with art: in Japan, he developed a passion for Edo-period woodblock prints, while in Paris and Florence he spent his days at the Louvre and Uffizi, immersed in quattrocento Italian painting. Gertrude had sailed out to meet him in Antwerp in the autumn of 1896, afraid she wouldn't recognise him after a year apart. But reunited in Baltimore, living together for the first time as adults, they soon drew an eclectic and erudite circle of friends around them.

Their closest allies were two wealthy sisters, Claribel and Etta Cone, whom they had met when they first arrived in Baltimore from California. Gertrude was fascinated by the dynamic between the pair: she felt a certain affinity with Etta, the youngest daughter dominated by her confident older sibling, but looked to Claribel – a professor in the university's pathology department – as an impressive example of female independence. The Cones held regular Saturday night parties, where Gertrude was able to experience the buzz of popularity: 'It is a toss up', wrote Etta to Gertrude, 'as to which, you or Sister Claribel, likes being lionized the most.' Some of Gertrude's Radcliffe friends, even those she had considered progressive, had questioned her plans for a medical career – 'A sheltered life, domestic tastes, maternity, and faith are all I could ask for myself or you,' wrote one. Gertrude, however, was already doubting that any aspect of this path was for her. Claribel not only offered a model of a powerful professional woman; she also encouraged Gertrude to join in her feminist activism, and even recruited her to deliver a speech to a group of (potentially sceptical) local women on 'the value of a college education for women'. The assignment was somewhat out of Gertrude's comfort zone – she warned her audience that her argument would lean heavily on Charlotte Perkins Gilman's recent book *Women and Economics* – but she made a strident case for 'the efficiency of the college woman', though couched placatingly in the argument that education would not impede women from fulfilling traditional domestic roles.

Gertrude Stein absorbed in scientific work
(with microscope and skull) at Johns Hopkins, *c.*1899

Stein's interest in feminist politics wasn't sustained: her time was occupied by scientific work. In her first two years at Johns Hopkins, Stein studied brain modelling and the history of neurology; her description of the nucleus of Darkschewitsch, a collection of cells near the top of the mid-brain, was good enough to be cited by one of her professors, Lewellys Barker, in his book on the nervous system. But in her third year (1900), after she began clinical work assisting with childbirth in local hospitals, Stein's grades began to slip. She was evidently uncomfortable with the work – perhaps due to squeamishness, the loss of her own mother, or its focus on the body rather than the mind – and she was vilified by one of her professors, a prominent obstetrician who expected a deference from his female students which Stein was not prepared to give. He called her 'the Battle-Axe', and awarded her a fail, forcing Stein to cancel the postgraduate work she had planned to do with a neuropathologist at the Massachusetts State Hospital for the Insane. Barker, generously, tried to help her to publish an article about her research on the brain stem, but Stein replied coolly that she was not available to attend to any edits a journal might require, 'as I am going abroad for an indefinite period . . . I do not expect to do any neurological work for some time to come.'

//

Stein later claimed she was 'openly bored' at medical school. She was also feeling the separation from her brother. Earlier that year, Leo had dropped out of his programme and moved to Florence, planning to write a book about the paintings of Andrea Mantegna. Instead of graduating in the spring of 1901, Gertrude sailed to visit him, accompanied by Etta Cone, who recorded long conversations with Gertrude about French literature and 'her pet subject of Human intercourse of the sexes'. Back in Baltimore that October, lonely and restless without Leo, Gertrude moved into a house with a former classmate, Emma Lootz Erving, who introduced her to a new crowd. Erving's friends were well-connected, sophisticated women from Smith, Bryn Mawr, and other eastern women's colleges: their leaders, Mabel Haynes and Grace Constant Lounsbery, cut striking figures in riding boots, scant skirts and bow ties.

At one of their dinner parties, Stein's attention was captured by a confident blonde woman, smirking conspiratorially with Haynes. May Bookstaver, she learned, came from an old Dutch family with a home in fashionable Newport; she had grown up in luxury, but her strict father – dismissive of women's education – allowed her no financial independence. Instead, it transpired, Mabel Haynes was Bookstaver's bankroller and lover: paying her bills, taking her on holiday, and jealously guarding her affections. Haynes and Bookstaver made it clear they saw Stein as gawkish, slovenly and naïve, but while Haynes's disdain was purely sneering, Stein sensed Bookstaver's was tinged with intrigue. Bookstaver intimidated Stein, but fascinated her too. Over long conversations – in Baltimore, and on weekends in New York at museums, restaurants or wandering around the streets and parks – Stein and Bookstaver hashed out their differences. They argued about class, about morals, about feminism: Bookstaver baulked at the way Stein intellectualised everything, chastising her for a lack of emotion, spontaneity, even humanity. Haynes, sometimes, watched their fights with amusement, as if their earnest debates were a play being acted for her benefit. She didn't see Stein as a serious rival.

Nowhere is it charted quite when and how Stein came to know she was attracted to women: her closest friends, in whom she might have confided, were still extolling the virtues of marriage and motherhood in their letters to her. To her new sister-in-law Sarah – Michael's wife – she wrote at length about sexual desire, though in relatively abstract terms. Sarah seems to have assumed she was talking about either masturbation or sex before marriage, and gravely offered Gertrude the details of her own gynaecologist. Elsewhere, evidently eager for experience, Stein lamented the fact that university studies tended to demand the most mental exertion at the moment when one's 'sexual desires are being constantly stimulated without adequate physiological relief'. The effort of repressing sexual feelings, she added – without going into specifics – is bound to affect the 'modern woman endeavouring to know all things, do all things and enjoy all things'. It's likely that May Bookstaver gave Stein her first experience of desire requited: a few years later, she described the frisson of their hands edging closer together, the electricity between them imperceptible to outsiders. Stein doesn't detail what they did in Bookstaver's New York bedroom, but their increasingly clandestine liaisons were cut off, abruptly, when Mabel Haynes – finally realising her pet was two-timing her – confronted Bookstaver, and ordered her to choose between them. Bookstaver wavered; Haynes remonstrated; Stein, alarmed at how complicated things were becoming, retreated. 'I have neither the inclination or the power to take Mabel's place', she wrote in a notebook, 'and I feel therefore that I have no right to step in between them.'

A couple of years after championing the value of a college education to Baltimore women, Stein composed another essay, angrier and more contrarian, titled 'Degeneration in American Women'. Perhaps in a dig at the snooty Haynes crowd, she expressed scepticism about the educated 'New Woman', and affirmed that a woman's natural place was, after all, in the home as a wife and mother. Just a few truly exceptional women, she suggested – clearly including herself in this category – ought to feel free to choose a different path. Was Stein differentiating herself from Mabel Haynes, in a provocative bid for May Bookstaver's attention? Bookstaver was a passionate campaigner for women's suffrage, who would undoubtedly have read Stein's essay and argued with her about it. The essay is strange, anguished and contradictory, but so were Stein's ideas about her sexuality, her gender and her own future. The misogyny she had faced at Johns Hopkins, as well as her exposure to feminist activism, had heightened her awareness of both the possibilities and the pitfalls of life as an educated middle-class woman. She felt simultaneously weighed down by the constraints of gender roles and determined to subvert them – but had not yet worked out how. Around this time, Stein resolved that her liberation would not be enacted within the academy or the organised women's movement. She would escape on her own terms.

//

In the spring of 1902, Stein sailed to Europe to meet Leo. They travelled around Italy before arriving in England at the end of the summer and joining Leo's friends Bernard and Mary Berenson at their country home in Fernhurst, West Sussex. Berenson, the celebrated art historian, had served as Leo's mentor since he first came to Europe: they welcomed Gertrude warmly and swept her into the household's vigorous debates over socialism and art, American and English politics. She was astonished to hear the Berensons and their friends – including Bertrand Russell and Logan Pearsall Smith – express unanimous surprise that she planned to return to America, which they all considered a sterile place, far behind Europe in artistic development. She had not yet considered an alternative: although she defended her country staunchly, the idea of living elsewhere quietly lodged in her mind. The Steins stayed at Fernhurst for several weeks, before travelling north to London: there, shortly before Christmas, Leo vanished to Paris to visit a friend, and Gertrude was left alone.

Holed up in rented rooms at 20 Bloomsbury Square near the British Museum, Stein began to record her thoughts in a notebook – descriptions of her surroundings, quotations from books she was reading, snatches of overheard conversation. Her first entry is an evocative sketch of London's East End – its greyness, its Indian restaurants, its pubs and music halls, laundries and tea shops – that slowly brings the buildings, and their interiors, to life. Lonely and anxious, she was people-watching intently, observing the way 'everybody talks to everybody', familiarising herself with social quirks and unspoken rules (how anyone will buy a drink for someone out of work, for example, but regular spongers will be despised). Stein applied for a six-month pass to the British Museum's reading room, where she devised a scheme to read through English literature from the sixteenth to the nineteenth century – extending the project she had begun as a teenager in California. She spent entire days at the museum, breaking only to eat: there she read the works of Fanny Burney, Bunyan's *Life and Death of Mr Badman*, several books about Chinese history and literature, and various studies of saints, including Mary Francis Cusack's *Life and Revelations of Saint Gertrude*. Among her notes from her reading, Stein tried out some titles for possible short stories, her first attempts at fiction since the Radcliffe composition classes: 'Maggie being the history of a gentle soul'; 'The Progress of Jane Sands being a history of one woman and many others'; 'The Tragedy of the Wirkin Sisters'. And she jotted down the beginnings of a narrative based on the ill-fated marriage of her older cousin, Bird Stein, who was then in the middle of a high-profile divorce case, involving numerous lawyers and private detectives, that was titillating the New York press.

In February 1903, Stein turned twenty-nine. The years since her adolescence, she reflected, had been spent in 'the strain and stress of the making of a personality'; now, slowly, the confusion that had often characterised her youth was starting to abate. She was still uncertain of her future, but felt she was finally facing down 'the straight and narrow gateway of maturity', ready to exchange 'uproar and confusion' for 'form and purpose'. After five months in Bloomsbury, Stein sailed back to America in February, glad to leave behind 'the dead weight of that fog and smoke laden air . . . the soggy, damp, miserable streets', and arrive in New York, its skyscrapers laden with snow. She moved into the White House, a sprawling mansion in uptown Manhattan shared by numerous single women, and spent her time reading about Japanese art, noting down names and dates in her notebooks ('Yeishin,' she wrote, 'Fra Angelico of Japan'). But her initial optimism faded when she learned that May Bookstaver was still enmeshed with Mabel Haynes; she found herself struck by a pang of jealousy she hadn't quite expected. The dynamic between her and Bookstaver had always been antagonistic, and she had thought her feelings weren't strong enough to merit a fight with Haynes: 'I am a hopeless coward,' she wrote, 'I hate to risk hurting myself or anybody else. All I want to do is to meditate endlessly and think and talk.' But now Stein felt dismayed at the way Bookstaver seemed simply to have forgotten her altogether.

Almost as soon as she had arrived in New York, she decided to return to Europe – only to discover that Bookstaver and Haynes were planning an Italy trip of their own, and would coincide with her in Rome. When they met there that June, Haynes seemed determined to dominate Bookstaver, to Stein's irritation; tensions mounted, and, though Bookstaver murmured regretful apologies, Stein found herself angry at Haynes's possessiveness and resentful towards Bookstaver's passivity. Now certain that the episode had run its course, she resolved to put them both out of her mind. She confirmed her plans to stay in Europe with Leo, who was setting up home in Paris. After one brief final trip the following spring – whether she saw May Bookstaver is unrecorded – she did not return to America for thirty years.

2 : *VITA NUOVA*

L eo, now determined to become a painter, had enrolled in art classes at the prestigious Académie Julian. He would stare for hours at a single plate in an effort to teach himself 'creative seeing'; he wandered the halls of the Louvre entranced by the marble statues, before rushing home, stripping nude before the fire, and drawing from life. At the suggestion of their uncle Ephraim Keyser, a sculptor already living in Paris, he had taken an apartment on the Left Bank near the Luxembourg Gardens. It was not a fashionable district – the vermin-catcher had to be called on more than one occasion – but rents were low, and the flat (unusual for Paris) had a bath. The apartment was entered through a peaceful courtyard set back from the street, and consisted of two storeys: four small rooms, a kitchen and bathroom, and – standing separate to the main apartment, with its own entrance – a cavernous atelier, higher than it was wide, with dingy white walls, heated by a solitary stove. The address, soon to become famous, was 27 rue de Fleurus.

Paris, in 1903, was a city unrecognisable from fifty years earlier. A renovation of its urban design was in progress, begun in 1853 by the politician Georges-Eugène Haussmann on the orders of Emperor Napoleon III. His challenge was simple: to make the city beautiful. The dark, putrid medieval quarters immortalised by Balzac and Hugo – where disease spread fast among overcrowded populations – were replaced by wide, airy boulevards and public gardens. The embankments of the Seine became paved walkways lined with book-stalls, new footbridges connected the two halves of the city, and the river – formerly the repository of the local sewers – was cleaned up. The Steins moved into a city whose architecture was fresh, ornate and unified; newly manufactured Renault cars were beginning to crowd out horse-drawn carriages on the streets, and the thousands of gaslights, individually illuminated each night by a uniformed band of workers, were gradually being swapped for electric street lights. Leo had chosen a home in the heart of Montparnasse, crowded with cheap cafés and snug bistros, though not yet the centre of the city's artistic life: for now, poets and painters congregated up north in Montmartre, a village-like enclave known for its low rents and unbridled nightlife. South of the river, a different sort of decadence predominated. Turning left out of the front gates, Gertrude could window-shop along the bustling rue de Rennes, and melt into the crowds thronging the enormous department store Le Bon Marché. Turning right, she was moments away from the calming green of the Luxembourg Gardens, lined with ornamental promenades and fountains. She spent hours in the Louvre, walking through art history, and would often go to meet Leo after his drawing class, watching the changing light on the building façades. The city held promise: Gertrude's next challenge was to find her place within it.

//

Friends and strangers speculated endlessly about the peculiar Stein siblings, in their matching loose brown corduroy outfits and Grecian leather sandals: Leo tall, red-bearded, bony and serious, Gertrude short and voluptuous, her long dark hair coiled in a bun on her head, invariably poised to break out in peals of deep laughter. On first meeting, many assumed they were husband and wife, not brother and sister. From Paris, they regularly wrote joint letters to friends, passing the pen between them, Leo's handwriting small and neat, Gertrude's unspooling across the shared page in a haphazard scrawl. Those who knew them well understood their mutual dependence: Leo a natural leader but self-critical and prone to depression; Gertrude more practical and vivacious, ready to take up her brother's passions as her own. One friend described Leo as a man with a 'never-satisfied question mark in his face'. Gertrude, too, was eagerly seeking a new outlet for her energies – and her affections. In an effort to purge herself of May Bookstaver, she spent her first two months in Paris – September and October 1903 – dissecting their relationship in a novel, lightly disguising names and details, but drawing directly on the letters she and Bookstaver had exchanged. Beyond licking her wounds, Stein wanted to analyse the power dynamic between herself, Bookstaver

Stein in the Luxembourg Gardens, *c.*1907

and Haynes, particularly the difficulty she had felt all along in discerning Bookstaver's real feelings, or even understanding her own. In one scene, she gave her character Dante's *Vita Nuova* to read: the experience, she considered, had exposed her to a new emotional world, painful but ultimately humanising. She called the novel *Q.E.D.* – an abbreviation of 'quod erat demonstrandum', the Latin phrase used at the end of a mathematical proof, as if the relationship were an impossibility, its potential finally exhausted by her novel's completion. She showed the manuscript to Leo, but she didn't want anyone else to see it (yet); when the novel was finished, she put it away in a drawer and resolved to forget about it. 'Good God no I am not angry,' she wrote, conciliatorily, to Bookstaver. 'No one is to blame.' Other projects – literary and artistic – were already beginning to consume her.

The siblings' recollections of their early years in Paris varied considerably. Both agreed that it was Leo whose craze for Japanese prints sparked their shared interest in 'junking': prowling around antique shops in search of affordable art with which to adorn the atelier's walls.

It was Leo who fell for the work of Paul Cézanne, the ageing painter he thought 'succeeded in rendering mass with a vital intensity that is unparalleled in the whole history of painting'. And it was Leo, on the recommendation of Bernard Berenson, who first rang the bell of the tiny gallery run by Ambroise Vollard on the rue Lafitte. For Leo, making contact with Vollard (an ardent champion of contemporary artists who had mounted Cézanne's first ever solo exhibition nine years earlier) was the natural consequence of his long-standing engagement with aesthetic theory. In Gertrude's version of events, the visits to this 'incredible place' were simply a delightful form of entertainment.

Over the autumn of 1904, they were regulars at the shop, rummaging through the heaps of pictures and sending the gruff proprietor running upstairs in search of more. At this point, the Steins' tastes were eclectic: they would buy what they could afford. Their brother Michael, still in California, continued to send them a monthly allowance from their invested inheritance, which covered their rent and living expenses comfortably – they were able to hire a housekeeper, Hélène, who cooked and managed the household budgets – and they preferred to buy art than eat lavishly or extend their wardrobes beyond their simple corduroy uniform. When Michael informed them that their stocks had outstripped all expectations and they had a surprise windfall of 8,000 francs apiece, they went straight to Vollard's, and kick-started their collection. Their early purchases covered a range of styles: the classical Romanticism of Eugène Delacroix, the Impressionists Monet, Degas and Renoir (controversial a generation earlier, now more palatable to contemporary tastes), and more daring works by Gauguin, Van Gogh and Toulouse-Lautrec, who rebelled against their predecessors' naturalistic use of form and colour. Finally, they told Vollard they had to stop – but wanted their final purchase to be something large, unusual and exciting. Vollard led them through to a back room – where Gertrude had speculated that an elderly charwoman sat churning out the canvases sold as masterpieces – and showed them a portrait of Cézanne's wife seated in a red armchair, holding a fan on her lap, her expression enigmatic. One side of her face appeared dynamic, the other half smooth and flat as a mask. A brief deliberation over honey cakes down the street, and the painting was acquired.

But it was the following year, at the annual Salon d'Automne of October 1905, that the Steins took their first great risk, making the purchase which marked a shift in their collecting habits from modestly priced pieces by acknowledged modern masters to the cutting-edge work of marginal young artists. By this point, Michael had joined them in Paris with his wife Sarah and their eight-year-old son Allan, taking an apartment just around the corner in a converted chapel at 58 rue Madame. Michael had quit his job on the San Francisco railway, finding himself on the side of the union workers rather than the management during the cable-car strike of 1902. He continued to manage the family's financial affairs, and was inclined to be cautious where Gertrude and Leo seemed reckless: dismayed to discover his siblings spending all their money on art, he reproached Leo into auctioning off some Japanese prints. But before long he embraced the idea of a family art collection, which he had come to see as a potentially shrewd investment, as well as a source of pleasure, intellectual purpose and new social horizons.

On the opening day of the Salon d'Automne, the Steins joined the animated throngs queueing down the Champs-Élysées to enter the Grand Palais. Once inside, they passed through several large halls and stopped at a small side room, where a commotion was brewing. On the wall hung Henri Matisse's *Femme au Chapeau*, an exuberant portrait of his wife, her feathered headpiece at a jaunty angle, composed from loose daubs of paint in an explosion of blues, reds, purples and greens. Leo initially considered it 'the nastiest smear of paint I had ever seen' – a view shared by the hordes who jeered and scratched at the painting's surface – but after thinking it over, decided the portrait was 'what I was unknowingly waiting for'. Gertrude claimed it was her idea to buy the painting, which she considered 'perfectly natural', for 500 francs. In her telling, she 'arranged the whole matter' with

Madame Matisse herself, who urged her husband – so distraught at the painting's terrible reception he had considered burning it for the insurance money – to command the highest price he could, since these buyers were clearly mad.

The Steins were soon seeing a lot of Matisse. Sarah joined his art class, and she and Michael rapidly became his major patrons, devoting their own collection exclusively to his latest work. But Gertrude and Leo's attention had already moved on. A few weeks after the Salon, the dealer Clovis Sagot showed them a painting of a nude girl posed side-on against a dull blue backdrop, clutching a basket of red flowers. Placidly chewing liquorice, Sagot informed them that this unknown Spanish artist – who was so destitute he slept on a shared mattress in a run-down Montmartre studio – was 'the real thing'. Here, unusually, Gertrude's and Leo's stories align. Leo immediately recognised the work of 'a genius of very considerable magnitude', but Gertrude was 'repelled and shocked' by the girl's legs and feet, to the extent that Sagot, anxious to make his sale, offered to guillotine the canvas and jettison the lower half. They bought the (complete) painting for 150 francs. But that dynamic slowly reversed after they were introduced to Pablo Picasso by their mutual friend Henri-Pierre Roché. By the end of their first dinner together, Picasso and Gertrude were play-fighting over the last slice of bread, Gertrude concealing her giggles as Picasso, under his breath, poked fun at curmudgeonly Leo's clichéd enthusiasm for fashionable Japanese prints. Soon, she was in and out of Picasso's studio, discussing his work with him, lending him money, and buying his work independently. It was Leo who led the way, but Gertrude who stayed the course. Before the end of the year, Picasso asked to paint her portrait.

//

Having arrived in Paris from Barcelona in 1900, Picasso was painting figures he encountered in the streets, cafés and cabarets of Montmartre: gaunt beggars, prisoners and prostitutes bathed in blue; sombre jugglers, harlequins and acrobats in a sensual rose-pink; melancholy self-portraits which hinted at his sense of isolation as a foreigner in Paris, an ambitious but dejected artist seeking his own visual language. Leo and Gertrude had begun to open their doors each Saturday night to the artists they collected and anyone else who wanted to see their paintings, and Picasso – usually accompanied by a macho band of poets and his girlfriend, Fernande Olivier – was always there, skulking moodily around the room's edges while his friends cracked jokes. Whenever he could disentangle himself from the crowd, he would stare at Cézanne's portrait of his wife so intensely that Leo imagined it might dissolve before his eyes. It was starting to spark in him ideas of how to depict people without simply replicating a likeness: to express, instead, an inner essence. This painting, too, was increasingly important to Gertrude.

'Cézanne', Stein told an interviewer in 1946, 'gave me a new feeling about composition . . . it was not solely the realism of characters but the realism of the composition which was the important thing.' Cézanne was the first painter whose work Stein truly studied. Looking at *Portrait of Madame Cézanne*, which hung above her desk, she saw how every aspect of the canvas was alive and equal; there was no 'centre' to the work, nothing consigned to the margins, but 'each part is as important as the whole'. She was fascinated by Cézanne's use of form, the way he flattened space into simple shapes somehow pulsing with life; his paintings appeared complete in themselves, referring to nothing beyond the frame. In the spring of 1905, half-heartedly trying to improve her halting French, Stein had begun to translate Flaubert's story *Un cœur simple*, the tale of a servant named Félicité whose life is characterised by barely acknowledged devotion to a widow and her children: she dies alone, mistaking her stuffed parrot for a vision of the dove of the Holy Spirit. But under the watchful eye of *Madame Cézanne*, Stein began to imagine a way of writing that would depart from the two centuries of realist fiction she had devoured since childhood: Samuel Richardson's *Clarissa*, which she later described as a perfect novel, and everything by Anthony Trollope, Henry Fielding and Henry James. By the time she began her visits to Picasso's studio, she had completed two long stories – each focused on a working-class woman in a fictionalised version of Baltimore – and was working on a third, seeking a form in which to convey, as closely as possible, her characters' immediate, constantly shifting experience.

Stein's version of Flaubert's Félicité morphed into a narrative of the 'arduous and troubled life' of Anna, a stoical German Catholic servant who works in a succession of households run by cavalier mistresses wilfully determined, despite her frugal management, to live outside their means. Her second story, *The Gentle Lena*, also described a working-class German immigrant, brought to America by her aunt to improve her prospects through work and marriage. Neither Anna nor Lena is in control of her own destiny; each is vulnerable to the whims of demanding employers, husbands and mothers-in-law. Both stories end with the death of their subjects: Anna after a long illness and Lena in childbirth, having lost all interest in life and deprived, even, of her ability to feel. Her husband and children hardly notice she is gone.

But it was the last of the three stories, *Melanctha*, which most dramatically marked Stein's departure from the conventions of nineteenth-century writing. Melanctha is mixed-race, possessed of an 'inborn intense wisdom', and given to 'wandering', a term which connotes both her wayward meanderings through Bridgepoint, loitering with men at the docks and on building sites, and the complex desires for experience and knowledge which prove her downfall. After an unhappy childhood, Melanctha finds her first experience of closeness in a friendship with an older woman, Jane Harden, who encourages her to seek 'something that would move her very deeply'. She finds that stimulus, not altogether happily, in her relationship with Jefferson Campbell, a black doctor whom she meets at her mother's deathbed. Over the course of long debates about the nature of love and the necessity – or danger – of surrendering to emotion, the pair come to realise that their temperaments are fundamentally misaligned. Jeff, who values decency, honesty and a quiet life, must grapple with Melanctha's accusation that he is 'afraid to let himself ever know real feeling', as well as his fear – compounded when the jealous Jane tells him about Melanctha's promiscuous past – that he 'did not know the least bit' about her.

'It was a struggle,' writes Stein, 'sure to be going on always between them. It was a struggle that was as sure always to be going on between them, as their minds and hearts always were to have different ways of working.' The story's drama plays out through this intangible struggle, as language itself becomes fluid. Cascades of simple, repeated words and phrases, nuanced by slight variations which heighten the reader's alertness to the rhythm of the text, convey the gradual evolution of Melanctha and Jeff's dynamic. 'Every day now,' Stein writes, 'Jeff seemed to be coming nearer, to be really loving. Every day now, Melanctha poured it all out to him, with more freedom. Every day now, they seemed to be having more and more, both together, of this strong, right feeling. More and more every day now they seemed to know more really, what it was each other one was always feeling.' Time moves forward almost imperceptibly – a stream of paragraphs beginning 'always now' locates the reader, and characters, in a shared present – as the characters' feelings slowly change: they keep 'feeling', 'talking', 'suffering', increasingly frustrated that what is 'inside' one of them cannot be felt by the other. *Melanctha* explores the experience of yearning, the possibilities of euphemism and innuendo, the power of words to expose some emotions and keep others hidden. The characters find language inadequate to express their feelings: long sentences pile up with minimal punctuation, syntax breaks down, phrases repeat, and a suggestive range of meanings begins to accumulate. A series of misunderstandings occasion the final break: Melanctha, like Anna and Lena, dies forgotten, renounced by her former friends.

//

In the spring of 1906, Gertrude and Leo went to visit the Berensons at their villa in Fiesole – Gertrude took with her *The Arabian Nights* and Swift's *A Tale of a Tub* – where she finished writing *Melanctha*. Satisfied with her achievement and eager to continue, she returned to a manuscript she had begun early in 1903 but abandoned after a few chapters – the story of her cousin Bird's unhappy marriage. (She had been reminded of the unfinished novel that April by a letter from Bird, announcing her engagement to her divorce lawyer.) Building on her stylistic breakthrough, Stein decided to expand the marriage saga into a more ambitious structure, intertwining the stories of two families of German Jewish immigrants – her cousin's and her own – as they gradually assimilate into American life. Since arriving in Paris, Stein had been reading the Russian novelists, which had warmed her to the idea of a multigenerational chronicle. She was thinking back to her childhood: the twin houses in Allegheny in which her family and Bird's had briefly lived, the schism between their respective sets of parents, and the complicated dynamics within her own household. In Fiesole, Stein began to write with renewed energy. Her close observation of Picasso and Matisse at work had broadened her sense of what art – or literature – could be. The story she had envisaged three years earlier – the 'history of a family's progress' – was suddenly displaced by an urgent new concern: to tell the history of everyone who had ever lived. The novel, she decided, would be called *The Making of Americans*.

Over her life, Stein gave several different versions of this novel's origin story. Looking back almost thirty years later, she located the foundations of her fascination with human character in her experiments at the Harvard Psychological Laboratory, where she had found herself less interested in her subjects' reactions to her tests than in the gestures, mannerisms and patterns of speech that defined the way they talked. Stein had concluded that people's varying attention spans were a product of their 'complete character' or 'bottom nature', a driving force deep within them which directed everything they did. 'I began', she wrote, 'to get enormously interested in hearing how everybody said the same thing over and over again with infinite variations . . . endlessly the same and endlessly different.' There was no such thing as repetition,

Stein argued; rather, the essence of human expression was insistence, or emphasis. However many times a story is told, whether by different people or the same person at different times, it undergoes changes which do less to reveal what actually happened than to provide an insight into the speaker's personality. Years after leaving the laboratory, she found herself preoccupied with the possibilities – now literary rather than scientific – contained within this insight. She had conceived of a novel portraying specific characters against the backdrop of their family history. But even as she started writing it, her mind was dreaming up something larger still: something like a cosmic map of humanity, with every kind of person she had ever met represented, written in a style which reflected her sense that 'everybody always is repeating'.

When she and Leo returned to Paris in the autumn of 1906, Gertrude cast around for willing subjects on whom to test the theories that were beginning to take shape in her mind. She was delighted when one fell into her lap. Earlier that year, Michael and Sarah Stein had returned to San Francisco to check on their property after the earthquake which devastated the city. They brought a guest back with them: Annette Rosenshine, the cousin of a friend of Sarah's, an awkward young woman plagued by anxieties and neuroses, who was hoping for a fresh start. Gertrude and Leo met the party at the gare Saint-Lazare in the pouring rain, and accompanied them back to Michael and Sarah's apartment on the rue Madame, dazzling Rosenshine with a running stream of commentary on the landmarks they were passing: the Champs-Élysées, the Place de la Concorde, the Louvre. Rosenshine later remembered being awed by Gertrude's 'dynamic magnetism', and the hearty laughter which 'seemed delightful, although rather disconcerting when it was directed against me'. With her crowd of artist friends, her medical experience and her intellectual, liberated lifestyle, Stein seemed to Rosenshine 'an island of emotional security'. Trusting that Stein's psychological studies qualified her as some sort of authority on matters of the mind, Rosenshine turned herself over to her, 'as years later I learned one turns oneself over to an analyst'.

Gertrude, for her part, pounced on Annette as an ideal patient. Rosenshine agreed to visit Stein daily at 4 p.m.; they would walk through the Luxembourg Gardens, while Rosenshine would pour out to Stein her fears and problems. Stein observed her more systematically and intensely than she had considered anyone before, aiming towards an understanding so complete that she could – so she thought – think and feel along with her subject. In her previous writing, Stein had explored the way character was revealed through power struggles and the fluctuation of interpersonal dynamics. Now, she pondered whether she might be able to express something even more fundamental about character by mirroring the small repetitions of language and gesture detectable through the kind of sustained observation she had first trialled in the laboratory, and was practising now with Rosenshine. By watching everyone this closely, Stein thought, she ought to be able to discern anyone's 'bottom nature': to perceive 'the kind of being in them that makes them'.

In the autumn of 1907, Stein began a fresh notebook, which she titled 'Diagram Book'. Here, her ideas for the novel's narrative development were overtaken by notes on character, jotted with palpable excitement. Using her observations of those around her, she aimed to build a comprehensive stratification of every possible 'type' of human character. She began to compare her friends' qualities in charts and group those with similar traits in complex webs, sometimes including historical figures or literary characters in her analysis: Vincent Van Gogh, Napoleon, Abraham Lincoln, Charlotte Brontë. She defined people's ethical codes, analysed their relationship to power and speculated on their attitude to beauty; she assessed different ways of expressing love, fear and anger, and weighed up their sense of freedom. Some notebook entries deliberated where individuals should sit in the developing scheme; others tried to establish the boundaries of particular 'types', drawing up long lists of the characteristics that denoted them, and assigning names to each. 'The Bazarofians are blind but not intolerant,' she wrote, referring to a group named for a character from Turgenev's *Fathers and Sons*.

'The free soul, mistress type are important to themselves inside them – they have a personal pride in them.' Stein established an important contrast between 'passionate women' who 'afflict their world with agitation, excitement and unrest', and those whom she deemed more timid and fearful – the disjunct she had explored already in the relationship of Melanctha and Jeff. Her notebooks were soon filled with analyses of old friends from America (including, of course, Mabel Haynes and May Bookstaver) and newer ones from Paris: Matisse, Picasso and their respective partners Amélie Matisse and Fernande Olivier; the ethereal painter Marie Laurencin and her sometime lover, the poet Guillaume Apollinaire; an assortment of odd characters who turned up at the Saturday nights, oblivious to the intense scrutiny of their sandalled host. From the winter of 1907, one more name began to appear in the book with increasing regularity: a new arrival in Paris, who had instantly caught Stein's attention. It was Alice B. Toklas.

3 : MAN OF LETTERS

At twelve minutes past five on the morning of 18 April 1906, San Francisco began to quake. Alice Babette Toklas left her bed and looked, bleary-eyed, out of the window, then ran straight to her father's bedroom: 'Do get up,' she told him. 'The city is on fire.' After checking on friends, visiting the bank and picking up a supply of cigarettes, Toklas packed the family silver into a chest and buried it in the garden — a preservation instinct that would serve her well — then took the ferry to Berkeley to spend the night with a friend, unable to bring herself to look back at her hometown blazing behind her. When she returned, Toklas stopped by a local flower shop: the heat of the flames had stirred hundreds of carnations into immediate bloom.

The San Francisco earthquake — the deadliest in American history — left the city in ruins, and indirectly changed the course of Toklas's life. Three years younger than Stein, she had grown up in the prosperity of San Francisco, just across the bay from Oakland; her father had arrived in America from Poland in 1865, aged twenty, while her mother had grown up in San Francisco, the daughter of Jewish immigrants from Prussia. Like Stein, Toklas travelled in Europe as a child, rolling hoops in the Luxembourg Gardens and watching Victor Hugo's casket process down the Champs-Élysées; as a teenager, she spent six years in Seattle, where her father's booming mercantile business had headquarters. A talented pianist, she enrolled in the local university's music conservatory at sixteen, but her life was put on hold when her mother died in 1897, when Toklas was twenty. Her father took her and her younger brother back to San Francisco to live with her grandfather and great-uncle, and she abandoned a promising musical career to wait on a household of demanding Victorian gentlemen.

Stein, in fact, knew of Toklas already. She was the older cousin of Annette Rosenshine, whom Stein saw daily for psychological interrogation. As part of her 'treatment', Stein had encouraged Rosenshine to show her all the letters she received from friends and family in San Francisco — so before she met Toklas, Stein had begun to form an imagined picture of her through reading her private correspondence, without consent. Stein could sense that the dynamic between the cousins was fraught. As an introverted teenager, Rosenshine had been awestruck by Toklas's glamour and sophistication. When Toklas accompanied her father to the opera in a tailored suit, an article appeared in the *Morning Chronicle*; when the two girls attended the local art school's Mardi Gras ball, shy Rosenshine was stunned at Toklas's easy confidence talking to a group of male artists, expounding charismatically on books Rosenshine was almost sure she hadn't read. Rosenshine visited Toklas often at her grandfather's house; they sat quietly while the men talked, cigar smoke seeming to saturate the wooden chairs and the drapes. As soon as they could, they retreated upstairs to light their own cigarettes, where Toklas told Rosenshine about fashion and Henry James's novels, and revealed that she was plotting her escape from the stifling household. In one of these conversations, Toklas mentioned her friend Sarah Stein, who had just arrived from Paris to check her husband's properties for earthquake damage – and was looking for a friend to travel back with her.

Toklas had been introduced to Sarah by their mutual friend Harriet Levy, a drama critic ten years Toklas's senior, who – at forty – was also chafing to free herself from the strictures of her upper-middle-class Jewish family. Sarah summoned them to admire three paintings by Matisse she had brought back with her – the first of his canvases to cross the ocean – which Toklas found both grotesque and fascinating. She encouraged Toklas to come back with them to Paris; reluctantly, Toklas replied that she couldn't afford it (she was in debt after buying a fox cape) and wasn't ready to leave her father, and suggested they take Rosenshine instead. A year later, in the summer of 1907, Harriet Levy told Toklas she was planning to join the Steins in Paris, and offered to loan her the money to accompany her. This time, Toklas said yes, and packed her extensive collection of feathered hats, taking a copy of Flaubert's letters to read on board ship. On arrival, they dropped their bags at their hotel and went straight to Michael and Sarah's apartment, where Toklas was introduced to Leo and Gertrude, who wore her customary brown corduroy suit and a distinctive coral brooch. At that first meeting, Stein wrote with a twinkle in *The Autobiography of Alice B. Toklas*, Toklas heard inside her the unmistakable clang of a bell that signalled – she understood instinctively – that she was in the presence of a genius. 'It was Gertrude Stein', Toklas wrote in her own 1963 autobiography *What Is Remembered*, 'who held my complete attention, as she did for all the many years I knew her until her death, and all these empty ones since then.'

Stein, as taken with Toklas as Toklas was with her, invited her over the next day. Held up by unpacking and Harriet's desire for a leisurely lunch, Toklas arrived at the rue de Fleurus half an hour late, to find Stein a 'vengeful goddess', furious to be kept waiting. Bemused and nervous, Toklas waited as Stein paced up and down, ranting, until she suddenly calmed down and led Toklas around the Luxembourg Gardens, chatting as they went, her mollification complete when they stopped for cake and ice cream. The following Saturday evening, Toklas knocked as instructed at the door of 27 rue de Fleurus, and was greeted by Leo, another brown-clad figure in sandals, who showed her into the atelier. Looking around her, Toklas was overwhelmed. The white-washed walls were filled from floor to ceiling with paintings, crammed together in an explosion of colour. She averted her eyes quickly from several enormous nudes: one by Felix Vallotton – a woman reclining on a couch who reminded her, scandalously, of Manet's *Olympia* – and two by Picasso, the girl holding a basket of flowers and a woman stepping forward against a rose-pink background, hands clasped demurely at her waist. One wall showcased Picasso's Harlequin and Rose periods: a naked boy leading a horse, a blue-green-tinted woman dozing off over a glass of absinthe, a lithe young acrobat balancing on a ball. And there, presiding over all, was his portrait of her host.

As they were finishing dinner, served in the main apartment by the housekeeper Hélène at a table hemmed in by bookshelves, the group heard footsteps in the courtyard, and Gertrude leapt up and vanished. When Toklas followed her back into the atelier, she found her new friend perched by the door, ready to respond to any knock, while Leo

27 rue de Fleurus, *c.*1907

took his place in a low armchair, his feet propped high on a bookshelf. Already, the room was filled with visitors, lifting lamps up to the walls and leaning over the table to examine the folios of prints and drawings, murmuring to one another not only in French and English but Hungarian, German, Russian. Toklas joined Gertrude and Matisse in time to hear the end of a story about a hilarious lunch party where each artist had sat opposite one of his own paintings; she was swept into an earnest discussion of hats with Picasso's partner Fernande Olivier, and found herself confusedly assuring Picasso that he did, as he passionately begged her to tell him, slightly resemble President Lincoln. Leo gesticulated animatedly at the paintings, light reflecting off his spectacles, while Sarah sat on the corner couch draped in antique jewellery, expounding with enthusiasm on the greatness of Matisse. Toklas was intoxicated by her glimpse of the life that the brother and sister led here. It was, Stein had her remember in the *Autobiography*, 'one of the most important evenings of my life'.

27 rue de Fleurus, *c.*1913

//

It's not easy to chart just how Stein and Toklas's relationship developed. In the *Autobiography*, their inseparability is presented as a simple, inevitable fact: there's no gradual courtship, no moment of self-revelation, no record of a first kiss, or of the private exchange of promises which cemented the relationship they described, matter-of-factly, as a marriage. What's clear is how deliberately Stein engineered her position in Toklas's new Paris life. First, she cast Annette Rosenshine aside. Rosenshine later remembered making an anguished confession to Toklas that she had shown Stein all her letters, and sensing displeasure from her cousin's stony silence. To her dismay, Rosenshine could see that Stein and Toklas were more interested in each other than either was in her: the ease with which Stein dropped her made clear to Rosenshine that their therapy sessions had never been for her benefit at all. Within a few months, Rosenshine's mother visited Paris, was shocked to find her gaunt and despondent, and whisked her back to San Francisco, as far away as possible from the destructive influence of Gertrude Stein.

Meanwhile, Stein arranged for Levy and Toklas to swap their hotel for one a few streets away from the rue de Fleurus, where Toklas began to spend every Saturday evening and much more time besides. Stein quickly brought her up to speed on the Paris gossip. There was the philandering Swedish American sculptor David Edstrom, who had commissioned a friend to ghostwrite his memoirs then got cold feet and destroyed the finished manuscript, and was now on the run from his seething biographer. There was the intense competition between Matisse and Picasso; the latter had returned from a trip to Spain to find Matisse's newest work, *Bonheur de Vivre*, installed by the artist himself in the rue de Fleurus dining room. He was now, Stein confided, working on something sensational that would far outshine Matisse. And there was the ongoing drama between Picasso and Fernande Olivier, both of whom sought advice and consolation from Stein as their relationship faltered. 'You are the only person who takes a little interest in me,' wrote Olivier, asking Stein to help her find pupils for French lessons to provide an income during one of several periods of separation from Picasso. Stein's French was patchy – she and Picasso (who spoke little English) communicated in a strange hybrid language only the two of them could understand – but if Olivier hoped Stein would become her patron, just as she was Picasso's, Stein didn't take the hint. Instead, she volunteered Toklas, who was soon counselling Fernande three times a week.

One non-lesson day in early 1908, Toklas went with Stein to Picasso's cluttered studio. There, leaning against the wall, she saw one of the works he'd completed in a flurry of energy after finishing his portrait of Gertrude Stein, painting straight over some of his older canvases in the rush to set down his vision. Five fleshy women, seven feet tall, loomed out of the canvas, which bore a curiously flattened perspective: their disjointed, angular forms and impossibly distorted features made it appear that they were all staring, defiantly, directly at the viewer. *Les Demoiselles d'Avignon* had already shocked several of Picasso's friends. Some, like Matisse, recognised it as radical while wincing at the ugliness of the figures. Others, like Leo Stein, found its boldness offensive, and told Picasso so. One argument between them, at the rue de Fleurus, became so heated that Gertrude, troubled by the discord between her two 'brothers', dropped a pile of books on the floor with a crash to startle the men into silence. She could not afford the enormous painting without Leo's support, but did buy a series of the sketches for it, indicating subtly to Picasso that she was on his side. She knew that her portrait had led the way to *Les Demoiselles*; that Picasso's iconoclastic attack on classical ideals of female beauty had materialised, first, in the stripped-back, androgynous features he had given her, inspired by the Iberian sculptures he had seen at the Louvre in the spring of 1906. He showed his appreciation by acknowledging her as an equal. An envelope, containing one of the many notes they exchanged in these years, is addressed to 'Gertrude Stein, Man of Letters'.

//

Stein, meanwhile, continued her investigations into human character, now using Toklas and Levy as her primary case studies. Her novel-in-progress, *The Making of Americans*, had begun to reject narrative entirely: since starting the 'Diagram Book', she had laid the bones of the plot aside and became completely absorbed in her efforts at classification. 'Writing books is like washing hair,' she noted, 'you got to soap it a lot of times before you start to rinse it.' In the spring of 1908, Stein threw away much of the work she had done on the novel since 1906. 'Begin this new thing,' she wrote in her notebook. 'Don't forget anything.' The new version of the novel retained the two families from earlier drafts, but the characters now existed primarily as examples of her psychological system. Writing a novel without any of the conventional crutches – plot, scenes, linear time – was a daunting task. But Stein felt vindicated in her mission by a book she read in May 1908, which both confirmed and clarified her thinking to date.

It was Leo who first read the Austrian philosopher Otto Weininger's *Sex and Character*, which had been published in 1903 and translated into English in 1906. The book was a sensation: although Sigmund Freud, doubting its conclusions, had advised Weininger not to publish, early reviewers in the Vienna press described it as 'full of truths' and 'one of the most original books ever written', while Ford Madox Ford recalled intellectuals discussing it in hushed tones in clubs and cafés, as if 'a new gospel' had appeared. Weininger argued that human nature could be charted on a sliding scale from 'total male' to 'total female', and that all humans contain a mix of male and female traits which determine their overall character. Just like Stein, Weininger had set out to develop a 'broad and deep characterology', propelled by the belief that character 'is not something seated behind the thoughts and feeling in the individual, but something revealing itself in every thought and feeling'. Leo and Gertrude discussed the book at length, pressing it on their friends, until Leo lost interest. But for Gertrude, Weininger injected her work on *The Making of Americans* with a new sense of purpose. She saw that they had, independently, been pursuing a similar aim.

Weininger's system was profoundly misogynist. Fundamental to his theory was the idea that 'female' traits were passive, sexual, devoid of logic and consciousness, while 'male' ones were active, deliberate and ethical. Only those with the greatest concentration of masculine traits approached his system's highest level, that of genius. Furthermore, although Weininger was Jewish, his scheme was viciously antisemitic: he argued that Jews and women possessed similar moral deficiencies, while the Aryan male represented the ideal. The 'Jewess', to Weininger, was the lowest of the low.

It's hard to imagine the young Gertrude Stein taking these statements at face value. As her own family history bore out, mass immigration from eastern and central Europe over the nineteenth century had brought Jewish culture into the American consciousness, not always in positive terms: around the turn of the century, when Stein was at college, numerous books, articles and pseudoscientific studies asked whether Jewishness was a religion, a culture, a race, with conclusions ranging from outright prejudice (the Jews as degenerate wanderers, unable to assimilate) to equally stereotypical ideas of Jews as superior, chosen, perhaps dangerously intelligent. Stein was well aware of these debates. At Radcliffe, noting the widespread preconception that Jews were predisposed to physical and mental illness – a pathology attributed, also, to homosexuals – Stein had asked her friend and collaborator Leon Solomons, also Jewish, whether he thought there was 'any special tendency toward melancholia among our people'. In the spring of 1896 she had written an essay titled 'The Modern Jew', in which she argued that Jewish identity was not a question of race or religion, but an ethical spirit: a feeling of kinship which transcends nationhood, and which must be preserved. There, she lamented that so many Jews – including three she knew at Harvard alone – were denying their roots and identifying as Christians. Jews, she explained, are accepted by Gentiles only as long as they make themselves amenable: 'The instant he does aught that is blameworthy,' she wrote, possibly drawing on personal experience, 'swiftly comes opprobation, not only to the man but to his race. People say of him, what can you expect he is only a Jew.' The student Stein, who was simultaneously discovering feminism through the work of Charlotte Perkins Gilman, was scornful of Orthodox Judaism's attitudes to women – 'I don't like to sit behind galleries with a fence around it,' she wrote that summer, 'even if they are considerate enough to leave peep holes in it' – but her essay reveals both a pride in her Jewishness and an ambivalence, born of her awareness of Jews' precarious status. Weininger's overt antisemitism, in the course of a book she so admired, would have registered as a painful blow.

But Stein was always capable of taking on ideas she liked and discarding their contexts – a cavalier approach that would, through her life, generate bewildering contradictions – and a different aspect of Weininger's diatribe caught her attention. Weininger proposed that character is not tied to sex: that a woman can possess masculine traits. What's more, he argued that the most 'masculine woman' might aspire to the category of genius, transcending the limitations of more feminine types. He considered lesbians more emancipated and intellectually advanced than 'feminine' women, thanks to their 'deep-seated craving to acquire man's character . . . and his creative power' – and cited Sappho as the forerunner in a history of 'sexually intermediate' geniuses, including Catherine the Great, Queen Christina of Sweden and George Sand. 'Homosexuality', Weininger wrote, 'is a higher form than heterosexuality . . . Homosexuality in a woman is the outcome of her masculinity and presupposes a higher degree of development.' In the notebooks where she continued to sketch out her system, Stein often replicated Weininger's gendered categories: she designated Fernande Olivier the 'maternal' type, Etta Cone a 'perfect spinster', her sister Bertha 'pure female'. But she described herself as a 'masculine type' – aligned with the artists she most admired. 'Pablo & Matisse have a maleness that belongs to genius,' she wrote. 'Moi aussi perhaps.' Weininger's book offered validation not only to her system, but to herself.

Reading Weininger also focused Stein's conception of character. She was coming to see personality not as a single immutable entity, but a system of interrelated forces within a person that collide and inflect one another, repeating, forming patterns. While Weininger's system focused on the individual, Stein sought to apply his ideas to her own fascination with interpersonal dynamics. One of the most significant distinctions she made was between those who need to love (subduing the other in the process, in order to 'own' them) and those who derive their strength from being loved by others. She called these types 'independent dependent' and 'dependent independent', and decided that they represented 'two ways of loving'. Overall, she identified twenty types, into which she placed all her friends. Several types were designated as Jewish: among these, she drew an important contrast between the 'moral Caliban', removed from experience and thus stuck in tradition, and the 'earthy' group, productive and engaged with the world, who is able to 'unconventionalise' and think originally – the true artist, now triumphantly recast as Jewish. In this latter category she placed Picasso, Cézanne, Flaubert, Matisse, and herself.

That year, 1908, Toklas and Levy joined the Steins for their regular summer sojourn in Fiesole – Toklas spontaneously tossed her corset out of the train window as they approached – where they rented two villas near I Tatti, the sumptuous Renaissance-style home of Bernard and Mary Berenson. (Gertrude, meanwhile, scandalised Mary by swimming in the lake 'clad in nothing but her Fat'.) Ever the elder brother, Michael enquired into Toklas's financial affairs, and – on learning she had a letter of credit, drawing on an inheritance from her grandfather, which was intended to last her ten months – set to stretching her budget to last a full year. Together, Stein and Toklas explored Florence's galleries (Stein fell asleep stretched out on the Uffizi's benches, claiming she liked to wake up surrounded by art); they travelled to Assisi and Arezzo to see paintings by Fra Angelico and Piero della Francesca, and climbed a mountain to the fabled meeting place of Saint Francis and Saint Dominic, where they munched sandwiches in the swirling clouds. During this trip, Stein showed Toklas some pages from her work in progress. Toklas responded positively, and Stein saw her chance. Would Toklas, she asked, take over the typing of her handwritten manuscripts? Toklas, who had been seeking a purpose in Paris, agreed instantly.

Previously, Stein had typed finger by finger on her ancient Blickensderfer typewriter; Toklas soon ran out of patience and sent Stein out to buy an enormous, modern Smith Premier machine. She would arrive at the Steins' in the morning, and – if Leo was out – set up her typewriter in the studio and work until Gertrude came down for her breakfast coffee at noon. In the afternoons, they would go out for walks and visit friends, and often return together to the rue de Fleurus. To the disapproval of Harriet Levy, who wanted Toklas home by midnight, she often stayed on long enough to witness the beginning of one of Gertrude's writing sessions, which started late (to be sure no one would knock at the door) and continued until four or five in the morning, when her concentration was interrupted by birdsong. While Toklas read quietly in the corner – receiving instant admonishment if she made a noise turning a page – Stein would pace around the room, circling the two small tables and the enormous desk in the centre of the studio, then suddenly sit down, seize her pen, and begin to write 'like sheet lightning'. *The Making of Americans* was forming before Toklas's eyes. 'It was like living history,' she recalled. 'I hoped it would go on forever.'

//

As she worked on *The Making of Americans* during 1908, Stein continued to ponder the fate of the three stories, *The Good Anna*, *The Gentle Lena* and *Melanctha*, which had met with mixed responses from the friends to whom she had tentatively shown them. An American editor friend of Leo's, Hutchins Hapgood, told her he was struck by the 'deep humanity' of the stories, and the 'really remarkable way you have of getting deep into human psychology . . . Somehow you have attained your end without any of the ordinary devices of plot, piquancy, conversation, variety, drama, etc.' He warned her, however, that the text demanded serious patience of a reader, and was 'not likely to be popular'. The weathered typescript passed between a succession of friends, agents and publishers, meeting with wholesale rejection. Hapgood sent it to another editor, who regretted that it was 'too unconventional' for his list, but recommended it to a literary agent, Flora Holly, who held on to the pages for six months then pronounced herself flummoxed. Stein, impatient, asked Holly to deliver it to her college friend Mabel Weeks in New York: 'I think it a noble combination of Swift and Matisse,' Stein explained to Weeks in a covering note. Having exhausted all her own ideas, Weeks turned the typescript over to another mutual friend – none other than May Bookstaver, who had recently married a stockbroker and was now known as Mrs Charles Knoblauch.

Stein had done her best to forget about May Bookstaver and Mabel Haynes since moving to Paris in part to get away from them. But she had been kept updated on their news by her friend Emma Lootz Erving, who saw their old crowd regularly in New York. 'May Bookstaver', Erving told Stein in May 1906, 'is running amuck with her instinct for melodrama.' Bookstaver, it transpired, had been telling everyone who would listen the saga of Stein and Haynes's rivalry for her affections. Despite the intensity of their bond, Haynes and Bookstaver both chose – as Stein did not – to marry men. When Haynes announced her engagement to an Austrian army captain in the autumn of 1906, Bookstaver made a last-ditch intervention to try to prevent the marriage, unable to let Haynes go. Two years later, Erving saw May in Washington, and reported back to Stein that she and her new husband seemed charmed with themselves, each other, and life: 'May has invested the past with a romantic mist of contemplation which is edifying.' If she felt any guilt for the pain she had caused Stein five years earlier, perhaps May Knoblauch saw the opportunity to help Stein find a publisher as a kind of recompense. In any case, she was more successful than Stein's other makeshift agents. She took Stein's manuscript to a New York company called the Grafton Press, which offered to print 1,000 copies of the book for a cost of $660, to be borne by Stein herself. 'I want to say frankly that I think you have written a very peculiar book,' a representative wrote to Stein, who had agreed to pay for the publication but refused their suggestion of employing an editor to assist her with grammar. 'It will be a hard thing to make people take it seriously.'

But the stories – published together as *Three Lives* in the summer of 1909 – were heralded with a reception beyond all expectations for a self-financed project of experimental writing. Toklas subscribed on Stein's behalf to a clippings bureau, and together they tracked the responses: the *Kansas City Star* called the book 'a very masterpiece of realism'; the *Nation* praised its 'quite extraordinary vitality conveyed in a most eccentric and difficult form', while the *Boston Morning Herald* concluded that the stories were 'something really new'. Some reviewers took umbrage with the subject matter, denouncing Anna, Lena and Melanctha as members of a 'sordid' class and suggesting that 'the pages devoted to a description of the habits of dogs and of maid-servants are both tedious and distasteful'. But *Three Lives*, to Stein's surprise and delight, was noticed. A Baltimore newspaper published a profile of Stein under the headline 'Eccentric Authoress Once a Student Here'; it conjured a vision of Stein striding around Paris in her brown corduroy suit and sandals, noting that 'the corset, that modern invention of the suppression of unruly flesh, is an unknown article in the simple wardrobe of the fearless Miss Stein'. She was starting to emerge as a public figure: not just as Leo's sister or Picasso's patron, but as a daring and serious writer. It was a triumph which spurred her back to her writing desk.

Stein continued to work on *The Making of Americans* over the next three years, during which time the book fragmented into several splinter projects, and her style – and her life – underwent a series of transformations. *A Long Gay Book*, an offshoot of *The Making of Americans* which she began in 1909, introduces itself as a 'discussion of pairs of people', and sets out to build on her study of paradigms, paying particular attention to the ways people form relationships, and the clashes that ensue when people of contrasting personality types collide. But towards the final third of the book, something uncanny begins to unfold. The vocabulary – previously restricted – suddenly expands. The sentences shift from the undulating repetitions which characterised *The Making of Americans* – 'Any one knowing anything is repeating that thing' – to brief, fragmented phrases that defy logical order, composed of an enigmatic array of words that jostle against one another in combinations that appear to reject rather than build sense. *The Making of Americans* sought to create an orderly system, but *A Long Gay Book* embraces chaos. Stein's writing, previously heavy with despair, is inflected with a puckish joy. The text careers into the kitchen – 'Please tell the artichoke to underestimate valor,' she writes. 'Spice the same handkerchief and season the tomato, it is no use to be silly and if there is spoiling why should an atlas show that' – and, thrillingly, the bedroom. 'A lovely love is sitting', writes Stein, 'and she sits there now she is in bed, she is in bed. A lovely love is cleaner when she is so clean, she is so clean, she is all mine.'

By now, it was becoming apparent to everyone around them that Toklas was more than Stein's secretary. Harriet Levy recalled Toklas using thirty handkerchiefs a day, weeping 'because of the new love that had come into her life'. At first, Stein had been fascinated by Harriet Levy, a deeply anxious woman of the type who 'feel their pulses to see if they are living', and observed her character as eagerly as she had Rosenshine's, meting out advice on how Harriet ought to face her fears. But her enthusiasm had waned after Levy, seeking guidance from a higher power than Gertrude Stein, turned to Christian Science, and Stein and Toklas were spending less and less time with her; Levy could tell that they were scheming for her to hurry up and leave Paris. In the summer of 1910, Levy returned to California, and in September, Alice B. Toklas came to live with Gertrude and Leo at 27 rue de Fleurus. Now she was on hand to monitor the door on Saturday evenings, to cook on Hélène's night off, and – when Stein realised that Toklas was an excellent and creative chef – to host dinner parties, including one where she served Picasso a memorable sea bass decorated with a design fusing hard-boiled eggs, mayonnaise and tomato paste (his only comment was that the colours were more suitable for Matisse).

That December, Stein wrote a short piece called 'Ada', which marked her first experiment in approximating Toklas's voice, and placed their relationship – and domestic routine – at the heart of Stein's writing practice. Ada, a young woman who loves telling stories, is made to keep house for disgruntled male relatives after the death of her beloved mother. For the first two-thirds of the text, Ada is a daughter and sister, with no identity of her own. Then, suddenly, she goes away from home, and 'came to be happier than anybody else who was living then'. Ada finds someone to be 'always completely listening' to her; loving, here, is figured as an exchange of words and stories, on and off the page.

The text inscribes Stein and Toklas together: it celebrates Stein's finding in Toklas both subject and audience, whose support – practical and emotional – made her writing possible. ('Ada' recalls 'aider' – a nod to Toklas's crucial role.) After Stein wrote 'Ada', she began copying out the text in a fresh notebook, only for Toklas to take over the pen and continue the task herself. Their voices harmonise on the page, Toklas storyteller and scribe, Stein listener and writer, both playing two parts in a single, ongoing, mutually nourishing dialogue. And as their intimacy deepened, Stein's work was becoming more domestic, more sensual, more erotic. *Three Lives* had displayed a bitter negativity towards female experience: while not explicit, there are enough hints to read each protagonist as a closeted lesbian, unable to express themselves or act on their own desires. Now, secure in her relationship with Toklas, Stein could shift her critique away from societal norms and towards the structures of language. Life and writing, for Stein, were becoming one shared enterprise; so too was their relationship becoming more public, and in the process, more artfully performative. During a trip to Venice, they had their photograph taken among a flock of pigeons in piazza San Marco, which they printed as postcards to send to friends. Those who had once asked Gertrude to pass their regards to Leo now enquired, instead, after Alice.

Following 'Ada', Stein broke off from her work on both *The Making of Americans* and *A Long Gay Book*. Her fascination with character found

Stein and Toklas in Venice

a new outlet in a series of short compositions she called 'portraits', taking their cues from 'everybody who came in and out'. Each text set out not to describe a friend, but to convey the essence of their character: to show how, in her terms, 'any one being one is that one'. Many of her first portraits dwelt on artists; Stein was working out, in her own way, what a creative life might look like. The sculptor Elie Nadelman, for example, she defined as 'one feeling light being existing . . . one who was completely thinking about expressing light being existing', while the ballerina Isadora Duncan – whose single-minded commitment to her art Stein evidently admired – is 'one dancing . . . In being one dancing this one is expressing that dancing is existing. In dancing this one is expressing anything.' Stein chose to lean on short phrases or single words – usually verbs, like 'loving', 'living' or 'struggling' – which contain within them a multitude of possible implications that build as the word is repeated in altered contexts. 'I like it', she wrote in *The Making of Americans*, 'when I am feeling many ways of using one word in writing . . . different ways of emphasising can make very different meanings in a phrase or a sentence I have made.' Later, she compared the incremental changes in her repeated phrases to the succession of unique frames in cinema, designed to bring out a sense of ongoing motion that would unfold on the page as if in real time. Her first portraits picked up on William James's idea that all knowledge is contained in the experience of the present, and set out to convey a person's inner state: no straightforward description or traditional narrative, based on memory or past events, but people slowly revealing themselves to her, until she felt so attuned to their rhythms it was almost as if 'I had the existence of that one inside in me'.

As Stein's enthusiasm for portraits grew, the manuscripts piled up. She enlisted the help of the same friends who had tried to interest publishers in *Three Lives*, and kept a small black notebook tracking the editors and magazines to which each text had been sent. After each rejection, she wrote 'returned' next to the title. In early 1912, May Knoblauch – who had regained Stein's trust by negotiating the deal with the Grafton Press for *Three Lives* – took Stein's portraits of Picasso and Matisse to the photographer and gallerist Alfred Stieglitz, whose 291 gallery on Fifth Avenue had held the first exhibition of Matisse's paintings in America. Stieglitz offered to publish the pieces in a special number of his magazine *Camera Work*, accompanied by images of paintings from the Steins' collection. The portraits, read together, contrast the pair as two titans of modern art, Matisse 'struggling' – the portrait's central word – to convince himself of the value of his art, buffeted by conflicting reactions from his audiences, Picasso the emerging leader 'whom some were certainly following', a man of charm and vision but possibly flighty: 'He was', she writes, 'not ever completely working.' 'You will be very careful, will you not,' wrote Stein to Stieglitz, 'that no punctuation is introduced into the things in printing. It is very necessary as I have put in all of it that I want and any that is introduced will make everything wrong.' Stieglitz promised, and in his preface to the publication, he declared that in Stein's work 'the Post-Impressionist spirit is found expressing itself in literary form'.

//

In the spring of 1912, around the time of her thirty-eighth birthday, Stein finally completed *The Making of Americans* – the project which had consumed her, on and off, for a decade. Since beginning the novel again in the summer of 1908, Stein had used the text to reflect on her experiences of listening deeply to Annette Rosenshine, Harriet Levy and Alice Toklas. 'There was one,' writes Stein, probably thinking back to reading Toklas's private letters before they met, 'I knew some things about this one . . . I had heard descriptions of this one, I was interested but not more than I am in every one . . . Then I looked intensely at this one . . . it gave new meanings to many things.' Around the end of 1909, she had reached an impasse in her work, struggling to realise her character Alfred Hersland, a combination of herself and her brothers Leo and Michael: 'I am all unhappy in this writing,' she confessed. After 600 pages, she tried to articulate – to herself as much as to her imagined reader – one of her underlying motives for trying to devise this huge character scheme. 'It makes it simple to be certain,' she wrote – words which recall her realisation, after her mother's death, that 'nothing is safe'. The idea that everyone has a place in the grand system of the universe, Stein tentatively suggests, is 'comforting to me just now when I am thinking of every one always growing older and then dying'. But hard as she tried, she was beginning to wonder if a 'history of everyone' might never be possible to write. Her loss of faith in the system posed an existential threat as well as an aesthetic one: at stake was not just the future of her novel, but the world view that had sustained Stein in her grief. The narrator persists, despite her crisis of confidence, but her belief is shaken. As she reworked the Alfred Hersland chapter, Stein introduced the haunting refrain which would dominate the final section, 'Dead is dead.'

By the autumn of 1911, Stein had made peace with the flaws in her scheme. Living happily with Toklas, her confidence bolstered by the praise for *Three Lives*, she was willing to accept that there would remain mysteries in people's personalities that could not be contained in schemes and diagrams. The last chapter told the story of David Hersland, a mix of Gertrude, Leo and her old friend Leon Solomons, who had died, tragically young, following an operation. Writing it was an emotional and tense process for Stein, who knew her enormous project was nearing its end – 'I have a flush from feverish feeling,' she wrote, 'I never will live more with every one.' In that rush of writing, Stein laid out her hero's inner life from birth to death, leaving behind all the scaffolding, types and descriptive terms which had, after all, come to clutter her vision. 'Don't understand others,' read one of the last entries in her 'Diagram Book'. The enormous novel was done.

The Making of Americans is a strange, sprawling, incantatory text: a work of art in restless dialogue with itself, that seems to be constantly shedding its own skin as it expands and morphs under the reader's eye. The first pages (retained from one of the earliest drafts) introduce a cast of characters whose life stories Stein suggests we will come to know:

the Dehning parents and their children Julia, George and Hortense; the Herslands and their children Alfred, Martha and David. The novel announces itself as a classic immigrant narrative: 'The new people made out of the old,' Stein writes, 'that is the story that I mean to tell.' As the novel opens, eighteen-year-old Julia Dehning – who, like Melanctha, is eager for 'real experience' – is planning to defy her father's wishes and marry the rich and cosmopolitan lawyer Alfred Hersland, whom she considers 'a master in the art of life'. Stein sets out to offer a bourgeois tale of social advancement and the accumulation of wealth, imbued with tensions between three generations.

But after thirty pages, Stein's own voice suddenly – almost shockingly – intrudes. 'This that I write down a little each day here on my scraps of paper for you', she warns the reader, as if out of nowhere, 'is not just an ordinary kind of novel with a plot and conversations to amuse you.' From this point, the family's story becomes less and less important, its climax endlessly postponed, as Stein first sets up then confounds expectations of structure and narrative development. Stein comes back to her characters every so often as if reminding herself where she started, offering snippets of information about them and others they know – the dissolution of Julia's and Alfred's marriage; Martha's desertion by her husband; David's death – but the book's driving force becomes, instead, the narrator's effort to construct her comprehensive characterology. 'Soon,' she insists, 'there will be a history of every kind of men and women . . . there will be a history of them and now there is here a beginning.'

As the book progresses, Stein explains and refines her scheme again and again, adding new details as they come to her. She reiterates and builds on several fundamental ideas, to which she constantly returns as if laying down anchors for her own reassurance: that every individual is 'different from all the other millions made just like him'; that each person is defined by their 'bottom nature', which governs every aspect of their behaviour. That 'bottom nature', she continues, can be discerned by listening, carefully, to the characteristic gestures and ways of speaking which 'everybody always is repeating'; most pressingly of all, a 'complete history of every one', such as the one in progress, will ultimately produce 'complete understanding of men and women'. 'Repeating is the whole of living', she adds, 'and by repeating comes understanding, and understanding is to some the most important part of living.'

The Making of Americans is less a novel than a constellation of the human mind, a map of reality that yields its most pressing insights into the mind of its anxiously questing narrator, convinced she is on her way to a revelation of deep importance, but struggling to keep her text from spiralling out of her control. She writes viscerally of the euphoria of fresh ideas: 'Each one slowly comes to be a whole one in me, slowly it sounds louder and louder and louder inside me through my ears and eyes and feelings . . . a louder and louder pounding . . . I am filled full of knowing and it bursts out from me.' But the reader senses, too, her despair when doubts creep in and the enormity of the undertaking overwhelms her. 'Perhaps no one ever will know the complete history of every one. This is a sad thing . . . this is very discouraging thinking. I am very sad now in this feeling . . . A very melancholy feeling.' As the novel draws towards its close, the narrator reaches 'complete desolation', certain, at last, that her project is impossible. 'Sometimes', she laments, 'it is a very wearing thing bringing my feeling to the realisation that I have been wrong about something.' Yet with *The Making of Americans*, Stein had engineered a radical redefinition of the novel. Over the course of its writing, Stein claimed a style all her own, which blended scientific and literary innovation, showed its workings, and defiantly named the guiding force behind its composition: the narrator's pleasure in her task, in the gradual discovery of her voice, in the release of her intellectual powers. If *The Making of Americans* began with an uncertain Jewish daughter yearning for new horizons, it ends with a triumphant writer-scientist, in the process of learning what it means to make reality out of words.

MAN OF LETTERS / 67

4 : EXTREME CUBIST LITERATURE

Near the beginning of *The Making of Americans*, Stein breaks off abruptly to address her reader – 'but truly,' she adds, 'I never feel it that there ever can be for me any such a creature, no it is this scribbled and dirty and lined paper that is really to be to me always my receiver'. She knew the novel was long, repetitive and unwieldy; that it was wholly unlike anything written before. But as the novel progressed, her desire for affirmation only swelled. Throughout, Stein – or her narrator – contemplates the future of her work. 'I write for myself and strangers,' she admits, lamenting the indifference of those around her – thinking, perhaps, of Picasso's *Demoiselles d'Avignon*, which still languished in his studio, disdained and unsold. She implores her readers to be patient and eager, to trust her intuition and follow her in her quest. At this early point, Stein was already setting herself up as a kind of Cassandra, harbinger of a significant message yet doomed to be misunderstood and ignored. 'I want readers', she reiterated, 'so strangers must do it.'

In the summer of 1912, Stein and Toklas travelled together to Tangier and Spain. It was a period of enormous creativity for Stein, enhanced by the sights and sounds of Spain, the warmth of the people she met – who admired Stein's cane with its amber head, and speculated that she belonged to a religious order – and her pleasure in Toklas's company. They adored Ávila, the home of Stein's favourite saint, Teresa; in Madrid, they discovered Spanish dancing and bullfighting (which Stein watched with relish while Toklas hid her eyes beneath the brim of her flowered hat). Bulls charge into the latter part of *A Long Gay Book*, blood mingling with rain; in 'Susie Asado' and 'Preciosilla', short poems inspired by the whirling skirts of flamenco dancers, Stein's rhythm accelerates like the clashing of feet and castanets. In Granada, Stein 'worked terrifically' on a flurry of fresh pieces that marked a definitive shift in her style. Up to this point, Stein later recalled, her interest had been primarily in 'people, their character and what went on inside them'. Having moved away from typology, during that Spanish summer she 'first felt a desire to express the rhythm of the visible world'.

For the first time, Stein explained, individual words began to feel 'more important than the sentence structure or the paragraphs'. Drawing, perhaps, on her neurological research at Johns Hopkins as well as William James's ideas of thought as a stream of consciousness, Stein was thinking deeply about perception, and the way the brain processes language. She briefly experimented with inventing words, but soon went back to English: Stein was beginning to imagine a kind of writing so original that to read it would almost require a rewiring of the brain's neural architecture, to unlearn all the ways we expect written language to behave. After *The Making of Americans*, Stein's desire to wring every ounce of meaning from a limited set of words transformed into an even bolder ambition: to shed language of all its previous associations, so that her words would mean something fresh and specific, unique to the particular context she was giving them. In the *Autobiography*, Stein described this impulse as her 'intellectual passion for exactitude', and linked it to her need to realise a thought perfectly before putting it into writing: 'The more exactly the words fit the emotion', she wrote elsewhere, 'the more beautiful the words.' Later, Stein defined this urge as her reaction to the falsity she had begun to see in purely representational art, and the alternative possibilities being put forward by Picasso, who was by now experimenting with geometric compositions (soon to acquire the label 'Cubism') which invite viewers to identify familiar shapes, but reject straightforward imitation of the object in favour of fragmentary distortions. 'I was alone at this time in understanding him,' Stein wrote later, 'perhaps because I was expressing the same thing in literature.' Just as Picasso sought to convey the essence of a person or object without simply creating a replica, Stein wanted her writing to feel not like a description of sounds, colours or emotions, but an 'intellectual recreation' of the 'thing in itself'.

In Spain, Stein began to write a series of short vignettes, each headed with an enigmatic title – 'A CARAFE, THAT IS A BLIND GLASS', 'GLAZED GLITTER', 'A SUBSTANCE IN A CUSHION'. By the time she finished, Stein had filled three notebooks, scratching their titles on to the front covers: Objects, Food, Rooms. Within their pages, Stein had created something entirely new. Each word in *Tender Buttons* – as it came to be called – was recognisable in itself, but here words follow others not to advance any story, but to propel the text forward through verbal echo, surprise or pure insistence. 'Objects' appears, perhaps, to be rooted in a domestic space: a cluttered, dusty but welcoming atelier arranged with bottles, tasselled furnishings, chairs and tables, an inviting closet, boxes stacked in corners, and freshly cut flowers. A reference to 'Mildred's Umbrella' gives a hint at guests, perhaps divested of their hats, canes and cloaks, sharing coffee and cigarettes and proceeding to the table where 'a dinner set of colored china' is laid out for the ensuing feast. 'Food' opens with 'Roastbeef' and proceeds through a series of luxurious food-stuffs – mutton, rhubarb, asparagus, cream, salmon – though the surreal spread appears to be less for eating than for visual dissection: 'Sausages in between a glass,' writes Stein. 'Cold coffee with a corn a corn yellow and green mass is a gem.' The final section, 'Rooms', begins with a statement that might be read as Stein's aesthetic manifesto, following her study of Cézanne: 'Act so that there is no use in a center.' *Tender Buttons* is a cele-bration of mutability, a rejoinder to rules, where words are set free from the shackles of meaning and grammatical function, made unfamiliar, and charged with power to make the world afresh.

If *Tender Buttons* has a subject, it lies somewhere in the small sensual pleasures of daily life: the tactility of materials (ribbon, silk, copper), the textures and colours of food, the routines – and erotics – of shar-ing a home with a partner. 'In the inside there is sleeping,' writes Stein in 'Food', 'in the outside there is reddening, in the morning there is meaning, in the evening there is feeling.' But the primary pleasure of the text lies in its language. Stein delights in defining things, and pos-ing questions that cannot be answered because their component words bear little obvious relation to one another – 'Why is a feel oyster an egg stir,' she writes. 'Why is it orange center.' She attempted to empty her mind of what she called 'associational emotion' – the meaning a word conventionally bears, which holds within it a memory of all the previous times it has been used in that way. 'I took individual words and thought about them until I got their weight and volume complete and put them next to another word,' Stein told an interviewer in 1946, 'and at this same time I found out very soon that there is no such thing as putting them together without sense.'

Stein had come to see words as living entities with physical properties of their own, like the materials a painter or sculptor might take on and shape into something new, or the neurons in the brain, processing information and connecting with one another through synapses. 'Writing', she wrote, 'may be made between the ear and the eye': now, her inspiration tended to come not from the external world, but from the sounds and shapes of words themselves. 'Give known or pin ware,' opens a text titled 'Guillaume Apollinaire', Stein sounding the syllables in her mouth and re-making her friend's name into something else – almost translating the French words into English, matching them to equivalents not by meaning but by sound. 'Susie Asado' borrowed the Spanish word *asado*, meaning 'roasted', which rhymes with *helado*, ice-cream; the enigmatic final line of its companion portrait, 'Preciosilla' – 'Toasted susie is my ice-cream' – shows Stein revelling in the possibilities of her own multi-lingual puns, recycling and reanimating the earlier text, imbuing it with erotic delight. As Stein's words are loosened from association with one another, they brighten a little in themselves; they arrest both eye and ear as the reader is forced to pause on them, look and listen, rather than fit them automatically into a sentence. There's no discernible narrator in these texts, as there was in *The Making of Americans*, yet Stein is present in every sentence, forming and re-forming language, and celebrating the space and love she was sharing, now, with Toklas.

//

Stein's appearance in *Camera Work* had drawn the attention of a woman whose Greenwich Village parties offered bohemian New York a gathering place akin in spirit to the rue de Fleurus, with the Steins' austerity replaced by lavish quantities of Scotch, bowls full of cigarettes and trays mounted with piles of ham and Gorgonzola sandwiches. Like Gertrude Stein, Mabel Dodge sought to make her life a work of art: she surrounded herself with writers and artists, whom she gathered at her Fifth Avenue apartment and at the Villa Curonia, her fifteenth-century palazzo outside Florence. A mutual friend brought Dodge to a Saturday evening salon while she was visiting Paris, and the pair immediately hit it off, Stein eager for enthusiastic readers and practical help with publishers, Dodge seeking to ally herself with the newest ideas that crossed her path. Stein showed Dodge the latest version of *The Making of Americans*, and was immensely gratified when Dodge responded (despite having nearly lost the entire manuscript after dropping it on a train platform) that it was 'one of the most remarkable things I have ever read'. 'It is as new & strange & big as the post-impressionists in their way,' she wrote. 'I am perfectly convinced, it is the forerunner of a whole epoch of new form & expression. It is very morally constructive for I feel it will alter reality as we have known it.'

In the autumn of 1912, shortly after their return from Spain, Stein and Toklas visited Dodge at the Villa Curonia. Stein was still grappling with the ideas unlocked by *Tender Buttons*, and had returned to portraiture with new energy. Dodge had already poured out her heart in letters to Stein, expressing her dissatisfaction with her husband and her passion for her son's handsome young tutor. Stein's bedroom adjoined the room where Dodge would visit her lover at night; kept awake by the murmurings and moans, Stein lit a candle and composed a portrait of her host. Dodge was thrilled, and immediately had 300 copies printed and covered in Florentine wallpaper, which she placed on a table in her hallway for guests to take. Back in America, she reported her friends' (often bewildered) reactions to 'The Portrait of Mabel Dodge at the Villa Curonia', and urged Stein to visit New York: 'On account of my judicious scattering of the Portrait,' wrote Dodge, '*everyone* is saying "*Who* is Gertrude Stein? *Who* is Mabel Dodge at the Villa Curonia."'

Dodge's flattery was certainly self-serving – the connection of their names through the portrait meant she was well positioned to bask in Stein's reflected glory – but she operated shrewdly to build Stein up as the literary counterpart to the new, non-representational, Post-Impressionist art. At the start of 1913, New York was consumed with preparations for the Armory Show, which Dodge described to Stein as 'the most important public event that has ever come off since the signing of the Declaration of Independence'. Among the 1,300 works brought over for the exhibition, which was conceived in order to introduce American audiences to the modern art being made in Europe, was a roster of loans from 27 rue de Fleurus, including Matisse's *Blue Nude* and two Picasso still lifes. Dodge – who joined the organising committee a few weeks before the opening, and instantly started to call it 'my own little Revolution' – told Stein she had been raving to the organisers about her friend's work, and that she intended to write an article about Stein and Picasso for *Arts and Decoration* magazine, which was devoting its entire March 1913 issue to the show. Although she admitted her interpretation might be 'not at *all* what you mean', 'it *will*', Dodge gleefully wrote, 'make your name known by & large – as the writer of "post impressionistic literature" . . . So there Gertrude is my confession. *I* am your faithful & incomprehending Boswell.'

Stein, for now, was happy to accept Dodge's enthusiasm. After the success of *Three Lives*, she was hungry for more attention. 'You have made an audience for me alright, it's been a real triumph. I can't thank you enough,' wrote Stein to Dodge. The article – Stein's most significant piece of publicity yet – conjured a vibrant picture of the Stein salon, and made the case that Stein 'is doing with words what Picasso is doing with paint. She is impelling language to induce new states of consciousness.' After it came out, Dodge wrote triumphantly to Stein, claiming magazine editors were flocking to her asking for examples of Stein's work to publish, and that she was demanding Stein be paid for every opportunity. No chances were taken: she sent a lawyer round to visit a publisher who held on too long to a manuscript, and insisted, on Stein's stipulation, that any contract signed should contain a bankruptcy clause to prevent the copyright going to creditors if the company went bust. One friend, she boasted, had just declared that 'the name of Gertrude Stein is better known in New York today than the name of God'. Stein replied, 'Hurrah for gloire.'

In Paris, friends were bemused at the turn Stein's work had taken, and at New York's alleged appetite for what seemed to many like incomprehensible jumbles of words. Leo called the 'Portrait of Mabel Dodge' 'damned nonsense', while Mary Berenson sent her family a copy of 'Gertrude Stein's latest amazing (and horrid) production', expressing wonder that 'many people take it seriously as a new worthwhile "departure." It isn't even funny, only horrible.' But insulated by support and encouragement from Toklas and Dodge, Stein was able to ignore dissenting voices and focus on her work. She asked the American friends – including May Knoblauch – who had copies of her manuscripts to send everything to Dodge, so she could henceforth field all enquiries for Stein's work. 'I am working like a dog over you,' Dodge told her. 'It has to be done subtly. I have made all NY as well as suburbs talk about you. Now is the time for the publishers & *they* know it.' 'It takes lots of shoving to make them take me,' Stein replied matter-of-factly, 'but I guess you will do it.' But Dodge's position as Stein's exclusive representative was shortly to be superseded.

On 24 February 1913, Dodge sent Stein a short article in the *New York Times* under the headline 'Cubist of Letters' – unsigned, and inexplicably published only in the financial section of the paper's early edition, but written at Dodge's encouragement by a new friend of hers, a young dance critic making his name as a champion of the avant-garde. 'This is post-impressionist, or cubist, or futurist literature . . . a new attempt at feeling a thing,' he wrote, quoting an unnamed friend – Dodge – who had declared that Stein's writing 'demands an entirely new point of view'. Stein was delighted with the publicity, and intrigued when its author, Carl Van Vechten, wrote beguilingly to tell her his original article was 'three times as long and four times as amusing', and to ask if she would meet him in Paris that June. 'He wants me to tell him about myself,' she told Dodge. 'I hope I will be satisfactory.'

Like Stein, Van Vechten knew the value in self-mythologising, and like Dodge, he saw the advantages of yoking his own name to Stein's fast-growing legend. Their first meeting was a hit. Van Vechten reported to his wife that Stein was 'a wonderful personality . . . She lives in a place hung with Picassos and she showed me some more sketches of his including men with erect Tom-Toms much bigger than mine.' In later years, he claimed that they had met in a box at the premiere of Stravinsky's *Rite of Spring*, where riots broke out among the audience appalled at the discordant music. It was a sly elision of the truth which placed the two of them together at one of the most notorious moments in avant-garde history. In fact, they had attended the second performance, but – as Van Vechten cheerfully wrote to Stein – 'one must only be accurate about such details in a work of fiction'. Six years younger than Stein, Van Vechten was eager to ally himself with anything that seemed to upend tradition: his debut as an arts critic was a glowing review of Strauss's adaptation of *Salome*, notorious for a nine-minute-long striptease, and he was one of the first to praise Isadora Duncan's fluid dance movements. And he had connections at many of the leading small magazines, where Stein most wanted her work to appear. As their correspondence continued, Stein began to sound out Van Vechten about the possibility of finding an audience for *Tender Buttons*. 'I tried to get a combination of sound and picture that would make the effect,' she told him. 'I worked over them awfully hard, and I think I succeeded.'

Van Vechten complimented *Tender Buttons* lavishly, and swiftly obtained an offer of publication from his friend Donald Evans, a dandyish poet who had founded Claire Marie Press to print what he called 'New Books for Exotic Tastes'. Stein was enthusiastic, but Dodge – sensing that her grip on Stein's image was slipping – wrote to express her concern at the choice of press, which she considered 'absolutely third-rate'. The association, she argued, risked the public inferring 'that there is something degenerate & effete & decadent about the whole of the cubist movement which they *all* connect you with'. When Stein didn't change her mind, Dodge wrote again, with renewed desperation: 'I really believe you will give your work a set back and make further publishing & understanding of it more difficult unless you withdraw what he has from D. Evans.' But Stein remained resolute: the contract was signed in March 1914, and she asked Dodge to return the short pieces in her possession. Dodge attempted to keep their correspondence up, but Stein's replies grew more and more infrequent, and further invitations to the Villa Curonia were coldly refused.

The publication of *Tender Buttons*, in May 1914, sparked debates across America. 'Officer, She Is Writing Again,' announced *Detroit News*. The *Pittsburgh Dispatch* denounced it as 'a scramble of meaningless words' from a writer, nonetheless, who appeared to be 'the most talked-about creature in the intellectual world today'; the *Boston Evening Transcript* lampooned a library for classifying *Tender Buttons* under 'literature'; while one critic claimed that three typesetters had quit their jobs rather than attempt to set the text, which 'can be read either backward or forward, for it produces the same impression either way'. Evans was delighted to trade on Stein's controversy, describing *Tender Buttons* in his press release as 'one of the most unique books of the twentieth century' and Stein 'the patron saint of the new artists'. Whether or not the work was genius, mad or a hoax, he declined to confirm: 'It is idle to attempt to pass judgment at the present moment. Time alone can give the verdict. For us it is merely that she is a real force that must be reckoned with – she cannot be ignored . . . The effect produced on the first reading is something like terror.'

Whether ecstatic or vitriolic, the attention the book garnered was unprecedented. Newspapers, both local and national, devoted not just reviews but columns and opinion pieces to Stein and *Tender Buttons*. Those who praised the book – or at least sought to appraise it on its own terms – claimed Stein had found 'an entirely new use for words', only to be accused of posturing, in a pathetic attempt to demonstrate pseudo-sophistication. The well-known humorist and poet Don Marquis started to quote lines from *Tender Buttons* as a running gag in his *New York Evening Sun* column, while the *Chicago Tribune* invited readers of 'extreme Cubist literature' to send in their own attempts at 'futurist poetry', urging them first to 'use a vacuum cleaner on your brain'. One commentator spoke for many when he noted that the scale of discourse had long since transcended the question of Stein's actual merits (and that far more people were opining on the book than could actually have read it, given its limited print run): 'It will not do to say that nobody takes her seriously; newspapers do, or they would not give up so much space to her.' As the poet Alfred Kreymborg put it, 'Gertrude Stein has provided the world with a new kind of entertainment.' Whether you defended or attacked or simply laughed at her, he wrote, 'Miss Stein will have benefited you. She has given you a new sensation.'

Van Vechten saw his moment to assert his status as Stein's primary promoter and interpreter. He set out his position in an article in *The Trend* magazine of August 1914, titled 'How to Read Gertrude Stein'. 'Miss Stein has no explanations to offer regarding her work,' he informed his readers. 'I have often questioned her, but I have met with no satisfaction. She asks you to read.' He painted a colourful picture of a mysterious eccentric, 'massive in physique', who stalked Paris in brown velvet robes and carpet slippers and wrote by night. Stein, he explained, had taken on English, a language 'of hypocrisy and evasion', and 'turned language into music, really made its sound more important than its sense'. To Mabel Dodge, Van Vechten's article, coupled with Stein's ongoing silence, made clear that she had been supplanted. When Dodge complained to Leo Stein that his sister had cut her off without a word of explanation, he speculated that Gertrude felt threatened by the publicity Dodge herself garnered from the connection: 'There was a doubt in her mind', Dodge remembered Leo telling her, 'about who was the bear and who was leading the bear.' But by this time, Leo too had ceased to be his sister's confidant.

The three of them – Toklas and the two Steins – had lived uneasily together since 1910. Leo had long since retreated from the regular

Saturday nights: when Stein and Toklas visited London early in 1913, on a trip Stein called their honeymoon, he refused even to open the door to expectant visitors. He was preoccupied with two matters: his diet, and his girlfriend. When Toklas joined the household, Leo was engulfed in what he called a 'perfect whirlpool of tragicomic romance': an on-again-off-again relationship with Nina Auzias, a singer and life model whom he had met at a party and immediately asked to pose for him nude. In February 1910, Leo reported that Nina had several men desperate to marry her, all threatening to kill themselves and each other if she didn't choose them. Gertrude disapproved of Nina: her portrait 'Elise Surville' portrayed her would-be sister-in-law as a prostitute, selling her wares *sur ville*, a clear reference to Paris's red light district. As his relationship faltered, Leo had become possessed with faddish diets; he began with Fletcherism – chewing food thoroughly to optimise digestion – and soon was fasting for twenty or thirty days at a time, which left him weak and practically delirious. Gertrude watched her brother alienate his friends, sapped of mental energy and increasingly cantankerous. Worst of all, he thought her work was ridiculous, and said so. Cubism, he insisted, was 'tommyrot . . . whether in paint or ink'; he added, crankily, that he supposed his opinion counted for nothing since he was a 'rank outsider . . . no longer a prophet'.

On 7 February 1913, Leo Stein had written to their mutual friend Mabel Weeks that 'one of the greatest changes that has become decisive in recent times is the fairly definite "disaggregation" of Gertrude and myself'. 'The presence of Alice was a godsend,' he continued, 'as it enabled the thing to happen without any explosion. As we have come to maturity, we have come to find that there is practically nothing under the heavens that we don't either disagree about, or at least regard with different sympathies.' That spring, he left Paris for Florence. He told Weeks how relieved he was to have moved out: that his health and memory were improving, he was beginning to unravel 'impenetrable mysteries' of mathematics, and was very happy living simply, eating just bread and fruit, and seeing nobody.

In *The Autobiography of Alice B. Toklas*, Stein elided the emotional import of Leo's departure, focusing only on practical matters: 'During the winter Gertrude Stein's brother decided that he would go to Florence to live. They divided the pictures that they had bought together, between them.' Gertrude had the paintings appraised by Picasso's dealer Daniel-Henry Kahnweiler, who estimated the value of the collection at 158,550 francs. She took possession of all the Picassos (she sold three to Kahnweiler for 20,000 francs and a new painting), while Leo left with all the Matisses, with the exception of the *Femme au Chapeau*. Leo wrote from Florence to remind Gertrude, who had evidently challenged his right to a Cézanne painting of apples, that he had paid a 'grossly disproportionate' share of the household expenses, and that the apples were irreplaceable for him. 'I hope that we will all live happily ever after,' he concluded, 'sucking gleefully our respective oranges.'

In her autobiography, Mabel Dodge laid the blame for her schism with Stein firmly on one person. The split, she declared, was 'Alice's final and successful effort in turning Gertrude from me'. From her first visit to the rue de Fleurus, Dodge had considered Toklas a malevolent presence in the household. She had made herself indispensable, Dodge thought, by doing 'everything to save Gertrude a movement . . . and Gertrude was growing helpless and foolish from it and less and less inclined to do anything herself'. Dodge assumed that insecurity was Toklas's motive for insisting Stein cease contact: she claimed to have felt an attraction from Stein – 'such a strong look over the table that it seemed to cut across the air to me in a band of electrified steel' – which had ignited Toklas's jealousy. Toklas appeared, Dodge wrote, to be 'so self-obliterating that no one considered her very much beyond thinking her a silent, picturesque object in the background, but lo and behold, she pushed Leo out quite soon'.

Leo's assessment of Toklas was no more positive. 'She's a sort of all-important second fiddle,' he raged in a letter to Mabel Weeks, 'a kind of abnormal vampire who gives more than she takes.' In the summer of 1913, Carl Van Vechten met Leo at the Villa Curonia, and recorded in his diary that Leo said he had told Gertrude 'that any manifestation of homosexuality of any kind annoyed him and he asked them to refrain . . . as they were accustomed to being rather careless in their affection before him'. Leo had also, apparently, told the gathered group that Toklas was 'a stupid girl' and that 'some day she will do harm to Gertrude': 'It sickened me', Leo concluded, 'to see the weaker nature getting the better of the stronger.' Van Vechten, when he came to know Stein and Toklas better, came to agree superficially with these interpretations of their interdependence: Stein, he admitted, could not 'cook an egg, or sew a button, or even place a postage stamp of the correct denomination on an envelope'. But Van Vechten saw what the others did not: that Toklas's devotion created the conditions essential for Stein's writing. Now, visitors to the rue de Fleurus would see that Leo's old door was plastered up, and Picasso's portrait of Gertrude had taken centre stage above her chair. No longer was this the shared salon of Leo Stein and his eccentric sister: this was the home, and the workplace, of the internationally renowned writer Gertrude Stein and Alice B. Toklas, her secretary and wife.

5 : A PUZZLE PICTURE

After Leo's departure, Stein and Toklas found themselves alone together, for the first time, at 27 rue de Fleurus. Slowly, shyly, they started to feel out the contours of the familiar rooms anew, transforming the apartment into a space shaped entirely for them. Over the first months of 1914, as she passed her fortieth birthday, Stein's attentions were focused on the home she and Toklas were creating together – rehanging the remaining pictures to mask the gaps Leo had left behind, measuring themselves for personalised chairs, building a corridor between the atelier and the main apartment so they no longer risked a soaking when passing from one to the other in the rain, and printing shared calling cards ('Miss Stein | Miss Toklas | 27, rue de Fleurus') which Picasso – now experimenting with collage – promptly immortalised in a *trompe l'œil* still life.

Amid the bustle of renovations, Stein subscribed to the *Daily Mail*; for now, the stories of escalating tensions between European states made less impression on her than the tales of courageous British suffragettes. She was planning another trip to London, during which she hoped to cement friendships with writers and artists who might help

Dice, Packet of Cigarettes, and Visiting-Card by Pablo Picasso, 1914

her find a British publisher for *Three Lives*. She had sent the book to several leading popular novelists – H. G. Wells, Arnold Bennett, John Galsworthy – hoping their praise would open new commercial prospects; Toklas recalled later that Stein cherished Wells's warm reply more than any other letter she ever received from a stranger, 'because it was the first from anyone whose judgement she appreciated'. Stein had met a few members of the Bloomsbury Group who visited the rue de Fleurus to see the art collection: Roger Fry borrowed several of her paintings for the era-defining Post-Impressionist Exhibition he curated at London's Grafton Galleries in December 1910, and he now arranged an interview for Stein with the renowned publisher John Lane. Lane's office, near Piccadilly, was their first stop in London, in July 1914; Stein talked to him while Toklas examined shop windows outside, and she emerged triumphant with an invitation to return at the end of the month to sign a contract. After ten days in Cambridge and a further fortnight in London, they planned to spend the August bank holiday weekend at the cottage of the mathematician and philosopher Alfred North Whitehead in the Wiltshire village of Lockeridge. They had hardly unpacked their belongings when they heard the news: Germany had entered Luxembourg, and Winston Churchill, as First Lord of the Admiralty, had mobilised the British fleet. The German army was marching apace on Paris, where Stein's precious paintings and manuscripts remained, unguarded, in the apartment.

After a dash back to London to collect their trunks, obtain what reserves of money they could and cable to family in America, Stein and Toklas stayed with the Whiteheads for six weeks. Stein and Whitehead passed the time in long walks talking about philosophy and history, while visits from Lytton Strachey (who wanted to discuss Picasso and the Russian ballet) and Bertrand Russell (who debated fiercely with Stein on the merits of the educational systems in England and America) offered brief reprieves from the overbearing anxiety. Prompted by her conversations with Whitehead, whose work she greatly admired, Stein's style began to take a new turn. Surrounded by bustle – the regular radio reports, the family tradition of reading the newspapers aloud at breakfast, the amusing dynamic between the cerebral Whitehead, his worldlier wife Evelyn, and their lively teenage daughter Jessie – Stein began writing dozens of short texts incorporating snatches of conversation, creating fragmented collages of phrases dislodged from their contexts. 'The search for food and fuel became secretly cooking potatoes,' declares a hungry speaker in one piece, titled 'Painted Lace'. 'I'll make literature about the old lady tomorrow perhaps,' opens another, called 'Gentle Julia', its author-speaker attempting to remain focused in the face of distraction. Stein's early war style captured the heightened tension of this summer, where news was scarce, the future uncertain, and maintaining daily routines paramount for staying sane.

By October, the German army had retreated, and it was safe to return to Paris. But Stein was worried about money. The long-awaited British publication of *Three Lives* had been put on hold indefinitely due to paper shortages; the prospects of earning money through her work now seemed more futile than ever. 'The worst of it was determination,' she wrote in a piece she called 'No', in which she lists her financial resolutions: 'To make a pleasant home. To arouse feeling. To purchase linen.' For the first time, too, Stein articulated her life's ambition, which she was already starting to fear might be beyond her grasp: 'I was determined to succeed . . . It was very simple. I meant to be famous.'

The theme of economising seeps into several texts of these years, balanced by the pleasure of arranging household matters with Toklas. 'We are examples of moderation,' she wrote in another short text, 'Let Us Be Easily Careful', debating how many meals a leg of mutton can make, and what can be substituted for lobster. Early in 1915, she sold Matisse's *Femme au Chapeau* to her brother Michael, to raise money for domestic needs; he continued to administer her income, and had impressed on her with renewed urgency the gravity of tax bills and the risks of fluctuation in the stock market. Toklas had some money of her own from an inheritance, but Stein's income kept the household afloat. In other texts she casts herself as a beleaguered husband, determined to provide 'furs, a hat, kinds of purses, and nearly something new that we have not yet been careful about' for her wife.

Paris was abuzz with patriotic demonstrations and makeshift refugee shelters; machine guns were planted in the structure of the Eiffel Tower, while streams of taxis carried men off to the front. Prices of electricity and groceries rose sharply, and the social world of 27 rue de Fleurus was broken up. Stein and Picasso (excused from military service, as a Spanish citizen) would meet at night to walk, distractedly, around Montparnasse: 'That is Cubism!' Picasso exclaimed, when they spotted a camouflaged truck on the boulevard Raspail. As Zeppelins droned over the city, terrifying everyone, Stein got a letter from William Cook, an artist friend who was living in Palma, Majorca. Intrigued by his reports of the low exchange rate, blossoming almonds and the fact that 'the war doesn't seem to exist down here', she and Toklas decided to visit. They arrived on 8 April 1915 – their landing reported in the 'Society' section of the local newspaper – and ended up staying a year. After three months hopping between hotels, Stein and Toklas rented a small cottage by the sea, growing their own vegetables and enjoying the local produce – lobsters, fish, figs, oranges – while Stein read aloud to Toklas all of Queen Victoria's letters. Shortly after they arrived, Stein told a friend that they were 'very content and peaceful'; by November, she reported that the spring vegetables were planted, the landlord had built them a chimney, and her work was progressing. She had started to play with the arrangement of words on the page, inserting headings and indenting individual words and phrases. Her speakers – unnamed and unlocated – began, for the first time, to communicate with one another, evoking scenery and action through their voices. There's no urgency in their dialogue, few responses to questions, no clear setting or dramatic arc – but she called the texts 'plays', and they marked an important new development in her writing. 'In my portraits I had tried to tell what each one is without telling stories,' Stein wrote later, 'and now in my early plays I tried to tell what happened without telling stories.'

But the longest and most significant text which Stein began in Majorca was a love poem to Toklas. Its title – and central refrain – was *Lifting Belly*. Addressed from one lover to another, the poem is a diary-like evocation of the anxious war years, containing references to the Battle of Verdun, the sinking of boats, the knitting of stockings, all anchored in the sensual pleasures of their relationship. 'I love cherish idolise adore and worship you,' writes Stein to Toklas. 'You are so sweet so tender and so perfect.' Stein revels in the mutual satisfaction of their lovemaking; she gives and seeks praise and compliments, congratulates herself on her prowess ('He cannot understand women. I can . . . I do not lift baby carelessly') and recounts the joys of 'stretches and stretches of happiness': 'Kiss my lips. She did. Kiss my lips again she did. Kiss my lips over and over and over again she did.' Running throughout is the phrase 'lifting belly' – by turns a physical action, a stand-in term for the relationship as a whole, and a private language, containing within it a multitude of meanings, pleasures and feelings. Stein did not seek publication for this text, perhaps because she knew it would risk censure, perhaps because its sentiments simply felt too private to share. Away from Paris, enveloped in a 'permanent caress', Stein was happy – their Majorcan respite all the sweeter because they knew it couldn't last.

Stein and Toklas returned to Paris in June 1916. It was time, they decided, to help their adopted country hands-on. They enlisted as volunteers with the American Fund for the French Wounded, the largest American relief organisation aiding French hospitals, which headquartered in a nightclub off the Champs-Élysées. Stein's cousins in America shipped her a Ford car, which they christened Auntie after Stein's efficient and reliable aunt Pauline; their Majorca friend Cook (now working as a taxi driver in Paris) taught Stein to drive (she claimed she could do everything except reverse), and in March 1917

Stein and Toklas at work for the
American Fund for the French Wounded, *c.*1918

she and Toklas were sent to Perpignan in the south, then in October
on to Nîmes, where they worked until December 1918. Their duties
were mostly administrative and morale-boosting, though Stein – to
her horror – was asked to pitch in with operations when doctors got
wind of her medical training. They spent two years touring military hospitals – Toklas would wake Stein early, and for efficiency
would hand her a cold chicken leg to eat in one hand while driving
– distributing equipment and relief packages to the wounded 'like a
continuous Christmas', and befriending young soldiers who called
them 'godmothers'. When news of the Armistice came through, they
decked Auntie out in American flags and raced through the villages
spreading the festivities; they returned to Paris to watch the celebrations from Jessie Whitehead's hotel room overlooking the Arc de
Triomphe. In the spring of 1919 they travelled east to Strasbourg
and Mulhouse in Alsace, where they visited devastated villages and
supplied blankets and clothes to refugees, orphans and widows. Stein
wrote little in the second half of the war, engrossed and exhausted

by her aid work. But when they settled back in Paris that summer, glowing with official commendations for their wartime efforts, she 'began to work very hard'.

//

Stein did her best to keep up her public profile during the war, as the brief notoriety surrounding *Tender Buttons* inevitably faded. Now forty-five, she still felt as though her career had hardly begun. She told Carl Van Vechten she got sad every three months at the lack of interest in her work: 'I make so much absorbing literature with such attractive titles,' she wrote. 'I've got ten years' work and I want to dispose of some of it.' 'Your name pops up in current journalism with great frequency,' he reassured her, kindly, from New York. 'You are as famous in America as any historical character.' The war had been a serious setback to her publication hopes – but Stein had seized any opportunities that came her way. She sent several pieces to *Vanity Fair*, whose editor, Frank Crowninshield, saw no reason why avant-garde poetry should not sit alongside luxury advertisements: in March 1919 the magazine published a series of four short texts, with an introduction calling Stein 'one of the genuinely interesting figures among those who have attacked the task of revolutionising modern verse'. Meanwhile, *Life* magazine – a popular outlet with a circulation of 150,000 – took a poem with the deceptively straightforward title 'Relief Work in France' after Stein wrote in to point out that a series of parodies in 'mock-Steinese' they had printed were neither as amusing nor as interesting as the real thing.

But most mainstream magazines consistently rejected Stein's work. 'Your poems, I am sorry to say, would be a puzzle picture to our readers,' wrote Ellery Sedgwick, editor of the *Atlantic Monthly*, a response at the politer end of the scale. Stein, bullish, wrote back to admonish him. Sedgwick had lamented that her work was for 'illuminati or cognoscenti' exclusively; she retorted that this was a snobbish assumption, and her work was for ordinary readers. 'I may say without exaggeration that my stuff has genuine literary quality,' she insisted, 'frankly let us say the only important literature that has come out of America since Henry James.' Sedgwick, amused by the bravado, offered to print a poem alongside Stein's letter 'and let *The Atlantic*'s public be judge and jury'. But Stein felt the suggestion was an insult: her talents were not up for debate. 'My work is legitimate literature,' she reiterated, 'and I amuse and interest myself in words as an expression of feeling as Shakespeare or anyone else writing did.' She continued to send her work to Sedgwick; their barbed correspondence – increasingly respectful, then friendly on both sides – became a mainstay of the 1920s for Stein, though he continued to turn down her writing. 'There is a public for you but no publisher,' wrote her friend Henry McBride in sympathy from New York. It deeply frustrated Stein that her work was presumed to be esoteric, an acquired taste: it was publishers' preconceptions, she started to think, that were forming a barrier between her and her potential readers, who would surely enjoy her work immensely, if only she could find a way to get it into their hands.

As Stein's hopes for publication stalled, her reputation as a personality was rising exponentially. Paris, after the war, was buoyant with new circles of international artists. It was a few more years before Josephine Baker was lighting up the Folies Bergère in her skirt of beaded bananas, but Picasso was designing stage sets for Sergei Diaghilev's sensational Ballets Russes, who danced to music by Erik Satie; silent cinema was galvanised by Fernand Léger's experimental *Ballet mécanique*, while American writers found a convivial place to mingle with their French counterparts at Sylvia Beach's English-language bookshop and lending library, Shakespeare and Company, which opened its doors in 1919 – and soon moved to a location across the street from the French bookshop owned by Beach's lover, Adrienne Monnier, enveloping all who strolled down the rue de l'Odeon in a lesbian literary enclave.

Beach remembered customers asking directions to 27 rue de Fleurus, treating it like a stop on a tourist map: they came, now, not to hear Leo discourse on the history of art, but to bring their manuscripts, secrets and dilemmas to Gertrude Stein. They had read *Tender Buttons*, had heard rumours of the Saturday night parties and the apartment which was practically a museum of modern art – and treated Stein like a cult leader. No one was turned away on a first visit – but deference was expected. One visitor found the atmosphere there 'almost ecclesiastical': every aspect of Stein's appearance, he noted, projected 'remarkable power', from the folds of her floor-length gown which resembled the pillars of a temple, to the way she sat, leaning slightly forward in a pose that to several friends recalled the Buddha. The paintings on the walls, one guest remembered, lent Stein a certain authority: testament to her aesthetic judgements – vindicated by the passage of time – and her high regard among artists. Her Picasso portrait, hanging highest of all, reminded visitors that Stein would outlive them all; they were mere humans, she had been rendered immortal. The artist Man Ray visited Stein in 1922, and – with an eye to the publicity potential – she granted him exclusive rights to photograph her: he captured her seated next to her Picasso portrait, posing for a full-size sculpture by the artist Jo Davidson, and writing at her desk, surrounded by Catholic ornaments she had picked up in Spain. She looks out, confidently, at the camera; Toklas, barely perceptible in the distant doorway, looks at Stein.

But however successfully Stein developed her own personal mythology – however many admiring visitors she received, praising her work effusively and breathlessly telling her how her sentences had shaped their own – publishers' rejections stung only more sharply. 'Being only one, having only one pair of eyes . . . I cannot read your ms,' one editor wrote mockingly, returning a manuscript. 'Hardly one copy would sell here. Hardly one. Hardly one.' Another, less amused publisher, who had received an unsolicited package containing a typescript of *The Making of Americans*, wrote tetchily to Stein requesting $1.32, 'the amount of the charges which we had to pay upon receipt of the box containing the book'. 'Nobody knows what I am trying to do,' wrote Stein ruefully, 'but I do and I know when I succeed.' Finally, the Four Seas Company of Boston, a small outlet known for taking risks on avant-garde poetry, agreed to publish a new collection of Stein's work, on the condition that she – once again – pay the costs, this time amounting to $2,500. With no other publisher interested, Stein agreed. She took painstaking efforts to put together *Geography and Plays*, choosing fifty-two short pieces which she felt best represented each stage of her thought to date. To accompany the texts, Stein composed her own biographical note, mentioning her 'brilliant work on the origin and direction of brain tracks', her 'revolt against science', the 'profound influence' of Cézanne, and her friendship 'as brother and sister' with Picasso. 'Gertrude Stein is still experimenting and still renewing her realisation of people and things, ways of revealing something,' she concluded. '*Geography and Plays* is a book of examples.'

Stein was confident that this was her most important offering yet. Sherwood Anderson – a well-known American writer who had come to pay homage at the rue de Fleurus – contributed a preface, arguing that her work 'consists in a rebuilding, an entire new recasting of life, in the city of words'. Grateful, Stein quickly changed the attribution of a love poem she was drafting to Toklas, which became 'A Valentine for Sherwood Anderson'. But *Geography and Plays*, released in December 1922, was greeted by some of the most hostile reviews Stein ever received. 'Miss Stein Applies Cubism to Defenceless Prose', announced the *Baltimore Sun*, with the subheading 'Induces Nightmares'. *Bookman* called it 'a garish collection of wordy flotsam and jetsam, an olive branch to the futurist, but a puzzle to the uninitiated'; one critic denounced the book as '419 pages of drivel', while the *New York Herald Tribune* compared Stein to the emperor with no clothes. Carl Van Vechten – whose own 1922 novel *Peter Whiffle*, in which characters visit the rue de Fleurus, had been an instant bestseller in America – leapt to correct the record, insisting that 'Gertrude Stein is not only the founder of the modern movement in English literature, she is also at the present time far ahead of her boldest follower'. Stein could only take solace in the fact that her public profile was higher than ever – though not for the reasons she wanted.

The negative reactions to *Geography and Plays* rankled particularly because they rounded off a year widely considered a watershed for modernist literature. In 1922, Willa Cather later declared, 'the world broke in two'; Ezra Pound referred to it as 'Year One', reforming the calendar after the publication, in February, of James Joyce's *Ulysses*. The first English translation of Marcel Proust's *In Search of Lost Time* had followed in September, two months before the author's death; T. S. Eliot's poem *The Waste Land* and Virginia Woolf's breakthrough novel *Jacob's Room* both appeared in October. These works mounted a radical challenge to established forms: in their different ways they each explored how language might match the unfolding of experience, fluidly shifting perspective to offer readers access to characters' inner lives. These ideas – the workings of consciousness, the nature of perception – were the very preoccupations that had concerned Stein, now, for almost twenty years, and she was frustrated to see others celebrated while her own work was so bitterly derided. She was pleased when a friend told her he had heard Joyce's close associate Oliver Gogarty read aloud from Stein's 'Portrait of Mabel Dodge' in a crowded Dublin café some years earlier – and chose to believe this indicated Joyce had been influenced by her work. Some critics did acknowledge her precedent – one review of *The Waste Land* complained that it 'seems to us a bad example of the thing that Gertrude Stein did years ago' – but Stein was well aware that a group was forming, of which she wasn't part.

Stein had already identified Joyce as a particular rival. Starting in 1914, the same year as *Tender Buttons* appeared, Joyce's novel *A Portrait of the Artist as a Young Man* was serialised in *The Egoist*, a small but influential London-based periodical whose high-octane literary editor, Ezra Pound, was eager to promote work he saw as modern and vital. In March 1918, the New York magazine the *Little Review* – edited by a lesbian couple, Margaret Anderson and Jane Heap – had begun serialising Joyce's newest novel, *Ulysses*; in September 1920 a complaint was lodged against the magazine for a scene in which the young Gerty MacDowell enjoys the lascivious gaze of Leopold Bloom, and the editors were plunged into a highly publicised obscenity trial, which led to the book being effectively banned in America. Writers and critics rallied round, and Sylvia Beach offered to publish *Ulysses* through Shakespeare and Company, soliciting subscriptions to fund the endeavour. When Stein heard this, she pulled up in her car outside the shop and informed Beach, coldly, that she was transferring her membership to the American Library, across the river. The success of *Ulysses* was particularly hard to bear: Stein's own epic, *The Making of Americans*, the book she personally considered 'the beginning of modern writing', remained unpublished more than a decade since its completion.

In public, Stein insisted she was unbothered by her peers' success. But they were encroaching on her territory, in more ways than one: both Pound and Joyce moved to Paris in the early 1920s, and it was hard to avoid them. Pound visited her at the rue de Fleurus: he rocked too vigorously on his chair, broke it, and was not invited back. 'He was a village explainer,' she wrote in the *Autobiography*, 'excellent if you were a village, but if you were not, not.' She refused to meet Joyce, though they shared many mutual friends. (When they were, eventually, introduced at a party, the conversation was painfully stilted. 'After all these years,' Stein said. 'Yes,' replied Joyce, 'and our names are always linked together.' 'We live in the same arrondissement,' continued Stein. Joyce said nothing, and Stein moved on.) Stein claimed that she wasn't interested in knowing literary people: 'I want to be included in other people's artistic lives while I develop my own by myself,' she explained, 'and so I only want to know painters who never read.' It was something of a resentful exaggeration, but with an element of truth. Stein's writing process had always been a solitary, nocturnal endeavour. She wrote in a state of deep concentration she called meditation: she might take her starting point from an object or person in her surroundings, but would then focus purely on the text unfolding on the page, following a train of thought to its conclusion, riffing and playing on words, absorbing distractions into the text as they arose, obeying her instincts. The intensity of her process left little room for dialogue with peers, even if she had wanted it ('talking', she wrote, 'has nothing to do with creation'). But she knew these other writers were reading and responding actively to one another's work. Pound connected Eliot and Joyce with rich patrons and influential publishers, and edited *The Waste Land* himself; Eliot reviewed *Ulysses* and declared Joyce the greatest living prose writer. Stein met Eliot only once, in November 1924, when they held a stiff conversation about split infinitives; she later recalled his long delay in publishing a piece she sent him for his magazine, *The Criterion* (he had asked for her very latest thing, and the following day, to ensure no doubt, she sent him a text pointedly titled 'A Description of the Fifteenth of November: A Portrait of T. S. Eliot'). Her anecdote betrays her frustration at having to plead with Eliot, and her sense of being shut out of a literary coterie, even as she presided guru-like over her own salon. 'I know I am doing more important things than any of my contemporaries,' wrote Stein to her friend Mabel Weeks in New York. 'One does so badly want to be published,' she added, 'that one is unreasonable.'

//

In March 1923, the mirthful reactions to *Geography and Plays* still resounding, she decided it was time to renew her efforts to publish *The Making of Americans* – the work whose fortunes, perhaps, felt most tied up with her own. She had written it over formative years, beginning her relationship with Toklas in the course of its creation; it brimmed with personal passion both emotional and intellectual, and in many ways represented her birth as a writer. She sent the first three volumes of the typescript to Carl Van Vechten, who declared her achievement 'a very big thing, probably as big as, perhaps bigger than James Joyce,

Marcel Proust, or Dorothy Richardson . . . It is a little like the Book of Genesis.' Buoyed by his enthusiasm, Stein showed the novel to a new friend – a pugnacious twenty-three-year-old foreign correspondent who had recently knocked at the door and asked Stein, winningly, to look at his writing. The leader of a pack of young expatriates to be found each night barging into bars in pursuit of the next gin fizz, Ernest Hemingway brought energy and new friends to the rue de Fleurus, including F. Scott Fitzgerald – Toklas's favourite of the 'young men' – who asked Stein's advice on *The Great Gatsby* (she told him he was 'creating the contemporary world'). Hemingway appointed Stein and Toklas godmothers to his first child, and wrote that he and Stein were 'like brothers'. In Stein's telling, Hemingway read *The Making of Americans* and declared that anyone who cared about literature 'had but to devote their lives to seeing that it was published'.

As Stein turned fifty, in February 1924, Hemingway told her that he had persuaded the writer and publisher Ford Madox Ford to print her novel over several issues of the *Transatlantic Review*, for the handsome fee of 30 francs a page. 'I made it clear it was a remarkable scoop for his magazine obtained only through my obtaining genius,' Hemingway wrote. 'He is under the impression that you get big prices when you consent to publish. I did not give him this impression but did not discourage it.' Since the only typescript was with Van Vechten in America, Toklas and Hemingway together re-typed the entire manuscript, proofread the text, and sent it off to Ford. The collaboration was not entirely harmonious – Ford complained that Hemingway had misrepresented the length of the book, and financial straits forced the magazine to close before the serial was complete – but Stein was satisfied with its reception. 'There seems no doubt of its market', she wrote to Van Vechten, 'because everybody likes it in the Transatlantique even its worst enemies say it is like Dostoievsky which is none so dirty from an enemy.'

The following January, Stein cabled to New York in triumph: she had found a publisher for the novel herself. Robert McAlmon was married to the enormously wealthy lesbian writer Bryher – who used McAlmon to mask her sexuality from her conservative family – and was able and inclined to use his father-in-law's fortune to support writers he admired through his own publishing venture, Contact Editions (earning, from Hemingway, the nickname 'Robber McAlimony'). When McAlmon wrote to Stein to praise *Melanctha* for its 'zip of intelligence, and whoop of personality power', she saw the opportunity, and invited him to tea. He agreed to publish *The Making of Americans* in an edition of 500 copies, canvassing subscriptions (as Beach had done with *Ulysses*) to help defray the enormous printing costs. A cavalier Stein promised at least fifty of her friends would buy copies, and immediately began to send out order forms to anyone she could think of. Rereading old work, she told Sherwood Anderson, was a pleasure but strange to do: 'It is a bit monumental and sometimes seems foolishly youthful now after 20 years but I am leaving it as it is after all it was done then.'

Stein quickly fell out with McAlmon, who she judged was not doing enough for the book's publicity. He was already frustrated that his printing budget had been well exceeded, and was furious when he heard via his printer, Maurice Darantière, that Stein had been negotiating privately with an American publisher for a separate edition of the novel, and had asked Darantière, behind McAlmon's back, to export 400 sets of the sheets. When he refused to allow his copies to be sold off cheaply for another publisher to market, Stein retaliated: 'You know I want it to go big,' she told him, 'and I want to get my royalties.' Of the fifty copies Stein had promised to sell, he complained, at least forty had been given out for free to the friends who represented 'her only substantial public'. He threatened to pulp the rest of the edition, and pointed out that he had taken on the project as a 'philanthropic enterprise': 'Incidentally,' he added with a sneer, recalling the publications of *Three Lives* and *Geography and Plays* which Stein had paid for herself, 'you have never been financially incapable of putting your work before the public if your art is of prime importance to you.'

Yet *The Making of Americans* was greeted by significant press attention – even if most reviewers confessed they hadn't actually finished the book. The most important review Stein received – perhaps the best of her career – was from Marianne Moore in *The Dial*, who compared it to *The Pilgrim's Progress* and called it 'a truly psychological exposition of American living'. Katherine Anne Porter, in the *New York Herald Tribune*, described it as 'a very necessary book', and stated that 'next to James Joyce she is the great influence on the younger literary generation, who see in her the combination of tribal wise woman and arch-priestess of aesthetic'. But the bulk of reviews expressed incredulity at the book's length, repetitions and lack of plot: the *Boston Post* compared her duped readers to a lover realising the person they have brought home is drunk.

//

Stein's magnum opus was published at last, but her reputation was only more violently contested. She saw new manuscripts continue to pile up unread, and her ledger book swell with rejection slips for the portraits, plays and poems she was producing almost daily. She had always been reluctant to speak on behalf of her work: for Stein, words existed on their own terms, and not as keys to some hidden meaning. She repeated insistently that her writing required no interpretation, no external context, in order to be enjoyed: besides, any explanation would suggest a coherence that her work sets out to deny, affording Stein as creator an authority she deemed false. But, now in middle age, she was increasingly concerned about her writing's chequered reception, and its uncertain future. It was time to take an unprecedented step towards securing her literary legacy: to meet her readers in person, and stand up – literally – for her work.

In December 1925, Stein had turned down an invitation to give a lecture on her work in England to the Cambridge Literary Club. But a month later, she changed her mind. The response to *The Making of Americans* had confirmed her fears that the press preferred to caricature her as a personality rather than take her seriously as a writer, and she knew her future work was unlikely to find publishers if she did not

Stein posing for Jo Davidson, *c.*1922
(photo: Man Ray)

make efforts to change the status quo. She mentioned the conundrum to Edith Sitwell, the most recent addition to her enthusiastic band of promoters, who urged her to take up the opportunity to speak. Sitwell was a professional critic, well connected within London's literary circles, and – having won Stein's attention after a positive piece on her work in *Vogue* – was delighted to turn her considerable energies to 'propaganda' for her new friend. She had tried to persuade Virginia Woolf to consider *The Making of Americans* for her own publishing house, the Hogarth Press, but to no avail: 'We are lying crushed under an immense manuscript of Gertrude Stein's,' wrote Woolf to a friend. 'I cannot brisk myself up to deal with it.' Stein agreed to speak at Cambridge in June 1926, and Sitwell secured her a twin invitation from Oxford, assuring her that her work was being discussed everywhere. She and Toklas were welcomed to London with a party, hosted by Sitwell and attended by a starry group of writers including E. M. Forster and Woolf, who described the evening as 'an anxious, exacerbating affair': throned on a broken settee, she wrote, Stein 'insists that she is not only the most intelligible, but also the most popular of living writers'.

The occasion marked the first time that Stein had addressed an audience, directly, as herself. She was very nervous about it – would they like her? Would they understand? – but told Van Vechten she thought her talk was 'a pretty good address . . . really clarifies I believe'. The lecture – a turning point in Stein's conception of her career – both looked back over her past work and forward to a future in which it was celebrated: in it, Stein set out her theory of avant-garde aesthetics and made a bold case for her work's importance. She began by positing that each generation looks at art in a different way. Art that pushes boundaries and shatters conventions, she argued, will inevitably appear 'ugly' before people have got used to it. She called for audiences to be brave in their responses to modern art, recalling her own early adoption of Picasso and Matisse – 'Beauty is beauty', she repeated, 'even when it is irritating and stimulating not only when it is accepted and classic.' She led her listeners through her career to date: for the first time, she defined her use of repetition as her way of 'groping for a continuous present', creating texts with their own sense of time, ongoing and immediate. Above all, she positioned herself as a writer cruelly neglected by her contemporaries, but destined for future recognition. 'It is really too bad,' she insisted, 'naturally for the creator but also very much too bad for the enjoyer, they all really would enjoy the created so much better just after it has been made than when it is already a classic.'

Stein felt the Cambridge lecture 'went off very well'; by the time the Oxford iteration was over – standing room only, with an hour and a half's discussion following – she felt 'just like a prima donna'. Her host, the writer Harold Acton, recalled Stein appearing on stage like 'a squat Aztec figure in obsidian, growing more and more monumental as soon as she sat down'; Sitwell's two brothers, who flanked Stein as she entered the hall in a Chinese brocade robe designed for the occasion, remembered with delight Stein's brisk responses to heckles from the audience. 'For a very long time everybody refuses and then almost without a pause almost everybody accepts,' Stein had written in the lecture, which was published by Woolf's Hogarth Press as *Composition as Explanation*. It was true for Picasso, whose work, once shocking, had begun to command high prices and lavish praise – but not yet for Stein. Her breezy prediction contained within it her desperate hope that this public performance, carried out with some reluctance, would help bring her a wider readership. When they returned to Paris, she asked Toklas to cut her hair to a sharp crop. Monkish and masculine, Stein was entering a new phase of life, projecting confidence in her public and private self.

6 : SHOVING THE UNSHOVEABLE

The three and a half years since the publication of *Geography and Plays* had been among Stein's most productive. During a long stay in Saint-Rémy in 1922–3, she had set to work on a new series of plays, suffused with the sights and sounds of Provence. There, Stein wrote later, she 'really began to make words move in themselves, as apart from the thing they move with'. A regular theatregoer as a child in Oakland, Stein had hardly been inside one since she moved to Paris. In a conventional theatre, she argued, everything is set up to remind one of the essential artifice of proceedings, from the physical space (curtain, stage) to one's awareness of other audience members and inability to take part in the action. Above all, Stein found it hard to feel emotion in the theatre, since the action always seemed to be happening in a time and place entirely removed from that of the audience. The plays Stein had begun to write in 1913 sought to counter this temporal disjunct by expressing the 'complete actual present', as she had attempted to do in her portraits; having taken this idea as far as she could, Stein had largely set plays aside. But a decade later in Saint-Rémy, struck by her sense of 'light and air and air moving and being still', Stein began to contemplate a new conception of the play: as a landscape, a static expanse where elements – trees, hills, fields, sky – are 'always in relation'.

'In Saint Remy,' wrote Stein, 'they grow roses for seeds, flowers for seeds, lilies for seeds and saints for seeds.' The plays she wrote there evoke pastoral idylls: bountiful meadows and mountains, an abundance of fruit and flowers. Stein does not describe these landscapes, but creates a sense of movement and music, making and populating a world out of words. 'A girl with a rooster in front of her and a bush of strange flowers at her side and a small tree behind her,' she wrote in 'A Saint in Seven', as if setting up a stage. A series of declarative statements then evoke an atmosphere, a place, brought into being not by action but by language: 'In days and nights beside days are followed by daisies. We find them and they find them and water finds them and they grow best where we meant to suggest.' Just as her earlier work had sought release from the pressure of representation, taking leave of dramatic conventions allowed Stein to focus on her efforts 'to really completely and exactly find the word for the air and sky and light and existence down there'. Over the rest of 1923, Stein wrote 'quantities of portraits' with an ease that surprised and thrilled her. The concept of the landscape play had proved a breakthrough, and she was eager to apply the idea of a text as an expanse of space, rather than a chronological span, to other forms of writing. Away from the literary drama and social whirl of Paris, she relished the solitude with Toklas. In the margins of one notebook from these months, she doodled their names together, merging their identities: 'Gertice. Altrude.'

During the years immediately after the success of her lecture, Stein composed some of the most romantic texts she had written since her stint in Majorca. Perhaps middle age, and her new hairstyle, had loosened her inhibitions; as they approached the twentieth anniversary of their first meeting, Stein was reflecting, too, on the life Toklas had made possible for her. Writing the Oxbridge lecture had marked Stein's first foray into the anxiety-inducing field of public writing; with that done, Stein was happy to retreat into composing, first and foremost, for an audience of one, whose enthusiasm was not in question. *A Book Concluding With As a Wife Has a Cow A Love Story* (1926) recasts the intimacy of 'Ada' with triumphant eroticism: 'There is a key to a closet that opens the drawer,' writes Stein, evoking both Toklas's meticulous management of their household and the shared secret of their sexual life. The text opens up like an accordion, with short entries composed under headings, each replete with puns and double entendres. Snatches of dialogue give a sense of the witty repartee they sustained when no one else was around, and its final lines celebrate the fifteenth of October, the feast day of Saint Teresa of Ávila, anchoring their relationship in the Spanish hilltops where they had spent such joyful months in 1912. In many of her erotic works, sex is linked with food, in reference to Toklas's culinary skills. Cooking, writing, sex are all presented as creative, nurturing, pleasurable activities which, together, make up the domestic life Stein sings to celebrate. 'My wife is my life is my life is my wife,' wrote Stein in 'A Lyrical Opera / Made by Two / To Be Sung', a poem celebrating Toklas's birthday and the 'choice' of their union. Here, Stein acknowledges Toklas's contribution to her work, a shared act of creation 'made by two': the text creates a performance of love akin to a wedding, bursting with songs, flowers and kisses.

//

In the spring of 1927, Stein received an invitation from Natalie Barney, the debonair lesbian poet whose lavish salons in her home at 20 rue Jacob had acquired an international reputation. Known as 'the Amazon', Barney idolised Sappho, spent holidays on the island of Lesbos, and played her many glamorous lovers against each other. While Stein had become a *salonnière* by default, welcoming anyone who wanted to see her paintings and hear her talk, Barney's parties were carefully orchestrated, and featured entertainments from readings to concerts to dance performances. Stein and Toklas liked Barney, but stood somewhat outside her circles: their conspicuous monogamy set them apart from the *ménages à trois* and bedhopping of the 'Paris Lesbos' lovingly lampooned in Djuna Barnes's exuberant satire *Ladies Almanack*. Radclyffe Hall's 1928 novel *The Well of Loneliness* (which featured a character based on Barney) offered a vivid description of Paris's flourishing lesbian subculture – bars and nightclubs well out of the purview of Stein and Toklas, who preferred to socialise at home.

Now, Barney invited Stein to inaugurate her new venture, Académie des Femmes, a series of gatherings in celebration of women writers (so called because the Académie Française refused to admit women). The first evening, she announced, would be devoted to Gertrude Stein. Stein was not usually concerned with empowering displays of sisterhood, but graciously accepted the idea of an homage. Two hundred guests crammed into Barney's courtyard garden (adorned with its own Doric temple) as jazz wafted on the breeze and champagne flowed. The evening's highlight was a live rendition of Stein's poems 'Susie Asado' and 'Preciosilla', set to music by an up-and-coming composer named Virgil Thomson, who had recently arrived in Paris and declared his passion for Stein's writing. Stein admired his settings, which she felt showed real sensitivity to her style. So when Thomson proposed they collaborate on an opera, Stein writing the words and he the music, she agreed. Looking around the atelier, filled with porcelain models of saints collected on Stein's travels, they settled on the sixteenth-century Catholic reformers Teresa of Ávila and Ignatius Loyola as their protagonists. The theme, Thomson recalled, would be 'the working artist's working life, which is to say, the life we both were living'.

Stein worked on her libretto through the summer of 1927. *Four Saints in Three Acts* populates a bucolic landscape – 'pear trees cherry blossoms pink blossoms and late apples' – with a chorus of leisurely saints, who move in and out of buildings and gardens as they engage in a beatific series of games, processions, prayers, miracle-workings and 'idle acts'. It's a raucous celebration of the mystical and the mundane, which continually questions its own status as a play. 'How many acts are there in it. How many saints in all,' asks Stein; scenes follow no strict numerical sequence, while some contain no more than a single word, and stage directions often appear simply as vehicles for Stein's own pleasure in wordplay ('Scene One. And seen one. Very likely.'). Despite such ambiguities, Stein harboured hopes that the collaboration would be a commercial hit. 'Neither you nor I have ever had any passion to be rare,' she wrote to Thomson, 'we want to be as popular as Gilbert and Sullivan if we can, and perhaps we can.'

But before Thomson could finish his score, their burgeoning friendship hit a stumbling block. He had introduced Stein to his friends, a young, cosmopolitan and ambitious group of artists and writers who were eager to position themselves as a new generation of Stein's protégés, conscious of her reputation as a tastemaker. One of them, the Surrealist poet Georges Hugnet, ran his own deluxe publishing house (underwritten by his wealthy father): to Stein's delight, he proposed to translate a sample of *The Making of Americans* into French. Since Hugnet spoke little English, Stein composed a literal French translation of around sixty pages from the novel, with Toklas – the better French speaker – checking her accuracy; they then passed the text to Hugnet to rework the French into a more artful form. 'Young France has discovered me,' she wrote proudly to a friend. 'It reads me it translates me it admires me and it is printing me.' In gratitude, she began to translate a sequence of Hugnet's poems into English; her letters to him, at this time, brim with pleasure at this collaboration. But she found the experience of working from someone else's text disturbing. The excitement of writing, for Stein, lay in solving the 'internal troubles' that arose as she contemplated the page: having the direction of the composition already fixed, she found, gave her writing a smoothness that she always sought to avoid. The translation morphed into a sequence of original poems, in an unmistakably Steinian register. 'I dunno,' she wrote to Thomson, 'I think its interesting its a mirroring of it rather than anything else a reflection of each little poem.'

Hugnet sportingly declared the 'translation' better than his original. But when the question of publication arose – the plan had been for the French and English to appear on facing pages – Hugnet was horrified that Stein insisted her own name appear most prominently on the front cover, and the work be billed not as a translation but an 'adaptation' or 'transposition', foregrounding her artistry over his. A furious quarrel ensued, with Thomson attempting to mediate and Stein refusing to countenance compromise. A deal was nearly reached, whereby both names would appear in equal size – but this time Toklas would not hear of it, coldly reminding Thomson that this was not what had been requested. Negotiations reached an impasse when Stein sent Thomson a calling card; beneath 'Miss Gertrude Stein', centred in print, she inked 'declines further acquaintance with Virgil Thomson'.

One by one, Stein cut off the rest of Thomson's circle, on various more or less flimsy pretexts. Perhaps she doubted their talents, perhaps she was jealous of their youth and promise, perhaps she was simply fed up with their company. The men weren't sure – but they were bewildered, and asked each other (and themselves) what had possibly caused these sudden banishments, the most minor of infractions met with a conclusive telephone call or an ice-cold reception on their next attempted visit. Even Hemingway was no longer part of her inner circle. Stein never gave a reason – friends cited her disgust when he turned up drunk at the apartment one night, recalled her displeasure at his lampooning a Sherwood Anderson novel in one of his own, and suspected that she was frustrated that his success had outshone hers – but he blamed Toklas, speculating she disapproved of his intimacy with Stein. Gradually, others pointed the finger in the same direction: some ostracised friends began to call Toklas 'the Executioner'.

Few people recorded their first impressions of Toklas. Those who did tend to recall being unnerved by her scrutiny. The artist Françoise Gilot remembered Picasso, a few months into their relationship, taking her to meet Stein, menacingly telling his twenty-one-year-old lover he had 'a lot of confidence' in Stein's judgement. Two decades later, Gilot retained a visceral memory of the door opening 'a crack, almost grudgingly' and Toklas's face looming through the slit, shaded by an enormous hat. Stein – seated underneath her portrait – waved Gilot to the divan facing her; Picasso perched on the window ledge, his eyes gleaming, while Toklas took the far side of the divan, as distant from Gilot as she could get. 'She looked hostile, as though she were predisposed against me,' Gilot wrote. 'She spoke infrequently, occasionally supplying Gertrude Stein with a detail. Her voice was very low, like a man's, and rasping, and one could hear the air passing loudly through her teeth. It made a most disagreeable sound, like the sharpening of a scythe.' Several tables were covered with plates of petits fours, cakes and cookies, which Toklas darted at Gilot whenever she started to speak, frowning at any answers that didn't seem respectful enough. At the end, Stein invited Gilot back to visit on her own, which occasioned another dark look from Toklas. 'I might have gone back if I hadn't been so terrorised by Miss Stein's little acolyte,' she wrote, 'but I was and so I promised myself never to set foot in that apartment again.'

For some time, visitors to the rue de Fleurus had noticed that anyone Stein didn't want to speak to was swiftly deflected to Toklas. Several friends recalled straining to eavesdrop on Stein's conversations while Toklas distracted them with a determined stream of questions, steering them away – sometimes before they noticed what was happening – from the woman they had come to see. It was obvious that women, especially those who had turned up with their husbands, were the ones most consistently sidelined. How, many wondered, could Stein – a woman who prided herself on her modern thought – so callously replicate the repressive structures of heterosexual patriarchy in her own home? To surprised guests, this bizarre ritual seemed like one of several strange tests that made the atmosphere of 27 rue de Fleurus uneasy. Another was the way anyone who asked for a liqueur over tea (a smoky souchong) would be innocently proffered a glass of an eighty-year-old Marc de Bourgogne, well known as the strongest alcohol in Paris, which tasted 'like swallowing a lighted kerosene lamp'. Did Stein want friends at all, people wondered, or only disciples? Was Toklas – the silent presence skulking in the shadows – the master puppeteer here? Or was she entirely in thrall to the whims of her megalomaniac partner?

In the *Autobiography*, Stein made light of this. 'The geniuses came and talked to Gertrude Stein', writes 'Toklas', 'and the wives sat with me.' In the salon, where people thronged to hear her speak, Stein had begun to perform a role: 'Gertrude Stein', the icon, who expected subservience from her guests. Her cropped hair, in a way, was part of the performance, helping Stein project a masculine power through her Caesar-like silhouette (it's probably revealing that she often used 'Caesar', in her writing, as a code for orgasm). But this persona was highly playful, too. Stein's haircut was actually modelled on that of a female friend, Élisabeth de Gramont, a socialist duchess and one of Natalie Barney's lovers. Unlike Gramont, Romaine Brooks or Janet Flanner, who dressed in men's suits, silk cravats and top hats, Stein's wardrobe was somewhat ambiguous. On arrival in Paris in 1903 she had swapped her tailored 'Gibson Girl' suits for androgynous, unbelted corduroy robes. After meeting Toklas, these were renounced in favour of long skirts and dress shirts, usually fastened with a glinting brooch at the throat, topped with one of her signature flamboyantly patterned waistcoats – she owned more than twenty. Toklas, who cared more about fashion (and probably sewed the waistcoats) chose floral dresses, lace collars, enormous necklaces, fur coats. She wore her hair in a sharp bob and manicured her nails meticulously; she did not alter her pronounced moustache, which one friend recalled made other faces look nude. Stein didn't mind what others made of her appearance or their set-up: Toklas, she implied in a piece of doggerel which gestures, as Stein's writing often does, at a deeper psychological significance, was in on every joke. 'I am a husband who is very very good I have a character that covers me like a hood and must be understood which it is by my wife whom I love with all my life and who makes it understood that she isn't made of wood and that my character which covers me like a hood is very well understood by my wife.'

'Psychologically and emotionally Gertrude Stein was not a woman nor a man,' Toklas wrote, years later, to a student who asked how Stein's gender had affected her work. 'She was really both – in her thinking and in her feeling.' Stein was interested in masculinity as something that could be assumed, even earned: it was part of her public role as the genius writer who talked to men and ignored their wives, but it was also – paradoxically – inextricable from her desire to defy assumptions. Stein refused to be pinned down by labels. She sought the privileges of masculinity, while also setting out to subvert them. And Toklas's feminine subservience, as anyone who underestimated her found out, was a performance too. This was no straightforward imitation of heterosexual marriage, as some suggested: it was a knowing reconfiguration, its codes kept strictly private. 'Play, play every day,' wrote Stein in 1909, 'play and play and play away, and then play the play you played to-day, the play you play every day, play it and play it.' Stein played with gender like she played with language: she knew the rules, but found greater meaning in upending them than following them. 'The world is a theatre for you,' Matisse once said to Stein. When people were watching, Stein enjoyed performing a larger-than-life character, the front door her curtain and the salon her stage. Yet she liked, also, to shed her costume, fade into the crowd and watch others – and the demands of the role were starting to wear her down.

Too many obsequious young men, she decided, were distracting: her real life was conducted in private, with Toklas, their dogs, and her notebooks. They had another reason to slim down the social life at the rue de Fleurus; they were spending less time there. In the summer of 1924, on their way to visit Picasso, his wife Olga and their young son Paulo in Antibes, a recommendation in the Michelin gastronomic guide had led them to Belley, a small town in the foothills of the Alps not far from the Swiss border. After eating their first meal (poached fish with brown butter, salad and raspberries) at the Hôtel Pernollet, they cabled to tell Picasso they were going to be late. They spent the next four summers at the hotel, enjoying the gourmet delights of its restaurant and exploring the villages, waterfalls and Roman ruins of the Bugey region. In 1928, they spotted a seventeenth-century stone house looming over the Rhône valley from the hilltop hamlet of Bilignin. Covered in ivy, the house resembled a small chateau: French windows opened on to a large garden, landscaped with ornate box hedges, separated by a low wall from the open valley below. Without ever seeing the inside, Stein was determined that it should be theirs. There was only one hitch: the house was occupied, by a French lieutenant. Stein – after registering with the landlord her desire to take over the lease whenever it became free – mentioned her predicament to friends with military connections, and within six months, the lieutenant was promoted and transferred to a new regiment in Morocco. Stein claimed she never knew whether she had manipulated events or the timing of his transfer was a happy coincidence (either way, the anecdote shows the extremes to which she was willing to go in order to accomplish her wishes), but she signed an

Stein and Basket in the gardens at Bilignin, June 1934; Stein's
favourite photograph of herself (photo: Carl Van Vechten)

agreement to rent the house on 11 March 1929. A few months later, war
broke out in Morocco. 'Alice Toklas's conscience troubled her,' Stein
wrote. 'Mine did not trouble me.'

Stein and Toklas now stayed in Bilignin up to six months at a time.
Before they left Paris each summer, Toklas would order a selection of
books from the library – including quantities of detective stories, Stein's
entertainment of choice – and they would pack into the car along with
their white poodle Basket (a new addition, named because he looked like
he could carry a basket of flowers in his mouth) and Spanish chihuahua
Pépé, stopping on the way for a glass of the first May wine. They usually
employed a live-in servant – the application process involved the cooking of a perfect omelette – who would follow on the train to manage
the household budget and cook, under Toklas's exacting supervision:
around this time they hired Trac, a chef from what was still known as

French Indochina ('we love him', wrote Stein, 'and he loves us'), the first in a succession of East Asian employees at the rue de Fleurus. Chosen friends – including Picasso and his family; the painter Francis Rose; the writer Paul Bowles – would visit individually or in small groups for days full of good food and conversation, setting up easels and picnic blankets near the hills and waterfalls, roaming around the local market towns and lakes in search of the freshest fish and other local delicacies: crayfish tails with cream, country pâtés with truffles.

'I like ordinary people who don't bore me,' Stein once told an interviewer. 'Highbrows do, you know, always do.' While they warred with artists and writers back in Paris, Stein and Toklas became popular figures in the countryside, where they were comparatively anonymous – where people liked them for themselves, not for their celebrity. At first, the locals were suspicious of this strange couple: there were rumours that one of them was a man, or that they were descended from the Mohicans because they seemed so different from other American tourists. But soon, the local children were playing with Basket and Pépé; Stein offered her neighbours English lessons, and they were both joining in local events – the annual harvest at the vineyard in Béon; the unveiling of a statue to the famous gourmand Brillat-Savarin in his birthplace of Belley. Toklas would get up early in the morning to pick strawberries, wearing white gloves that were soon stained red as blood. By eight she would be arranging vases of flowers, a cigarette hanging from her lips; she then spent an hour washing Basket, and unsuspecting guests would be inveigled into helping dry him off by submitting to a game of chase in the garden, Stein leaning out of an upstairs window urging them to run faster. After conferring at length with their cook on the day's menu, Toklas would retire to the small kitchen table and type the pages Stein had finished the night before. After lunch, they would set out in the car for adventures, Stein driving, Toklas in the back seat, surrounded by empty shopping bags to fill with vegetables or antiques. In the country, Stein rarely continued writing texts she had begun in the city. Her work arose, always, from her present surroundings – and Bilignin generated an energy very different from Paris.

Stein invariably wrote about what was on her mind. Virgil Thomson once asked her why she had mentioned him in a text; she replied that he had walked through the door while she was writing. Sometimes, references in her texts are clearly private jokes or fleeting moments shared with Toklas or other friends; at other times, a new word is suggested by the sound or appearance of another word on the page, or via a mental association or thought only Stein herself could explain. But, often, Stein's abiding preoccupations seep into both her subject matter and the emotional register of her pieces – and wills, families and houses recur over and over in her writing of the late 1920s. The extra expenditure of taking on the Bilignin house had made her think seriously about her income, which relied on the old investments managed, now, by her cousin Julian Stein, who worked for the Baltimore bank established half a century earlier by their uncle Meyer. In 1927, clearly unsatisfied with the arrangement, she had contacted Julian about the possibility of handling her own finances; he had counselled caution, warning her that her affairs were in very healthy shape and 'the question of making you richer is a very dubious one in the present state of the universe'. She was also, for the first time, planning to draft a will, and reflecting on the practical implications, for Toklas, of their legally unrecognised partnership. 'We sign our checks with our maiden names because we are not married,' wrote Stein, her matter-of-fact tone belying indignation at the double standards that rendered their union technically illegitimate. In a 1928 text called 'Finally George', she pondered the fate of offspring 'born in wedlock even although the marriage is not legal by any arrangement', concluding that 'nevertheless the child of such a marriage is without doubt legitimate if they like and anybody can like'. She was contemplating the future of the manuscripts she and Toklas called their 'babies' – and of Toklas, who would not officially inherit their shared possessions if Stein predeceased her. In several works of these years, Stein figures family as a grammar: if heterosexual marriages produce legitimate children, she seems to suggest, their unorthodox marriage creates a new blueprint for language, producing poems as formally radical as the relationship they celebrate. Stein's writing betrays the anxiety, as well as the joys, of living outside traditional structures. Still, she defiantly writes back to detractors: 'We are a model to every one. We are wonderfully productive.'

//

'Alice is making tapestry in our leisure moments, I am making sentences in my leisure moments and darn good sentences they are,' wrote Stein from Bilignin. 'I have a new conception of prose which interests me profoundly . . . I am getting rid of sight and sound as well as sense.' She told Sherwood Anderson that she was 'making a desperate effort to find out what is and isn't a sentence', and reported, 'I think the intensive study I am doing of the sentence is bearing fruit.' Stein later claimed that during this period she had made a discovery she considered 'fundamental': 'that paragraphs were emotional and sentences were not'. While an individual sentence might express a single idea, a paragraph was more like a mood, a state of mind, or a landscape: a context in which relations between distinct, even contradictory, elements might emerge. In a series of works – 'More Grammar for a Sentence'; 'Saving the Sentence'; 'Sentences and Paragraphs' – Stein relentlessly probed the possibilities of syntax, placing parts of speech under the microscope and systematically dissecting them. 'Think in stitches. Think in sentences,' she wrote, evoking a sense of her writing as an expanding tapestry of words and phrases – a counterpart to Toklas's domestic labour. Stein's work from this period is stuffed with epigrammatic reflections on structures of language: 'Grammar. Fills me with delight.' 'I am a grammarian I do not hesitate but I rearrange prepositions.' 'I return to sentences as a refreshment.' 'Grammar if complicated is widened.' She moved increasingly away from nouns, whose meanings were disappointingly preordained, and from punctuation, which she found didactic. More interesting to her were articles and prepositions, whose signification depended most on context, and verbs, which contained the greatest possibility for slippage and ambiguity. She never pursued an idea further when she felt it had reached its natural limit: 'Forget grammar', she wrote one day (perhaps around dinner time), 'and think about potatoes.'

Stein struggled to interest publishers in her grammatical enquiries. But she was beginning to find some more success with her backlist of older manuscripts. Between April 1927 and March 1932, fifteen of her pieces were published in *transition* magazine, a small avant-garde outlet edited by Maria and Eugene Jolas, based in Paris and styled as 'An International Quarterly for Creative Experiment'. 'Realism in America has reached its point of saturation,' read one of the magazine's first editorials. 'We need new words, new abstractions, new hieroglyphics, new symbols, new myths . . . Without unrest we have stagnation and impotence.' Gertrude Stein, it added – along with James Joyce, André Breton and Louis Aragon – is 'showing us the way'. To critics' mirth, the editors failed to notice that the first piece of Stein's published in the magazine was printed with its pages in the wrong order. But a subsequent issue reprinted *Tender Buttons* in its entirety, and in February 1929 the magazine published 'Bibliography, 1904–1929': Stein's own assessment of her oeuvre to date, with every title of every piece she had written listed by its year of composition. Many of these texts had never appeared in print at all, and she hoped the bibliography would serve as an advertisement to potential publishers, as well as a guide for completists. Her only disappointment with *transition* was the fact that her old rival, James Joyce, appeared in its pages even more often than she did.

But the pages of *transition* – as well as providing a showcase for Stein's writing – soon became a battleground over its merits. In 1927, the same year *transition* started, the belligerent artist and critic Wyndham Lewis had launched his own satirical magazine, *The Enemy*, which set itself firmly against the corrupting literary force of 'Stein and the *steinizing* foreign garrison in Paris'. In a series of increasingly ferocious essays, Lewis described Stein as a 'highbrow clown' and an 'arch-fraud', and her work as 'a gargantuan mental stutter' and 'a cold, black suet-pudding . . . the same heavy, sticky, opaque mass all through'. Her influence, he argued, had blighted both Joyce and Hemingway; he concluded that *transition* was nothing less than a 'shrewdly organised' Communist conspiracy, and that the Paris literary world was dictated by a 'Gipsy Queen' (Stein) and an 'Irish Exile' (Joyce), marking an assault on Western civilisation and risking the dawn of a 'New Philistinism'.

The editors of *transition* leapt to defend Stein against Lewis's attacks. They pointed out the outrageous misogyny and prejudice of his rhetoric, and took pains to counter the way he had lumped Joyce and Stein together, asserting that the two of them stood 'at opposite poles of thought and expression'. While Joyce's characters, like Proust's, are saturated with their own pasts, and he charged his words with a wealth of accumulated meanings – to preserve 'all the crackling short circuits of idea associations which have existed between sounds and signs throughout the long evolution of our language' – Stein (the editors argued) set out to wring those associations out of language entirely, in order to afford her words 'an absolute or static quality', and hold an exact moment in sharp focus. Stein herself remained silent on the controversy, but Joyce replied to Lewis within the pages of *Finnegans Wake*, which was then being serialised in *transition*. He denied any connection with 'that eyebold earbig noseknaving gutthroat' – clearly identifiable, to readers familiar with the saga, as Gertrude Stein.

Lewis's scaremongering argument that Stein's work represented a threat to intellectual civilisation was echoed, in somewhat less vitriolic but no less serious form, by T. S. Eliot. In a 1927 essay sketching out possible future directions for literature, he noted that 'there is something precisely ominous about Miss Stein'. Her rhythms, he argued, 'have a peculiar hypnotic power', but if future writers should attempt to emulate her style, he warned, then a 'new barbarian age' of literature was likely to dawn. Eliot did not deny her significance, but positioned her work as a dead end, an aberration that needed to be stamped out. While Lewis sneered openly at the 'Jewish lady' (he also described her as 'a whale out of water', and drew implicit links between her idiosyncratic use of English and her family's history of immigration), Eliot's suggestion of Stein's 'kinship with the saxophone' aligned her perceived degeneracy with African American jazz music. Ezra Pound stayed out of the melee, but wrote privately to Eliot disparaging Stein as an 'old tub of guts', elsewhere suggesting – in blatantly antisemitic terms – that 'Gertie Stein . . . writes yittish wit englisch wordts'.

By now, Stein's work was the subject of a tense battle waged between the leading lights of modernist literature. She found her most enthusiastic defenders, notably, among her female peers, whose work, like hers, lurked on the margins of respectability. In an essay titled 'The New Barbarism and Gertrude Stein', the poet Laura Riding responded directly to Eliot's attack with an insightful defence of Stein's poetics, arguing that his critique betrayed a wilful misunderstanding of Stein's technique and ambitions. While Eliot's appraisal of aesthetics cast backwards to a stale literary tradition already looking inward on itself, Riding argued, Stein's work uses words that 'are no older than her use of them' to break free of the past, 'creating the possibility of poetic thought to come'. Eliot had condemned Stein for cleansing language of human experience. But Riding saw this tendency as a democratising resistance to traditional structures, which made stimulating creative demands on her audience. The poet Mina Loy, too, praised the 'fresh significance' of Stein's language, and compared Stein to Marie Curie, extracting 'a radium of the word' from 'the tonnage of consciousness'. If Lewis and Eliot saw Stein as something sickening, excessive and unhealthy ('suet-pudding'), Riding and Loy positioned her as a scientist-healer, purging language in order to create something new, exciting and alive.

Stein didn't engage in the debates, though she must surely have followed them. 'I don't like attacks and I don't like controversy and I like to mind my own business,' she wrote. She was pleased when Riding solicited her work to publish with Seizin Press, a new outlet she was editing with her partner, the poet Robert Graves. But she baulked at the intensity with which Riding pursued a friendship, and eventually stopped replying to her letters, once she had ensured her royalty statements were in order. Her focus, as ever, was on her work. Her latest collection, *Useful Knowledge* (compiled for an American editor she had met during her visit to Oxford), almost bankrupted the publishing house; the editor regretfully declined her novel *Lucy Church Amiably*, an emotive pastoral evoking the countryside around Bilignin. By now, Stein was fed up with publishers: approaching them, being turned down by them, falling out with them. In the summer of 1930, seeing no other way to keep her fast-accumulating work before the public, she took matters into her own hands.

'We have decided to publish ourselves,' she wrote to Van Vechten. 'Alice is managing director I am author, and we hope there will be purchasers.' They sold Picasso's *Lady with a Fan* to finance the endeavour, and the Plain Edition was announced, ambitiously, as 'an edition of first editions of all the work not yet printed of Gertrude Stein'. There was precedent for this in Leonard and Virginia Woolf's Hogarth Press, an in-house endeavour designed to offer Woolf total creative freedom – but while Hogarth's catalogue included the work of other like-minded writers, and sales were sufficient to take on employees, the Plain Edition was an entirely Stein-focused project. 'Here we are in business,' Stein wrote, 'in despair at using up our energies to shove the unshoveable we have concluded it will take less energy and get more results if we do it ourselves.' Toklas wrote to bookshops and made arrangements with printers; she sent blank subscription forms to friends to distribute, and asked for names of librarians likely to make orders. Once the strain of negotiating with commercial publishers was lifted, Stein entered some of the most creatively fertile months of her career. She could write without any external pressure, confident that her writing would be shepherded into the world by the publisher she had long dreamed of: someone utterly devoted to her work, who understood and cared about it like no one else.

The Plain Edition released five titles between 1930 and 1933, each with simple covers modelled on the school copybooks Stein liked to write in, as if readers were receiving the texts directly from her pen. *Lucy Church Amiably*, subtitled 'A Novel of Romantic beauty and nature and which Looks Like an Engraving', was first to appear, followed by Stein's versions of George Hugnet's poems, under the pointed title *Before the Flowers of Friendship Faded Friendship Faded*. *How to Write* contained a selection of her recent meditations on sentences and paragraphs, while *Operas and Plays* included work dating back to 1913, as well as two sur-realist works inspired by noir cinema: 'A Movie' and 'Deux sœurs qui ne sont pas sœurs'. In 1932, Stein looked back to some of her earliest writing: the final volume they published contained *A Long Gay Book*, *Many Many Women* and *G.M.P.* (*Matisse Picasso and Gertrude Stein*), all written between 1909 and 1912. 'It is interesting', she wrote, 'because it shows the transition from *Making of A* to *Tender Buttons*.'

Like the bibliography she had published in *transition*, the Plain Edition programme offered Stein an opportunity to assess her career to date, trace the various stages of her writing, and showcase the breadth of her output to new readers. Working with Toklas turned their domes-tic partnership into a professional alliance centred on Stein's work: Toklas's tireless support now provided not only the environment Stein needed to write, but also the transformation of that writing into a sell-able commodity. Stein enjoyed coming up with slogans, press releases and advertising copy for her titles: publicity, now, was embedded firmly in her practice. But this, too, bred new anxieties, both existential – whether her creative independence was compromised by commercial reality – and practical, when negotiations with printers proved complex, spines fell apart, and errors were introduced. She received a boost in 1931 when the influential critic Edmund Wilson included a chapter on her work in his acclaimed study *Axel's Castle*, placing her among Yeats, Joyce, Eliot and Proust as 'a literary personality of unmistakeable origi-nality and distinction', and singling out for particular praise *Three Lives*, which showed her 'masterly grasp of the organisms, contradictory and indissoluble, which human personalities are'. Wilson's assessment of her career was not entirely positive – he saw her work as displaying a 'fatty degeneration' of imagination and style from *The Making of Americans* onwards – but the fact that he had picked her out as one of several modern writers worthy of deeper analysis showed that Lewis and Eliot's attacks had not entirely damaged her critical status. But the print run of 1,000 copies for the first two Plain Edition titles was halved for the final three, as Toklas attempted to cut losses. And most reviewers were as bemused as ever: one declared *Lucy Church Amiably* 'as hard to read as the telephone book and not much more interesting'.

In the summer of 1932, Stein told a friend she was 'trying to write a long dull poem'. Since she had begun her intensive study of grammar, Stein's writing was becoming increasingly liberated from the external world: events, places, names and objects appear less and less frequently. *Stanzas in Meditation*, which grew to fill six French notebooks each longer than the last, represents the culmination of decades of practice in loosening language from the scaffolding of syntax. Over 1931, Stein had begun working with single words, lifting them from their contexts and breaking them down into their elements, playing with individual syllables, sounds, even letters, in an effort – more audacious than ever before – to strip language of 'associational emotion'. 'A sentence', she wrote, 'should not be familiar.' In a draft letter of 27 May 1932 to a researcher who had asked about her method, Stein wrote that she sought to achieve 'exactness and as far as possible disembodiedment if one may use such a word, creating sense by intensity of exactness'. Her stanzas mirror the gradual dawning of perception, with certain images cutting in, fresh, through the hum of background noise.

But that summer, a surprise discovery changed Stein's course dramatically. While they were packing up for their annual sojourn at Bilignin, Stein was rifling through her cabinets looking for some early drafts of *The Making of Americans* to show a friend who was interested in translating it into French. As she rummaged, she pulled out a notebook she hadn't seen for almost thirty years. It was the novel she had written during her first months in Paris, in 1903, describing her painful

On the back of this photograph, Toklas has written 'Gertrude Stein commencing to write the *Autobiography*', October 1932.

relationship with May Bookstaver and her rivalry with Mabel Haynes. Turning the pages of this long-forgotten manuscript – 'was it hidden with intention?' Stein asked herself – she was overcome with a mixture of shame, anxiety and intrigue. But she held back from showing it to Toklas. Though the language of sexual desire was restrained, a quick flick through the pages would make the novel's theme palpably clear: 'The first recognition of mutual dependence . . . intensely kissed on the eyes and on the lips . . . the pain of passionate longing was very hard to bear.' Stein had not told Toklas about the strength of intimacy she had once shared with May Bookstaver, who had been so helpful with her manuscripts in the early years, and had even visited them once in

Paris, though she hadn't been in touch for a long time. Perhaps Stein had anticipated Toklas's jealousy; perhaps she simply hadn't thought it needed mentioning – either to keep the youthful affair as a private memory, or because it no longer felt relevant now her life had moved on. But she and Toklas had promised not to keep secrets from one another, and Stein knew this discovery would undoubtedly manifest as a betrayal, invite awkward questioning, possibly cause serious distress. Still, despite herself, she couldn't help but wonder if the manuscript might be publishable. She thrust it at a friend, Louis Bromfield, who happened to be visiting. When he reacted positively, she showed it to William Bradley, a Paris-based literary agent she had hired in 1930 to advise on the Plain Edition. He agreed the novel was well-written, but – given the notoriety, four years earlier, of Radclyffe Hall's explicitly lesbian novel *The Well of Loneliness*, the subject of a highly publicised obscenity trial – warned her that publication might be difficult. So several months passed before Stein gave the manuscript, finally, to Toklas – who was used to receiving work almost directly from Stein's pen. Toklas was silent. Stein was filled with remorse – and knew only a dramatic gesture would restore her partner's trust.

'History', Stein had written two years earlier, 'is made by a very few who are important.' Approaching sixty, stung by her contemporaries' scorn and success, Stein was aware that she was at risk of becoming a mere footnote to literary history. With her frustration at years of thwarted efforts for publication now compounded by the slow and stressful disintegration of the Plain Edition, she was worried about money, about her legacy – and, now, about her relationship. At a crisis point in her life and her work, Stein set the *Stanzas* aside. Her quest to push language to its limits was set, more directly than ever before, against her lingering desire for commercial success. It was time, she decided, for a bestseller – and one which would reassert Toklas's place at the very centre of her life.

7 : KNOCKOUT AND A WOW

Early in the summer of 1932, Stein and Toklas were sitting out on the terrace at Bilignin, examining the cheques in Stein's purse and anxiously calculating their future income, when they heard the faint but unmistakeable call of a cuckoo down in the valley. Stein immediately announced that things would not be as bad as they feared, because the first cuckoo had arrived while she had money in her pocket. Then, she later recalled, the bird flew up to the terrace, perched in a tree at the corner, emitted one emphatic cuckoo directly towards her, and swooped away. 'I was a little scared, I really and truly was,' she remembered. 'And then late that fall I wrote the autobiography.'

//

Stein had always insisted she would never write a memoir. 'No,' she wrote in a notebook after a literary agent suggested she could find a healthy readership for one. 'I am not interested in autobiography messages experiments. I am interested in literature.' She never explained, in public, what sparked her total shift from the work that had engrossed her up to this point – except to say that had it not been for six 'beautiful and unusually dry' weeks at Bilignin, from the start of October to the middle of November 1932, *The Autobiography of Alice B. Toklas* might not have been written at all. She spent those weeks sitting at a table on the terrace, writing five hours a day – uncharacteristically long, daytime stints for Stein – until the book was done. Stein was writing with an eye deliberately to the marketplace, aware (from long experience) that reputations were manufactured by the media. The *Autobiography* was Stein's arch rejoinder to her doubters, and a triumphant declaration of how she wanted to be seen.

The Autobiography of Alice B. Toklas is a joke, a myth, an audacious act of knowing artifice. It contravenes every rule of autobiography – and, in doing so, draws attention subtly to its own act of creation. Narrated, simply and charmingly, in Toklas's voice, the book is a portrait of Stein through the eyes of her most intimate observer. Although she is the book's ostensible subject, 'Toklas' reveals little of herself – she is, she declares, a 'pretty good housekeeper and a pretty good gardener and a pretty good needlewoman and a pretty good secretary and a pretty good editor and a pretty good vet for dogs'. The book begins with a brief account of Toklas's childhood in San Francisco before skipping, within a couple of pages, to her transcendental meeting with Gertrude Stein, already hard at work on *The Making of Americans*. From here, the narrative presents a selective sequence of events from their charmed life together: raucous dinners in Montmartre studios, nights at the Russian ballet, European travels, and evenings at home, the salon teeming with distinguished visitors eager to pay homage. Friends are praised or skewered at will, scores are settled cheerfully; well-known figures are less likely to be celebrated, here, than scolded for an ancient petty crime towards Stein they had in all probability forgotten. As a history of the Parisian avant-garde, it's deliberately abstruse: Toklas, humorously, tends to miss the point, noting personality quirks and oddities rather than the new directions in art and literature being pioneered before her eyes. ('I like a view,' she declares early on, 'but I like to sit with my back turned to it.') The only genius fully recognised as such is Gertrude Stein. On the final page, the ruse is revealed with a wink: Gertrude Stein, writes 'Toklas', had always encouraged her to write her autobiography, but had given up hope that she was ever going to do it. Stein decided to write it for her, 'and this is it'.

What no one knew was that the book had been written as a form of reparation. Toklas's fury about the hidden manuscript had driven Stein to compose a work that would affirm her commitment to Toklas once and for all, uniting their names, publicly, for ever. Every person who had caused strife between them was either excised from the narrative entirely or witheringly dismissed. Hemingway was demoted to a former friend whom Stein was faintly embarrassed to have encouraged in his writing; Leo Stein was not mentioned by name; May Bookstaver was smoothly erased from Stein's personal history. Instead, Stein wrote into being a version of her life in which their roles were defined only by each other: Stein the genius husband, Toklas the adoring wife. On one level, it's entirely Stein's story: she dominates every page, bragging brazenly about her achievements. But at a second glance, Stein's identity is contingent on Toklas's recognising and declaring: it is she who creates Stein, who makes possible everything Stein does. Toklas's invisible household labour – the cooking, the sewing, the typing – is brought to the fore: Stein celebrates the wifely work which enables – even guarantees – her own achievement.

Stein sent the manuscript to her agent, William Bradley, in November 1932. He immediately saw the potential – after sending Stein a telegram, halfway through reading, to clarify which one of them had written it. 'With a little clever handling,' he wrote to the American editor Alfred Harcourt, 'this book could be made into a best-seller.' Harcourt replied in raptures: 'It is an extraordinary and extraordinarily interesting book,' he told Bradley, 'and we are looking forward eagerly to the sensation its publication is apt to cause.' Within weeks, Bradley had struck lucrative deals with Harcourt, Brace & Company in New York and the Bodley Head in London for the book's publication. Flush with the proceeds, Stein bought a new Ford car, the most expensive Hermès coat she could find, studded collars for Basket and Pépé, and a telephone for Bilignin, so she could stay up to date on all matters of publicity. They hired an Italian couple who began work on a deep clean of the apartment – its first since 1914. 'After these years of faith,' Stein wrote, 'to know that I have a public gives me what the French call a *cœur léger*, it makes me not light-hearted but it leaves me unburdened.'

'Affirmation is what one needs, in poetry and in prose,' Stein wrote to a friend after receiving Bradley's enthusiastic response, 'as I have always said an artist needs appreciation not criticism.' Harcourt began to promote the book months before its publication, teasing readers that the latest book by Gertrude Stein would upend all their expectations. Since 1919, Stein had kept up sporadic communication with Ellery Sedgwick, the literary editor of the *Atlantic Monthly*, who had consistently rejected her work, with good humour on both sides. To her delight, he now offered to print the *Autobiography* in four instalments over May 1933, for the substantial fee of $1,000. 'During our long correspondence,' he wrote, congratulating Stein on her persistence, 'I think you felt my constant hope that the time would come when the real Miss Stein would pierce the smokescreen with which she has always so mischievously surrounded herself . . . Hail Gertrude Stein about to arrive!' With an eye for suspense, Stein asked that the serial should appear under the name of Alice B. Toklas, and that the book's final pages – where Stein is unveiled as the true author – should not be included. (When the book was published, Stein's name was not listed on the cover – but the US edition's cover image, Man Ray's photograph of Stein writing at her desk with Toklas standing at the door, dropped a strong hint.) Readers queued at newsstands for the first issue, and within days both Stein and Toklas were besieged by fan letters, as well as – most gratifyingly – orders for Plain Edition titles. By the time the book was officially published, on 1 September 1933, the entire first American printing of 5,400 copies had already sold out, since it had been selected as the September choice of the Literary Guild, one of America's largest and most influential subscription book clubs (an honour for which Stein was paid $3,000). On 11 September, a photograph of Stein at Bilignin appeared on the front cover of *Time* magazine. The caption, a quotation from the *Autobiography*, read 'My sentences do get under their skin.'

To Sedgwick, and to many others, this new, clear and highly readable style marked a happy ending to the uneasy mystery of Gertrude Stein. She had, at last, begun to make sense. Finally, it seemed, Stein had dropped the impenetrable wordplay, and those who had felt they were never quite in on the joke could laugh together in hearty relief. 'As you read her', wrote one columnist, 'you have a terrible feeling that she will drop off any moment into such sentences as Gertrude is a stein. Stein is a stone . . . But Gertrude doesn't go steinish once.' *Newsweek* called the book 'as clear as a comic strip', while *Time* rejoiced that readers 'may begin to understand why Gertrude Stein's importance as a writer has received so many reiterated testimonials from writers of accredited sanity'. Stein's delight in the attention helped suppress her disappointment at the open disdain for her earlier work which praise for the *Autobiography* seemed, inevitably, to entail. 'I am as happy as happy can be,' she wrote to a friend. 'I will tell you a dark secret, I am adoring being successful, completely and entirely adoring it. I always thought it might be nice and I am grateful that it did not come too soon but now is just soon enough.'

The pleasure of the *Atlantic* publication was undercut only temporarily when the same magazine published an article by the American psychologist B. F. Skinner entitled 'Has Gertrude Stein a Secret?' Skinner had searched through old issues of *Psychological Review* to find the scientific papers she mentioned, in the *Autobiography*, writing at Radcliffe under the supervision of William James. He proposed – rightly – that her early psychological studies had been deeply influential to her writing practice. But he went further, suggesting that Stein's work was actually produced using the automatic methods she had investigated in the laboratory: readers baffled by Stein's writing could rest assured that it was simply the babbling of the unconscious mind. Stein rarely commented on criticism of her work, but such an egregious misunderstanding bothered her. She never liked the term 'experimental' to be used of her output: it implied that the writing was merely a haphazard means towards achieving desired, yet uncertain, results. To Stein, composition was deliberate. 'Everything I write', she asserted, 'means exactly what it says.' She wrote to Lindley Hubbell, an American poet working on a more sympathetic article about her methods, asking him to reply to the *Atlantic* on her behalf. The experiments she had conducted with Leon Solomons, she explained, aimed to detect the effects of distraction on the motor functions, not to induce subconscious literary creation, as Skinner seemed to imagine. 'There are no real cases of automatic writing,' Stein stated, 'there are automatic movements but not automatic writing. Writing for the normal person is too complicated an activity to be indulged in automatically . . . There is no good nonsense without sense and so there cannot be automatic writing.'

The comments had struck a nerve. Since the start, critics had called Stein's sanity into question. Speculation abounded that she wrote lying languid on a couch sipping absinthe, or sequestered in a dark room letting her fingers wander freely. 'The idea is not to think,' declared one critic, authoritatively. To Stein, whose work was all about thought process, the insinuation that her work was produced unconsciously could not be allowed to stand. 'NO,' wrote Stein to Sedgwick, 'it is not so automatic as he thinks. If there is anything secret it is the other way . . . I think I achieve by xtra consciousness, xcess, but then what is the use of telling him that.'

//

After the *Autobiography*, Stein struggled to write. In part, her days were now taken up with the professional business of being a successful writer: negotiating contracts, responding to interview requests, tracking reviews. Having lived comfortably but frugally, selling or trading paintings when funds were required – in 1935 Michael (who filed her returns for her) told her she had not been liable for tax for years, since she didn't have enough income above the personal allowance – Stein enjoyed having money to spend: 'There is no pleasure so sweet as the pleasure of spending money,' she wrote, hurriedly adding, 'but the pleasure of writing is longer.' The influx of cash was well-timed: the Depression had begun to hit France, and her American investments had suffered a sharp fall when Roosevelt suspended the gold standard in April 1933. But the popularity of the *Autobiography*, ironically, exacerbated Stein's anxieties over the status of the work she cared about most. For the first time in her career, her writing was in demand – but the voice readers wanted was not her own. She had finally achieved the fame she had long desired, but for the wrong reasons: she was being appreciated not as a serious writer, but as the comic heroine of Alice B. Toklas's fictional autobiography. The book had been marketed as a tell-all confessional affording privileged access to a coterie of celebrities: the publisher's full-page newspaper advertisements featured photographs of Stein alongside lists of names of 'the people who crowd her atelier', whetting readers' appetites for gossipy revelations about Hemingway, Fitzgerald, Picasso, Matisse. At no point were readers informed that the *Autobiography* was written with cunning self-awareness and a large dose of irony: that it lampoons the very celebrity culture to which Stein had now fallen prey, which reduces artists to cartoonish, two-dimensional figures, and privileges the personality over the work. Stein's main fear was existential. By writing as Alice B. Toklas, had she killed off Gertrude Stein?

'I began to think about how my writing would sound to others,' she wrote, 'how could I make them understand, I who had always lived within myself and my writing.' Stein had finally found her audience, but belatedly realised that it was stifling her. As she had intimated to Hubbell and Sedgwick, writing was a very private activity for her, difficult to describe and requiring absolute isolation from the outside world. When no one wanted her writing, she had been full of ideas; now that her work was worth money and her personality was a public

Literary Possibilities No. 4
Gertrude Stein interviews herself about "The Autobiography of Alice B. Toklas."

Cartoon by Irma Selz, *New York Post*, 14 September 1933

commodity, she had none. 'If you are a genius and you have stopped writing are you still one,' she wondered. In response to pressure from Bradley and Harcourt for another memoir, she tried to sketch out 'what happened from the day I wrote the autobiography to to-day', pressing four-leaf clovers into her notebook and trying out titles on the cover – 'A Confession', 'Beginning of another biography', 'A True Story' – but couldn't find the motivation. 'The other book was gay,' she noted, 'this one will not be so gay . . . It is going to be rather sad.'

Stein's heightened anxiety over the second half of 1933 was magnified by several strange events in the countryside. Madame Pernollet, whose hotel had been their sanctuary for several summers, was discovered one morning dead on the pavement, having apparently fallen from a window. In Belley, rumours abounded: was this an accident, suicide or murder? Around the same time, a newly hired servant – without obvious motive – tampered with the engine of Stein's car and with the telephone wires at Bilignin. Shortly after attending Madame Pernollet's funeral, Stein and Toklas were shaken by the discovery in a ravine of another body, an English woman whom they had recently had to lunch, her torso pocked with bullets. For Stein, these sudden and unexplained deaths merged with the confusing after-effects of her unprecedented success, and the mystery in her own life: the disappearance of her ability to write. As Stein attempted to make sense of the summer, she turned to detective fiction, which she called the 'only really modern novel form' (since the hero is dead from the start, 'so you have so to speak got rid of the event before the book begins'). Her short novel *Blood on the Dining-Room Floor* was written in a burst of energy over the uncertain weeks following the local deaths, and exudes a palpable sense of unease. The novel couldn't be further from the plot-driven page-turners of Agatha Christie, Raymond Chandler or Stein's own favourite, Dashiell Hammett. Rather than moving towards a solution, it only raises questions. Stein opens in a scene of domestic chaos: hair and dust scattered all over the desk, cement clogging the piano keys, the car not starting, the appearance of a mysterious stranger. There is no detective, no culprit or witnesses, just gossip, coincidences and suspicion. It's up to the reader to draw conclusions from the fragments of information offered, as the investigation proceeds without logical progression.

'It always did bother me that the American public were more interested in me than in my work,' Stein wrote later. 'And after all there is no sense in it because if it were not for my work they would not be interested in me so why should they not be more interested in my work than in me.' The *Autobiography* is sprinkled, deliberately, with references to Stein's earlier writing; like the bibliography she had published in *transition*, she hoped the memoir would serve as a kind of textual archive, and an advertisement to future readers and publishers of the pieces she considered her 'real' work. Stein urged her agent William Bradley to put pressure on Alfred Harcourt to reissue *The Making of Americans*, which had not been published in America. Harcourt was reluctant, citing the inevitable dent in profits it would cause in a time of economic depression; he eventually compromised by agreeing to publish an abridged version, but refused Stein's request that he take on the distribution of Plain Edition titles. Bradley encouraged her to offer publishers a synopsis of a work in progress, so they might strike a deal and pay her in advance of its completion, but this required a level of planning totally at odds with her usual process. Having changed her mind about writing another autobiography, Stein began to compose a long work she called *Four in America*, a new approach to portraiture which set out to explore American genius. The book took on four American heroes and imagined them swapping roles, presenting Ulysses S. Grant as a religious leader, the Wright brothers as painters, Henry James as a general, and George Washington as a novelist.

When Bradley duly proposed the project to Harcourt, the publishers confessed to being 'a great deal puzzled' by the book, which threatened to be 'hard reading for most of the readers of the *Autobiography*'. Despite Stein's hopes, the abridged *Making of Americans* hardly sold, and Harcourt was reluctant to put out anything that might further discourage readers just when 'the American public had begun to realise what an extraordinary personality Miss Stein is'. Instead, the bemused editor told Bradley that Harcourt wished to 'confine ourselves to publishing what may be called Miss Stein's more open books'. Stein was furious at the betrayal: 'Do try to make him see that what he calls open and public books are really illustrations for the other books,' she wrote to Bradley, 'and that illustrations should be accompanied by what they illustrate.' But Bradley admitted defeat, and Stein broke off their professional relationship with a series of vehement letters.

With Bradley and Harcourt out of favour, Stein placed high hopes on Bennett Cerf, one of the founders of Random House. Cerf was an experienced promoter, confident in his ability to make ostensibly niche literature appeal to a wide readership. He had already found popular success in 1933 with an edition of *Ulysses*, the first to be printed after the lifting of its government ban; through word of mouth, extravagant advertising campaigns and a sense of humour, he was convinced that he could find an American audience for Stein, just as he had for Joyce. To coincide with the *Autobiography*, he had reissued *Three Lives* in Random House's Modern Library collection, which mass-produced cheap volumes of 'the world's best books': it swiftly became his best-selling title, selling 4,500 copies within a month, including 1,300 to the department store Macy's. Where Harcourt had faltered, Cerf declared himself ready for the challenge, and pledged to publish a new volume of Stein's work every year. His programme would begin, they agreed, with a new collection of short pieces, including examples from twenty years of work. 'The readers of the autobiography', Stein wrote, triumphant, 'will not only read the autobiography but they will read and see everything that has made the autobiography. And so all this which has pleased and contented me will please and content them.'

//

Since their falling-out in December 1930 over the translation of Georges Hugnet's *Enfances*, Stein and Virgil Thomson had maintained a frosty silence. But Thomson had continued to work hard to find a venue willing to stage their opera. He performed his one-man rendition of *Four Saints in Three Acts* in numerous clubs and living rooms around Boston and New York, while Carl Van Vechten had endeavoured to talk up the opera at fashionable parties, within earshot of possible funders. Towards the end of 1932, Thomson mentioned the opera to Arthur Everett 'Chick' Austin, an energetic young curator who had recently taken on the directorship of the Wadsworth Atheneum in Hartford, and was doing his best to transform the museum into a home for avant-garde art. Austin was in the process of raising funds for a new wing of the museum, and immediately lighted on the idea of inaugurating its subterranean theatre with a week-long run of *Four Saints in Three Acts*, to complement the exhibition he was secretly planning for the upstairs galleries: the first American retrospective of Picasso's work. Thomson performed the opera in Austin's living room to a group of potential sponsors – a society dubbed the Friends and Enemies of Modern Music – and plans were set in motion for an opening in the spring of 1934.

When Stein heard of the production plans through Van Vechten, she wrote to Thomson, enquiring after a contract: 'I do not wish to be critical,' she said, 'the great thing is to get it done and successfully done.' After a heated disagreement over the division of profits – despite Thomson doing all the work to stage the production, Stein insisted on fifty–fifty, informing him imperiously that 'the commercial value of my name is very considerable' – they agreed that Thomson would find and rehearse a cast in New York. Thomson's partner, the artist Maurice Grosser, devised a scenario for the opera, creating a stage setting that would give the singers some sense of activity and purpose. Act One would represent a pageant, set on the steps of the cathedral at Ávila, where Saint Teresa would enact a variety of scenes: being serenaded with a guitar, painting giant pink Easter Eggs, being photographed holding a dove. Act Two would present a garden party in

Four Saints in Three Acts at the 44th Street Theatre (left, photo: Carl Van Vechten) and the Wadsworth Atheneum (below)

the country near Barcelona, where the saints watch a performance from an opera box. Act Three would take place near a monastery, where Saint Ignatius would describe his vision of the Holy Ghost – using Stein's enigmatic, repeated line 'pigeons on the grass alas' – to a heavenly assembly. Thomson selected an eager if inexperienced director, John Houseman, a conductor, Alexander Smallens, and recruited an all-black chorus through Eva Jessye, musical director of a Harlem choir, who – perhaps sensing that Thomson had chosen her singers with an eye for spectacle – ensured her cast were well paid for rehearsals, as well as for performances. The choreographer Frederick Ashton was summoned from London to arrange the staging; he scouted unsuspecting dancers performing the Lindy hop in Harlem's Savoy Ballroom – a lifeguard, a boxer and a taxi driver – and created movements designed to turn the opera into a baroque extravaganza.

Thomson's casting decision invoked a nostalgia for the black churches in Missouri where he had spent his childhood, and a nod to the exhilaration of Harlem nightlife. His pride in his singers was often expressed with fetishistic, romanticised ideas of blackness: he wrote later that he had hoped the singers would approach Stein's surreal text without self-consciousness, that they would bring a 'simplicity' and 'dignity' to their roles. But the cast, for the most part, were glad of the opportunity to sing parts far removed from the stereotypical roles usually available to black singers – one singer later recalled his relief at not being required to fall down, wave his arms and sing Hallelujah – and they were soon conversing in lines from the opera. Within weeks of rehearsals beginning, in the basement of Saint Philip's Church on 134th Street, the building was besieged by journalists eager for a scoop on these unconventional proceedings. The *New York Herald Tribune* reported that 'it begins to look as if the mysterious woman so long laughed at would at last be justified to the world – and by Harlem'.

Thomson arrived in Hartford on 1 February 1934, to find a cache of Picassos leaning against the museum's walls (scrambled together from American collections after a planned shipment of loans from Europe had failed to arrive), and Austin hastily trying to raise final funds to pay the opera's cast and crew on time. The week before the scheduled opening was hectic and stressful for all involved. The choir and orchestra had never rehearsed together; the score, copied out by Thomson by hand, was full of errors. The final rehearsals took place amid the chaos of trucks dropping off rigging and ropes for the new theatre, and seeing off the dance critics and society columnists who had rushed up from New York in such droves that the train line laid on extra parlour cars for their comfort. Thomson had co-opted the reclusive artist Florine Stettheimer to design the sets and costumes, after performing a private rendition of the opera at the family home she rarely left. She created a high-camp spectacle featuring palm trees, archways of stringed crystal beads with curtains of starched lace to represent Ávila's cathedral, and a mass of cellophane gauze draped in cloud-like puffs for the backdrop, flooded in white light from bare bulbs.

'Since the Whisky Rebellion and the Harvard butter riots there has never been anything like it,' reported the *New York Herald Tribune* of the opening night, 'and until the heavens fall or Miss Stein makes sense there will never be anything like it.' The *New York Sun* described 'a gasp of astonishment and delight' when – to a resounding drumroll – the red velvet curtains parted to reveal Saint Ignatius kneeling resplendent in purple silk against the shimmering 'Botticellophane'. The music took its cues from a hodgepodge of American vernacular – Southern Baptist hymns, nursery rhymes, drinking songs and marches – creating a cheerful tapestry of moods and registers both traditional and modern, sacred and secular. Thomson was hauled to the stage at curtain call amid a stampede of celebration for the saints, who were dressed in bright-coloured robes with golden haloes. Their performance – the first time many in the audience would have seen black singers perform opera – was by all accounts sensational.

Van Vechten – who had travelled from New York for the occasion – reported to Stein that the opera was 'a knockout and a wow': 'I haven't seen a crowd more excited since Sacre du Printemps.' Fifteen minutes of the Holy Ghost aria were broadcast across the nation, thanks to radio microphones embedded in the cellophane. Two weeks later, the show transferred to one of Broadway's largest theatres, where it played for six weeks to sellout houses, the longest run for an opera in the city's history. To comply with New York's stringent fire regulations, Stettheimer's set (described by one critic as 'a child's dream of rock candy') had to be doused in noxious fire-resistant chemicals, but the show went on, deemed by the *New York Times* to be 'the most interesting theatrical experiment that has been made here in many a season'. That Easter, department-store windows up and down Fifth Avenue were festooned with *Four Saints* references ('Four Suits in Three Acts', read one); it was quoted in Fred Astaire and Ginger Rogers' movie *Top Hat* and in the beloved Charlie Brown comic strip, and Van Vechten sent Stein photographs of her name in electric lights on Broadway. Six months on from the publication of the *Autobiography*, Stein was firmly embedded in American popular culture – she had made modernism mainstream.

//

Due to the coolness of her relations with Thomson, Stein had held the opera somewhat at a distance: she had declined to loan any of her Picassos to the Wadsworth exhibition, and refused Chick Austin's invitation to stay with him for the premiere. But its success, in tandem with that of the *Autobiography*, stirred in her an interest to return to the US for the first time in thirty years, to appear before her new admirers and account for her work in person. Van Vechten urged her to 'come to America where you can properly smell your triumphs': he painted an irresistible picture of her and Toklas whizzing around the country in automobiles and aeroplanes, meeting celebrities and enjoying 'one big taste of America'. Stein was apprehensive. Her experience of writer's block had left her anxious that facing an audience in person would set back her tentative recovery. But she remembered how her lectures in Oxford and Cambridge, back in 1926, had renewed her sense of purpose. What's more, the prospect of a new lecture series – the chance to elucidate her method to a far wider audience than before – seemed to hold an enticing opportunity to turn readers' attention away from her personality and back to her work, once and for all.

Her lecture tour of America was part-planned by Bernard Faÿ, a close confidant over the past few years. They had met in 1924 through a mutual friend, and had begun to correspond two years later when Faÿ wrote, in gushing terms, to tell Stein he had 'read eagerly everything that you have written'. From a French Catholic family of lawyers and bankers, Faÿ was a star professor of American history, and the youngest person to be elected to the Collège de France. He had published biographies of Benjamin Franklin and George Washington – their discussions of American politics and genius had fed into Stein's *Four in America* – and having taught widely in American universities, was considered an expert conduit between French and American cultures and institutions. He had already lectured on her work in America, and translated *Melanctha* and *The Making of Americans* into French, to her enormous pleasure. Stein shared Faÿ's admiration for Washington and his disdain for Roosevelt, and was flattered by his attention to her, which morphed into obsequious ingratiation: he called her 'Saint Gertrude' and referred to her home, unironically, as 'the chapel of Our Lady'. 'I always did say an artist does like appreciation', she told him, 'and yours is appreciation and how.' Unlike the cases of Hugnet and Thomson, this was a collaborative relationship where Stein's primary position was never in question. He was a regular visitor at Bilignin, and over long dinners they conversed in a way Stein did with few people: as equals.

Before their falling-out, Stein's agent William Bradley had introduced her to a tour operator, telling him she had written a bestseller: 'Interesting if true,' the man replied, looking her snootily up and down. Affronted, Stein declared she would have no one else make money out of her: 'Jo Davidson always said one should sell one's personality', she wrote, 'and I always said only insofar as that personality expressed itself in work.' On her behalf, Faÿ – who insisted he could manage the task without involving any mercenary agents – began to seek invitations from colleges, universities, schools, galleries and members' clubs across the United States. Stein set out her terms: no more than three lectures a week; no more than 500 people in any audience; no ticket sales to benefit any causes; a $100 fee to her for talks at schools, $250 for members' clubs; hotel rooms to possess two beds and a bath, not higher than the sixth floor. The sailing date was set for October 1934. 'I am so pleased and we are so busy,' she wrote to Van Vechten, 'that I have no time to worry about how it will be to lecture.'

Faÿ's prominence in Stein's life had come as a sharp sting to Van Vechten, who had considered himself Stein's principal champion and promoter for two decades, and feared that her new friend was threatening to usurp his position. Van Vechten had not seen Stein in person for years – in some ways, their close friendship may have depended on this distance, which both permitted written intimacy and foreclosed the possibility of disappointment – but he remained proprietorial over her work and image. That summer, determined to reassert his status, he dashed to Bilignin to see Stein and Toklas at home, photographing them cavorting with Basket and Pépé, sitting on the terrace with the mountains behind them, playing croquet in the back garden. 'My dearest Carl,' Stein wrote to him that August, 'you do so much for me that I just hoggishly go on asking for more but then I always did like pigs, and you have so encouraged me in that.' Back in New York, on Stein's behalf he corrected the proofs of the new collection of her older work – *Portraits and Prayers* – which Random House was rushing through the press to be in shops for her grand arrival.

Stein devoted the summer of 1934 to writing a series of lectures designed to equip doubting readers to appreciate what she considered her 'real' writing. Each talk would be longer and more direct than 'Composition as Explanation': one was dedicated entirely to *The Making of Americans*, another to the history of English literature and the relationship of her work to the nineteenth century; one was titled 'Portraits and Repetition', another 'Poetry and Grammar'. House guests at Bilignin were enlisted to help draft her press releases, while Stein worked on the lectures themselves, a task which gave her pre-emptive 'stage fright'. Friends in America sent menus from the hotels they planned to stay in, which all their neighbours pored over, trying to establish whether the food was more or less expensive than in France. Stein corresponded with her cousins Julian and Rose Ellen Stein, letting them know which relatives to inform of her homecoming ('the only ones I want to see are Aunt Fanny Keyser, the Rosenberg cousins, that is the Keyser nieces and Uncle Eph, all the other miscellanies no please'). As their departure date grew closer, and Stein's nerves intensified, Toklas wrote to each host explaining that Stein preferred not to be honoured at lavish dinners but to eat a light supper alone before each event. Stein, meanwhile, wondered how changed she would find America from the country she had left thirty years before. 'What will I say to them,' she asked, 'those who make my native land my native land . . . will they listen to me and will I listen to them.'

//

As Stein and Toklas packed their bags and prepared to board an ocean liner for their seven-day crossing to Manhattan, the US press worked themselves into a frenzy over their latest *cause célèbre*. 'One of the most talked-about authors in the world returns to America this week,' declared *Newsweek*. 'Some people call her the "most intelligent American woman alive today"; others say she is crazy.' Articles scrutinised Stein's clothes, driving, haircut; newspapers reported on Basket, 'the French poodle, who has his own toothbrush and who likes to sit in Gertrude Stein's lap', and claimed authoritatively that Stein and Toklas spent their holidays driving around the countryside looking for cows to serve as Stein's muse. When Stein and Toklas disembarked from the SS *Champlain* on 24 October 1934, the docks were lined with journalists jostling to question her. To everyone's surprise, she launched into a virtuoso performance, batting back their jibes with candid good humour.

Van Vechten and her editor Bennett Cerf bustled Stein and Toklas into a taxi bound for the Algonquin Hotel. As they drove past Brentano's bookshop, Stein spied *Portraits and Prayers* displayed in the window alongside Van Vechten's photographs from the summer, her own face looking out at her as if through a mirror. The next day, the newspapers commented on her tweed hat, which 'gave her the appearance of having just sprung from Robin Hood's forest', and her 'disappointingly intelligible' answer to the question 'Why don't you write as you talk?' ('Why don't you read as I write?' she had, reasonably, shot back.) The *New York Times* headline declared that 'Gertrude Stein Arrives and Baffles Reporters by Making Herself Clear'.

For American audiences, the greatest mystery remained Stein's 'secretary-stooge', Alice B. Toklas. Many readers of the *Autobiography* had assumed she was a literary invention altogether, a cipher for Stein's inflated ego. Van Vechten had written stern ripostes to columnists who speculated that her name was an anagram, while Harcourt took out an advertisement confirming that 'Alice B. Toklas really exists'. To reporters who had wondered whether Toklas would make the journey at all, or whether the hoax would finally be revealed, her appearance at Stein's side – silent while her partner cracked jokes – provided fresh fodder for a stream of articles, all concluding that the pair were 'inseparable as ham and eggs'. One interviewer described Toklas as 'a microscopic person who seems interested only in two things – solitude and Gertrude Stein'. Cerf – spotting the opportunity to capitalise on the papers' fascination – tipped off a reporter to a story that an elevator operator, mistaking Stein and Toklas for cooks, had dropped them not on the floor of the Random House offices but at the Swedish Maids Employment Bureau. No journalist dared suggest the two women might be lovers. Only one, who had trailed them as far as he could, revealed his scoop triumphantly: Stein and Toklas, in private, called each other 'Pussy' and 'Lovey'.

Stein enjoyed her encounters with the press enormously, and their reports emphasised her likeability, her infectious laugh, her emphasis on common sense. 'If you enjoy it you understand it,' she assured a reporter bemused by *Four Saints*. 'And lots of people have enjoyed it, so lots of people have understood it . . . If you do not enjoy it, why do you make a fuss about it? There is the real answer.' Within a few weeks of her arrival, the *Washington Post* deemed her 'undoubtedly the most popular and accepted visitor New York has had this winter'. Just as at the rue de Fleurus, access to Stein was mediated, carefully, through Toklas. 'You people should have interviewed Miss Stein many years ago,' she chided one reporter, 'when she was not so well known and not so busy.' There was a scuffle with a photographer who wanted a picture of Stein doing something active: Stein matter-of-factly pointed out she could not be shown talking on the phone or unpacking her bags, because 'Miss Toklas always does that'. They settled, eventually, on her drinking a glass of water. At a press conference, one reporter asked Stein to tell them about Toklas. 'She scolds me when I'm indiscreet,' replied Stein, 'and makes life comfortable for me.'

Above all, Stein enjoyed her meetings with the public: fellow diners at restaurants who sent notes via waiters requesting autographs, taxi drivers who hummed tunes from *Four Saints* and refused to accept her fare. As they wandered up and down Manhattan's avenues, passers-by caught their eyes and smiled, and the women smiled back and remarked to each other that New York was not, after all, so different from the French countryside. On one occasion, they turned into a grocery store and the owner glanced up. 'How do you do, Miss Stein,' he said casually, as if he'd been expecting her. 'It must be pleasant coming back after thirty years.' As they passed on through Times Square, squinting at the garish billboards advertising Chevrolet, Wrigley's and Coca-Cola, Stein and Toklas looked up, together, at the ticker tape snaking around the *New York Times* building, flashing breaking news to all who passed beneath. 'Gertrude Stein has arrived,' it read in electric lights.

Stein's tour lasted seven months, taking in thirty-seven cities in twenty-three states. They watched the Rockefeller Center rise from building site to skyscraper, avidly followed the FBI's search for gangster John Dillinger's notorious associates, and noted the signs of economic decline – high prices and levels of unemployment – after four years of depression. As they zigzagged across the country, her audience ceased to be an object of fear and became, instead, her friends. Wherever they went, Stein and Toklas were welcomed as guests of honour: they attended a meeting of the Raven Society in Edgar Allan Poe's old room at the University of Virginia, they took tea at the White House with Eleanor Roosevelt (despite Stein's scepticism towards the President), and cheered from the stands at the Yale–Dartmouth football game. In November, they flew to Chicago, escorted by Van Vechten, to see *Four Saints*, which had transferred there for a limited run of five performances, with Thomson conducting the original cast. It was Stein and Toklas's first time on an aeroplane: their tickets were provided free of charge by Curtis Air, and Harry Moses, the businessman who had financed the opera's Broadway transfer, filled the cabin with roses. Looking down at the landscape from above reminded Stein of the shapes and forms of Cubism: 'The twentieth century', she wrote, 'is a century which sees the earth as no one has ever seen it.' In her mind, she idly connected the flatness of the American land with its democratic promise: a free environment, she thought, conducive to genius. After the show – she moved back and forth between seats around the auditorium to see it from all angles – Stein told the press it was 'perfectly extraordinary how they carried out what I wanted'.

Rumours of Stein's penchant for crime fiction had reached Chicago, and one night they were invited to ride in the back of a squad car with a battalion of homicide police detectives, searching for criminals at large. They were collected from a lively dinner where Stein had ignited a heated debate with several academic philosophers over the relative merits of various eighteenth-century writers: she made the case for Swift, and professed for good measure that it was more important to teach students the history of literature than of politics. 'Government is the least interesting thing in human life,' she argued, rising to her feet, 'creation and the expression of that creation is a damn sight more interesting . . . the real ideas are not the relation of human beings as groups but a human being to himself inside him.' Just as Toklas was trying to calm her down, the maid burst in to announce the police were at the door – which caused momentary commotion, until everyone realised this was merely Stein's next entertainment ('no murders,' she lamented, 'but lots of fun'). She was thrilled, too, at a different brush with the world of crime, when the writer Dashiell Hammett – the person she claimed she was most eager to meet in America – joined her for dinner in Beverly Hills, along with Charlie Chaplin, Lillian Hellman and Anita Loos. 'It is very nice being a celebrity', wrote Stein in *Everybody's Autobiography*, her memoir of the tour, 'a real celebrity who can decide who they want to meet and say so and they come or do not come as you want them. I never imagined that would happen to me to be a celebrity like that but it did and when it did I liked it.'

//

Stein's purpose, on her tour, was to shatter the assumptions and misunderstandings that had clouded her reception. Over and over, she insisted that her work required no prior knowledge or intellectual framework; there was no secret to be unveiled here, no key to the riddle. In the course of ten talks, Stein mounted a defence of her work which formed a counterpart – even a corrective – to the *Autobiography*. She staked her claim to be the pre-eminent modern writer, creating the quintessentially twentieth-century American literature in the lineage of Walt Whitman and Henry James. To anyone who reproached her for writing with no awareness of tradition, she described her decades spent reading through eighteenth- and nineteenth-century English literature and her immersion in art history, from her early collecting of Japanese prints to her gradual acquaintance with Titian, El Greco, Courbet and Cézanne. She explained her antipathy to 'servile' commas, which enfeeble sentences by imposing a pause, and made a passionate case for 'long complicated sentences', which force readers to linger on the words, listening out for rhythms to break up the stream of phrases. She suggested that narrative has lost its meaning in an age where newspapers, cinema, photographs and radio bombard us with 'what is happening': we don't need more stories about what people have done, she argued, when 'the thing that is important is the intensity of anybody's existence'. She meditated on the difference between American and English literature, proposing that England – being on an island, and the centre of a global empire – had its own distinctive relationship to language, embedded over centuries. In America, she suggested, words can have a 'vitality of movement' that offers writers a tantalising freedom.

A major theme, running across Stein's lectures, was novelty: what it meant for writing to be immediate, fresh or modern. Each generation, she argued, must find its own language anew: words become stale and saturated from overuse, sapped of meaning and unable to produce any original effects. 'Nothing could bother me more than the way a thing goes dead once it has been said,' she claimed, insisting that since *The Making of Americans* she had been 'trying in every possible way to get the sense of immediacy'. 'The business of Art', she explained, 'is to live in the actual present, that is the complete actual present, and to completely express that complete actual present.' More explicitly than ever before, she laid out her theory of the function of memory in language, which she aimed to break down: that each appearance of a word invokes, in the reader, memories of its previous uses – and the process of remembering, the mental formation of an association between the word and what it has described before, creates a gulf between the reader and the text before them, holding the word in bondage. At the University of Chicago, in response to a student's question about her much-parodied line 'rose is a rose is a rose' (which had first appeared in her 1913 text 'Sacred Emily', and recurred across her work) Stein summed up her approach in characteristically bullish style. The repetition, she argued, distilled the image to its essence. 'You all have seen hundreds of poems

Stein and Toklas travelling, holding good luck
charms from Carl Van Vechten

about roses and you know in your bones that the rose is not there . . . I'm no fool; but I think that in that line the rose is red for the first time in English poetry for a hundred years.'

'I am delighted really delighted with the way all the audiences take the lectures, and it makes me happier than I can say,' wrote Stein. But it was something of a stretch to infer that the lectures had shifted her reception back to her work entirely. Early reports – which treated her talks like theatrical performances – tended to focus on Stein's appearance: her 'enigmatic countenance', her androgynous wardrobe, the mysterious 'secretary' lurking just offstage. *Portraits and Prayers*, whose publication coincided with Stein's arrival, received a lukewarm reception from readers who felt infuriated to see her persisting with her former style after proving she could write so delightfully. The *San Francisco Chronicle* complained that the book contains 'the precise babbling, the formless irrelevancies, the elaborate abracadabra which we have come to recognise as Miss Stein at her purest', while the *Journal of Medical Associations* even published a paper diagnosing Stein with palilalia, a speech disorder characterised by involuntary repetition. Still, Stein held on to her belief in her audience, whose attention and enthusiasm had buoyed her through her tour. She had reaffirmed her sense that she was writing for readers, not for publishers or critics who persisted in disparaging her. The enormous popularity of her lectures, especially with young people, presaged well, she was sure, for her work's endurance.

Stein and Toklas returned to Paris in May 1935, to a rapturous reunion with their dogs and friends there. Most significantly, the tour had cemented their friendship with Carl Van Vechten, who had accompanied them around the country, relaxing them with wisecracks and providing a genial foil to their dynamic. As their intimacy deepened, the three had established nicknames – Papa, Mama and Baby Woojums (the name of a cocktail described in Van Vechten's novel *Parties*) – which united them as a family: Toklas and Van Vechten as carers and protectors to their mutual interest, Stein. He had photographed them throughout the tour, releasing promotional images to newspapers as canny and crucial branding. That Christmas, he sent to Paris tiny photographs of the three of them together: his role as primary promoter was firmly restored. Stein's erstwhile tour organiser Bernard Faÿ, meanwhile, had to deal with an embarrassing hiccup. An acquaintance of his, an actor named Jean-Jacques Rousseau Voorhies, had been passing himself off as Stein's representative and – until caught – had been attempting to solicit fees from groups and institutions. After the tour, in a bizarre act of revenge, Voorhies had begun giving interviews branding Stein – as one newspaper put it – 'as the world's biggest faker, and her triumphal tour of America as the world's biggest hoax'. Faÿ had to issue a press release rebutting Voorhies's assertion that the *Autobiography* was a practical joke created by himself, Stein and Faÿ over a wine-fuelled dinner party to 'test American gullibility'. Even Faÿ's terse denial could not stop Voorhies publishing a two-part interview stating that Stein drove drunk, that the Four Saints were based on Stein, Toklas, Faÿ and himself, and that Faÿ had conferred a diploma from the Collège de France on Stein's dog Basket – this last was, in fact, true, though not information intended for public consumption. But Stein was on a high: with the tour concluded, she was ready to get back to work. 'I can't get over it,' Stein wrote, recalling the exhilaration of the past months. 'It is a funny experience . . . it has made me come out all different and I am wondering what that will make me do.'

//

Not everyone in Paris was thrilled at Stein's success. 'We are public figures with private lives,' said the artist Marie Laurencin to Toklas, expressing a widely felt indignation that Stein had been indiscreet. Reading the *Autobiography*, Ernest Hemingway – already smarting from a cold telephone call from Toklas making clear, without explaining why, that he was no longer welcome at the rue de Fleurus – was incensed at Stein's comment that she and Sherwood Anderson had profoundly influenced the rhythms of his prose, and that they were 'both a little proud and a little ashamed of the work of their minds'. Picasso's former partner Fernande Olivier complained that Stein had plagiarised her own memoir: Stein brushed off the accusations, but was more seriously wounded by Picasso's own disdain for the book, which he thought trivialised the avant-garde by treating it as gossip. Her disappointment at his reaction was compounded when he casually told her he had begun to write poetry, trespassing, as she saw it, on her territory. 'Things belong to you,' she explained, 'and writing belonged to me.' After the *Autobiography*, they didn't speak for two years.

'God what a liar she is,' wrote Leo Stein to Mabel Weeks. 'Practically everything that she says of our activities before 1911 is false both in fact and implication.' Now married to Nina and living near Florence, Leo's resentment of his sister had only hardened over the years. As she made her way around America, he annotated newspaper clippings with sarcastic asides, and enumerated the *Autobiography*'s errors and omissions in snide marginal notes. A few friends who knew of the siblings' quarrel wrote to Leo to commiserate. 'As I read her book,' wrote the art collector Albert Barnes, 'I recalled often your reply, way back in 1913 or 14, to my question – why are you leaving Paris to live in Italy? You said – in effect – "Gertrude is crazy. I can't stand her any more."' Leo attributed her decision to leave him out of the book to pure pettiness: Gertrude, he wrote at the time of the split, 'hungers and thirsts for *gloire*, and it was of course a serious thing for her that I can't abide her stuff and think it abominable'.

If Gertrude Stein was now the arbiter of history, friends and acquaintances began to ask, whose voices would be left out? If her version of events was going to be authoritative, who was doomed to become a minor character, pushed to the periphery of Stein's story? Her old Baltimore friend Etta Cone was a case in point. Cone was deeply hurt to see herself described in the *Autobiography* as a 'distant connection' of Stein's: a rich acquaintance who could be relied on to buy paintings if the Steins needed money. In 1906, Cone had typed up the manuscript of *Three Lives* as a favour to her friend, before being called away from

Paris for a family emergency: when she returned, Stein rebuffed her, having found a new typist in Toklas. To add insult to injury, Stein had contacted Cone again in 1922, after a long period of silence, having heard that the manuscript of *Ulysses* had just been sold to a Philadelphia book collector for an enormous sum. She was now offering Cone the chance to purchase, for $1,000, the manuscript of *Three Lives* – the very pages she had spent thankless hours typing. Incredulous, Cone refused. In the summer of 1933, travelling around Europe with her teenage niece and nephew, Cone saw Leo, Michael and Sarah Stein – but stiffly refused Gertrude's invitation to lunch. Her young companions, eager to meet the famous Gertrude Stein, were disappointed, but Cone sternly told them that Gertrude wasn't worthy of meeting them.

The most sustained criticism came, ironically, from the pages of *transition* magazine. Stein had fallen out with the editors, Maria and Eugene Jolas, after she accused them of favouring Joyce's work over her own. When they read the *Autobiography* (published in France in Bernard Faÿ's translation), the Jolases were furious at what they perceived as numerous slights and inaccuracies towards them and their contributors. Stein presented the magazine as a doomed enterprise, which had failed after it stopped printing her work. Fuming, the Jolases struck back. In February 1935, *transition* published *Testimony Against Gertrude Stein*, a document of intense vitriol, putting Stein on trial. In his introduction, Eugene Jolas dismissed the *Autobiography* as 'hollow, tinsel bohemianism' full of 'egocentric deformations', and declared that the aim of the pamphlet was to challenge Stein's inaccuracies 'before the book has had time to assume the character of historic authenticity'. Inside, Matisse compared the book to a harlequin's costume, its parts sewn together 'without relation to reality'. He corrected a series of minor factual points – that he had not come to Paris to study pharmacy but law; that Braque, not Picasso, had made the first Cubist painting – but above all, he wanted to correct the record on his wife's features, which Stein had compared to a horse (she claimed it was a compliment): 'Madame Matisse was a very lovely Toulousaine, erect, with a good carriage and the possessor of beautiful dark hair.' Other contributions, from Tristan Tzara, Georges Braque and André Salmon, argued that Stein was more of a tourist than an authority on the epoch: that she was too self-centred to see accurately what was going on around her. It was a concerted attempt to consign Stein to the margins of history: to write her out, as determinedly as she had written herself in. The reaction was widely publicised – the *New Yorker* ran an article called 'Latest Dirt on Gert' – but Stein claimed to be unbothered. Where once publicity had thrown her, now she thrived on it. 'My French publishers', she wrote grandly to Van Vechten, 'are naturally very pleased.'

8 : PUBLICITY SAINT

Gradually, Stein and Toklas eased themselves back into their domestic routine. 27 rue de Fleurus seemed somehow smaller when they returned from America – the rooms felt stuffy, permeated by fumes from the garage next door – so when the landlord told them he wanted the apartment back for his son, it was not such a wrench to part with it. 'We are moving,' wrote Stein. 'I guess 27 got so historical it just could not hold us any longer.' The new apartment they found stood on the upper floor of an elegant seventeenth-century building on a short street two blocks back from the Seine near the Île de la Cité. 5 rue Christine was twice as big as their former home and cost half the rent, with a roof terrace looking out over the chimneys of Paris. Soon they were drawing up plans for a fresh hanging of the paintings, and covered one room with wallpaper dotted with white doves, to recall a beloved line from *Four Saints*, 'pigeons on the grass alas'. It was, Stein wrote, 'the apartment of our dreams'.

The American tour had prompted a period of self-reflection for Stein. She was no longer hampered by the intense self-questioning that had compounded her unsettling period of writer's block, but her experience of fame now generated a series of introspective, genre-bending prose works, centring on questions of identity and the relationship between writer and audience. Throughout her sixties, Stein mused at length about what her writing meant and what it means to write at all, contemplating her readers both present and future. In the summer of 1935, still exhilarated from her aeroplane rides across the American landscape, Stein began work on a long text titled *The Geographical History of America*, which she described as 'a detective story of how to write' and 'a poem of how to begin again'. At the heart of *The Geographical History* – a constantly shifting work incorporating dialogues, plays and elements of autobiography – is a distinction between human nature and the human mind, two parts of the self which Stein insisted have 'nothing whatever to do with' one another. Human nature, Stein suggested, is personal identity, assured by memory and external validation; the human mind, by contrast, stands outside of personality, and is the element capable of artistic creation. Separating her public and private selves like this helped Stein return to her writing desk after the excitements of the past two years; to make sure the business of being a public figure did not distract her from the work which still lay ahead of her. She had mooted the distinction a couple of years earlier, reflecting on her own writing practice, which required her to clear her mind entirely of disturbances in pursuit of clarity, such that she could forget where, or even who, she was: 'Begin again,' she often instructed herself when her concentration momentarily broke, refocusing her thoughts to take fresh aim at what she was trying to say. 'I am I not any longer when I see,' she had written. 'This sentence is at the bottom of all creative activity. It is just the exact opposite of I am I because my little dog knows me.' Over the next few years, this last phrase – drawn from the Mother Goose nursery rhyme – became a touchstone for Stein, as she wrestled with her competing desires for solitude and for appreciation.

//

Stein's ideas about the human mind and human nature were shaped by long conversations with a writer who, like her, had catapulted to disconcerting celebrity. In 1928, aged thirty-one, Thornton Wilder had won the Pulitzer Prize for his novel *The Bridge of San Luis Rey*, immediately resigned from his teaching position and signed a five-year contract with a lecture bureau. Stein had met Wilder during a tour stop in Chicago, and promptly enlisted him as her 'secretary, errand boy-companion', which he gamely considered 'a great treat'. After the tour, Wilder became a major source of long-distance support to Stein. He promised to write about her work and promote her with publishers – 'I am resolved that my pleasure shall be contagious,' he wrote, while confiding to other friends he could endure 'only a bundle of pages' of *The Making of Americans* – and they corresponded gaily about the prospects of a Hollywood film of the *Autobiography* for which the whole Paris household, dogs included, would return to America for champagne and oysters. Stein discussed writing more deeply with Wilder than with anyone else. 'I am not leading him,' she wrote, pinpointing where their relationship differed from that with most of her acolytes, 'I am confiding in him.' But Wilder's most valuable act of assistance to Stein was persuading her, in the summer of 1937, to take concrete steps to secure her literary legacy.

The year had begun with an exciting trip to London, where her 1931 play 'They Must. Be Wedded. To Their Wife' had premiered as a one-act ballet, choreographed by Frederick Ashton, who had worked on *Four Saints*. Stein, by now, was accustomed to being praised and celebrated in public, but was painfully aware that much of her older work lingered out of view in her own filing cabinets. That August, Wilder received a letter from an old schoolfriend, Wilmarth Sheldon Lewis, who was chairman of the Yale Library Associates, asking him to put a proposition to Stein. Over the past few years, a team of scholars at Yale University had been soliciting a collection of archival materials relating to contemporary American literature, amassing the papers – manuscripts, letters, diaries – of writers they felt would draw researchers to the library and cement Yale's status as a shaping force in literary culture. The idea that papers previously consigned to wastepaper baskets should be accorded the status of scholarly artefact was a relatively new phenomenon, which had begun to take off amid a boom of rare book collecting after the Depression: several universities around the US had begun to establish collections, and Yale was determined to position its own holdings at the forefront of this new field, evaluating literary history in progress, and guiding readers' interpretations. The collection's chief curator, Norman Holmes Pearson, was eager to build an archive reflecting a distinctly American literary tradition, and was especially interested in the work of under-recognised women modernists: he was already cultivating the poets Marianne Moore and Hilda Doolittle, and set his sights now on Gertrude Stein.

The previous year, Stein had written that she was less bothered about her writing not being published than she used to be: she had already begun to conceive of a posthumous readership. 'If it is not printed', she wrote, 'some one will discover it later and that will be so much more exciting.' Stein and Toklas had, for years, been building their own private archive, a document of their relationship as well as of Stein's work:

not only the manuscripts, letters and notebooks stacked neatly in filing cabinets, but the photographs they posed for, the clippings they kept, even the headed notepaper and napkins Toklas embroidered with their own motto – a circular emblem reading 'rose is a rose is a rose'. Self-archiving, for Stein, was a way to assert herself as a serious writer, a person worthy of future study. Some, of course, saw her determination to keep every piece of paper she wrote on as a marker of inflated ego. The poet William Carlos Williams remembered once attending a tea at 27 rue de Fleurus during which Stein went to her cabinet and began to pull out manuscripts, reading out their titles and asking Williams what he would do if he faced her difficulties in getting published. There was a stunned silence when he replied, boldly, that he would select the best and throw the rest in the fire – before Stein, witheringly, replied: 'No doubt. But then writing is not, of course, your *métier*.' So the Yale library's interest appeared finally to offer vindication to her hoarding tendencies – and, what's more, the pleasure of having her work's status verified by a prestigious institution. On 23 November 1937, Stein wrote formally to Yale, offering to donate outright the manuscript of *A Long Gay Book* and deposit the rest of her papers there as a loan – retaining the option of retrieving and selling them at any point, should she need the money.

The idea of an archive fascinated Stein: she approached the task of creating a collection with energy and playfulness. The move was designed to give her the immortality she wanted: it removed the pressure to find willing publishers for the texts she had been flogging unsuccessfully for decades, knowing they would be safe at Yale for perpetuity. Through packing her texts into boxes, Stein was able to imagine a reality in which they would be received with pleasure, not derision: recovered, examined, celebrated. And by constructing the archive herself, Stein had control over what those future readers would find. Now, the prospect of her own dedicated repository, a kind of time capsule where facts and secrets could be buried in order to be excavated, offered enticing possibilities. This was Stein's chance to create a paper trail: to project a version of herself into the future.

The process of archiving proved a productive stimulus to new writing, too. Stein was always magpie-like in her compositions: she would often reuse and recast lines from earlier work, as if dropping clues for the reader and linking her texts together ('pigeons on the grass alas', in *Four Saints*, was a verbal echo of 'chicken made of glass. Alas', a phrase written four years prior which she had rediscovered in 1927 while preparing the text 'Mildred's Thoughts' for publication in an anthology). As Stein packed up her old manuscripts for Yale, she began to borrow snippets and fragments from them to insert into the new novel she was writing, as if showcasing her whole career as one ever-evolving continuous present. Following her experience in America, and the saga of the divorced socialite Wallis Simpson's constitutionally fraught engagement to King Edward VIII (which she had followed avidly), Stein had grown fascinated by what she called the 'publicity saint': a class of celebrity 'who achieves publicity without having done anything in particular'. In *Everybody's Autobiography*, Stein had explored the power of the media to create caricatured versions of people that render subjects unknowable to themselves; now, she told a friend she wanted to write a novel where 'a person is so publicised that there isn't any personality left'.

Ida follows a woman who wins a nebulous beauty contest and finds herself famous simply for being famous; nobody knows anything about her, yet she is recognised everywhere she goes. The better known she becomes, the less familiar Ida feels to herself — yet she is plagued by the fear that if she ceases to be recognised, she will stop existing even in this reduced form. *Ida* is full of doubles and phantoms, split selves and segmented identities. In Ida's fears are Stein's own — that her personality had superseded her work and made her too self-conscious to write as she once had — but here, those anxieties are expressed with humour, sympathy and a degree of distance. The novel transforms into a comedy, finally celebrating Ida's two successful relationships, which mirror Stein's: with her partner, and with her beloved dogs.

//

Stein worked on *Ida* all through 1938 and into 1939 – until her peaceful routines were ruptured, in the summer, by global events far beyond her control. She had followed Adolf Hitler's rise to power in Germany, but didn't comment, in her letters, on the increased precarity in Europe. Instead, she blithely told friends she didn't believe there would be a war. As early as 1936, her brother Michael (who had returned to California in 1929) had suggested they send paintings to America for safekeeping. 'There is no use in being too forethoughtful,' Stein replied, 'if you are too careful you are so occupied in being careful that you are sure to stumble over something.' It's a casual statement that smacks of denial – yet which chimes with Stein's long-standing ability to tune out anything she didn't want to hear. Along with at least 5,000 other Americans in Paris, she and Toklas ignored the Ambassador's warning of 24 August 1939, urging citizens to return to the US. They were at Bilignin with the photographer Cecil Beaton, who recalled that they refused to countenance any talk of war until the butcher telephoned to inform the household that he couldn't supply the joint they had ordered, since the army had requisitioned all local meat. On 1 September, they heard the announcement that Germany had invaded Poland, and war had been declared: the Louvre had begun to evacuate its treasures, and Parisians were either fleeing the city or gearing up for siege. Quickly deciding they would be safer for now in the countryside than in Paris, they obtained a thirty-six-hour permit to return to 5 rue Christine, where they bundled up winter clothes, their passports and other important papers, and seized two paintings to take, wrenching them with some effort from their frames: *Portrait of Madame Cézanne*, and Picasso's Stein. The art dealer Daniel-Henry Kahnweiler helped them wrap some larger paintings in paper and store them in cupboards, and carried the chosen cargo out to the car – tying Picasso's masterpiece to the roof. With no time to waste, they sped through the dark roads to their rural sanctuary.

'There is so little to do here xcept be a comfort to each other that is the village and us,' Stein wrote to Wilder in October. The countryside around Belley housed a close-knit community: about twenty families lived in Bilignin, all of whom Stein had known for a decade ('and they know me,' she wrote, 'and my car and my dogs'), and she and Toklas had a wide network of long-standing friends in the surrounding villages. Immediately, they were enveloped in a sense of camaraderie, and a grim determination to support one another through whatever was to come. As the nights drew in, and restrictions intensified, Toklas planted radishes and potatoes and began preserving fruit for a 'liberation fruit cake', while Stein obtained her first radio, and became fascinated by the 'entirely new' sensation of listening to someone talk from far away. They had never spent the winter in the countryside, so soon discovered there was no way to heat the house except by open fire, but they found a supply of coal, tore up some Henry Miller novels for kindling, and adapted. 'Really it is xtraordinary how quickly the time passes,' she wrote to Kahnweiler. 'I am sawing wood and Basket and I walk and Alice sits by the fire and sews and Pépé sits by the fire and sleeps, and I work right along and sometimes I wonder if I could ever care again for a city life,

Gertrude Stein and Alice B. Toklas by Sir Francis Rose, Bilignin, 1939

the hills and the stars and the trees are such a pleasure and the sky.'

During the first winter, the air thick with rumours, Stein worked primarily in her 'lighter' mode, too distracted to plan a longer-term project. Between September and Christmas 1939 she wrote *Paris France*, a love letter to her adopted 'home-town', and began a children's book called *To Do: A Book of Alphabets and Birthdays*, which she composed in her head while pacing up and down the terrace, making Toklas laugh with her rhymes and wordplays. The first eight months of the war, where hardly any military action occurred, were known as the Phoney War, or *drôle de guerre* (literally 'funny war', a pun which struck Stein as quite profound): a tense period of waiting for something to happen. At this point, Stein wrote, the war felt more like a dream or a novel than real life: 'It is a thing based on reality but invented.' Her chosen comparisons betray, interestingly, her lifelong tendency to escapism: to seek comfort by avoiding any head-on confrontation with fear. Stein was used to protection; from childhood she had been Baby, and for thirty years Toklas had made sure her life proceeded, as far as possible, without undue perturbation. Although she (or Toklas) ended friendships easily, she shied away from direct conflict, preferring to remove people from her sightlines and pretend they had never existed. She could argue cheerfully for hours with trusted friends, but would shut down debates when her convictions (and, implicitly, her authority) were too robustly challenged – perhaps, when she felt out of her depth. Yet privately, she had always been prone to anxiety and rumination, and the outbreak of war had left her 'terribly frightened'. 'There are enough things to be afraid of, nobody wants to be afraid,' wrote Stein. All that she – and anybody – wanted was 'to be free, to be let alone, to live their life as they can, but not to be watched, controlled, and scared, no no, not.'

She had always found it hard to conceive of suffering in the abstract; only what was immediately around her ever seemed real to Stein. Even as she gradually began to acknowledge the rapid expansion of Germany's military power, and the antisemitism at the core of Nazi ideology, her first recourse, still, was to the realm of fantasy, and to sources of optimism, however unlikely. As 1940 dawned, Stein became obsessed with predictions. She discovered an astrological book by Leonardo Blake called *The Last Year of War and After*, and was especially taken by his story of a long-dead curé who had foretold that 1940 would bring a war, and that the women would have to sow the grain alone but the men would be back to bring in the harvest. She read the book in bed every night, and took comfort from its prophecies – that Tuesdays would be bad days for the Nazis, and May would mark the beginning of the end for them. She collected, too, predictions from other prophets ancient and modern, in particular the medieval Saint Odile of Alsace: 'They all agree', she wrote, 'that the war ends with the defeat of Germany.'

On 9 May 1940, Hitler's army advanced across north-west Europe, sweeping into northern France. German trucks entered Paris in the early hours of 14 June. From her flat above Shakespeare and Company, a short walk from the empty apartment on the rue Christine, Sylvia Beach heard the ominous beat of boots on the pavement, and watched from her window as a column of tanks, armoured cars and motorcycles processed through the blacked-out streets. Paris clocks were put an hour ahead to Berlin time, French flags were replaced with swastikas, antisemitic flyers were pasted to lampposts, and martial parades began. A few days later, Stein and Toklas were out shopping in Belley when they heard a commotion and a rumbling noise, and turned to see tanks rolling into the market square, with swastikas painted on their sides. The following day, an explosion on a nearby bridge blew all the electricity pylons: now there was no petrol to be found, newspapers ceased to arrive, an eight o'clock curfew and nightly blackouts were imposed. 'No one alive today', wrote their friend Janet Flanner sombrely in her *New Yorker* letter from Paris, 'can know which side's dead men will win the war.'

Philippe Pétain – the eighty-four-year-old former general who was hurriedly inaugurated as premier of France in the wake of the invasion – signed the Franco-German Armistice on 22 June 1940, and France was split into two. Paris was now part of the Occupied Zone, the section of the country under German rule, while Bilignin lay in the southern,

Unoccupied Zone, administered by the French from the spa town of Vichy. Pétain pledged that France's collaboration with Germany would not be military, but people had quickly to absorb the moral quandaries of living in an occupied and divided country. Within months, Pétain had established a new administration, replacing previous officials with his own allies. Among those appointed to influential positions in Vichy was Stein's friend Bernard Faÿ, who was made general administrator of the Bibliothèque Nationale in Paris, France's most prestigious library, and given responsibility for preserving France's cultural heritage.

Many in France greeted the Armistice with jubilation, persuaded by Pétain's insistence that his actions were shielding millions of French people from the ravages Germany had already executed across northern Europe. (He was already a national hero for his decisive action during the Battle of Verdun in the First World War.) Others were ambivalent, and wondered if capitulation had come too soon. Many more considered the deal an act of unforgivable moral cowardice. The exiled politician Charles de Gaulle sounded the first call to resistance in a broadcast delivered from London, calling Pétain 'the father of defeat'. 'So many points of view about him, so very many,' wrote Stein. 'I had lots of them, I was almost French in having so many.' But Stein's predominant reaction to the Armistice was one of relief. Several young men from their village had been called up – Toklas had knitted woollen socks for them, and she and Stein consulted regularly with their mothers for updates – and two mothers in Bilignin, both widows whose husbands had died in the last war, had already lost their sons in the fighting. Stein hoped this news would bring the surviving troops home; she also hoped, less altruistically, for minimal disruption to her own routines. In 'The Winner Loses', an essay she wrote that August for the *Atlantic Monthly*, she remembered awaking from a nap on the sunny terrace and hearing the news that Pétain had asked for an armistice, and thinking that 'he had saved France and everything was over. But it wasn't, not at all – it was just beginning for us.'

//

Friends in America were deeply concerned for Stein and Toklas's safety. In September 1940, Van Vechten told a mutual friend that he had heard nothing from her since June, and that her letters up to that point had indicated that she knew very little of the situation in Paris: that food rationing had been introduced, that unoccupied apartments in Paris were being filled with Germans, that Jews' property was being seized there, and many Jews were leaving the city, either for other countries or the comparative safety of the southern Unoccupied Zone, where Stein was. He knew that he couldn't write to her freely or expect frank replies, as the letters would be read by censors. 'What I cannot understand,' he wrote, 'is how she thinks she can stay on under these circumstances.'

In fact, Stein and Toklas had seriously considered leaving for America. Stein's main anxiety was that she would not be allowed to return to France, where – as a journalist who visited her at Bilignin put it – she had found 'the calm and peace that are necessary to her work'. Some years earlier, when asked why she chose to live abroad, Stein had explained that the United States is 'a country the right age to have been born in and the wrong age to live in': it's the greatest country in the world, she insisted, but 'your parent's home is never a place to work'. So she was reluctant to countenance an indefinite return – but had accepted, grudgingly, that it might be necessary. The American embassy had issued a second advisement on 14 May 1940, urging citizens to make their way to Lyon in order to arrange onward transport from Bordeaux. Stein and Toklas did not immediately react, but when Italy entered the war in June, with Bilignin in the direct path of Mussolini's forces, they joined the droves of cars and set out with their passports towards Lyon – only to turn back, spooked, when they found the military preparing to blow up bridges. As they approached home, they met their neighbours paying for the next year's fishing rights at the local lake, and were struck by this gesture of simple faith in the future. They explained their dilemma, and asked for their friends' honest advice. 'Everybody knows you here; everybody likes you,' the doctor replied, 'we all would help you in every way. Why risk yourself among strangers?' Local friends agreed they were as safe here as anywhere: 'Here in this little corner,' one farmer told her, 'we are *en famille*.' Stein vowed to turn off the wireless and devote herself to gardening. 'Dear me,' she wrote in August 1940, 'I would have hated to have left.'

The initial goodwill many felt towards Pétain soon paled. Over the summer of 1940, his regime swiftly became authoritarian, the collaboration with Nazi Germany more and more involved. Stein and Toklas had to grow used to the sight of German soldiers in the town – 'familiar because we had seen their photographs in illustrated papers all winter', Stein wrote, 'and unfamiliar because we never dreamed we would see them with our own eyes'. On 15 September 1940, all Jews who had fled Paris during the initial invasion – including Stein and Toklas – were forbidden to return to their homes, while businesses in the Occupied Zone had to display signs denoting themselves a 'Jewish Enterprise'. On 3 October, Pétain instituted the first Statut des Juifs, which – for the first time in French history – offered a legal definition of the Jew, meaning Jews could be barred from public and professional posts, and arbitrarily arrested. Three weeks later, he was photographed shaking hands with Hitler. Stein didn't comment on the increased precarity into which she and Toklas were now plunged: instead, she remembered feeling 'filled with sorrow and despair and a little hope and a complete certainty that after all, the Germans were not going to win'.

Towards the end of the year, Stein began work on a haunting new novel, which she described as 'a kind of history of our time': she considered titling it 'My Emotional Autobiography'. From its opening line – 'It takes courage to be courageous' – *Mrs Reynolds* is a psychologically acute account of the way war infiltrates every aspect of the mind. A couple, Mr and Mrs Reynolds, wait anxiously for some unspecified yet ominous event to occur at the hands of shadowy figures named Angel Harper and Joseph Lane – unmistakable apparitions of Hitler and Stalin. Angel Harper is a looming harbinger of unknown evil: the non-specificity of his threat allows the imagination free rein to speculate on the worst possible horrors. 'Eighty percent of the people are afraid', says one neighbour, 'and of the remaining twenty percent half are imbeciles and the other half fanatics.' Villagers are powerless against this force which has come to dominate their days: they can only carry on with their business, and look for language into which to trammel fears that defy words. As daily life became the stuff of nightmares, Stein captured in real time her and Toklas's own heightened state of tension during these years: the everyday oscillation between desperate anxiety, boredom and moments of happiness that kept them from losing their minds.

//

In New York, Carl Van Vechten – making his own preparations for 'death, bombs, destruction and disasters' – decided it was time to send his letters from Stein somewhere where they would be '*kept safely* in vaults'. In January 1941, he presented the Yale library with a box bound in chintz with a rose design, containing 392 letters from Stein, as well as 137 photographs taken at Bilignin and in America. 'Let's write lots more letters for Yale!' he wrote to Stein. To celebrate the acquisition, the curator Norman Holmes Pearson announced an exhibition which would unveil the Stein papers to the general public with fanfare. To speed up the process of cataloguing the material which Stein had stuffed unmethodically into suitcases – and to alleviate the librarians' consternation at her often indecipherable handwriting – Pearson enlisted the help of a young man named Robert Bartlett Haas, who held the distinction of being one of the world's leading experts on the work of Gertrude Stein. As a bookish teenager in California, Haas had been given a Plain Edition catalogue by a local librarian, and went wild for Stein's work. They struck up a correspondence in 1937, and Haas told Stein he was working on a thesis he hoped would serve as 'a guide to your ideas' for 'that vast body of disbelievers who must be converted to Gertrude Stein'. Haas raised the idea of his editing 'a good fat anthology of your work'; Stein responded enthusiastically, and over the coming months and years she regularly sent him copies of her unpublished manuscripts as they discussed the anthology's potential contents. Now, summoned by Pearson, Haas flew to New Haven, and set up a workstation in the Sterling Memorial Library. As librarians passed him scraps of paper directly from Stein's trunks and boxes, he identified fragments and drafts and marked each item with a date – derived from his encyclopaedic knowledge of the different phases of her style – before passing them back to a librarian, who carefully placed the pages in labelled folders on one of twenty-four tables, each representing a single year in Stein's output.

On 22 February 1941, visitors poured into the library's austere halls to find those messy tables now replaced by sleek glass cabinets. The show represented Stein's career as a chronological narrative, telling the story of her life not through her personality but through her work. There was the manuscript of Stein's early portrait, with the name 'Alice' crossed out and replaced by 'Ada', and the notebook in which she charted her first rejections (next to 'Matisse' and 'Picasso' she had written, in 1912, 'May – Stieglitz published'). Among the most intriguing documents revealed for the first time were the manuscripts she had composed during writing classes at Radcliffe: short pieces, marked by misspellings and erratic punctuation and annotated in the margins by her disgruntled tutor, now upgraded to the status of 'early work'. Her process was laid bare as never before: viewers could examine the soft-cover French exercise books in which she wrote in her slanted, spidery script, and pore over her hand-scrawled corrections to Toklas's typescripts. Stein's work had achieved a significant stamp of institutional approval: here, at Yale, she was presented as no mere eccentric, but a notable literary figure.

Friends kept Stein informed of the show's enormous success: Thornton Wilder wrote to tell her of its 'beauty and wit and thoroughness and dignity', while Van Vechten sent photographs of the display which she and Toklas examined under a magnifying glass. But America had begun to seem very far away. On 11 December 1941, after months of speculation, Germany declared war on the United States.

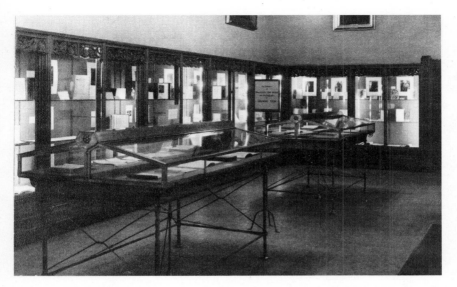

An Exhibition of Manuscripts, First Editions, and Photographs of Gertrude Stein, 1941

Washington retained diplomatic relations with Vichy, allowing life for Americans in the Unoccupied Zone to continue relatively unchanged, but Americans in occupied Paris (2,000 remained there, down from 30,000 before the war) were forced to register with the authorities or risk arrest. Van Vechten's fears for Stein and Toklas were compounded in spring 1942, which saw an extremist turn in Vichy policy towards Jews. From May 1942, Jews in the Occupied Zone were made to wear a yellow star of David, marking them humiliatingly as outsiders. The French police had begun to arrest Jews on behalf of Germany, and on the night of 16–17 July, over 13,000 Jews were rounded up in Paris. Some were sent to a detainment centre at Drancy, a northern suburb, while others were penned into an indoor velodrome used for winter cycling events, where they were kept in appalling conditions for several nights. From there, most were deported to Nazi concentration camps. In September, a mass arrest of American women followed: Stein's friends Sylvia Beach and Katherine Dudley (a neighbour who was looking after the rue Christine for them) were among those interned at Vittel for several months, though both were eventually released. Vichy now imposed its own distinct and brutal measures of discrimination: Jews across the country had to present themselves at police stations for their identity cards to be stamped.

At this point, the French populace did not know the full horrors of the Nazi extermination camps, though warnings had begun to leak through the underground press: it wasn't until 1945 that the ultimate fates of so many Jews from all over Europe started to become public information. The cruelty and unsanitary conditions at domestic detainment camps were common knowledge, as was the fact that many were sent on from them to an unknown destination (surmised, despite assurances to the contrary from the Nazis and from Vichy, to be highly unpleasant, if not deadly). But amid so much rumour and propaganda, it was impossible for even local information to spread reliably, especially in remote villages. 'We hear stories', wrote Stein, 'and do not know whether they are true . . . we are completely isolated.' The deportation of Jews in Paris, however, caused widespread outrage. Heartrending images of children separated from their parents stirred the consciences of a previously lethargic public; police reports noted a shift in public opinion towards criticism of Pétain's government, and in August 1942, the Catholic archbishop of Toulouse delivered an impassioned plea for mercy, which was broadcast in Britain and printed in the *New York Times*. Although antisemitism and xenophobia were prevalent in France – having increased over the 1930s – there was pervasive discomfort at the fact that it was hard to distinguish, now, between Nazi and Vichy policy. The Nazis relied on the co-operation of their French counterparts to enact the persecutions. In the Unoccupied Zone, local officials generally retained a high level of autonomy in their districts; practices and attitudes varied significantly. But many – especially in rural areas like the Bugey region, where Catholic traditions were strong – were shocked by Vichy's participation in these deportations, and chose to quietly protect the Jews in their areas, rather than condemn them.

Stein's district was one of these. In a notebook, she told the story of a Parisian Jewish woman who took refuge in the nearby town of

Chambéry 'when the persecutions against the Jews began in Paris'. This unnamed but 'well-known' woman, Stein wrote, went to the prefecture to have her ID and ration card stamped 'Jew'. The official asked for proof she was Jewish; when she said she had none, he simply told her to leave. 'Most of the French officials were like that really like that,' wrote Stein, moved by the act of tacit civil resistance. It's likely that this anecdote was her own experience, told in disguised form. Stein and Toklas had the steadfast support of Maurice Sivan, the sub-prefect of Belley, and Justin Rey, the mayor of nearby Culoz, both of whom they knew personally. She later told a journalist that Rey had remained silent when the Germans began rounding up 'enemy aliens' in his area. 'You are obviously too old for life in a concentration camp,' she remembered Rey saying. 'You would not survive it, so why should I tell them?'

The alliance between Vichy France and Germany soon proved unstable. In November 1942, following the Allied invasion of Algeria and Morocco, Hitler ramped up the pressure on Vichy to declare war on the Allies, which Pétain refused to do. On 11 November, German troops invaded Vichy France, and occupied the whole country, bar a small section – including Bilignin – under more lenient Italian control. The US treasury immediately restricted the transfer of funds to France, and all communications between the countries were cut off. The fascist sympathiser Pierre Laval was appointed Prime Minister in place of Pétain, who fled: both Jews and Americans in France now faced the most serious peril yet. The Hôtel Pernollet in Belley, where Stein and Toklas had spent several summers, was requisitioned as headquarters for occupying troops, and soldiers patrolled the tiny town centre.

Did her neighbours know Stein was Jewish? If so, they treated her with a compassion starkly absent from their government's policy. As one local Resistance fighter explained in an interview years later, everyone vowed to rally round them if these eccentric but charming women ever needed help. Many survivors have similar stories. Of approximately 320,000 Jews in France in 1940, 240,000 – three-quarters

– survived the war, one of the highest rates in occupied Europe. The majority lived, like Stein and Toklas, in remote countryside communities; some went into hiding or used false identities, often with the help of organised Resistance movements, but many simply carried on with life as best they could. No amount of local trust and support could take away the danger: close to 80,000 Jews in France were deported and killed by the Nazis, with the direct assistance of their own government. Denunciations were increasingly common: at any moment, any Jew in France might have been arrested. But quiet acts of solidarity, often rooted in personal friendships, were not exceptional in Vichy France – and Stein and Toklas knew well that they were, as Stein put it, 'rather favoured strangers' in their local region.

Stein was a well-known figure in the area around Bilignin. For years, she had tramped miles with her dogs through the fields and villages; now, with food increasingly scarce, Stein walked up to sixteen kilometres a day to procure supplies. She would stop to talk to the people she met, listening with an intensity that recalled her first years in Paris: asking about their families, their survival strategies and their politics, genuinely curious – and non-judgemental – about what they had to say. She heard stories of escaped prisoners, of altercations with German soldiers, of a café owner who was forced to serve the occupiers, one of whom smirkingly thrust out a hand for her to shake. Without newspapers or post, with the telephone lines suppressed and many radio broadcasts known to be propaganda, these conversations were Stein's major source of information; they also won her widespread friendship. The baker supplied Stein with extra flour, jam and morels because she talked to him about Hungarian cooking with such interest. A policeman sent over a goat to ensure they never lacked for milk. Friends found a French sergeant who could siphon off cigarettes for Toklas; when his reserves faltered, they set to growing their own tobacco. Neighbours loaned them money when they ran out of francs, until Stein and Toklas – reluctant to prevail on this kindness indefinitely – sold the portrait of Madame Cézanne to a Parisian dealer, who made a clandestine trip to collect it. It was a major sacrifice – the painting had watched over Stein her entire writing life – but there was no time, now, to be sentimental.

'Nowhere in the world', wrote Stein, after hearing of someone who went out to buy bread and never came home, 'should those who have not committed any crime not live peacefully in their home, go peacefully about their business and not be afraid.' From the end of 1942, Stein charted her reflections on life under occupation in a fresh notebook. On the inside front cover she wrote, 'I am really writing my autobiography.' This habit of daily writing sustained her through the upheavals of 1943. In April, their landlords – a family living in Belley – reclaimed the Bilignin house, and Stein and Toklas reluctantly made arrangements to move to Culoz, a nearby railway town nestled in the foothills of Mount Colombier. When the negotiations for the new house were concluded, Stein went in to Belley to thank her lawyer, who greeted her anxiously. He had been in Vichy the day before, he told her, and saw the local prefect Maurice Sivan, who had pressed him to tell Stein and Toklas to leave at once for Switzerland, 'otherwise they will be put into a concentration camp'. Stein recalled feeling 'very funny', and raced home to talk to Toklas. They weighed up the relative dangers of leaving and staying, but the comforts of home, and the friendship of their neighbours, confirmed their sense that it would be unwise to go somewhere 'where nobody can help us if we are in trouble'. They walked back down to Belley, in the dark, and told the lawyer they would move to Culoz as planned – having first dried, powdered and jarred all the herbs from the Bilignin garden. 'They are always trying to get us to leave France', Stein added, 'but here we are and here we stay.'

//

Throughout the war, Stein's work was sought out by some of the leaders in the intellectual resistance to the occupation, who were working to maintain freedom of expression under impossibly dangerous circumstances. They knew Stein remained in France, and considered her an ally. In October 1941, her book *Paris France* was published in French (translated by May d'Aiguy, a countryside neighbour of Stein's) by the radical French Algerian editor Edmond Charlot. A piece on the American language was solicited for *L'Arbalète*, another overtly anti-fascist journal run from a print shop in Lyon regularly raided by police, and her poem 'Ballade' – which, in its imagery of small birds under threat from large ones, might easily be read as anti-Nazi allegory – appeared in *Confluences*, edited by René Tavernier, a poet, philosopher and Resistance fighter who had escaped from the internment camp at Drancy. But this stream of publications ended abruptly after 10 May 1943, when Stein's name appeared as a 'Jewish author' on the Liste Otto, a Nazi catalogue of French books to be banned from sale and removed from libraries. Tavernier wrote to offer his regrets that he could no longer risk including her work in *Confluences*, which had already been temporarily banned by Vichy for its subversive content. 'The literary magazines of the southern zone have always manifested, more or less slyly, the greatest tenderness for the defunct Third Republic, its Jews, pederasts, and Freemasons,' sneered the fascist writer Pierre Drieu la Rochelle. 'To write for this magazine it is sufficient to be an American Jewess, without talent, like Gertrude Stein.'

Culoz, a town significantly larger than Bilignin, was now a thorough-fare for occupying forces. In August, German soldiers knocked on the door and presented military passes entitling them to accommodation. Stein and Toklas, and the two servants who already worked at the house, had to live alongside them for several tremendously fraught days, trying to hide their English books and stretch their food supplies. A few weeks later, they had to go through it all again when a phalanx of Italian sol-diers turned up. Nevertheless, in September 1943 the locals harvested their grapes as ancient custom dictated, calling it the victory wine.

Yet that month, the surrendering of the Italian Zone plunged the region into even deeper fear: they now lived, Stein wrote, with 'the ter-ror of the Germans all about us'. Stein and Toklas were now confined to Culoz: they could no longer even reach Belley, only a few miles away, without passing through twenty-three barricades. But despite their isolation, there was cause for hope. The local Resistance movement (known as the Maquis) gathered strength, led by young men who refused to join the Compulsory Work Service and hid out, instead, in the surrounding mountains. Stein applauded their 'Robin Hood' actions – coming down to steal a pig from an unpopular local aristocrat, supplying butter to all and sundry – and wrote, in her private notebook, of her admiration for their bravery. The first months of 1944 were marked by a series of terrifying incidents close to home: mines placed at Culoz station; an explosion in Chambéry, where they used to go each week for shopping, in which the arcades and the famous elephant statue were 'bombed to bits'. They joked with the baker about the number of stars he could fit on a cake decorated with the American flag when the war was over, and Stein commiserated with Justin Rey, the town mayor, who had to negotiate curfew regulations with the Germans, and deal calmly with their demands, rules and threats.

Random raids and deportations began to increase across France in early 1944. On 6 April, a Jewish children's home in Izieu, a tiny village thirty kilometres from Culoz, was raided overnight: fifty-one children and carers who had been living there peacefully, under the protection of the Belley authorities, were deported. No one knew who had ordered or organised the arrests. Years later, a neighbour of Stein's remembered they had never heard about either the home or the raid, but Stein's writings make clear her awareness of the peril around her. She never mentioned the Statut des Juifs specifically in her war writings, but she reckoned, in her notebook, with historical and ongoing antisemitism, which struck her as 'a plunge back into medievalism'. She recalled the horrifying persecutions of the Boer War and the Dreyfus affair, as well as the recent 'Jew baiting' in England led by Oswald Mosley's Blackshirts, and wondered whether Germany was not 'desperately clinging' to a 'strange delusion' of Jewish power. In the same passage, she remembered her shock at Oscar Wilde's trial, in 1895, when she was twenty-one: 'the first thing that made me realise that it could happen, being in prison', she wrote, implicitly linking her sexuality and her Jewishness, the two aspects of her identity which she knew made her suspect in the eyes of occupying forces. As her notebook progresses, her sense of vulnerability is palpable, as is her admiration of the local Resistance. 'We who lived in the midst of you salute you,' she wrote, aligning herself firmly with the community. She knew, by now, that her survival was out of her control: all she could do was carry on writing.

But this most perilous phase of the war was, mercifully, interrupted. As spring turned to summer, rumours of the Normandy landings aroused hopes that freedom was not far off. In the final weeks of the occupation, locals began openly mocking the Germans, singing the 'Marseillaise' in the country lanes and cheering on the Resistance fighters, who were pelting the occupiers with stones from the hills and robbing collabora-tors' shops, redistributing money to villagers whose livelihoods had been destroyed. With the war over in all but name, the Germans stopped car-rying weapons, and since they were no longer receiving army pay, even started asking around for work and trying to sell their wagons; some told the mayor they hoped to return to Culoz, before long, as tourists. Stein's tone, in her notebooks, turned from gloomy to emotional and excited, as they waited, giddily, for the signal that celebrations could truly begin. Finally, military cars rolled into town bearing noisy Americans equipped not with weapons but with cameras and typewriters. Culoz was liberated.

//

On 1 September 1944, the American journalist Eric Sevareid left his tent and rounded up a group of idle colleagues to join him in a mis-sion: finding Gertrude Stein, who was rumoured to be somewhere in the Alps. As they drove around the poplar-lined roads near Bilignin, the men encountered a colonel in an army jeep who had spent the previous night in Culoz, and directed them north-east. On arrival, after making local enquiries, the mayor personally conducted them up the hill, where they found Stein and Toklas in the middle of a leisurely lunch with a group of

On steps of her house in Southeastern France, Gertrude Stein (left) poses for "Life" with her companion-secretary, Alice B. Toklas, and their pet poodle.

Author Stein and friend, Miss Toklas, stroll through liberated village. Miss Stein lost weight under Nazis. She had to walk 7½ miles to town and back for her food.

Village children dance for joy when Miss Stein tells them Allies are driving Nazis all the way back to Berlin. Villagers knew who she was but never told the Germans.

Mayor Justin Rey calls on Miss Stein to celebrate the liberation of his town. Said Miss Stein: "What a day is today, that is, what a day it was day before yesterday."

Photos and captions from 'The Liberation of Gertrude Stein', *Life*, 1944 (photos: Carl Mydans)

American soldiers they had just met in Belley, the Picasso portrait hanging cheerily above them, and frangipani tart about to be served (planted, as promised, with French and American flags). Sevareid remembered Toklas requesting a single cigarette, and Stein asking eagerly for news of Thornton Wilder. He noticed that Stein had 'a faint tone of sorrow that Pétain had turned out so miserably . . . Laval was unspeakable, and for Darnand's vicious Gestapo not even Gertrude had adequate words.' How, Sevareid asked, had she and Toklas kept themselves safe and hidden, when the Germans were literally on their doorstep? Stein replied that the local people, who knew perfectly well 'who and what' they were, had chosen not to alert hostile authorities to their presence.

One of Sevareid's colleagues was flying to New York the next day, and offered to take as much of Stein's wartime writing as he could carry with him. Overnight, Toklas typed up the writing Stein had been careful to hide throughout the Occupation – they hadn't worried about the Germans finding her notebooks, Stein said, since they were sure they wouldn't be able to read her handwriting. It amounted to a full-length book, an account of life in France from 1942 to 1944, which Stein titled *Wars I Have Seen*. In the morning, the *Herald Tribune* broke the story – 'Gertrude Stein Safe in France With New Book' – and Stein was taken by the journalists to their press centre at Voiron, where she delivered a broadcast for American radio. 'I can tell you that liberty is the most important thing in the world,' she announced. 'I who spent four years with the French under the German yoke tell you so.' Over the coming weeks, more newspapers published photographs of Stein: writing at her desk, handing out sweets to the children of Culoz, strolling with Basket through the town. She and Toklas sent Van Vechten a radiogram – 'Joyous Days Endless Love'. To her cousins in America, she claimed they had been so busy they had not had time to be scared: 'Now that it is all over, what might have happened does sometimes frighten us, anyway it was a wonderful experience, and in a kind of way we did enjoy every minute of it.' She asked after her sister-in-law Sarah Stein, widowed since Michael's death in 1937, and her nephew Allan, now a father himself, 'and do you know what happened to Leo, I heard from Italy just before we came into the war but since then not a word'.

Stein was determined to return to Paris as soon as possible, and reclaim 5 rue Christine. Trains were not yet running, and most cars had been commandeered by the army, but in December a local taxi driver offered to take them back. They loaded the Picasso portrait on to the back seat, and left Culoz at midnight, with the roads flooded and snow on the ground. Several times, they had to get out and push the car up the twisting mountain lanes; the tyres burst every couple of hours, and they were stopped for questioning by a Resistance fighter with a gun, who leaned menacingly on the canvas until Toklas indignantly informed him he was damaging a Picasso. They finally arrived home, on 15 December 1944, to find the apartment ransacked. The Gestapo had invaded twice, and their stamp was still on the door. But although a few small items were missing and several paintings were tied together, ready to be taken away, the collection was intact. Their neighbours in the building rushed in to welcome them back, and the concierge ran down the street to summon Picasso from his home around the corner. 'We were very moved when we embraced', Stein remembered, 'and we kept saying it is a miracle, all the treasures which made our youth, the pictures, the drawings, the objects, all there.'

Picasso told them the whole story. When the Gestapo had invaded on 19 July, brandishing photographs of Stein and Toklas and demanding to know how two Jewish women had managed to retain their home and possessions, the concierge had sent her son to alert him. As a Communist, who had been subjected to Gestapo questioning himself, Picasso detested the Vichy authorities – but for his old friend's sake, he had immediately telephoned Bernard Faÿ at the National Library, and implored him to use his influence to save the collection. The next day, Faÿ let him know it was all arranged. Playing for time, aware the war was waning, he had alerted two German agencies – the Department of Jewish Property and the department for sequestering American goods – and suggested that each of them should assert authority over Stein's paintings, thus stymieing the removal process in bureaucratic confusion. Before the Gestapo could establish which department was responsible for the paintings' seizure, both sets of officials had left Paris, and the collection was safe. But Stein could not thank Faÿ in person. On 19 August 1944, armed police had entered his office, where they found him destroying documents at his desk. While Stein was celebrating with American soldiers, Faÿ was taken to prison at Drancy. There, he awaited trial as a collaborator with the Nazi regime, and a traitor to France.

9 : TO BE HISTORICAL

*S*tein and Toklas returned to Paris just as a stunned and split France was starting to reckon with its complicity in Nazi war crimes, the worst depravities of which – the death camps at Auschwitz – were still emerging. Gaunt prisoners had started returning from the camps, many hardly recognisable after their ordeals: from around May 1945, the world knew that the Nazi camps were, in fact, sites of systemic extermination, and that the rumours of horrors which had circulated in the underground press were not exaggerations, as many had assumed they had to be, but actually underestimates. Over the freezing cold winter (the electricity and water were turned off for most of the day, while the lack of butter was quickly deemed a national crisis) the French people began, slowly, to recognise the atrocities their government had not only enabled but, in many cases, perpetrated. Many were eager to forget the fact that support for Pétain and the Armistice had been so widespread in 1940, and preferred to imagine that with the exception of outright collaborators, France had stood united against the enemy.

As the country began to rebuild under Charles de Gaulle's provisional government, streets were renamed after military heroes and plaques celebrating the Resistance were erected; meanwhile, France began a purge of those who had condoned the Nazi regime. Much of the recrimination was extrajudicial and ad hoc – the *épuration sauvage*, which saw the public humiliation and, regularly, assault of suspected collaborators by vigilantes – but a series of highly theatrical trials was established in late 1944, conducted in a fraught atmosphere of recrimination and grief. Pierre Laval was executed, while eighty-nine-year-old Philippe Pétain's death sentence was commuted, due to his age, to life imprisonment. During his emotional three-week trial, his obsequious letters to Hitler were revealed for the first time; the jury dismissed his avowal that the Armistice was 'a necessary act of salvation' to prevent France suffering the fate of Poland. He was stripped of all military honours and spent the last six years of his life in a remote castle on the Île d'Yeu.

In a letter sent from prison, Bernard Faÿ asked Stein to write a deposition to be read at his own, as-yet-unscheduled trial. His defence was to hinge on the argument that he had spent the war defending French culture, pointing as evidence to the library treasures he had kept safe from looting – and to the art collection at the rue Christine, which he took credit for protecting. Stein obliged, and in careful French she recorded Picasso's words on finding the collection intact: 'It's a miracle,' he had told her, 'thanks to Bernard Faÿ.' Her statement is short and slightly guarded, but she insisted that Faÿ was a consummate patriot who had always remained faithful to both France and America, his twin passions. 'We held rather different opinions,' she wrote. 'Bernard Faÿ was a conservative, and I a radical, but we were always in agreement on Franco-American relations.' To her friend Francis Rose, she wrote that Faÿ 'certainly did certain things he should not have done, but that he ever denounced anybody, no, that I do not believe, in fact I know he did not'.

She was wrong. During the 1930s, while corresponding regularly with Stein and spending holidays with her at Bilignin, Faÿ was building ties with increasingly militant far-right organisations in France and across Europe. Faÿ believed that French traditions were under threat from a shadowy and nefarious elite who were secretly consolidating power: he argued for a new Europe based on the defence of Western civilisation against the corrupting forces, as he saw them, of Communism and Freemasonry. He saw the 1940 Armistice as an opportunity to effect the moral reform he believed France needed, and within weeks of his appointment as general administrator of the Bibliothèque Nationale under Pétain, Faÿ began to use his position to further his own agenda. In August 1940, Vichy passed a new law dissolving all secret societies and proclaiming Freemasons enemies of the state; Faÿ became one of the chief prosecutors of this law, tasked with seizing Masons' property, creating and spreading anti-Masonic propaganda, and editing an official Vichy journal set up to publicise, and gather support for, the government's anti-Masonic crusade. On the journal's cover was a star of David: one of its guiding mantras was the idea that Jews and Freemasons were co-conspirators in a plot to overthrow France. Faÿ had ordered surveillance to be carried out on all library employees; in September 1942, he had written to the ministry of education about a 'communist conspiracy' at the library, and personally dismissed twenty employees, of whom eleven were arrested and transferred to an internment centre. Among the documents found after his arrest was a cache of erotic poems addressed to an officer named William Gueydan de Roussel, whom Faÿ had taken on as his secretary. Roussel was a Gestapo agent, paid 6,000 francs for every Freemason he denounced: prosecutors estimated that under his and Faÿ's programme, 6,000 Masons were sent to jail and almost a thousand were delivered to concentration camps.

Stein almost certainly did not know what Faÿ was doing in his position. She saw him in September 1939, when she returned to Paris to pick up her things, and it's possible he promised to keep an eye on the art collection then – though Pétain wasn't yet in power, so Faÿ had no official influence. They had kept in sporadic touch through the war, though their extant letters offer little insight into Faÿ's work. 'I spend a week every month in Vichy to call on the Marshal and advise him how to run his business,' Faÿ wrote to Stein in September 1941. 'He is very nice, and says "yes, yes" – and I go home feeling great. We do it every month.' They spent an evening together in Lyon in December 1941, their first meeting in two years, and in early 1942, he wrote to her again: 'My responsibilities are growing and will grow steadily in the coming months. It's not dull.' In September 1943, he spent two nights with Stein and Toklas at Culoz – how freely he discussed his activities cannot, now, be known. They did not meet again, but Stein sent him sweets in jail – along with a copy of her new publication.

Touted by her publishers as 'written secretly right under the very noses of the Nazis', *Wars I Have Seen* was published in March 1945 – one of the earliest first-hand reports of the war from Europe. It is a diary-like account of the last two years of the war, in which the heroes are the local community: the friends who shared predictions and prophecies, the shopkeepers who kept cakes aside for them, and the 'mountain boys' who made the Bugey region a stronghold of the Resistance. Into her chronicle of 'daily living' in extraordinary straits, Stein mingled recollections from her childhood, reflections on her disillusionment with the nineteenth-century ideals of permanence and progress, and her musings on several European and American wars. 'The village of Culoz is the whole of France in microcosm,' read the press release, 'and its story is the story of the French nation.' The first reviews were rapturous. 'Nobody else,' wrote the *New York Times*, 'among all the writers who have told us about life in occupied France, has made the story so intimate, homely, immediate, as if a squad of Germans were quartered in your own kitchen and the Maquis were prowling the roads outside your door.' Foreign rights quickly sold to Italy, Sweden, even Germany, and it became far and away Stein's bestselling title.

Most reviews portrayed Stein uncomplicatedly as a triumphant hero. But one piece, by the philosopher Jean Wahl, who had managed to escape from the internment camp at Drancy and spent the rest of the war in the US, raised the question of exactly what politics her narrative espoused. He singled out a passage about Pétain which he considered 'almost unbelievable in its naïveté'. 'I always thought he was right to make the armistice,' Stein had written in the autumn of 1943, long after most of his supporters had rescinded their initial enthusiasm. 'Pétain then did save France and saving France defeated Germany.' But even Wahl did not know how closely Stein had once allied herself with the disgraced Maréchal. Towards the end of 1941, Stein had written to her editor Bennett Cerf, informing him of a new project she was beginning: to translate a collection of Pétain's speeches, from 1936 to the present, which had recently been published in French. 'I found the book convincing and moving to an xtraordinary degree', she told Cerf, 'and my idea was to write an introduction telling how my feelings have changed about him, I have had strong ups and downs and I think it would all do a lot of good.' She doesn't say whether this was her own idea, but Faÿ was certainly involved: on 7 February 1942, he wrote to tell her that he had discussed the proposed translation with Pétain himself, who was pleased with the idea. Stein described the translation as a 'fascinating occupation'; in August her neighbour Paul Genin, who had translated her introduction into French, was communicating about the project with a Monsieur Cusset of the Comité France-Amérique, indicating that the project had an official stamp of approval.

In her draft introduction, which Faÿ forwarded to Bernard Ménétrel, Pétain's private secretary and personal physician, Stein reiterated her belief that in agreeing the Armistice, Pétain had achieved a 'miracle'; she urged readers, French and American, to keep faith in the hero who has 'held them together through their times of desperation'. Stein wrote this several months before Pétain's capitulation. When she asked American readers to 'have faith in him and in the fact that France will live', it's plausible – given her psychology and her situation – that she was trying to will that eventuality into being. Translation does not, of course, entail agreement with everything written. Apart from his decision to sign the Armistice, Stein never praised Pétain's actions or policies; her attachment to Pétain was primarily iconographic, focused on the idea of him as a protective symbol of hope. But it remains astonishing that she was willing to engage in a project of active propaganda for the regime, even beyond the point at which Vichy's antisemitic policies had been signed into law.

Was this project intended as a bargaining chip for her protection? Was she pressured into it – or did she believe in its value? Faÿ's involvement raises the possibility that Stein's safety, during the war, was a matter of concern to the highest Vichy authorities. Years later, in his self-exculpating 1961 autobiography, Faÿ claimed that he had been instrumental in protecting not only the art collection at the rue Christine, but Stein and Toklas too. When he learned that Stein was determined not to return to America, he wrote, he resolved that his 'duty was to keep her safe'. Over a long lunch with Pétain at the newly established Vichy headquarters, he claimed, he had mentioned his concern for Stein: her genius, their long friendship, the dangers she was facing now and those to come in the freezing winter. At once, Faÿ alleged, Pétain dictated a letter to Maurice Sivan, the sub-prefect of

Belley, ordering him to take special responsibility for Stein and Toklas, and ensure they had everything they needed to stay warm and safe through the coldest months. 'During this horrible period of occupation, misery, and nascent civil war,' Faÿ wrote with pride, 'my two friends led a peaceful life.'

Faÿ's account is impossible to verify. At the time he wrote his memoir, he was desperate to clear his name, and his association with Stein was his most valuable riposte to the accusations of antisemitism that continued to plague him. Stein and Toklas never mentioned his protection, apart from the specific occasion in July 1944 when he stepped in to prevent the collection's seizure, which she outlined in her statement to the court. In all her own accounts of the war, Stein attributes her survival to the local people – including Sivan, who was already a personal friend of hers – who could at any point have denounced them (which Faÿ would have been powerless to counteract), but who instead chose to keep them safe. It's possible, of course, that with hindsight she preferred not to acknowledge the help of a Vichy collaborator – or that she was unaware of efforts he made behind the scenes. But even if Faÿ had offered Stein assurances in 1940, his influence would have diminished significantly when Pierre Laval – who distrusted Faÿ, and tried to have him fired from the library – replaced Pétain as leader of France. After November 1942, Stein had to survive on her own.

Within weeks of Pétain's fall, her translation project faltered: the notebook in which Stein had translated twenty-seven of the fifty speeches (in a strange, literal English), ends mid-sentence. Whatever her motivation for the project, she made no further attempt to finish or publish it. Perhaps she saw Pétain could no longer help her, perhaps she was advised to keep her head down, perhaps she decided to stop of her own volition. Her later, published writing makes clear that she was beginning – belatedly – to change her mind about Pétain: by the end of the war, she certainly thought better of associating her name with his. The letter she had sent Cerf announcing the translation project was caught by wartime censors, and not delivered to Random House until February 1946. Since it was undated, Cerf assumed it had just been sent, and replied immediately expressing his unqualified shock that Stein was proposing to ally her name with this 'appeaser, collaborator, Fascist'. 'Don't go upsetting the apple cart,' he urged her, citing the success of *Wars I Have Seen* and the new heights her reputation had reached. When Stein received his letter, she replied with a cable: 'KEEP YOUR SHIRT ON BENNETT DEAR LETTER RE PÉTAIN WAS WRITTEN IN 1941.'

Toklas, later, told Van Vechten that the translation project had arisen from genuine feeling. 'Baby believed in his speeches,' she wrote, 'as literature as well as good political acumen. She thought that he more than likely saved France from complete occupation in 40.' This attitude was widespread in the summer of 1940 – but required a wilful blindness to sustain as the war beat on. It's clear from *Wars I Have Seen* that even as her awareness of her vulnerability, as a Jewish lesbian in France, increased, Stein retained a lingering affection for Pétain, founded on nostalgia for that brief, dramatic, hopeful moment of the Armistice. Slowly – too slowly – she came to accept the fact that the rest of the war had not borne that hope out. Her later comments about him express ambivalence, disillusionment and regret; she did not express any sorrow at his trial and conviction, and laughed heartily with a relieved Cerf about the idea of the translation being published. By the end of *Wars I Have Seen*, it's the Maquis, not Pétain, who are her heroic symbols of hope and freedom. But she never quite acknowledged the full cost of the 'peace' she had blithely celebrated in 1940.

Many people in occupied France had to make their own compromises for survival: the spectrum between outright collaboration and total resistance was wide. In November 1942, the philosopher and Resistance activist Simone Weil spoke out against the self-righteousness of those in America who treated 'as cowards and traitors those in France who are struggling as best they can in a terrible situation'. Weil saw the popular embrace of the Armistice as an act of 'collective cowardice', but argued that 'one should not use the word "traitor" except for those people whom one is certain desired the victory of Germany'. When Sylvia Beach – who had refused to sell her last copy of *Finnegans Wake* to a Gestapo officer, and proudly employed Jewish staff at Shakespeare and Company – was sent to a detention camp in 1942, her distraught lover Adrienne Monnier made an appeal to Jacques Benoist-Méchin, an early customer at their bookshops and a French translator of Joyce, who now held a prominent position in the Vichy government. Beach was duly released, but hated the fact that her life had been saved by a collaborator. As she began to reflect on the past five years, this sort of dilemma became Stein's subject. She didn't comment much on Faÿ's situation in letters, but she pointed out that many collaborators had also helped people, citing the case of a Resistance fighter who was trying to secure the release of a Nazi interpreter who had saved his life. 'My point of view is simple,' she wrote to a friend, 'anybody who denounced anybody that's different, but opinions . . . well well well, this is not for publication but for understanding.' Stein prided herself on having friends with 'all shades of opinion': she was close to several

Stein writing at the rue Christine, *c.*1945

notable Communist intellectuals, including Picasso, René Crevel and Élisabeth de Gramont, but also with neighbours in the countryside who were members of the right-wing Croix de Feu. Her resolute open-mindedness was both a strength and a weakness: her ability to get on with all her neighbours may have saved her life, but her more radical friends were disturbed, over the 1930s, by what they started to see as reactionary tendencies in Stein's own thought.

Throughout her life, Stein's politics were highly inconsistent, and difficult to assess coherently – especially since she relished making outlandish statements tinged with so much irony or pure contrariness that it's dangerous to take them at face value. She tended to react for or against individuals, rather than movements; she was fundamentally more interested in people, and in specific moments of high drama (like the Armistice), than in long-term trends or ideologies. In American politics she was a lifelong Republican, bar a brief moment at college when she became fascinated by the Democratic president Grover Cleveland; she told an interviewer in 1934 that only Cleveland and Woodrow Wilson had possessed the 'singular seductiveness' required to make her Republican allegiance waver. She expressed a strong dis-like of the French socialist prime minister Léon Blum and the Popular Front – despite her closeness with Picasso, she told a friend in 1937, in an only semi-facetious tone, that she wasn't sure whether communism was not even worse than fascism – and often expressed nostalgia for the lost eighteenth-century spirit of 'individual liberty', as represented by George Washington, which she contrasted positively with the paternal-ism of Roosevelt's New Deal.

After the American tour, she had written a series of short, glib articles for the *Saturday Evening Post* about money, warning of the dangers of state intervention. She argued that Roosevelt, in 'thinking for us' with his interventionalist economic policy, was forcing Americans to submit to governmental authority and depriving them of the freedom to live a 'private life'; she likened him to 'father Mussolini and father Hitler . . . and father Stalin and father Trotsky and father Blum and father Franco'.

Perhaps Roosevelt's regime reminded her, uncomfortably, that her own money had always been doled out by a father figure, until she began to earn a living through her writing in her sixties. The series, to her dismay, was widely criticised as flawed and tone-deaf, betraying Stein's bourgeois background and rentier mindset. Yet – as she wrote in her statement for Faÿ – she considered herself a 'radical', and often sounded perturbed that anyone could think otherwise. An FBI agent who visited Stein in Paris in 1937, investigating possible left-wing activities, departed bemused: 'She did not seem to be pro any nationality,' he reported, 'but she was anti-Roosevelt.' Stein herself cheerfully admitted she was 'most generally always wrong'. 'Writers only think they are interested in politics,' Stein told the *Partisan Review* in 1939, 'they are not really, it gives them a chance to talk and writers like to talk but really no real writer is really interested in politics.'

It's another contrarian statement – a wild generalisation, with a kernel of deep truth for Stein. 'I cannot write too much upon how necessary it is to be completely conservative that is particularly traditional in order to be free,' she wrote in *Paris France*, paraphrasing a line from Flaubert's letters: 'Be regular and orderly in your life, like a bourgeois, in order to be vigorous and original in your work.' Stein's radical writing was made possible by her stable domestic life, which the war threatened to rupture. In *Wars I Have Seen*, she wrote that 'a long war like this makes you realise the society you really prefer, the home, goats chickens and dogs and casual acquaintances'. This need for privacy, for peace and quiet and concentration, was at the root of her decision to stay in Bilignin; it might also explain (though not excuse) her callous behaviour to those around her when their demands on her attention grew too intense. She tried to block out the reality of the war as long as she could: not to disrupt her routines, but stubbornly – in hindsight, recklessly – to stand her ground. Over the course of the war, as she reluctantly accepted that her trust in Pétain was misplaced, Stein's position changed. She had always cited her need for a truly private life – but her war experiences had shown her that it was impossible for 'daily living' not to be political.

As she settled back in Paris, she poured her conflicting emotions about the war into new writing. *Yes Is for a Very Young Man* is a drama of divided loyalties and moral dilemmas, the most direct of all Stein's plays. It stages dialogues among the inhabitants of a small village, whose values and relationships are thrust into crisis by the war: a reactionary aristocrat whose family supports Pétain, her husband who fights for the Resistance after his father is killed by the Germans ('Pétain is a cretin,' he sneers), a complacent American who chooses to stay in France, and a young man sent off to work in German munitions factories. Each is desperate for survival, each resistant to the irrevocable changes to their previously peaceable lives. Nothing, here, is black-and-white: neighbours must live alongside one another, even when they find themselves at loggerheads. During the occupation, Stein wrote in her programme notes, she had been reminded of stories her mother had told her about growing up in Baltimore during the Civil War: 'the divided families, the bitterness, the quarrels and sometimes the denunciations, and yet the natural necessity of their all continuing to live their daily life together, because after all that was all the life they had'.

//

During the war years, Stein had reflected at length on her affinity with France, her affection for her adopted country and her gratitude for its ongoing welcome. But at the end of the war she expressed a renewed pride in her American identity, feeling – perhaps – a sense that it was in America, rather than in France, where her legacy would lie. Stein had always bristled at the suggestion that her expatriate status made her somehow less of an American. 'My patriotism is fundamental, instinctive,' she told an interviewer. 'I have lived in France the best and longest part of my life', she wrote, 'and I love France and the French but after all I am an American . . . one's native land is one's native land you cannot get away from it.' After the Liberation, her home became once again a mecca for young men, now of an altogether different generation.

A stream of GIs, dismissed from active service, knocked on the door, bringing with them their manuscripts, drawings and questions, helping themselves to Toklas's delicious cakes and homemade chocolate ice cream, buying up leftover stock of Plain Edition titles, and answering Stein's questions about their hometowns. 'All the boys I know in Europe are worshipping at her shrine,' wrote Van Vechten to a friend. 'They take tours of Paris from Belgium, Berlin, and Marseilles, and then spend their forty-eight hours' leave on the rue Christine.' One of her visitors was Hemingway, who said to her, 'Hello, Gertrude. I am old and rich. Let's stop fighting.' Stein replied: 'I am not old. I am not rich. Let's go on fighting.' Cecil Beaton remembered her wondering aloud why the GIs were so fascinated by her and Picasso, and concluded that 'for some reason she and Pablo stand for humanity'. 'To think how hard it used to be to get anybody to do anything,' Stein wrote, 'anyway it's nice to be glorious and popular in your old age, and to buy bones for Basket and be admired by the young.' To her own surprise, Stein had become a symbol of survival.

Stein began to deliver regular talks to enormous groups of GIs – at libraries, at the Sorbonne, at Red Cross clubs, at jitterbug dances. She had lost a lot of weight during the war, but came back to Paris with a new and refined wardrobe: in 1940 she and Toklas had met a young designer named Pierre Balmain, whose mother owned a shop near Bilignin and let them know her son was a great admirer of Stein's work. He tailored them each several elegant outfits, cycling ten miles to their home for fittings. In August 1945, Stein and Toklas flew to Germany with twelve members of the army, to report for *Life* magazine on the beleaguered country, as some of the first civilian visitors. After driving through Frankfurt, Cologne and Salzburg, they went to take photographs at Hitler's abandoned bunker in Berchtesgaden, where Stein and Toklas lounged on his balcony in garden chairs, while the GIs climbed on the furniture and hunted souvenirs. Her report on the trip is jarringly jingoistic, focused on the excitement of travelling with American soldiers and displaying little compassion for the ordinary people whose lives the war had destroyed. Was she trying to compensate for having supported Pétain too long – or carried away with glee at her popularity? To all appearances, Stein was invincible: the consummate survivor, finally revelling in her hard-earned celebrity. But it's also possible that Stein, already, knew she was ill.

//

Meanwhile, she poured her friendships with the GIs into a new novel, *Brewsie and Willie*, which approximated their voices, concerns and anxieties about their futures and that of America, now facing economic depression. Over the course of 1945, she had befriended the black American writer Richard Wright, who had written a long and praising review of *Wars I Have Seen*. In it, he recounted stumbling upon *Three Lives* in a Chicago public library and finding himself entranced by *Melanctha*, hearing in it his grandmother's voice. Pleased, Stein wrote to thank him for the review, and they struck up a correspondence; Stein helped Wright obtain a visa to bring his family to Paris, where he hoped to rebuild his life away from the virulent racism of his home country. Wright even urged Stein to return to the US to address white audiences on the subject of racial justice, insisting the nation was feeling guilty and would take notice of Stein's opinion. She should challenge the nation's white artists, he suggested: 'You'd tell them . . . I was the first to treat Negro life seriously in my *Three Lives*; now what in hell have you . . . been doing since I showed you the way?'

It's difficult to imagine Stein touring America as an anti-racism crusader. Her complex, articulate, intriguing mixed-race protagonist was a significant departure from the clichéd, two-dimensional black characters in most books by white authors at the time – but *Melanctha* displays some extremely crude racial stereotyping, particularly in its physical descriptions, not unusual for 1906 but still highly jarring with the sensitivity shown to the characters' inner lives. Stein's language betrays an unexamined prejudice hard to square with

Wright's positive assessment of her racial politics. But forty years on, perhaps eager to live up to his praise, Stein ordered a copy of Wright's recent memoir *Black Boy*, which charts his upbringing in poverty in the South, and his 1938 novella *Uncle Tom's Children*. In October 1945, Stein told the black newspaper the *Chicago Defender* that she considered Richard Wright 'the best American writer today', and a few months later she told an interviewer that 'his meditations on the American scene are the most interesting I have heard from anybody'. It may well have been the influence of reading *Black Boy* that led Stein to reflect more deeply on racism in her last works. In *Brewsie and Willie*, characters ponder the legacy of imperialism and slavery and the future of segregation, after one soldier reports a black colleague telling him America is no place to raise a child. Since the army was segregated, she made a point of visiting black troops: 'Goodness,' she told an officer, tacitly connecting racism with antisemitism, 'are we going to be like the Germans, only believe in the Aryans that is our own race.' In an essay published in the *New York Times* magazine, titled 'The New Hope in Our "Sad Young Men"', she expressed her wish that Americans should realise that Jim Crow laws can lead only to 'persecution and to a sense of imprisonment'. And her final work explored questions of equality more explicitly than ever before.

//

'When the war is over, we must write another opera,' Virgil Thomson had written to Stein in December 1941, their old resentment having dissipated after the success of *Four Saints*. In the summer of 1945, he returned to Paris from New York with a proposal for her: Columbia University had invited them to collaborate on a new commission. For her libretto, Stein decided to explore the life of a heroine far removed from Saint Teresa of Ávila: Susan B. Anthony, the nineteenth-century suffrage campaigner and abolitionist. Unusually, Stein threw herself into research: in September, she told Thomson she had exhausted the

American Library in Paris's holdings, so had ordered 'all the literature of the period' to be sent to her from the New York Public Library. 'If it comes off', she added, 'it will be a most erudite opera.' She showed him the first two scenes in October, but worked on the libretto until March 1946, when she sent Thomson the full text. Thomson reported back that it was 'sensationally handsome, and Susan B. is a fine role'.

The Mother of Us All, in many ways, was Stein's valediction. She peopled the stage with an impossible company of historical figures and the people around her – GIs figured, in the characters of Joe the Loiterer and Chris the Citizen; her old friend Constance Fletcher, the subject of one of Stein's early portraits, is embroiled in a comic flirtation with the former president John Adams; and 'G.S.' and 'Virgil T.' comment from the sidelines. While *Four Saints* portrayed religious devotion as a metaphor for an artist's commitment to their work, *The Mother of Us All* presents Susan B. Anthony as a woman consumed by resolute dedication to her cause, convinced that her words can make a difference, and determined to make her voice heard. Her impassioned demands for equality – drawn from her real speeches, and staged through a debate with the anti-suffragist Daniel Webster – are vindicated, in the final act, with the posthumous unveiling of her statue at the US Capitol. Susan B. Anthony appears in the final scene as a ghost, mingling unseen with the crowds who have gathered to reminisce and celebrate her achievements. As the opera closes, she sings alone of the battles, passions and achievements of her long life. She calls on the mourners, who file past her statue, to honour her legacy by continuing her struggle.

The subject marked an intriguing departure for Stein. Her writing, lectures, letters and behaviour displayed little sense of solidarity with women as a political or social class. Only once, in *The Geographical History of America*, did she define herself explicitly as a woman writer – 'in this epoch', she wrote, 'the only real literary thinking has been done by a woman' – but this served less to celebrate women than to highlight her own exceptionalism. She often seemed drawn, surprisingly, to male leadership: despite her damning critiques of Roosevelt's paternalism, she consistently wrote favourably of George Washington – 'the father of his country' – whom she depicted as a hero on horseback, like Pétain, who had described himself as his country's shield. Inconsistent as ever, she appreciated some symbols of patriarchal protection, but decried others. 'Fathers are depressing,' she wrote in *Everybody's Autobiography*. 'The periods of the world's history that have always been most dismal ones are the ones where fathers were looming and filling up everything.' Her most overt challenge to the gendered dynamic of literary, familial and nationalistic tradition came in her 1927 poem *Patriarchal Poetry*: 'Patriarchal poetry needs rectification . . . patriotic poetry is the same as patriarchal poetry is the same,' she writes, in a rallying cry for fresh artistic expression. But *The Mother of Us All* was the first time Stein identified with a historical foremother, a crusader for equal opportunities.

In her version of Susan B. Anthony, Stein created both a mother figure and a cipher. Over the first months of 1946, Stein was contemplating her own legacy with a pressing sense of mortality, looking back over her long struggle to find readers for her work, partly with satisfaction, partly with a sense of work still to be done. For a long time, she had been urging Bennett Cerf to reissue her early works, to capitalise on the huge success of *Wars I Have Seen* and her new-found role as 'grandmother to the American army'. 'I think some of my books should be treated like classics and left on sale,' she had written to him in September 1945, to which he replied with a cable: 'Keep your pants on letter that will delight you is on way.' That letter announced his intention to celebrate her with a 'BIG BOOK': a one-volume edition of her selected works, to be edited and introduced by Carl Van Vechten. Stein had long dreamed of such a career survey. 'I always wanted to be historical, from almost a baby on,' she wrote in her preface. 'I felt that way about it, and Carl was one of the earliest ones that made me be certain that I was going to be.'

Stein had one further opportunity to reflect on her career in its entirety. Robert Bartlett Haas, the young scholar who still harboured hopes of putting together his own Stein anthology, was eager to include an interview with Stein in the eventual book. From Ohio, he sent a series of questions to a friend, William Sutton, on military assignment in Paris, who visited Stein at the rue Christine for two sessions of several hours over the weekend of 5–6 January 1946, and returned to Haas a verbatim transcription of her responses. 'You got a scoop!' Stein told him. Their conversation ranged over her whole life, and lingered on her fascination with people, from the period of intense listening that produced *The Making of Americans* to her conversations with villagers charted in *Wars I Have Seen*. 'I was not at all interested in the little or big men,' she told Sutton, 'but to realise absolutely every variety of human experience that it was possible to have . . . I have always had this obsession, and that is why I enjoy talking to every GI. I must know every possible nuance.' In a way, she recast her career as a democratic enterprise premised on a sense of equality stemming from examination of Cézanne's canvases, in which 'one thing was as important as another thing'. She argued that everyone, including children, should have the vote: anyone who exists 'has a stake in what happens'. Towards the end of the interview, she contemplated more explicitly than ever before the chequered reception of her work, a subject – as she entered her seventies – at the forefront of her mind:

> You see it is the people who generally smell of the museums who are accepted, and it is the new who are not accepted . . . It is much easier to have one hand in the past. That is why James Joyce was accepted and I was not. He leaned into the past, in my work the newness and difference is fundamental.

Why, Sutton asked her at the end of their interview, was she so eager for her work to be appreciated by others, when her process indicated that her texts were really written for herself? 'There', Stein replied, 'is the eternal vanity of the mind . . . Anything you create you want to exist, and its means of existence is in being printed.' In February 1946, she asked Yale to make arrangements to collect her remaining manuscripts.

'There are a lot of mice here', she wrote, 'and they do get at papers.' On 11 July, she reported that most of the materials she had accumulated since 1940 had finally been dispatched. 'I hope they get there alright,' she wrote, 'there has been a delay because I have not been quite well, had some intestinal trouble but now we are going off to the country for a couple of months and hope to get a real rest.'

At the start of 1946, Stein had complained of exhaustion, which Toklas attributed to 'the occupation and seeing nearly the whole American army'. Cecil Beaton had noticed how much thinner and shrunken Stein was on her return to Paris, but against doctors' advice she continued as though nothing was wrong. Toklas tried to cut down on visitors, but Stein would not hear of leaving Paris again, and the social demands became so overwhelming that when they were alone, Toklas reported, 'it was necessary to put one of her detective or crime stories near her and not have her talk'. In April, she was diagnosed with a form of uterine cancer, and was offered an operation, which she staunchly refused. On 19 July, hoping for a period of rural rest, their GI friend and 'adopted nephew' Joseph Barry drove them with Basket to Bernard Faÿ's house – which was empty, since he remained in prison awaiting trial – in the Sarthe region of the Loire valley. In the car, Barry remembered, Stein was in discomfort, clutching her stomach while Toklas studied the map. A few days later, Stein was in such pain that they rushed back by train to the American Hospital in Neuilly, just outside Paris; Stein kept leaping from her seat and crossing the carriage to drink in the passing land-scape from both windows. From her hospital bed, she received the first copies of *Brewsie and Willie*, which was published on 22 July. On 23 July, she drafted a document headed 'Last Will and Testament'. In lucid moments, she told Toklas how Carl Van Vechten had been her most loyal friend from the beginning; she had 'all confidence' in appointing him her literary executor. On 27 July, she died.

'She was furious and frightening and impressive – like she was thirty years and more ago when her work was attacked,' wrote Toklas to Van Vechten.

And oh Baby was so beautiful – in between the pain – like nothing before. And now she is in the vault at the American Cathedral on the Quai d'Orsay – and I'm here alone. And nothing more – only what was. You will know that nothing is very clear with me – everything is empty and blurred. Papa Woojums – she said it to me twice – you are to edit the unpublished manuscripts and I am to stay on here and the Picasso portrait goes to the Metropolitan Museum – and on Sunday Jo Barry takes me down to the Sarthe to bring back Basket and the trunks.

PART 2 AFTERLIFE

'Gertrude Stein, famed woman writer and one
of the most controversial figures of American
letters, died at 6.30 o'clock tonight (Paris
time) at the American Hospital in Neuilly, a
suburb of Paris.'

'Gertrude Stein, seventy-two, American writer
who set a style of literature all her own,
died at 7.30 o'clock tonight in the American
Hospital.'

'Miss Gertrude Stein, American novelist, poet
and playwright whose artistic enthusiasm gave
encouragement to two generations of writers and
artists in Paris...'

'Gertrude Stein, 72, the beloved but puzzling
American writer who opened her heart and her
home to hundreds of American soldiers during
World War II...'

'Gertrude Stein, whose prose sometimes
exasperated and mystified readers but
profoundly influenced other writers, and whose
more than 40 years in France never lessened her
love for her native United States...'

'Miss Stein, whose strange style of writing
produced such phrases as "A rose is a rose is
a rose" and bewildered her wide following of
readers...'

'Miss Stein, whose works were incomprehensible...'

'At her deathbed were her lifelong friend, Alice B. Toklas, a nephew and niece, and a physician.'

'At her bedside was Miss Stein's close friend and secretary, Miss Alice B. Toklas.'

'Her companion of many years, Alice B. Toklas...'

'Alice B. Toklas, secretary and biographer of Gertrude Stein...'

'Her admirers held that she wrote the most profound prose of the twentieth century, others, who did not pretend to understand her books, said she wrote gibberish.'

'Devotees of her cult professed to find her restoring a pristine freshness and rhythm to language. Medical authorities compared her effusions to the rantings of the insane.'

'In some she stimulated a fierce, undying admiration; others looked on her as an amusing poseur and a charlatan. History alone will judge who was right.'

'That she was one of the most forceful personalities of her age in cosmopolitan literary and artistic circles few have even sought to deny.'

'Certainly she is not really dead: legends never die.'

RECKONING RECKONING RECKONING RECKONING RECKONING RECKONING RECKONING

Gertrude Stein's death was announced on American radio that same evening. The following day, friends opened their morning newspapers to discover a terrible shock within. Few had known she was ill. Those who telephoned the apartment, or tentatively knocked at the door with flowers or murmured condolences for Toklas, were met with silence. The *New Yorker* writer Janet Flanner was one of few friends who managed to see her in those first blurry days of grief: she described Toklas as 'the most widowed woman I know'.

In the days and weeks that followed, Toklas began to receive letters from Stein's friends, old and new, and from strangers around the world, fans of the *Autobiography* who felt they knew Toklas well and couldn't imagine how she would ever cope alone. 'Please remember', read one letter from a GI, 'that there are thousands of us who join you in your bereavement.' To those she trusted, Toklas made few attempts to disguise her pain. 'I wish to God we had gone together as I always so fatuously thought we would,' she wrote; 'a bomb – a shipwreck – just anything but this.' Buffeted by grief, she took three months to organise the funeral, but finally selected a plot for Stein on the outer edges of Paris's Père-Lachaise Cemetery, close to the tombs of four Resistance officers, not far from Oscar Wilde. On the overcast morning of 22 October 1946, Stein's body was driven along the Seine from the crypt of the American Church on the quai d'Orsay to the cemetery out in the east of Paris, passing the limousines crawling towards the Senate, where representatives from twenty-one countries were concluding negotiations for the post-war European peace. A handful of friends, including Natalie Barney and Joseph Barry, comforted Toklas – tiny in black – as the coffin was lowered into the ground. Stein had left no instructions for her funeral, but Toklas commissioned a tombstone from their friend Francis Rose to bear her own name too – on the back – as if a part of her had died with Stein.

//

Over the final days of her life, two matters had been foremost in Stein's mind: Alice B. Toklas's future, and her own literary legacy. In her will, she bequeathed the Picasso portrait to the Metropolitan Museum of Art in New York, ensuring that her likeness would take its place among masterpieces of art history. She left her art collection to her nephew Allan – the only child of her brother Michael – with the proviso that it was to stay with Toklas until her death, and that she was entitled to sell art whenever she needed money for her own upkeep. Finally, she ordered Toklas and Allan Stein, as executors of her will, 'to pay to Carl Van Vechten of 101 Central Park West, New York City, such a sum of money as the said Carl Van Vechten shall, in his own absolute discretion, deem necessary for the publication of my unpublished manuscripts'. Should her cash reserves not prove adequate for the project, Stein stipulated, Toklas was authorised to sell as many paintings as required to ensure that every word Stein had ever written should, finally, reach print.

All her life, Stein had remembered a line from a George Eliot poem she had read as a child: 'May I join the choir invisible | Of those immortal dead who live again.' She quotes the poem in *Everybody's Autobiography*, after admitting that 'Identity always worries me and memory and eternity.' In that book, she recalls the jolt she experienced on reading the Old Testament and finding there was no mention of a future life. Her work – from the all-encompassing characterology of *The Making of Americans* to her later musings on identity – was Stein's way of affirming her existence against that early sense of her own insignificance. Otto Weininger, whose work had been so formative to Stein back in 1908, had argued that a mark of a genius is his 'passionate and urgent desire for immortality' (he suggested that this drive is lower in women, who lack 'reverence for their own personality'). Stein considered herself a genius; in her writing, geniuses (like saints) are always portrayed as 'most intensely alive', standing somehow outside of time due to an ability to see themselves beyond mortal existence, which she called 'a future life feeling'. Stein had always been afraid of death: the deaths of her older siblings and parents, the creative death of writer's block, the wartime persecutions, all mingled in her mind with her fear that her work would be forgotten, that she would die without leaving her mark. 'Listen to me,' runs a plaintive refrain, never answered, which recurs in Stein's work across the decades, from the anxious young narrator of *The Making of Americans*, disheartened that no one seems to recognise the significance of her insight, to the elderly Susan B. Anthony in *The Mother Of Us All*, pondering whether her life's work has made the impact she hoped for.

In her 1933 book *Four in America*, writing about Henry James – and reflecting on the disjunct of being celebrated for the *Autobiography* without her 'real' work being understood – Stein had argued that it's not clarity that's necessary in writing, but force. 'Nobody listens', she wrote,

> and nobody knows what you mean no matter what you mean,
> nor how clearly you mean what you mean. But if you have vitality
> enough of knowing enough of what you mean, somebody and
> sometime and sometimes a great many will have to realise that you
> know what you mean and so they will agree that you mean what you
> know, what you know you mean, which is as near as anybody can
> come to understanding any one.

Understanding, Stein had written in *The Making of Americans*, is 'the most important part of living' – to die without being understood meant a truly permanent extinction. She was satisfied with her work – she knew what she meant, always – but she was not satisfied her achievements had been properly acknowledged yet. 'When this you see remember me,' read one of her favourite mantras, scattered across her work. Stein didn't believe in an afterlife; her fervent desire for posthumous recognition was her bid for immortality.

For years, Stein had predicted that her work's fullest appreciation lay in the future – if only readers could find it. As it was, her writing remained best known through contextless snippets ('rose is a rose'; 'pigeons on the grass alas'): widely discussed, but little read. Her published texts had always appeared in piecemeal fashion, subject to the constraints of space and editors' patience – she would invariably try to squeeze extra pieces into her collections – so the distinction between her published and unpublished work was somewhat arbitrary. To Stein, all her work was important: she chose carefully every word she wrote, and cared about each of them. Certain texts, of course, were special to her, or stood out as distinct entities. But she conceived of her life's work as a single body, one long progression of intellectual effort, in which – like a Cézanne canvas – no one part was more significant than the whole. Only with the publication of all her writing, Stein was adamant, could her achievements be assessed: without it, the public perception of her output would not only be wildly distorted, but unfairly diminished. Since the *Autobiography*, most of the work she had published was in her 'open', accessible style; conversely, most of the unpublished texts – *A Novel of Thank You* (1925–6), *Stanzas in Meditation* (1932), *Four in America* (1933) – represented the 'real', more hermetic writing publishers had resisted printing. If Stein was to achieve her aim of having her ideas more widely understood, these were the texts she most eagerly wanted to make available. She saw no reason why her death should halt that mission.

//

'Is Gertrude Stein serious?' another novelist had once asked Alice Toklas. 'Desperately,' she replied. Toklas, famously, was the only person who could reliably read Stein's awful handwriting. In life, every one of Stein's texts had passed through Toklas, on its way to readers: her typing labour transformed each handwritten scrawl into a literary product. With no more new texts to type, her role as intermediary had shifted – but her work for Stein continued. By all accounts, Toklas had lived entirely for and through her partner. Even if she had run the show all along, as some suspected, no one could deny that she had devoted herself to Stein with a self-effacement few relationships could have sustained. Approaching seventy, not only did she have to redefine her relationship to herself; she had to reframe that devotion, focused now not on the living person but on her memory.

'Dead is dead', Toklas wrote to a friend, quoting a line from the end of *The Making of Americans*, 'but that is why memory is all and all the immortality there is.' It was up to Toklas, now, to steward Stein's legacy. One part of her role, she knew, would be proactive: to bring

Gertrude Stein in San Francisco, 1935 (photo: Imogen Cunningham)

Stein's work out of the Yale library's locked cabinets, and place it in the hands of the readers she and Stein had always believed she deserved. But she knew, also, that there were parts of their life she would want to keep hidden from prying eyes. Over the next twenty years, Stein's desire for publicity would be set directly at odds with Toklas's deep-seated instinct for privacy. Already, Toklas had turned into a myth, even as she tried to disappear into Stein. She had lived in the public eye – widely photographed; a household name – without revealing anything of herself except through Stein's words. Left to uphold the Stein legend on her own, Toklas soon saw that the task would force her to look back over aspects of their shared past she might have preferred to forget.

In the popular imagination, their images had long since solidified as polar opposites: Stein cheerful and commonsensical (Mabel Dodge claimed to witness her devouring chunks of raw meat with unseemly relish); Toklas silent, dainty, enigmatic. Toklas had few friends of her own; she had lost touch with her family in America, and both her father and her brother had died since she left San Francisco, having swapped a life attending to their needs for a life taking care of Gertrude Stein. Her brother, Clarence, an army engineer, had died by suicide in 1937, leaving a son she never met; a newspaper report mentioned his sister Alice, 'authoress and companion to Gertrude Stein'. At Yale, her few personal papers – some letters, some recipes, her wartime tobacco registration card – mingled almost imperceptibly with Stein's huge archive. Even at the rue Christine, the lease and all bills were in Stein's name: it was as though Toklas were a passenger in her own life, legible to the world only via her partner. 'Gertrude never left home in the same way I did,' Toklas told a friend. 'She was always at home through the language, but I was at home only through her.'

Many of their friends freely admitted they hardly knew Toklas, so vivaciously had Stein sucked up all the attention. But now that Stein was dead, people started to question the depth of their friendships with her, too. Friends and strangers – over drinks, in letters, in their memoirs – began to piece together a picture of Stein that was very different from the one she herself had put forward. 'She was surprisingly modern in some ways and surprisingly naïve in others,' wrote Richard Wright, whose tentative friendship with Stein had imploded, weeks before her death, when he was swindled by a friend she had told him to trust. 'When you knew her she was so real that you had to contend with her . . . you could not ignore her. Not at all. But what she really stood for, I really do not know.' As the news of her death spread, friends began to call Wright to ask if he knew what had happened – people Wright had assumed were far closer to Stein than he was, but who turned out to consider themselves, as he did, on the outer fringes of her circle. No one, he concluded, really knew Stein at all.

One reviewer of the *Autobiography* had pointed out, perceptively, that Stein had found an approach which 'permits the writing of an autobiography without self-revelation'. After reading, he concluded, 'one knows the life history of Gertrude Stein, [but] one still does not know Gertrude Stein . . . I do not think she wants to reveal herself.' Storytelling, myth-making, had been central to Stein and Toklas's shared life since the beginning. In the *Autobiography*, Stein had invented a version of Toklas: in the process, she had created a protective sheen which rendered both of them, paradoxically, unknowable to all but their closest intimates. From now on, it was Toklas's turn to tell the stories. Who was Gertrude Stein? Who would Alice B. Toklas be without her? The next two decades would begin to answer some of those questions – and raise many others – as researchers entered Stein's archive, new texts appeared, her work (and her legend) took hold among new generations of readers, and Toklas began to speak.

10 : POISONED WHEAT

O n 23 February 1947 – seven months after Stein's death – a doorbell rang on the rue Christine. Toklas hadn't been expecting visitors until later in the afternoon, but when she opened the door, she wasn't surprised to see that Picasso had appeared early. She led him down the narrow corridor, lined with small paintings, and into the sun-drenched sitting room, where his portrait of Stein still hung over the fireplace, facing the sofa where its subject had always sat, such that Toklas used to imagine the two Steins talked to each other when no one else was there. 'He stood alone in front of it quite a few minutes,' Toklas reported back to Carl Van Vechten, 'drinking it in as only his eyes can and then he saluted it quite seriously – quite simply – and he kissed my hand and said *au revoir chérie*. After all the portrait is their youth – its intensity and theirs are all one – and I mind its going so very very much.' As he left, Picasso shrugged and said to her, 'Neither you nor I will ever see it again.'

Later that day, the president of the Paris Guaranty Trust arrived to collect the portrait on behalf of the Metropolitan Museum of Art. He had called at 5 rue Christine a few days earlier, but left empty-handed: on his arrival, as he explained in a cable to his colleagues back in New York, Toklas had begged to keep the portrait another week to allow time for friends to say goodbye. She had refused the lawyer's 'insulting' request for a signed guarantee of authorship: 'Good God,' she exclaimed, 'don't they know it's Gertrude by Picasso.' The painting was unhooked from the wall – the first time it had left its position since September 1939, when Stein and Toklas had grabbed it along with a jumble of clothes and papers as they fled the city – and hauled out of the apartment. 'Baby is going away again,' wrote Toklas, anguished, 'and to strangers.'

Across the Atlantic, friends and admirers waited in eager anticipation of the portrait's arrival. 'The rue de Fleurus will seem to live again,' Van Vechten promised Toklas. On 22 August, the portrait was unveiled in the Metropolitan's grand Fifth Avenue atrium, the sole artwork displayed in the lofty hall, with a discreet plaque nearby telling the story of Stein and Picasso's friendship. To the visitors who passed through the lobby, or saw the portrait's grainy reproduction in the evening newspapers, the display was a curiosity; a historical encounter between two now-familiar figures, a relic of bygone days. But to Toklas, alone in Paris, the rupture felt 'like another parting' – representing both Stein's enduring vitality and her ineffable absence. The portrait – which had 'so much of her in it' – was now public property. Stein, too, was no longer a real, living person, but a character of legend.

//

'Without Baby', Toklas wrote to Van Vechten's wife, Fania Marinoff, 'there is no direction to anything – it's just milling around in the dark – back to where one was before one was grown up.' Alone in Paris, Toklas slowly began to form a new routine. Thin, hunched, dressed in a heavy tweed suit and thick stockings, she began her days with black coffee and ended them with a plate of cooked fruit. Most mornings she set out from the rue Christine with umbrella in hand and Basket on a leash to shop for groceries at the Marché de Buci. (Both Pépé and the original Basket had died before the end of the war; this dog, unsentimentally, had been named Basket II.) The poodle, she told friends, showed no sign of missing Stein at home, but as soon as they left the apartment he would drag Toklas's miniature frame along the routes Stein used to take him: across the river and down the rue de Rivoli, on the edge of the Tuileries Garden, past Galignani's bookshop and Rumpelmayer's famous patisserie, barking for Stein as he went. The city was still grappling with the lingering effects of the war: food prices had trebled, rationing had intensified, wage stagnation had led to a paralysing wave of strikes across industries and public services, and the unswept streets were sporadically filled with demonstrations – some violent – between the battling forces of Gaullists and Communists. Post-war Paris hummed, too, with an invigorating atmosphere of change and freedom: new magazines were starting up and jazz clubs launching, Albert Camus and Jean-Paul Sartre were debating existential philosophy on the terrace of the Café de Flore, Simone de Beauvoir was starting work on *The Second Sex*. But all this was a blur to Toklas, whose life had closed in on her just as the city opened up.

In the first long months, Toklas faced 'a veritable invasion of friends and acquaintances' wanting to talk about Stein – so many that she left the telephone off the hook, though she couldn't stop Basket from barking when the doorbell rang. She enjoyed visits from Picasso, who opened up about his romantic troubles – 'he hasn't been so human for years' – and from his estranged wife Olga Khokhlova, lonely herself, who stayed talking for hours. Toklas appreciated the way Khokhlova ended every story by thoughtfully asking what Gertrude would have said, making her come alive again by including her in the conversation. Some visitors wanted simply to spend time in the rooms that held so many memories – like the art dealer Daniel-Henry Kahnweiler, she wrote, 'who is sad and just sits a while and goes away'.

But as time wore on, the calls gradually dried up. Some disconcerted visitors compared the apartment to a shrine, or a mausoleum; Toklas, distraught and hollow, seemed almost to fade into the furnishings. Many realised, to their embarrassment, that Toklas assumed they were only there to see the pictures or pay tribute to Stein (who was spoken of 'as a deity'), not to talk to her for her own sake. 'Welcome to Gertrude Stein's home,' she said at the front door. Often she would trail off from an anecdote and stare into the distance, as if watching a silent film of her past flashing before her. Others noticed her habit, when asked questions, of deferring to Stein's opinions of people or places. To some, this self-effacement seemed almost sinister. One visitor was stunned to realise, in the course of a 'gossip fest' over cigarettes and Turkish Delight, that Toklas was quoting almost verbatim from the *Autobiography*, reciting entire passages with an uncanny sincerity. 'These word-for-word flights,' she wrote, 'puzzled, saddened, and, in a way, even frightened me.' It was impossible to say whether this 'bare-faced plagiarism' was evidence that Stein had ventriloquised her partner's voice perfectly, that Toklas had adopted Stein's version of stories as her own out of pure loyalty, or that Stein's account had now overwritten Toklas's own memories. Was Toklas enjoying the hoax? Was Stein manipulating her from beyond the grave? Or was she simply fed up of answering the same questions over and over again? The visitor hoped that one lingering alternative was not true: that Toklas felt, as perhaps she always had, that she had nothing of her own to offer.

//

In the first year after Stein's death, Toklas dispatched to Yale a monthly load of additional papers. Gradually, she dismantled the library – its shelves double-stacked – and wrapped up Stein's voluminous correspondence, though she warned the librarians that Stein 'didn't write about the method or meaning of her work'. Only Thornton Wilder, she wrote, 'prodded Gertrude with questions about method and technique and got the answers'. Meanwhile, she urged the lawyer for Stein's estate – the Baltimore-based Edgar Allan Poe, a distant relative of the Gothic writer – to release funds as quickly as possible, so that Van Vechten could start arranging for Stein's work to be printed. Stein had left an estate of $82,761.97, of which the most valuable part was the art collection; cash, stocks, bonds and royalties made up the rest of her holdings, which – after various expenses and taxes – were already fast depleting. Random House's volume *Selected Writings* – the planned compendium of forty years of published work – had appeared on 21 October 1946, the day before Stein's funeral, to characteristically mixed reviews: in anxious letters to Van Vechten, Toklas expressed the need to move soon, to cement Stein's legacy before it stalled irretrievably. Replying to Toklas, Van Vechten insisted that he was 'deeply touched' by the responsibility Stein had given him, as her literary executor. His championship of Stein's work had been a shaping force in his life, and the posthumous honour reflected Stein's gratitude. But in private, his initial apprehension turned to shock when he realised the extent of the unpublished material. At first, he had assumed he was responsible only for arranging the publication of Stein's most recent work – *Mrs Reynolds*, *The Mother of Us All*, and a few other short pieces. But Toklas calmly clarified that 'she certainly meant everything'.

Van Vechten's worst fears were confirmed in February 1947 when Donald Gallup, a curator at the Yale Collection of American Literature, reported the arrival of three large boxes of material which had turned the reading room into a 'wastepaper collection centre'. The hoard comprised newspaper clippings (she had kept a 1939 review of *Finnegans Wake* which suggested Joyce found precedents in 'Lewis Carroll and Gertrude Stein'), a series of fortune readings ('Very good news about a manuscript,' reads one, optimistically), instructions for maintaining old cars and a police citation for walking Basket without a muzzle, and several hundreds of letters, which Gallup described, with excitement, as 'almost every communication which she received from the early 1900s until the end of her life'. But the most extensive cache was the manuscript notebooks – hundreds of them, accompanied by Toklas's neat typescripts, preserving five decades of Stein's writing, much of it unpublished. The

Donald Gallup at Yale with the Gertrude Stein Papers, 1947
(photo: Frank H. Bauer)

boxes were littered with buried kernels of poisoned wheat; some manu-scripts had been nibbled by doughty mice. But the riches inside, Gallup concluded, represented not only the record of a 'remarkable personality' but summed up 'an entire period in the cultural history of Western Europe and America'.

Gallup's fresh energy tempered Van Vechten's irritation at the pros-pect of responsibility for the manuscripts' publication. If Van Vechten groaned as each fresh carton was unwrapped, Gallup cheered. As a junior curator he had helped organise the exhibition of Stein's papers at Yale in 1941, only to be drafted two days before the exhibition opened; when stationed in Paris at the end of the war, he had spent many happy evenings with Stein and Toklas and other GIs at the rue Christine, and felt personally invested not only in furthering Stein's legacy, but in doing so with Toklas's full blessing. He took time off from his work on a bibliography of T. S. Eliot to catalogue the Stein collection: his letters to Van Vechten are peppered with exclamation marks and infec-tious delight at new discoveries in the boxes he was slowly unpacking, from the annals of 'friendships and feuds' he discerned in the letters to the doodles Stein made while clearing her pen ('I am sure that the psychologists will be tremendously interested in these'). Perhaps in an effort to manage Toklas's ambitions, Van Vechten warned her darkly that she would surely need to sell a picture or two, to fund the publica-tion of so many volumes. But when Toklas calmly responded that this would be no sacrifice whatsoever, citing Stein's sale of Picasso's *Lady with a Fan* to finance the Plain Edition, Van Vechten resigned himself to the task ahead, aware that Toklas trusted him completely. 'How wonderful you are!' he told her. 'Your complete loyalty to Baby's wishes is a very beautiful thing.'

The two men who now controlled access to the Stein archive were polar opposites in many ways. Donald Gallup was in his early thirties to Van Vechten's sixty-six. Van Vechten made his trade in the realm of fiction and imagination, Gallup through a meticulous command of facts dredged from books and archives. While Van Vechten lived in luxury in the heart of New York City – a million-dollar inheritance had bolstered an already comfortable lifestyle – Gallup came from a humble background: he had arrived at Yale on a scholarship, and worked his way through university waiting tables in the college cafeteria. Van Vechten was flamboyant, a dilettante who loved hosting parties for his international network of friends and associates (sometimes swapping his customary ruffled silk shirts for Chinese robes or cowboy shirts); Gallup was studious and diligent, committed to the institution where he spent his whole career. Van Vechten hardly left Manhattan, where his marriage to the actress Fania Marinoff was supplemented by affairs with a revolving cast of younger men ('We have found that a sense of humour is better than separate apartments,' his wife told a journalist); Gallup's domain was the university town of New Haven, where he lived alone in a modest book-lined apartment close to the Yale library. But the men shared wit, sensitivity and a total commitment to Stein – and to Toklas. While Van Vechten covered his envelopes in novelty commemorative stamps, tossed off incongruous sign-offs ('Cornflowers and incunabula!') and imperiously numbered the Donalds in his address book, such that most letters to Gallup begin 'Dear Three', Gallup was thoughtful and precise, often concluding his letters with a chosen Stein quote ('It is very nice to change your mind about roses'). Their working relationship soon deepened into a trusting friendship.

Since his early work as a dance and theatre critic, Van Vechten had retained his reputation as a tastemaker with an eye for originality and an attraction to the unfamiliar, the clandestine, the outrageous. He had become a household name in the decade he later called 'the splendid drunken twenties' for a series of whimsical, plot-heavy novels, which often made reference to Stein. Over these years, Van Vechten's advocacy for the art of the Harlem Renaissance, both on and off the page, won him friends and enemies. He sought out black writers he admired – Zora Neale Hurston, Langston Hughes, Nella Larsen, James Weldon Johnson – and threw his energies into connecting them with publishers. He encouraged them to read *Three Lives*, and found them receptive:

Weldon Johnson praised the 'consummate artistry' of Stein's style, and expressed his surprise that Stein was the first white author 'to write a story of love between a Negro man and woman and deal with them as normal members of the human family'. Larsen, too, pronounced *Melanctha* 'a truly great story'; writing to Stein in 1928, she said she had read the book many times, always finding something new in it. 'I never cease to wonder', Larsen wrote, 'how you came to write it and just why you and not some one of us should so accurately have caught the spirit of this race of mine.'

Van Vechten invited his black friends to mingle with white literati at his famous parties, where George Gershwin played piano as Bessie Smith sang the blues – but increasingly, he spent his nights uptown, partying in Harlem's ballrooms, cabarets and speakeasies and holding court at the nightclub Smalls Paradise, where waiters performed the Charleston with trays of swaying whisky glasses on their heads. Van Vechten, who masked his sexuality downtown, was drawn to Harlem for what he saw (with a heavy dose of voyeuristic fantasy) as its permissive atmosphere of sexual freedom; he soon struck a familiar and controversial figure there. Those who trusted him credited his support with bringing their writing to wider audiences; others saw his insistence on involvement with their work (mediating with editors, writing introductions) as discomfiting paternalism, and pointed to essays where his appreciation is couched in retrograde ideas of primitivism and sensuality, rendering art exotic and foreign even as he praised it. But his work for the Harlem Renaissance and his lifelong loyalty to Gertrude Stein both issued from a desire to promote an interracial, queer solidarity – to channel funds and publicity where he felt them due, and to encourage audiences towards work which broke boundaries, whether of aesthetic norms or of racial prejudice.

The uneasy welcome Harlem extended Van Vechten had, by this point, splintered. In 1926, Van Vechten published a novel he titled *Nigger Heaven*. In the book, the phrase is tinged with heavy irony – a character uses it to describe the cheap gallery of a theatre, where black

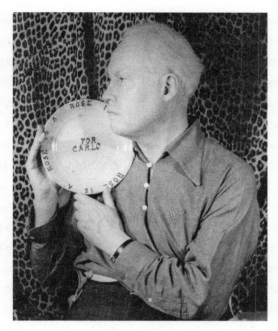

Carl Van Vechten holding a plate made for him to Stein's
design at a Bilignin pottery (photo: Saul Mauriber)

viewers are sneered at by white punters in the orchestra below – but
Van Vechten's decision to place this word in his title displayed a pre-
sumption (that, as an insider, he was allowed to use the word as his
black friends did casually among themselves) that was severely mis-
judged. W. E. B. Du Bois described it as 'an affront to the hospitality
of black folk', and copies were burned at an anti-lynching protest; Van
Vechten was banned from Smalls Paradise, while his effigy was hanged
in Harlem. But his friends stuck by Van Vechten: Hurston escorted him
back to Smalls, and Weldon Johnson wrote in praise of the book, which
he saw as a sincere and powerful challenge to American racism.

Over subsequent years, Van Vechten's notoriety had slowly faded.
Since the 1930s, he had published little writing, devoting his time
instead to photography (even Du Bois, old grudges set aside, sat for a
portrait). His dramatic images of artists and writers helped define his
subjects, who were often on the brink of stardom but not yet established

in the popular imagination; he crafted his photographs like stage sets, posing subjects with an eye to the projection of a distinctive personal image. His other passion – another form of image-making, in a way – became the archive. After James Weldon Johnson's sudden death in a car crash in June 1938, Van Vechten turned his energies to ensuring the lasting legacies of the black writers he admired. In 1941 he encouraged the Yale library to inaugurate a dedicated collection of black literature: in addition to bequeathing his own enormous stash of first editions, manuscripts, records, photographs and letters, he urged his friends to donate their own papers to the library, in order, as he put it to fellow writer Claude McKay, 'to insure your future immortality'. His work transformed the Yale Collection of American Literature, which had not previously contained any work by black writers; he campaigned for a black librarian to be appointed to oversee the collection, though the candidates he supported did not get the job.

By the late 1940s, his youthful energies were depleting. Now white-haired, he was experiencing circulatory trouble, and finding it difficult to walk. 'The tax man took all my money,' he complained, 'and now the doctor takes all my health and Baby's books will take all my time.' But he carried on for Toklas – who told Gallup how deeply grateful she was to him and Van Vechten. 'To know that you are both there taking care of Gertrude's future is my comfort – the one consolation in the general bleakness.' In her letters to Van Vechten, Toklas tended to adopt an anguished tone, by turns professing helplessness and displaying a shrewd command of the work she needed him to do. With Gallup, she was more relaxed, perhaps glad to have a younger correspondent whose enthusiasm for the task seemed unconditional. She told Gallup she would answer any questions about Stein and her work that arose as he catalogued the material: 'You realise surely that Gertrude's memory is all my life – just as she herself was before.'

//

Gallup, meanwhile, was engrossed in his own research, determined to enlarge the enormous Stein archive even further. He wrote to everyone whose name appeared among Stein's papers, asking for donations of any letters Stein had written to them. In some cases, his enquiries stirred up old antipathies. The writer Laura Riding, who had tried to establish an intimacy which Stein rebuffed, wrote that she was filled with 'sorrow and shame' when she contemplated her obsequiousness towards Stein, while T. S. Eliot admitted that his correspondence with Stein was 'trivial' and his compliments to her 'possibly more courteous than sincere'. Ernest Hemingway, writing from Cuba, told Gallup he didn't want his letters to Stein printed while Toklas was alive. To 'make the letter a collector's item', as he put it, Hemingway mentioned enigmatically that he had once overheard Stein and Toklas talking, thinking they were alone, and had had to close his ears to 'the terrible things she said and G.S.'s pleading'. Gallup – though privately intrigued by the insinuations (which Hemingway would, later, elaborate) – scrupulously returned the letter: his interest, he insisted, was enhancing the archive, not re-litigating distant quarrels. But, soon, he realised he couldn't stay out of such dramas.

As he pored over the material, Gallup began to note down odd discrepancies and mysteries thrown up by the archive. He spent a long time searching for a trace of Stein's first attempt to translate Flaubert's story *Un cœur simple* – which she had claimed was the origin of *Three Lives* – but came up short. Yet one larger absence niggled at his mind. In *The Autobiography of Alice B. Toklas*, describing her own arrival in Paris, Stein mentions that when she joined her brother at the rue de Fleurus in the autumn of 1903, she had immediately begun to write a short novel: the first full-length manuscript she had completed. The funny thing, the narrator continues, 'is that she completely forgot about it for many years'. Recently, Stein goes on, she came across the old manuscript in a drawer; she felt 'very bashful and hesitant', but gave it to her friend Louis Bromfield to read. His response is not recorded, and the narrative moves on. The novel is not mentioned again in the

Autobiography or anywhere else: the way it was casually dropped in, then immediately 'forgotten' once more, felt to Gallup like Stein seeding a clue, sure to mystify attentive readers.

Gallup was sure this novel had never been published, and it didn't seem to be among the manuscripts sent to Yale. But in Stein's clippings, he found a review of the *Autobiography* by the aforementioned Bromfield, an American novelist, gardener and gourmand who had struck up a friendship with Stein and Toklas in the late 1920s. Writing in 1933 in the *New York Herald Tribune*, Bromfield recalled having had 'the interesting good fortune to read a novel, unpublished, and written in an old copy-book, set down when Gertrude Stein was in her early twenties . . . The faded writing had in it the same fierce intensity of purpose and evidence of the same battle with words and grammar and meanings which has occupied her steadily since then.' Among Stein's letters from Bromfield, Gallup found one dated to the summer of 1932, which seemed to corroborate the *Autobiography*'s account of the novel's rediscovery, but added a further layer of intrigue. 'I have finished the early book you gave me to read and find it vastly interesting,' he wrote. 'I'm thinking of the possibilities of publishing . . . There are great difficulties certainly but they might be overcome.'

Did those difficulties refer to Stein's usual uphill battle to convince editors of her work's worth, Gallup wondered, or was something more private at stake? Once Gallup was certain that the mysterious manuscript was nowhere to be found at Yale, he decided to write casually to Toklas. He was hesitant to trouble her with questions he sensed might prove distressing, but the prospect of uncovering Stein's very first novel was impossible to resist. On 19 April 1947, Toklas replied. As he had discerned, it was a sensitive matter. 'It is a subject I haven't known how to handle nor known from what point to act upon,' she told him. 'It was something I knew I'd have to meet some day . . . But you are the *only* person who ever asked.' The manuscript, she confessed, remained with her in Paris. 'The only thing I know is I wouldn't want it read – that is therefore not published – during my life.' It was, of course, the account of Stein's youthful passion for May Bookstaver, latterly May Knoblauch: the bewildering love triangle which she had moved to Paris, in part, to leave behind.

That same day, Toklas wrote a letter to Van Vechten. She wanted desperately to talk to him, she began, but since he was so far away, she was bearing up to write 'as much as I can of it'. In the summer of 1932, Stein had found the old manuscript and shown it to various friends and her literary agent, before finally giving it to Toklas – 'and we never spoke of it again'. Stein knew that she had it, Toklas explained, but her silence was loud enough to ensure Stein never asked for a reaction. Stein would have known that Toklas 'couldn't have destroyed it', though the possibility would have crossed both their minds. Now that Gallup, 'with his lovely devotion to Baby', had brought up the question, Toklas acknowledged that she had to take action at last – but was adamant, without giving any hint at its contents, that this text could not be placed with the other papers at Yale, available freely for any curious scholar to walk in and read. Nor could it be considered part of the mass of manuscripts it was Van Vechten's duty to publish. 'Baby definitely did not expect it to be published while I was alive,' she reiterated.

The following morning, before sending the letter, Toklas added a PS. She had changed her mind entirely overnight: what had held her back were 'just memories of feelings'. She would type the manuscript and send Van Vechten both the original manuscript and the typed copy; he could decide their fates. 'Baby way back when I read it said it meant absolutely nothing to her except as literature and later when it still made me miserable and so unhappy Baby said that she wished to goodness it meant nothing to me too,' she wrote. She had read the manuscript again after writing to Van Vechten – 'and went to sleep knowing perfectly that it couldn't mean anything but one more adorable portrait of my own darling and that she was gone away'.

//

As soon as he received his letter from Toklas, Gallup wrote to Van Vechten jubilantly, expressing his relief that the manuscript had survived. Van Vechten, for his part, had to balance Gallup's enthusiasm with the distress Toklas had confided in him – though he remained baffled as to exactly why this novel had so severely upset Toklas, whose determination to see Stein's work in the world had up to now been her driving motivation. Her next letter gave a clue. 'The trouble about publishing *Q.E.D.*', she wrote, revealing the book's title for the first time, 'is that they were portraits.' The women depicted in it, Toklas told him, never saw the novel – but 'they and one or two others knew the portraits and the conversations afterwards in *Melanctha* to be literal'. Now, Van Vechten was even more puzzled. It had never been suggested that *Melanctha* – whose mixed-race, ostensibly heterosexual protagonist bore few resemblances to Stein – was in any way autobiographical. On 13 May 1947, Toklas posted the complete manuscript, along with a typed version, to Van Vechten in New York. She had typed for three days straight: the experience, she confessed, was 'heart breaking – all Baby's youth laid bare'. Van Vechten opened the envelope, its outside plastered with stamps and airmail stickers, to reveal a dark-green, square-lined notebook, with a map of France on the inside front cover. On the first page was written: '*Quod Erat Demonstrandum*, vol 1. G. Stein, 27 Rue de Fleurus, Paris.' On the last: 'FINIS Oct 24 1903.'

As he turned the pages, Van Vechten began to understand why Toklas had reacted so violently to the manuscript. Taking its epigraph from *As You Like It* – 'what 'tis to love' – *Q.E.D.* tells the story of a sexually inhibited young woman awakening to her own lesbian desires. The novel presents a psychological stand-off between three college students: the heroine, Adele, grapples with the conflicting feelings brought on by her attraction to Helen, which are complicated by her discovery of Helen's prior commitment to another woman, Mabel. Stein recounts Adele's agony in painstaking detail: the frustration of having to compete with a longer-established rival, the impossibility of knowing whether her feelings are reciprocated, and – above all – the difficulty of understanding and being understood by another, especially when one is not sure of oneself. In long dialogues with Helen, and 'thinking aloud' to herself, Adele works through her fear of surrendering control over her own emotions to another, as she debates whether to 'yield or resist': 'It's not easy', she concludes, 'this business of really caring about people'. *Q.E.D.* ends in deadlock, with Adele determined to make a clean break from Helen and Mabel, and 'set herself in order'. Toklas had clearly intimated that the novel was autobiographical. If so, Van Vechten realised, the failure of this affair – a fundamental mismatch between two women whose 'pulses were differently timed' – must have provided the bedrock for Stein's investigations into human relationships, the fascination with character and conflict which drove her early writing. But if the anguished, puritanical Adele, wrestling with passions she didn't fully understand, was a portrait of Stein – who was Helen?

Something else was clear to Van Vechten. As Toklas had hinted, *Q.E.D.* bore uncanny similarities to *Melanctha*, which Stein wrote a little over two years later. In fact, the echoes were strong enough to suggest that Stein had transformed the early novel into the later text, which had marked her first real aesthetic breakthrough. Many of Adele's thoughts are expressed, in *Melanctha*, by the stolid doctor Jefferson Campbell, while the shadowy Helen morphs into the impetuous heroine. Both Helen and Melanctha complain that their lovers prioritise words over emotion: 'Haven't you ever stopped thinking long enough to feel?' Helen asks Adele, while Melanctha admonishes Jeff: 'Don't you ever stop with your thinking long enough ever to have any feeling.' In both versions, the developing trust between two central characters is tested by the jealousy of a third: Melanctha's older friend Jane Harden tries to sabotage her relationship by dropping dark hints to Jeff about Melanctha's promiscuity, while in *Q.E.D.*, Mabel warns Adele that Helen is already 'bound', and any efforts to lure her away are doomed to fail.

But the changes Stein made between the texts, Van Vechten saw, were as profound as the similarities. *Q.E.D.* depicted a lesbian passion between 'college bred American women of the wealthier class', at least one of whom – Adele – is clearly marked as Jewish. It was relatively explicit about sexual desire – alone with Helen, Adele is aroused from slumber by 'a kiss that seemed to scale the very walls of chastity' – but Stein's narrative style remained conventional. Though something of the love triangle lingered in the subtle erotic overtones to Melanctha and Jane's friendship, *Melanctha* portrayed a heterosexual relationship. Its protagonists were a working-class mixed-race woman and a black Christian man, and its language marked the birth of Stein's own voice, her first rebellion against linguistic norms. Why, Van Vechten wondered, did Stein change her characters' races? Was she simply disguising the novel's autobiographical roots – in particular, the characters' homosexuality – by making her characters black on a surface level only? The discovery opened up new layers to *Melanctha*, a text which had long fascinated and troubled its black readers. While some – like Nella Larsen, Richard Wright and James Weldon Johnson – had seen the novella as a perceptive articulation of black language and experience, others had remarked on the incongruous fact that while Stein had depicted her protagonists with such sympathy, her portrayal of the wider black community was marred with crass stereotypes: the men violent and hypersexual, the women lazy and childlike. 'In the telling of the story I found nothing striking and informative about Negro life,' wrote Claude McKay. 'Melanctha, the mulattress, might have been a Jewess.' The Harlem Renaissance writer Eric Walrond had once told Leo Stein that 'Gertrude was the only white person who had given real Negro psychology'. Leo's reaction was scoffing: *Melanctha*, he had replied, 'was really not about Negroes'.

The date on the manuscript of *Q.E.D.* showed that Stein had written it immediately after her immersion in brain research at Johns Hopkins, a field abounding with eugenicist and pseudoscientific discourses connecting – and pathologising – blackness, Jewishness and homosexuality. If in *Q.E.D.* the young Stein had set out to explore the complexities of her identity as a Jewish lesbian, it's plausible that she saw a certain affinity between her own outsider status and that of the mixed-race Melanctha

– that in changing the characters' races, she had wanted to think through the experience of otherness without being immediately identifiable as the protagonist. Morphing Adele into Jefferson Campbell – the character whose over-thinking tendencies and lack of emotional self-knowledge drew on Stein herself – was another change that could be construed as self-protective. But what the discovery of *Melanctha*'s first draft showed most conclusively was just how radically Stein's style had shifted between 1903 and 1906, as she began to use syntax to express the inner processes and sensations of the mind: not just to describe her characters but to present them in full, complex humanity. She was not aiming to approximate realistic dialect, but to liberate language from literary conventions altogether. *Q.E.D.* seemingly set out to explore Stein's own feelings, but *Melanctha* explores the nature of feeling itself. Reading the two texts together made it possible, for the first time, to chart the emergence of Stein's distinctive voice: to see her leave behind the mannered prose of the story's first version, and – with some distance from the affair, and under the influence of her new stimuli in Paris – recast it entirely afresh.

For now, Van Vechten's primary reaction to reading *Q.E.D.* was twofold: intrigue about its origins, and anxiety about the distress its discovery had caused to Toklas. He reassured her that he would do nothing without her full consent – but asked, first, whether she would confidentially identify the women on whom the characters of Helen and Mabel were based, so he might consider their possible reactions to the publication, should they be living. 'You must realise', he added, 'that to most people it will be a completely objective work with no semblance of autobiography. As I believe you told me Baby said, "Regard it as a work of art."' Toklas complied. 'The characters', she wrote, 'were Mrs Charles Knoblauch and her friend Mrs Mabel Haynes Heissig.'

'Between us,' Van Vechten wrote to Gallup, 'you and I will own many Stein–Toklas secrets that cannot yet be shared with biographers . . . or anyone else.' Gallup travelled down from New Haven to read the manuscript of *Q.E.D.* in the seclusion of Van Vechten's home, stopping at the Metropolitan Museum of Art on his way to admire Picasso's portrait of Stein. He agreed with Van Vechten that the novel should be published, if Toklas was amenable: not only was it a psychologically rich examination of forbidden feelings, written with an appealingly ironic touch, it marked an important link in the development of Stein's prose from realism to abstraction, the first piece of writing she had composed in Paris. But Toklas's description of the work as 'portraits' confounded them both. Although she had clearly been a significant figure in Stein's life, neither Gallup nor Van Vechten could recall ever encountering Mrs Charles Knoblauch, either in person, in conversation with Stein, or in the archive. When Gallup told Toklas he was 'puzzled at finding no letters at all (save for one unimportant late one of the 30s) from Mrs Knoblauch', Toklas replied simply: 'Mrs Knoblauch's letters were destroyed years and years ago.'

Having released the manuscript from its hiding place, Toklas pondered her next moves. She knew that Stein's express wishes were that all her writing should be published. She had devoted her life to bringing Stein's work to readers – typing it, submitting it to editors, publishing it herself with the Plain Edition – and that moment in 1932, when Stein gave her *Q.E.D.* to read, was the only time she had responded to a text with anything other than pleasure. Her seething silence then had chastened Stein enough to let her keep the manuscript; when preparing her shipments for Yale, Stein had not asked for it back. Fifteen years later, with Stein gone, Toklas had the opportunity to suppress the manuscript, and May Knoblauch's name, for ever – and found she couldn't do it. She would not tell Van Vechten or Gallup why the manuscript had provoked such a strong reaction in her – though they deduced romantic jealousy from the mention of the destroyed letters. Being solely responsible for its publication added sting to that wound: she was being asked to make public a romance Stein hadn't even shared with her.

The main reason Toklas gave for her hesitation to publish *Q.E.D.* was her fear that the lesbian theme might 'make a scandal'. Van Vechten tried to reassure her – he loved scandal, but didn't consider this book raunchy in the slightest – to no avail. She had good reason to worry. As

Toklas pondered the manuscript's future, the novelist Patricia Highsmith was beginning to write *The Price of Salt*, which was rejected by several mainstream publishers for its depiction of a lesbian relationship and, in particular, for its relatively happy ending. Highsmith published the novel in 1952 under a pseudonym, and did not reveal herself as the author until 1990: the 1953 pulp paperback edition bore the tagline 'The Novel of a Love Society Forbids'. (The reader is given an early hint at the protagonist's sexuality when her boyfriend expresses his surprise that she has read Gertrude Stein but not James Joyce.) At that moment in America, thousands of government workers suspected of homosexuality were being dismissed from their jobs during the 'Lavender Scare', while Senator Joseph McCarthy's repressive crackdowns placed gay people across the country under extra scrutiny.

While homosexuality remained illegal in America and England, sodomy laws in France had been repealed during the Revolution in 1791 – though lesbian couples, particularly those in the public eye, remained alert to pervasive homophobia. Stein and Toklas never vaunted their sexuality as some of their peers did – Dolly Wilde, who turned up at parties masquerading as her uncle Oscar, or Natalie Barney, whose weekly salons, Sylvia Beach recalled, were a gathering place for 'ladies with high collars and monocles'. Nor did they disguise it, as did their friend Bryher or Vita Sackville-West, whose lesbian relationships were camouflaged by heterosexual marriages. Rather, Stein and Toklas presented themselves to the world as a couple as if it were entirely unremarkable. *The Autobiography of Alice B. Toklas* ironically gave little insight into the texture of their relationship: their mutual devotion is simply taken for granted. Stein, anticipating a wide and international audience for the book, had been deliberately discreet.

But through her 'real' writing, Stein had scattered intimate clues to their sexual life – which few readers had ever acknowledged. These were barely concealed, but reviewers had persistently lamented the abstraction of her references, the impossibility of deciphering what she could possibly mean. While the *Little Review*'s publication of extracts from

Ulysses had drawn the censors' opprobrium in 1920, Stein's tribute to Toklas in the same magazine a few years later – 'She is very lovely and mine which is very lovely,' wrote Stein, picturing Toklas gently snoring beside her in bed – had passed unnoticed. Her friend Mabel Weeks remembered Stein, shortly after meeting Toklas, reading her letters aloud with giddy excitement: 'Gertrude showed no reticence whatever about her homosexuality,' she recalled. 'On the contrary, she made no secret of it, talked with absolute frankness, and justified her sexual activity on the ground that the world was so askew and abnormal that abnormal things became perfectly legitimate.' Her comments suggest that it was Toklas, not Stein, who insisted on discretion: the chaste *Autobiography*, after all, was in Toklas's voice. Now, the possible publication of *Q.E.D.* threatened to invite prurient speculation on an aspect of their lives Toklas had always kept private. Although it would have proved surprising only to the most wilfully prudish, the prospect of being 'outed' horrified her.

Toklas never commented on Stein's erotic poems – whether she was proud to be celebrated, or embarrassed by them. But Stein, certainly, was aware she was testing taboos. 'I was overcome with remorse,' announces a speaker in 'Sentences and Paragraphs'. 'It was my fault that my wife did not have a cow. This sentence they cannot use.' 'This must not be put in a book,' says a speaker in Stein's 1916 poem 'Bonne Annee'. 'Why not,' replies the other. 'Because it mustn't.' One line near the start of *Everybody's Autobiography* hinted at Toklas's discomfort with Stein using her name: she would have preferred to be simply 'Alice Toklas' without the 'B', Stein belatedly acknowledged, 'if it has to be she at all'. She had, evidently, consented to appear in Stein's work, however reluctantly – but if she had done so for the sake of domestic harmony, that payoff no longer applied. As Gallup continued cataloguing Stein's papers, he found, to his discomfort, that these questions would have to be confronted. Some of the unpublished manuscripts were even more explicit about their relationship than anything Stein had published: *A Sonatina Followed by Another*, for example, which is full of rhyming pillow talk

('Little Alice B. is the wife for me'), sincerity ('To-day there is nothing but the humble expression of a husband's love. Take it') and relatively frank accounts of sexual passion ('Do you feel satisfied. Oh so satisfied. Have you pleasure in your point of view! Oh a great deal of pleasure.').

A cursory scan of Stein's small notebooks revealed how her writing process – passing the pages daily to Toklas for typing – served as a domestic ritual that both performed and cemented their mutual love and dependence. Often, Gallup saw, new notebooks would begin with a doodled dedication from 'little hubby' to 'wifie', as though Toklas were a talisman to guarantee Stein's creative powers. 'A little new book always has to tell and to tell very well very well of my belle,' she wrote, inscribing Toklas's presence permanently in her writing. In the margins of notebooks, on loose scraps of graph paper or pages carelessly torn from detective novels, Gallup found around sixty notes in Stein's handwriting addressed to 'darling wife', 'birdie', 'boss', 'little ball', 'little Jew', 'Baby precious', 'Sweet selected sovereign of my soul'. These notes – expressing love, seeking advice – seemed to have been left around the flat at night for Toklas to discover with Stein's manuscripts in the mornings: they nestled among shopping lists, requests for Toklas to order more candies from Chambéry, plans for dinner guests, and pencilled sketches of cheerful shapeless blobs labelled 'Mr and Mrs Cuddle-Wuddle'. Many of these private notes lay within the very pages that contained Stein's writing, sometimes physically inseparable from the literary text. Stein's pieces often present two speakers in dialogue, arguing and contradicting each other, such that reading her work can feel like eavesdropping on a conversation that has started somewhere outside the text: 'What are you doing my precious. Taking grease off my face my love.' 'Who's having tea. Who. It smells like sea-water. How do you know. By tasting it.' These notes, it was clear, were another form of private dialogue – a poignant record of ephemeral moments.

As Gallup opened new boxes, he uncovered more and more of these notes. Sometimes Stein pointed out that she had cut the ivy off the terrace, or oiled Toklas's sewing scissors, expectantly fishing for praise. She apologised for bringing cold air into bed when she joined Toklas, warned her the kitchen floor was slippery where Basket had been 'hunting slabs of butter', and let her know her work was appreciated: 'By loving her flowers and her food I tell my wifey how I love her, yes I do.' She reported on the progress of her day's writing, and expressed, over and over, her adoration. 'Precious baby I had an attack of working', Stein wrote, perhaps in apology for a sheaf of papers left strewn on the floor, 'and I wrote lots of pages and I loved my blessed wifie so completely so entirely that even dear sweet precious wifey is satisfied with all the love with which I love her.' 'Sweet pinky, you made lots of literature last night didn't you,' replied Toklas, when she returned the typed pages. 'You are doing most handsomely. Would you mind if I didn't think you a Post-Impressionist. You aren't lovely. You are not a cubist either. It's such very orderly literature. Much more so than Pablo's. *La Jolie* is quite messy compared to this. You never were messy lovie but it's more crowded now & I like it. You can almost say anything you please can't you.' In another note, Toklas reiterated her 'complete devotion' to Stein. 'Please be sure not to forget that you are the most illustrious and distinguished husband an industrious wife ever had,' she wrote in one. 'I have just looked up to see if you were as beautiful as I remembered,' read another, 'and I found that you were employed with a pencil and paper.'

Many of the notes were overtly sexual. 'I love her all night and I love her all day and every day and every night and in every which way,' read one. Stein compliments Toklas's hair on the pillow, describes climbing into bed next to her and moving the hot water bottle to hold her for warmth instead. Several make enigmatic references to 'cows', which seem to signify orgasms, while Stein's texts are the 'babies' that legitimised their unlawful marriage. In these notes, as in Stein's erotic texts, sex and writing merged into one joyful act of creation, with each partner's pleasure dependent on the other's. Some notes hinted at temporary strife in the home: 'My darling wifey, I am so sorry I was so hurtful and I love my wife so and I am all hers and nobody elses only my wifey's'. Sometimes Stein is imperious, ordering Toklas around; in other notes she is a bashful 'little hubby' who 'will do what he is told by little wifey'. Power shifts and balances as notes pass back and forth. Above all, the notes show their mutual delight in the ritual and rhythm of this intimate exchange, rooted in the shared home and life they maintained. 'I love you so much more every war more and more and more and more,' reads one of the last notes: moving acknowledgement of the most difficult times they had seen through together.

//

Gallup suspected the notes had been sent to the archive in error. Given Toklas's reluctance to have their relationship scrutinised, he doubted she would have freely sent such intimate material to Yale. But some of them had arrived in an earlier tranche of papers, sent directly by Stein: it was just as plausible that Stein wanted future readers to witness the fullness of the relationship, for her archive to anticipate a moment when lesbian sexuality would be more broadly accepted, even offer future lesbian readers a sense of their own history. Without telling the other librarians about the content of the letters, he arranged for them to be stored in a fireproof steel cabinet, attaching the only key to his own belt. Next, he decided to write to Toklas with a factual question, in order to let her know gently and discreetly that he had seen the notes, and to gauge her reaction. Many of the notes were signed 'Y.D.' or 'D.D.' Rather than mention the letters overtly, he asked her casually what those initials stood for – adding that, should she prefer, she might write the words on a slip of paper sealed inside an envelope, and he would ensure the seal would not be broken until after her death. As with *Q.E.D.*, he spoke of the notes to no one except Van Vechten, who speculated that Toklas had, in fact, sent them to Yale deliberately: 'She wants the whole story known soon or late.'

But Van Vechten's confidence was misplaced. A few days later, he received an anguished letter from Toklas, insisting that all those notes had arrived at Yale by accident – 'they were *not* oh but certainly *not* intended to be sent.' The first thing she had done when she returned to 5 rue Christine from the American Hospital after Stein's death, Toklas revealed, was to gather up their notes – 'the thousands and thousands we had over those long happy years written to each other' – and begin to destroy them. There were too many to dispose of at the apartment, so she had carried 'baskets and baskets' of them – thirty-nine years of daily correspondence – over to a friend's flat, where she had burned them. Now, she wrote, she wanted Gallup to do the same to those letters Yale had obtained 'through the most gross carelessness'. 'There is not a line in there that is literature or refers to her work,' she wrote. 'They are in a private language we used and no future student could gain any clue key or the slightest guidance of Baby's meanings in their perusal . . . there was never the slightest intention on Gertrude's part that they should ever be read by anyone but me.' She did, however, answer his question, after imploring once again that he burn every one of them. 'The D.D. was darling darling and Y.D. was yours dearest.'

Van Vechten, exhausted and exasperated by the emotions stirred up

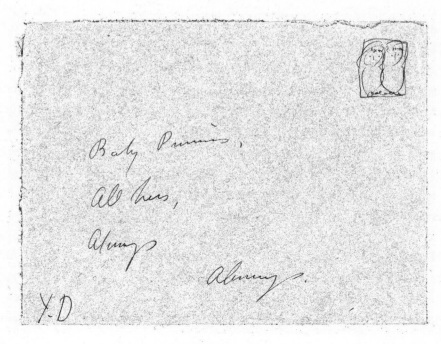

by the archive, suggested Gallup just assure Toklas her wishes would be carried out 'before the biography writers get their talons in'. But Gallup, ever the archivist, was horrified at the prospect of burning original Stein material. It was impossible, in many cases, to distinguish between literary manuscripts and their marginal love notes; what's more, several notes contained phrases and sentiments that overlap with texts that were either published or destined for publication. Gallup considered

Love notes (opposite and above) from Stein to Toklas

that 'these notes contain some of Gertrude's loveliest short poems', and afforded her work a greater emotional depth by laying bare its personal roots. Toklas herself had suggested as much in one of her replies to Stein: 'Notes are a very beautiful form of literature,' she wrote. 'They are never too frequent, do not fear to overwhelm me with them.' Gallup did not suggest they should be published, or even made available to re-searchers – yet. But the prospect of destroying them, he was convinced, cut off a potentially generative insight both into Stein's work and into the relationship which formed its primary context.

Gallup apologised to Toklas for the emotional turmoil his letter had caused, and reiterated that the material was locked safely away from prying eyes. But he asked that he might be permitted to follow his scholarly instincts, and keep them in the safe: 'The notes make clear the role which her love for you played in everything she wrote, charging it with a personal emotion, and a warm living humanness.' Van Vechten wrote to Toklas to support Gallup's pleas: 'Surely there will be no reve-lation in these letters to any reader about the relations between Baby and you. They will only serve to prove how very much she loved you.'

'I'm not being a Lady Burton – nor a Jane Carlyle – nor even Murray of Albemarle Street,' wrote Toklas contritely to Van Vechten, playing down her destruction of the notes in Paris. It's an interesting statement: a rare moment of self-reflection, from Toklas, on the fraught history of literary executorship, and her own place in that complex tradition. Isabel Burton devoted her life to supporting her husband, explorer Sir Richard Burton; after his death in 1890, she burned a quantity of his journals, letters and manuscripts, including an exposing series of notes on pederasty, and wrote a whitewashed biography portraying him as a model husband and a devout Catholic. John Murray, the renowned Scottish publisher, destroyed the manuscript of Lord Byron's memoir at his Mayfair office in 1824, obeying the wishes of Byron's surviving fam-ily, who were wounded by its contents, despite the poet having charged him with its posthumous publication. Jane Carlyle made a pact with her friend Geraldine Jewsbury that each would destroy the other's intimate letters on their death – though she died suddenly without upholding her half of the bargain. But Jane Carlyle's story has further layers, which make her a more intriguing comparison than Toklas perhaps intended. She published nothing in her lifetime, managing the household meticulously so her husband, Thomas Carlyle, could write in peace. After Jane's death in 1866, her husband read the letters she had written, privately, for years, and was struck by the devastating realisation that had she not spent her life catering to his every need, Jane might have been a novelist of a talent on a par with George Eliot. In grief and guilt, he devoted the rest of his life to celebrating her legacy, shepherding her letters into print: Virginia Woolf declared her one of the all-time great letter writers, and her fame eventually came to equal, if not eclipse, her husband's. In insisting she was no Jane Carlyle, was Toklas foreclosing the suggestion that she herself had anything of value to offer? Many of Jane's letters expressed understandable resentment at the drudgery she had taken on for her husband's benefit: was Toklas reminding Van Vechten that her devotion to Stein, by contrast, was selfless and eternal?

When Van Vechten replied, he cited the case of the artist Charles Demuth, whose mother had found a cache of erotic drawings of male nudes after his death, and – despite her shock – handed them over to his executors, saying she was sure anything her son painted was art. 'These letters are not obscene, but I think you will get the point,' Van Vechten added, 'everything Baby wrote was art.' The entreaties paid off. Gallup's promise to keep the notes sealed for her lifetime was enough to persuade Toklas that they could be allowed to stay in the archive. On 11 June 1947, Van Vechten wrote to Gallup: 'Eureka and blessed be the saints in heaven, Gertrude's love-letters are NOT to be destroyed, at least those that remain.' Gallup replied: 'Three cheers and thirty-three tigers for Alice!' Henceforth, Toklas told them, they need not even consult her on matters to do with Stein. The love notes could stay in the archive, and Q.E.D. could – if a willing publisher were found – be printed. She left affairs entirely in the hands of the two men whose devotion to Stein, she had convinced herself, was equal to her own.

11 : 'DIAGRAM BOOK'

In May 1947, almost a year after Stein's death, a GI telephoned Toklas to tell her he had found a photograph he'd taken of Stein the previous June. Walking past Rumpelmayer's café near the Tuileries Garden, he had glanced in through the window and spotted Stein inside having an ice cream, and snapped a quick picture from the pavement. Toklas was delighted by the prospect of a new image of Stein – perhaps the last photo of her ever taken – and asked him to bring it round at once. But when she saw the picture, she told Van Vechten, 'Everything just went blank. For there was Baby precious inexpressibly sad tired old and ill – as she didn't ever look – not when I said goodbye to her – it upset me completely and I put it away.' It was a bitter reminder that memories are fallible, and vulnerable to displacement: Toklas, who had just turned seventy, saw her past being reshaped before her eyes.

//

Both Toklas and Stein adored the work of Henry James. Stein had hoped to meet him during a visit to London in 1913, and had been disappointed when he replied, courteously regretting that he seldom socialised. Toklas had written to him even earlier: at nineteen, she had asked his permission to adapt one of his novels into a play, then been so embarrassed by his kind response that she had taken things no further. So it's likely that she'd read his 1888 novella *The Aspern Papers*, in which a monomaniacal American researcher rents a room in the 'sequestered and dilapidated old palace' in Venice occupied by an elderly woman who, in her youth, had been the lover of the late Romantic poet Jeffrey Aspern. Desperate to procure the revealing letters he suspects her of hoarding, he offers a false name, flirts unscrupulously with her niece, and prowls around the house at night, dislodging 'phantoms and dust'. Toklas must have wondered who would come for Stein's papers, looking for secrets and skeletons. Would they court Toklas, or treat her like an impediment to be dispensed with, along with her version of the truth? Every biographer knows their subjects are most amenable when they are dead. But while Stein, now, was a spectre to be reanimated from the mass of paper lying sealed and serene in her archive, Toklas was her living agent – with the power to decide what knowledge to pass on, and what to suppress. James had burned most of his papers, telling his nephew his only wish was to 'frustrate as utterly as possible the postmortem exploiter'. But Toklas's role was more complex. She had an unprecedented opportunity to get Stein's work more widely read and shape how posterity received her – but her new role opened her up to the scrutiny she had always avoided.

Both Stein and Toklas knew that the story a biographer can tell will always depend on the material made available to them; that narratives composed from shards of memory and whatever documentation the subject has left behind will always be partial and highly subjective. Some writers sought to direct the course of their posthumous reception even more explicitly than did Stein. Shortly before his death in 1941, James Joyce – who had previously railed against 'biografiends', grim reapers with murky motives – had commissioned the critic Herbert Gorman to write his 'definitive biography'. Joyce made clear what personal crises were off limits to Gorman, and corrected his manuscript himself, rewriting entire passages to ensure the book presented him as he wanted to be seen. Stein, by contrast, never considered appointing her own biographer: the idea would have been creative death. But while Joyce's personal papers were scattered among rival factions of family and friends, whose whims would direct what was accessible to scholars, Stein's – with the exception of what remained with Toklas – were safely collected at Yale. She had taken control of her material legacy by setting up her archive, but left it to her readers to interpret what they found there. It was up to Toklas, now, to help or hinder researchers who wanted to hear her perspective as they shaped their narratives: to offer readers as full, or as restricted, a picture of her life with Stein as she chose.

Gallup's gentle questioning about the love notes had forced Toklas to confront her own position in Stein's story. Her immediate instinct was to remain in her partner's shadow. Working quietly to ensure Stein's literary legacy felt more in keeping with her established role – and she was furious with the lawyer, Poe, whose administration of Stein's estate had proceeded glacially over the past year, holding up any hope of starting the publication programme. Meanwhile, rumours were fast spreading that the Stein collection was available at Yale: tantalising fodder for researchers whose interests ranged from the scholarly to the salacious. Toklas knew these inquisitors would play an important role in securing Stein's reputation for the next generation – her work needed new readers if it was to survive. But she hated the prospect of being interrogated about her personal life by eagle-eyed biographers in search of a story. She resolved that she would respond to questioners by directing them back to Stein's writing. Beyond that, she would be silent. They would soon discover that Toklas was as tough and tenacious as she was self-effacing: ready to block writers' access to material as she had once blocked artists' wives from talking to Stein.

Scholars did, indeed, flock to Yale's reading rooms hoping to examine the new archival riches. Some had known or corresponded with Stein and Toklas, while others were journalists or literary critics approaching Stein from a critical distance. As promised, Toklas welcomed those who aimed to shed light on Stein's writing, but the inevitable requests for her collaboration were met with stony refusal. She insisted she could not help the poet and would-be biographer John Malcolm Brinnin; she remained unmoved by his protestations that he had been reading Stein's work since he was fourteen, and some years previously had paced up and down the rue de Fleurus, but not summoned the courage to ring the bell. Her patience was more severely tested by Julian Sawyer, a longtime Stein admirer whose cultish adoration for Stein had already raised hackles. When Stein and Toklas arrived in New York in October 1934, the teenage Sawyer had turned up at the docks to meet their boat, introducing himself to Stein in mumbled tones. Over the course of her stay, he spent hours waiting in the lobby of the Algonquin Hotel with a suitcase of books for her to sign and an invitation (not accepted) to his solo rendition of *Four Saints in Three Acts*, performed in his own living room. Now, he spent his days in the Yale reading room, where Gallup and Van Vechten suspected he was looking for references to himself; he had, in fact, found one of his own letters to Stein, now covered with fragments of *The World Is Round* – a children's book she devised during the war for a young neighbour – in Stein's own handwriting. 'I hope,' wrote Gallup, 'he isn't EATING the mss!'

Toklas assumed Sawyer's interest was benign, until he sent her the text of a lecture he had delivered linking Stein, Greta Garbo and Frank Sinatra (representatives, in his eyes, of the mind, the body and the soul). She struck back at once, condemning his 'repeated references to the subject of sexuality as an approach to the understanding of Gertrude's work', and insisting that 'she would have emphatically denied it – she considered it the least characteristic of all expressions of character'. Sawyer replied undeterred, pointing out (correctly) that Stein's references to sex in her work were far from oblique, and that *Melanctha* and *The Making of Americans* both revolved around the subject of sexual repression. Toklas was furious, and condemned Sawyer as 'ignorant – unintelligent insensitive and pretentious'. His insights had touched a nerve. Even critical interpretations of Stein's work, Toklas saw, might stray into the psychological, and she would be powerless to halt them, however uncomfortable they made her.

For now, Toklas threw her support behind the projects she approved of. She was delighted to hear from Fernanda Pivano, a leader in Italy's underground anti-fascist movement, who planned to translate *The Making of Americans* into Italian, and who told her that Stein's work had been secretly passed among members of the Resistance during the occupation. And she was thrilled when Donald Sutherland – whom they had met as a student during the American tour, and was now a teacher of Greek at the University of Colorado – wrote to propose a scholarly book, 'dry as a bone', exploring Stein's attitude to consciousness with reference to her early work at Radcliffe. Sutherland was an exponent of the New Criticism school, which aimed to tease out meaning from a text through close reading, without recourse to the author's biography or possible intentions. He read Stein's as an 'intellectual and secular art', as much a scientific and philosophical enquiry as a literary project. Not only did she write 'in full consciousness', he argued – sharply dispelling the old idea that her writing might be automatic – but her work went further than anyone else's to express the movements of the human mind. 'I think one has to like freedom in order to like Gertrude Stein's work,' wrote Sutherland. 'One has to want a work to be itself . . . to find its own spontaneous logic and form its ideas on the way rather than follow out a preconception.' Toklas considered his ideas 'completely in accord with Gertrude's theories' – and appreciated, in particular, that he made no attempt to connect Stein's writings with her personal life. 'Knowing that your work is progressing is the only comfort these months have offered,' she told him.

She also encouraged William G. Rogers, a journalist whom she and Stein had met as a doughboy in France during the First World War and henceforth knew as 'the Kiddie', who was eager to write a memoir about his long friendship with Stein. 'He would write something SWEET, if not mystic or profound,' Van Vechten agreed, 'and whatever he wrote would be loving.' She read parts of Rogers's manuscript as he wrote it, and enjoyed his anecdotes, recounted with flair: of hair-raising drives down country lanes with Stein behind the wheel, lighting matches to read signposts in the dark; of Toklas walking quickly and Stein with a slow, deliberate tread. Rogers had argued at length with Stein about politics, and he wrestled with her contradictions in his memoir: 'Miss Stein', he wrote, 'was born into a bourgeois background, and was a Republican all her life. The wonder is that she was such a rebel in art and creative writing, where she won her unique reputation, not that she was so conservative in the unfamiliar fields of economics and politics.' But Stein, he wrote, was always open and honest, didn't mind if anyone disagreed with her, and was not averse to changing her mind. 'Her record in her last years was faultless.' It was a charming and sympathetic portrait – but Toklas was horrified to read, in his completed manuscript, that friends suspected 'her touch in the Stein genius' – and wrote to remonstrate with a bemused Rogers. Responding, contritely, Rogers told her that he knew there were opinions in the book she would not share – but, he added, 'There were so many things about you that you wanted taken out . . . I think I should be thanked for what I did omit.'

//

On 2 October 1947, Gallup received a new visitor to the Stein collection. A doctoral student from Columbia University had turned up out of the blue and asked to see 'all the correspondence'. Gallup was stalling him with letters he knew contained 'nothing inflammable', but wanted to warn Van Vechten the man might cause trouble. Van Vechten agreed that, given all the sensitivities, caution was best practice, especially with 'unimportant biographers and thesis writers': 'I certainly do not think you should permit anyone to rummage through correspondence you haven't very carefully checked on.'

Leon Katz had discovered Stein's writing as a theatre-mad thirteen-year-old living in the Bronx, after reading a review of *Four Saints* in the *World Telegram* and tracking down a copy in his school library. Barracked in England during his wartime stint in the 67th Fighter Wing, he wrote to a friend that he was spending his leave cycling around the countryside, going to the theatre as often as possible, and making regular forays to London to pick up more Gertrude Stein. Now in his late twenties, Katz was modest and ruminative, yet pincer-sharp and passionate about his work: colleagues complimented his 'first-rate' mind, 'inexhaustible' energy and 'winning' personality. He was working on a theatrical adaptation of *Melanctha*, a text he considered 'profoundly rewarding', and hoped in time to write Stein's biography. 'She will stand', he wrote in a scholarship application, 'as one of the two or three creative giants of her time who were capable of imagining and portraying the world exactly as it is. I must confess that it has become part of my private propaganda to make this widely understood.'

On 25 October, Katz contacted Van Vechten, asking his permission to delve more deeply into the archive. Gallup had warned him, Katz wrote, of the 'peculiar difficulties' in using the Stein papers, due to 'the problems of writing about people who are still living or recently deceased' – but he did not believe 'that a biography of Miss Stein that is essentially concerned with her accomplishment as an artist . . . need violate the reticence or private feelings of her surviving associates'. Van Vechten replied, briskly, that he could not give carte blanche to someone he knew 'absolutely nothing' about: 'as a matter of fact,' he added, 'the nature of the material – some of it – is so personal that I couldn't give anybody such permission at this time.' But he agreed that Katz might continue to examine letters and manuscripts at Gallup's discretion. He informed Toklas that Katz was 'the latest to want to write about Baby': 'We'll go easy with this fellow until we know more about him.' They didn't hear from Katz again until September 1948, when he reappeared, announcing his intention to commute daily to the library from New York. He had narrowed down his area of interest to Stein's early writing, 1906–12, and asked to see the manuscript of *The Making of Americans*.

As he rifled through the papers, Katz came across two unassuming brown paper packets containing a bundle of small, grey-covered notebooks. He extracted them carefully and began to turn the pages. Instantly, he was gripped. The notebooks were clearly related to the novel, but the writing they contained was not drafts, as he had expected. Pages were covered with diagrams, with familiar names from Stein's circle grouped under headings. Parallel lists connected characters from *The Making of Americans* with Stein's friends from Radcliffe, Baltimore and her first years in Paris. In some notes, Stein appeared to be ruminating on her own identity and relationships, in others, she described the personalities of those around her in strange, clinical language. As Katz began to assemble and order the books and scraps, he became convinced that this was a continuous stream of discourse: notes and comments written by Stein to herself across the course of her thirties, recorded without self-consciousness and not intended to be seen. It suddenly looked, to Katz, as though *The Making of Americans* was 'as much a diary as a novel'.

When Stein sent her papers to Yale during the last nine years of her life, she packed them haphazardly, often overturning the drawers that Toklas had carefully organised. It was not, therefore, surprising that the envelopes full of these early notes had escaped even Gallup's attention: no one had noticed them, let alone examined their contents. But as he read on, Katz became convinced that this material offered entirely fresh insights into Stein's first, formative years in Paris. One passage in particular jumped out at him from the scrawled pages. It was headed 'Alice Toklas', and appeared to have been written shortly after the pair met, in the autumn of 1907. In it, Stein unleashed her disapproval in vitriolic style. Alice, Stein insisted, was 'a liar of the most sordid unillumined undramatic unimaginative prostitute type, coward, ungenerous, conscienceless, mean, vulgarly triumphant and remorseless, caddish, in short just plain low'. She was an 'elderly

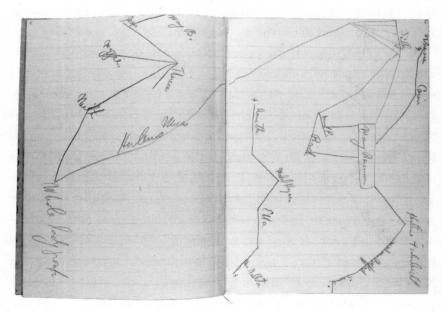

'Diagram Book'

spinster mermaid' with 'no distinguishing sense for people', possessing no 'moral purpose' or discrimination, yet not interesting enough to be considered 'evil'. 'Alice runs herself by her intellect', wrote Stein, 'but there is not enough intellect in her to go around and so she fails in every way.' Reading these lines forty years after they were written, Katz was faintly terrified at the intensity of Stein's critique. Yet he suspected also that the strength of her reaction betrayed – even at this early stage – her intrigue at the new arrival.

Gallup told Van Vechten he had added this notebook to the rapidly expanding safe containing the love notes and the manuscript of *Q.E.D.* 'I am convinced there is no time to be lost about editing the notebooks,' replied Van Vechten by return of post. He asked Katz to try to organise them into a preliminary chronology and create a full typescript of their contents, with the promise that should the notebooks be published in the future, he could be credited as their editor. Katz agreed, asking only that no one else should be allowed to see this material while he was working on it; Van Vechten – who had warmed to the young man's directness and discretion – acquiesced, instructing him to ask for help when he needed it and never to guess when he wasn't sure of a fact. 'Whew!' Van Vechten wrote to Gallup, once the negotiations were concluded. 'I'm dizzy.'

//

After careful scrutiny, Katz determined that these notebooks dated to the years between 1902 and 1912, during which time Stein travelled in Europe, left America, set up home in Paris, wrote *Three Lives* and completed *The Making of Americans*. In them, Stein dissected the characters of some 400 people, almost everyone she had ever known: family and friends from her childhood in California; fellow students at Radcliffe and Johns Hopkins; the writers and artists who thronged to the rue de Fleurus. As well as providing insight into her daily life, the notebooks revealed her judgements, often harsh, on others and on herself, and showed her grappling, across a decade, with the complex questions of human psychology that propelled her writing. Not only did they represent a stage in Stein's writing that had not been documented in any detail – tracing *The Making of Americans* from first draft to completion – but the notebooks were fascinating from a biographical perspective: these were raw notes, written with no sensitivity towards posterity. Here, Katz saw, was a version of herself Stein concealed in her autobiographies: a young writer, groping her way past significant self-doubt towards wholly new forms of writing, testing and surpassing the limits of language as she approached the certainty of her vision. And these notes, he believed, provided the keys to understanding *The Making of Americans*, still the most bewildering of all Stein's works. Deep within its pages of character types and schemes, he began – with the help of the notebooks – to excavate the buried remnants of a personal story.

In the *Autobiography*, Stein claimed she had begun *The Making of Americans* in Fiesole in the spring of 1906, while waiting for Picasso to finish her portrait. When she returned to Paris, not only was her portrait finished – establishing her likeness in legend – but she was entirely 'under the spell of the thing she was doing'. The front cover of the 1925 Contact Editions publication had, presumably at Stein's request, listed the work's date as 1906–8. But two facts were clear to Katz from reading the notebooks. First, that her work on the novel had begun much earlier than Stein claimed: he detected the two initial drafts which Stein had abandoned. And second, in contrast to the rosy portrait of the *Autobiography* – an immediately charmed life of trips to Vollard's and glitzy Saturday nights – he gleaned that Stein's first four years in Paris were 'a period of the most relentless despair, surrender of ambition, and psychological disorientation'. Many of the names that appeared regularly in the notebooks, attached to lengthy character assassinations as vociferous as Toklas's – Annette, Bird, Mabel, May – were entirely unfamiliar to Katz. But he was possessed of a detective's energy to follow clues. In order to start to make sense of the jottings contained in the notebooks, Katz decided to contact some of Stein's university friends, whose names he had obtained from the earliest correspondence in the archive.

The first to respond was Mabel Weeks, now an academic administrator at Barnard College, who invited Katz to visit her in Manhattan. She explained that she had met Gertrude Stein at a Radcliffe philosophy club, and was soon fast friends with both Gertrude and Leo, who seemed to her to think 'as one being'. With a raised eyebrow, Weeks told Katz that Gertrude's adulation of her brother was extreme: she claimed to remember Gertrude breezily saying that she would have 'been glad to have an incestuous relation with him . . . if Leo hadn't objected'. Leo, Weeks explained, presided over a circle of younger student disciples, whom he was teaching 'to free themselves of all conventions'; he and Gertrude spent their time plotting their friends' moral reform, having deemed them all 'sickened with dry rot'. At the time, Weeks thought Gertrude had 'no feeling for words at all', nor any discernible appreciation of art. But she was 'immensely interested' in human beings. Weeks had shared lodgings with Gertrude in New York for several months in early 1903, before she moved permanently to Paris; she recalled that their housemates liked Gertrude for her 'vitality, warmth, originality', but despaired of her disregard for cleanliness and domestic order. She had, Weeks remembered, already conceived her determination for renown. '"I'm out for glory! I want fame more than anything else in the world!" she would say. Of course, she always laughed about it, said it jokingly, but there was no question in her mind that it was *gloire* she wanted.'

At this point, Weeks told Katz, Stein was 'crazy about men' – but, she added cattily, 'her appearance was so utterly unattractive to the men whom she liked, that she turned to women'. In particular, she suggested that Stein had been in love with Leon Solomons, the brilliant scholar with whom she collaborated at the Harvard Psychological Laboratory. To some extent, Katz saw the idea corroborated in the notebooks for *The Making of Americans*. 'Make Jane Sandys not really in love with David,' Stein wrote in one note, referring to characters based on herself and Solomons. 'Describe the same amount of being in love that I had.' But

Weeks followed swiftly with another bombshell to Katz, who of course had not read *Q.E.D.*, and knew nothing of the May Bookstaver episode: Stein's relationship with Toklas, she told him knowingly, 'was not Gertrude's first homosexual experience by far'. Weeks had not noticed the depth of Stein's attachment to one particular woman until she met Gertrude and Leo in Siena in the summer of 1903. Gertrude was distraught: she had just bumped into the object of her affections, who was travelling through Italy with another woman. 'The whole time', Weeks confided, 'was given over to Gertrude's miseries on the subject.'

It was Emma Lootz Erving, Katz's second interviewee, who gave Katz that woman's name. Over tea and cake at her home in Hartford, Connecticut, Erving (a retired doctor) told Katz she had met Stein at Johns Hopkins, where they were members of a group of female medical students widely considered 'outrageously unfeminine and déclassé'. During Stein's last year, they had shared a house – cheap quarters in the run-down part of Baltimore, tactfully suggested by Stein since she knew that Erving, who had been disinherited by her father for choosing to study medicine, could afford nothing more luxurious. They had still employed a housekeeper, Lena Lebender, who – Erving told Katz – became the model for Stein's 'Good Anna' in the opening story of *Three Lives*. In the kitchen – where she used to deliver moral lectures to her dogs and pray for Gertrude and Emma, whom she considered irredeemable – Lena would tell them stories about a friend of hers, whom Stein transformed into the protagonist of her second story, confusingly named *The Gentle Lena*. Stein never met this woman, Erving said, but this did not deter her from making her the subject of fiction: referring to *Melanctha* and Stein's limited interactions with Baltimore's African American community, she reminded Katz that Stein 'habitually elaborated on people and circumstances with only the smallest knowledge of them'.

Erving told Katz that Stein had taught her how to live. She was 'so exhilarating and inspiring an example of complete and absolute independence', Erving remembered, 'that following her lead was irresistible.'

She was, however, 'lazy without conscience': she would lie on her back and call for Lena in various tones just to hear her own voice, aware that Lena was out of earshot. She took boxing lessons because 'she thought it would be fun to punch people', and was a fearless companion on the long night-time walks they used to take around Baltimore: when Erving expressed her lingering fear of being attacked, Stein suggested stabbing their assailant with a hairpin and jumping on him from a tree. 'Gertrude's idea of argument was to throw her shoes at you, pitch you down a flight of stairs, trample on you and leave you wordless and for dead,' said Erving. 'All figuratively. But if her assault didn't convince you, it left you permanently shaken and transformed.' Erving spent hours exploring the Steins' collection of Japanese prints, her first exposure to non-Western art; she remembered that despite Stein's disillusionment with her medical studies, most teachers recognised her 'extraordinarily original thinking'. She remembered Leo, too, who she felt 'was never quite fitted to live normally in the world – always unhappy in the tangle of his own thinking'.

In Baltimore, Erving confided, Stein had fallen wildly in love with a fellow student named May Bookstaver. She told Katz how Stein had taken an instant dislike to Mabel Haynes, who considered Bookstaver her own; that Stein had 'conceived a desire to wean her away from Mabel, and the tussle between them over May began'. From the note-books, supplemented by Erving's gleeful indiscretions ('I *knew* you were going to get to her!' she told Katz, who hadn't expected anything of the sort), Katz was able to piece together what happened next: fights and recriminations, Stein's retreat to Europe, a final ultimatum in Italy. May continued to figure in the notebooks: one of the human 'types' Stein identified in her characterological scheme was called May's Group, which she described as an 'emotional sexual aristocrat' with 'the intensest form of emotional sexuality, but . . . not actual sexuality'. Katz could only imagine the battles which had led to this diagnosis.

//

Despite these bombshells, Katz's primary interest lay in Stein's work, and the implications of his discoveries for understanding *The Making of Americans*. From the notebooks, Katz surmised that Stein underwent what he called 'a monumental aesthetic awakening' between 1904 and 1908, having moved to Paris and left her university friends, including Bookstaver, behind. In particular, he was excited to find proof of how meaningfully her immersion in modern art, and her exposure to artists' working processes, had influenced Stein's approach to representation. Friends often recalled that Gertrude remained quiet during the Saturday evening salons, while Leo held court, discoursing on art history to anyone who would listen. But after the artists had left, Katz discovered, she recorded her impressions of them at length, diagnosing what she saw as their successes and their struggles. A major theme in the notebooks was Stein's personal analysis of the Cubist revolution. Here, she connected her work on *The Making of Americans* with the 'ugliness' of Picasso's *Demoiselles d'Avignon* – and positioned the two of them as the nineteenth century's most formidable assassins.

'Our initiative comes from within,' wrote Stein in her notebooks, aligning herself with Matisse and Picasso, 'a propulsion which we don't control, or create.' Picasso was a regular object of her study: streams of scribbled notes – including a first draft of her portrait of him – analysed his art, his temperament, the possible application of his principles to literature. What she admired in his work, and sought to emulate in her writing, was his refusal to use objects 'as a point of departure' to suggest allegories or further meanings. Instead, he wanted to depict their essence, in and of itself. She connected him with Cézanne, 'the great master of the realisation of the object itself', and contrasted the two of them with Matisse, whose work she deemed 'lovely but not significant'. In the notebooks, she devoted a lot of space to wondering whether she and Picasso would remain on the same track artistically, or whether there was anything in his character ('his laziness and his lack of continuity') that would interfere with his commitment to 'object as object', and stymie his art by compromise.

'Pablo is never dragged,' she reassured herself, commending his 'emotional leap and courage': 'he walks in the light and a little ahead of himself like Raphael'. She and Picasso, she concluded, were the ones with 'the kind of originality that is genius'.

After breaking off to write *Three Lives*, Katz discerned, Stein had come back to *The Making of Americans* with new purpose, ready to inflect it with fresh psychological dynamism. Katz's breakthrough came when he was able to pinpoint to the spring of 1908 a moment of euphoria prompted by Stein's reading of Otto Weininger's *Sex and Character*. His interest was sparked by a letter, found in the archive, from Stein's college friend Marion Walker: 'By the way,' Walker had written, 'in an idle moment I read the book on sex which you said exactly embodied your views – the one by the Viennese lunatic.' A rival biographer working alongside Katz in the Yale library – John Malcolm Brinnin – had read the same letter, and assumed Walker was referring to Freud. But from his exclusive access to the notebooks, Katz not only identified Weininger correctly, but was able to appreciate the full significance for Stein of reading his book. As she ripped up her work and began *The Making of Americans* for the final time, stripping out the first draft's narrative for a full-hearted exploration of human character, Katz saw Stein transform from a disoriented 'minor writing talent' into 'one of the major innovators of her century'. The tentative and mannered scenarios of her earliest efforts at fiction had morphed into 'one of the most extraordinarily intense and complex investigations into the fundamental problems of writing itself'. The process charted in the notebooks, Katz argued, brought Stein to the brink of a form and style – that of the early portraits and *Tender Buttons* – which he considered one of modern literature's signature achievements.

From his sleuth-like investigation into the notebooks' biographical context, Katz now knew it was the debilitating uncertainty engendered by Stein's first relationship that pointed her towards the question of how to transcend the implacable gulf between individuals. But he saw, too, how the arrival of Alice B. Toklas in Paris had marked a sharp shift in

Stein's work. Unlike her friends Harriet Levy or Annette Rosenshine, who happily sat for hours with Stein discussing their personal problems, Toklas appeared indifferent to self-exploration. In the notebooks, Stein tracked her confusion at Toklas, whose character appeared to her 'in pieces', in contrast to the others' relative transparency. In large part, her bewilderment registered as invective. Her first entry on Toklas lambasts her 'lack of imagination and appreciation of the significant'; subsequent notes condemn Toklas's 'blind mind', and her character 'made up of every conceivable kind of weakness, crookedness, laziness, stupidity'. But beyond the barrage of insults, Stein's attraction movingly starts to shine through. 'Have to do miracle on another to win her,' she wrote, 'the worldly side of her, the appeal to her admiration of success.' The more time they spent together, the more her desire to 'win' Toklas took hold. 'Work out the drama between Alice and me,' she wrote. 'Me wanting to give but resisting being owned wanting the feeling of generosity but not wanting to be possessed.' In the 'Diagram Book', Stein contemplated the difficulty of assessing subjects who eluded her. 'To know surely in these cases one has to know the complete history and weigh it carefully,' she wrote. 'Almost one has to love them, to find out.'

//

As he completed his transcription of the notebooks, and typed up his notes from his interviews, Katz took stock. He knew he had material that revealed a wholly unknown Stein, and suggested significant new intellectual contexts to her work. Her visceral reaction to meeting Toklas – damning her as a 'prostitute type', the lowest group in Weininger's scheme – hinted at a far more antagonistic start to their relationship than anyone had imagined. Leaving America for Paris – and swapping the misery of yearning for the stimulus of living among artists – had emboldened Stein to take great leaps in her writing, borne out by the successive drafts of *The Making of Americans*, in which Stein developed the project from an intimate family saga to a vision of the whole of humanity, contained within a single structure: the novel. These first years in Paris – from 1904, when she began buying art, to 1912, when she completed 'the long novel' – were, Katz thought, the most crucial in Stein's career, the foundations of everything she did later. The note-books had, first and foremost, identified the people who inspired her early works; revealed the biographical context which lent life to even Stein's most opaque writing. But most meaningfully, they charted a crucial shift in her commitments, both personal and aesthetic: away from narrative fiction and towards a fundamental quest to understand the essence of character, time and perception. The isolation and confusion of her younger years had slowly dissipated as Stein's confidence grew – an emotional and intellectual upheaval Katz attributed in part to Otto Weininger, in part to Cubism, and in part to Alice Toklas.

But much remained unclear. The notebooks were full of names he still didn't recognise, mysterious allusions to events and stories he couldn't place. The awkward dynamic between Stein, Toklas and Annette Rosenshine seemed critical, but he hadn't been able to track Rosenshine down, and neither Weeks nor Erving seemed to know anything about her. There were some dark hints at Stein's schism with her brother, which Katz considered one of the defining moments of this period, but the details remained elusive. And the notebooks stopped just as Stein's relationship with Toklas was deepening, so he could only speculate on Toklas's role in Stein's 'aesthetic revolution'. The only way to find out, he knew, was to speak to her in person.

Yet the attitude his interviewees had displayed towards Toklas worried him. Both Weeks and Erving had kept in touch with Stein, if sporadically. Erving had visited her in Paris in 1929, and was shocked to find Stein 'revoltingly egotistical'. Erving sensed Stein's disappointment that she was not sufficiently impressed by Stein's achievements; when Erving did, weakly, remark on her friend's great success, Stein simply replied, 'Yes, I have become wonderfully famous.' In 1934, reading in the newspapers of the planned American tour, Erving invited Stein and Toklas to stay with her in Hartford (where the first performances of

Four Saints had taken place), but received no reply; she attended a lecture anyway, but Stein was whisked away afterwards and didn't speak to her. 'She cut all her friends in various insulting ways,' Erving complained to Katz. 'She knew she was a fake, and didn't want any of us looking at her.' Erving attributed this change to Toklas. 'After she was started with Alice, Gertrude's one ambition was to be notorious. She succeeded in making a great literary stir because people who met her mistook the woman for the writing, or at least took the writing on faith after they met her.'

Mabel Weeks, too, was stung by Stein's blatant disregard for her old friends, many of whom had devoted significant energies to helping her place early pieces in magazines. She told Katz that Stein 'had reached the point where she could not only bear no opposition to her work, but required the most abject kind of adulation from everyone about her'. Like others, Weeks blamed Toklas for creating a monster in Stein. She had visited Paris with Erving in 1929, and was stunned to witness Toklas's obsequiousness. 'Everything was for Gertrude, and there was no thought for herself,' she told Katz. 'She provided Gertrude with what she was evidently seeking with more and more intensity: adulation morning, noon and night.' (Toklas, as it happened, had recently told Van Vechten that Stein had outgrown her earliest friends and preferred not to see them when she returned to America. Shortly after the First World War, she recalled, Stein had joked that she was ready to put a notice in the *Herald Tribune*: 'The friends of Gertrude Stein whom she has not seen for fifteen years are requested not to make an attempt to renew the acquaintance.')

In particular, Weeks felt Stein should have made time to see May Knoblauch, whose husband Charles had died of a sudden heart attack shortly before Stein and Toklas arrived in America. Because – she told Katz, to his great surprise – Stein had, in fact, stayed in touch with May. It was May Knoblauch who had signed the contract for the Grafton Press to publish *Three Lives*. And it was May Knoblauch who had taken the portraits of Picasso and Matisse to Alfred Stieglitz and persuaded him to publish them in *Camera Work* – the 'huge woman leading a huge Boston bulldog' Stieglitz remembered, in his memoirs, bustling into his office with a bursting portfolio full of yellowing paper under her arm, sternly informing him that every publisher in town had told her there was only one man who might be crazy enough to publish them. Katz did not know about the existence of $Q.E.D.$, and Carl Van Vechten, as yet, knew nothing about May Knoblauch apart from her name. But if they had conferred, they would have begun to work out why exactly Alice Toklas had felt so betrayed when she read the manuscript of $Q.E.D.$ in 1932. The object of Stein's first affections had remained a part of Stein's writing life for some years, encroaching unforgivably – in her eyes – on Toklas's domain.

12 : A SACRED TRUST

While Leon Katz was hard at work on the notebooks, Carl Van Vechten was contemplating the future of Stein's unpublished writings. Despite constantly assuring Toklas that Stein remained as alive as ever in her admirers' hearts, no publisher had come forward to help him discharge his duty to her manuscripts. Toklas was eager to stick with Bennett Cerf of Random House – 'it would be the blackest villainy to think of anyone else' – but Cerf, deterred by the minimal sales of *Selected Writings*, and perhaps still shaken by Stein's late suggestion of the Pétain translation, finally refused to take on any more of her work. Van Vechten confessed that he was not surprised: 'Bennett, I am convinced, was devoted to Baby as a person, but he is very little, if at all, interested in her writing.' Cerf warned that the cost of publishing at the estate's expense would be around $5,000 per volume; mindful of conserving funds for Toklas's personal needs, Van Vechten was determined

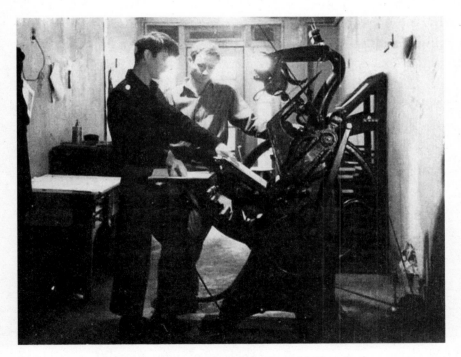

The Banyan Tots: Claude Fredericks and Milton Saul
with Theodora, 1947 (photo: David Leavitt)

to hold off from self-publishing as long as he could. But it was clear that her future lay outside of mainstream commercial publishing: that it would be small, avant-garde outlets who would carry Stein's torch forward. So when he received a letter out of the blue from two young men, a gay couple with their own printing press, saying they had heard he was Stein's literary executor and were wondering whether there was any unpublished material he might allow them to print, Van Vechten was intrigued enough – by their youthful charm, their sexuality and their literary tastes – to suggest he pay a visit to their premises, a rat-infested former butcher's shop in the basement of a tenement on New York's Lower East Side.

Claude Fredericks, 'cute looking and alert', and Milton Saul, 'dark and romantic looking, with a mop of hair over his left eye', had founded the Banyan Press in December 1946 with a battered Golding platen press they had bought for $250 and named Theodora after the Byzantine empress. They were eager to publish serious writers in beautiful, finely crafted editions, and Van Vechten – warming to them immediately – proposed they cut their teeth on a setting of Stein's detective novel *Blood on the Dining-Room Floor*, written during the strange brooding summer after the *Autobiography*, but never published. 'This is so like the things that were always happening to Baby,' he wrote to Toklas: 'two adorable boys falling from heaven at her feet.' At Christmas, they sent a card to Toklas, piling on praises for the novel's richnesses, and reporting on the curious abundance of the letter 'h', thanks largely to the roles of the horticulturalist and the hotel-keeper. 'C van V sent me a photograph of you,' she replied, 'and it's so right that you should be young and as you are. Gertrude Stein would have wanted you to be so – she always said that her work was for the young – that they knew what it was about because they had not gathered the prejudices of middle age.'

Pleased with proceedings, an idea struck Van Vechten. Would not the 'Banyan Tots', as he and Toklas had come to call them, be the ideal solution to the vexed question of what to do about *Q.E.D.*?

After her initial fears, Toklas appeared to have come to terms with the idea of *Q.E.D.* being published, but remained anxious about its possible reception, and was determined that publicity should be minimised, so as not to risk undue interest in the sexuality of its protagonists. If they entrusted the novel to this tiny two-man press, Van Vechten suggested, an edition could be strictly limited, announced discreetly, 'guided to the public gradually on gilded wings and there will be little danger of scandal of any kind'. Toklas agreed that 'just slipping it before the public' seemed an acceptable way forward, and Van Vechten told Saul and Fredericks he had a 'really stupendous' manuscript for them, refusing to reveal the title or author. Saul wrote back that they were 'in a state of complete hysteria', and speculated that it might be a lost Shakespeare play, a pornographic novella by Emily Dickinson, or 'the fifth dimension'.

In March 1948, following the successful printing of 600 copies of *Blood on the Dining-Room Floor* – the book was to be presented in an elegant slipcase, with a splash of bright red staining the title page – Van Vechten invited himself to a celebratory dinner 'wearing my new belt (not chastity) and my new (Puss in) boots'. There, he swore the pair to secrecy and told them of his plan. A few weeks later, they visited his apartment to read the manuscript. Van Vechten took pains to impress upon the Tots the importance of keeping the project 'an utter secret' until a month before publication: 'It is a very delicate matter and if it got gossiped about before it came out and something smutty was said Alice would be furious.' The young men were nonplussed by the cloak-and-dagger – this was hardly erotica – but did their best to assuage Toklas's worries. Fredericks told Toklas the book 'should be considered one of Miss Stein's permanently valuable works': it captured, he wrote tactfully, a sense of deep suffering he had known himself, 'that situation where people hurt each other and hurt themselves without understanding what is happening . . . without wanting to hurt at all'.

A period of illness for Fredericks put publication proceedings temporarily on hold. He and Saul were also preoccupied with renovating a remote house and garden in Pawlet, Vermont, where they planned to live, write and publish books together. Toklas sent radish and basil seeds from Paris; she fondly recalled the days of the Plain Edition, when she and Stein turned their home into a workplace, their relationship an all-encompassing collaboration just like this one. But the idyll was short-lived. In early 1950, Fredericks confessed to Van Vechten that *Q.E.D.* was to be the Banyan Press's final book. That winter, he had fallen madly in love with a young poet named James Merrill, and planned to travel with him to Europe, leaving Saul and the press behind. Van Vechten was shocked. He liked both men immensely, and had considered their relationship rock solid; he had hoped they would continue to publish Stein indefinitely. In particular, he was concerned about the arrangements he had made so carefully for *Q.E.D.* 'It is a book that needs a special publisher and that is why you have it,' he wrote coldly to Fredericks, forbidding him from selling the rights, and instructing him to inform Toklas of the changed situation immediately. Her response was conciliatory: their kindness, she told Fredericks, had made the publication far less of an ordeal than she had expected.

From the start, all involved had agreed that the book would be accompanied by no introduction, which might 'make it seem *historical* rather than *vital* and *present*'. They debated the wording of the press release, which Van Vechten insisted should not offer any suggestions of titillation or personal revelation, and decided simply to print the passage from the *Autobiography* mentioning the 'forgotten first novel', adding that it 'will unquestionably take its place with *Three Lives* and *The Making of Americans* as one of Gertrude Stein's most important works'. Van Vechten felt the title *Q.E.D.* was a little obscure for a modern public, and lit upon *Things as They Are*, a line taken from the final page. More vexing was the question of characters' names, and whether any identifying details would embolden readers to assume autobiographical roots. With Toklas's approval, they changed the name 'Mabel' to 'Sophie', to further mask any connection to Haynes (let alone Weeks or Dodge), and swapped two mentions of Adele's brother – lest anyone imagine a reference to Leo – to a cousin. Toklas, meanwhile, reported from Paris that she had seen Stein's college friend Grace Constant Lounsbery for the first time in fifteen years, and had mustered the courage to ask her whether 'the two women' of the novel were still alive. Mabel Haynes was back in Boston, having lost a husband in each world war, but 'Helen' – May Knoblauch – was dead. Lounsbery 'must never see *Q.E.D.*,' she added, 'for she'd recognise the portraits and the situation and she'd talk. Helen of the book displaced her with Mabel.'

In fact, May Knoblauch was not dead. A small edition of *Things as They Are* was quietly published at the end of April 1950; she died, in New York, on 28 November that same year. Unlike Stein, she had sustained her early feminist activism: after a decade in the suffrage movement – she once made headlines for riding a white charger down Fifth Avenue in a parade – she had campaigned for birth control, working in the office of Margaret Sanger. And she had kept up her literary interests after her success placing Stein's work with publishers: the *Little Review* had printed her translations of poems by Apollinaire, and in April 1921 she had participated in a symposium organised by the New York Surrealist group Société Anonyme, where Mina Loy and Marsden Hartley read from Stein's work and Knoblauch, according to one tantalising report, 'told of her friendship with Miss Stein'. After the death of her husband, she had lived in New York with another old university friend: her life had taken a very different path from Stein's. It's tempting to imagine her reading *Things as They Are* in the last eight months of her life, perhaps recognising her youthful self and cringing at distant passions – but it's just as possible she didn't see the book at all.

'I burn to see the reviews,' wrote Van Vechten to Gallup. But none appeared, and a month after publication, Milton Saul reported forlornly to Toklas that 'No one seems to have read *TATA* yet.' Few bookshops placed orders, and by June Saul had not recouped enough to pay the binder, while the half-dozen friends to whom Toklas, heart in mouth, had sent copies, had neglected to react. 'You will understand how I dreaded hearing anything,' wrote Toklas to Gallup in July 1950; 'now the silence infuriates me – which shows a radical change in the personal barometer but explains nothing in the way readers are taking it.' She took solace in a visit from Fredericks and his new lover James Merrill, who were delighted to meet her and Basket ('the most famous animal I've ever met,' remembered Merrill); she had them to lunch with the writers Paul and Jane Bowles (crab au gratin, veal and homemade strawberry ice cream). Fredericks found Toklas 'fabulously opinionated' on subjects ranging from cooking techniques to Picasso's love life: brittle, unsentimental, and strangely seductive, she reminded him of 'some small species of owl – with great blinking liquid eyes'. Saul, back in Vermont, kept sending copies out to potential reviewers, ruefully wondering if their carefully discreet publication strategy had actually backfired.

Toklas had controlled the release of *Q.E.D.* as closely as she could. With the reassurances of Van Vechten and Gallup, Fredericks and Saul, she had grown used to the idea of the book, and the ardent, agonised young Stein it represented, going out into the world. Letting go of the manuscript, which she had guarded fiercely since 1932, had marked a significant stage in her grief, too. The process had helped her see that her relationship with Stein was inviolable: that no publicity could erode or invalidate the private life they had shared. She wanted Stein to remain a public figure – and had come some way to acknowledging the intrusions this choice would entail for her, now that she had to speak and act on her partner's behalf. Above all, Toklas was resolute in her mission: to celebrate Stein's work, to help her writing find readers, to allow these archival documents to deepen the public's understanding of Stein, as Stein must have hoped they would. By letting *Q.E.D.* be published, Toklas had begun the heart-wrenching task of letting others see Stein at her most vulnerable. But mere months after its subtle launch, another, very different book appeared on shop shelves – one written with a vengeance, which threatened to lure readers' attention away from Stein's writing and back, once again, to an old quarrel Toklas would rather have suppressed.

//

Leo Stein had read of his sister's death in *Newsweek*, at his home in Settignano, near Florence. 'I can't say it touches me,' he wrote to a friend. 'I had lost not only all regard, but all respect for her.' The fact that no one had thought to inform him of her death recalled two previous slights that Leo had never forgotten: first, the dark cloud under which he had left the rue de Fleurus in 1913; second, that the *Autobiography*, written in the voice of the woman who had replaced him in his home, had omitted to mention Leo's name at all. From afar, Leo had followed his sister's career, and complained bitterly about her 'ghastly twaddle' and 'delusions' in letters to friends. Neither had collected art with the same zeal, or eye, after they separated. Since leaving Paris, Leo had earned a living as a critic, moving between Europe and America before settling in Italy and publishing his only book to date, *The ABC of Aesthetics* (1927). The book had taken twenty years to write: Leo's career had been set back by poor health – chronic sleeplessness, progressive deafness, mysterious digestive troubles – which he had attempted to remedy through a long series of raw food diets, systematic purging, extended fasts and long periods of psychoanalysis. It's tempting to suppose that the increased prominence of his sister's voice was another factor in his own prolonged silence. As soon as he heard of her death, Leo began to write, making public his side of their story for the first time.

The book he had drafted at speed over the last months of 1946 – *Appreciation: Painting, Poetry and Prose* – took its cue from the *Autobiography* and didn't mention Gertrude by name. Its first half set out Leo's thoughts on art and aesthetics, while the second part described his own route to 'appreciation', subtly making the case that it was he who possessed a real understanding of art, and who should be credited with the taste-making attributed, in so many obituaries, to his sister.

Yet when his book appeared, in July 1947, reviewers chose to rehash speculation about the causes of the schism instead of engaging with his aesthetic theories. The *New York Herald Tribune* headline referred to the author as 'Leo, Known as Gertrude's Brother, Stein', while another review, leaving Leo out of his own book altogether, was titled 'Gertrude Stein's Feud With Her Brother'. Irritated at newspapers 'looking for scandal', he told his cousin Fred that he would have included more piquant anecdotes if Gertrude hadn't already mistold the most amusing ones.

By this point, Leo was seriously ill. Motivated, now, to set down his feelings about his sister more explicitly, he asked Fred Stein to send him Gertrude's 'assorted works' by registered post. Worried for his cousin's health, Fred enclosed food packages alongside copies of *Paris France* and *Wars I Have Seen*. But just six days after *Appreciation* was published, Leo Stein died. 'A year and two days after Gertrude,' wrote Toklas. 'It was more of a shock to him than he would have cared to acknowledge I'm sure – there had never been a closer tie than theirs – in their years of early devotion – up to about '11.' The book he had planned about himself and Gertrude – the culmination of a lifetime's musings on their differences – never materialised. All that remained of it was a scrap of paper titled 'Last Notes'. 'The differences between Gertrude's character and mine were profound,' Leo wrote there, citing her interest in people and his in ideas. 'Some reviewers speak of a feud or quarrel between us. We never quarrelled except for a momentary spat. We simply differed and went our own ways.'

Gertrude had said little in public about the split. Writing once to her friend Louis Bromfield's wife Mary, she thanked her for being 'such a sweet wife of a genius': 'I once did that,' she added, surely referring to her period living in Leo's shadow, 'and I know how difficult it is for wives of geniuses to be sweet about it.' In Los Angeles, in April 1935, she opened up to David Edstrom, a good friend of hers and Leo's in their early days in Paris, who was interviewing her for the *Los Angeles Times Sunday Magazine*. 'When I wrote that sketch about you, Matisse,

Picasso and others,' she told Edstrom (referring, probably, to her early text *G.M.P.*), 'he began to heckle and abuse me. When I finally got some of my stuff into print he went completely off his head. He became so abusive we had to separate.' Her most explicit comment came in *Everybody's Autobiography*, in a passage where she recalls confused friends asking her, over dinner one night, to explain what had happened between them. 'The only thing about it', she wrote, 'was that it was I who was the genius, there was no reason for it but I was, and he was not there was no reason for it but he was not and that was the beginning of the ending and we always had been together and now we were never at all together. Little by little we never met again.'

After his death, Leo's friends – led by Fred Stein and Mabel Weeks, who had stayed in touch with Leo long after Gertrude stopped replying to her letters – turned their minds to his posthumous reputation, indignant on his behalf that Gertrude's outsized persona dwarfed her brother's intellectual achievements. At first, they encouraged Leo's distraught widow, Nina, to write about her life with 'Steiney'. But she refused, admitting she didn't know how she would tackle 'many things which bother me much having to do with Gertrude's and Leo's affection for one another, things I realised too late'. She didn't elaborate, and died by suicide two years later. Among the papers sent to Yale by the executor of her and Leo's estate – alongside numerous newspaper clippings about Gertrude annotated with Leo's contemptuous asides – was a letter from Leo to Nina written in the 1920s, describing a dream in which he and Gertrude were interrupted, in the course of having sex, by Alice Toklas opening the door.

In lieu of what might have been a richly revealing memoir, *Journey into the Self* appeared in June 1950, less than two months after *Things as They Are*: a collection of Leo's letters, journals and other miscellaneous writings, edited by a group of his friends. In his preface, Edmund Fuller wrote that the volume was designed 'with one goal in mind, that Leo Stein should emerge from these pages as he really was'. But the ulterior motive was apparent from the first pages. Weeks, in a foreword, contrasted Gertrude's magnetism with Leo's shyness, her thirst for glory with his 'thousands of frustrations', while Van Wyck Brooks maintained that 'he was the aesthetic discoverer far more than she was'. It was clear to any reader that this was a book with a score to settle – though both the competitors were dead.

To those who knew the legend of 27 rue de Fleurus only through Gertrude's telling, *Journey into the Self* filled out a less familiar story, detailing Leo's movements after leaving Paris. He had contacted Gertrude a few times after the split. In February 1916, he wrote to her from America (where he was lecturing on art at Bryn Mawr and spending weekends at Mabel Dodge's farm in the Hudson Valley) remonstrating with her for not replying to letters from Nina, who was stuck on her own in Europe, her application for a passport having been denied. He wrote again in December 1919, informing Gertrude that 'the antagonism that had grown up some years ago' had dissipated: a period of psychoanalysis, he told her, had taught him that '"the family romance" as it is called is almost always central in the case of a neurosis, just as you used to get indigestion when we had a dispute'. In June 1922 he told Fred Stein he considered his life 'an utter failure', blaming the 'foundations': he felt that his undisciplined upbringing had left him unmoored, unable to focus on a single course or fulfil his intellectual potential.

After the death of his beloved brother Michael in 1937, Leo had begun to write down his memories of childhood, which appeared here in fragmentary form. It was a way to reclaim a narrative of personal distress his siblings had tended to dismiss. Michael had always been annoyed when Leo described the pain of his early years: 'Nothing could have been happier than our childhood,' he chided his brother briskly. Gertrude claimed to remember Leo's unhappiness, but not that she had shared it. But after the split with Leo, she avoided contact with most of her family. She hadn't kept in touch with her brother Simon, who had died in California in 1913, and exchanged cordial but superficial letters with Bertha only once a decade, until her sister's death in 1924. She showed little interest in Bertha's children, even her namesake Gertrude Stein Raffel, who supposed her aunt 'preferred nephews to nieces'. (Raffel lamented the fact that Gertrude and Leo wrote Bertha off so quickly: she was a 'wonderful person . . . little troubled by the divine discontent that shot Leo and Gertrude out of America'.) In her later writing, Stein distanced herself from her childhood, referring readers back to *The Making of Americans*, as if by writing there the 'story of family living' she had achieved catharsis and didn't have to think about her family of origin again.

The notebooks, Leon Katz had discovered, were more revealing. In one entry, Stein noted the 'disagreeable condition at home after death of mother', and reminded herself to make a father character in *The Making of Americans* 'angry the way pa was with me'. 'It was not easy for them to be free of him,' she wrote in the novel, describing the father pounding on the table at mealtimes, his wife cowering and his children resentful. 'Sometimes he was very angry with them . . . he was the father, they were his children, they must obey him, he was master.' Another disturbing notebook entry describes a father character approaching his daughter one night 'to come and keep him warm', which Gertrude connected with 'my experiences with Uncle Sol'. She doesn't elaborate, and the context is somewhat ambiguous, but the passage hints at sexual abuse. Transgressive daughters and domineering fathers are regular figures in Stein's early work. *The Making of Americans* opens with the overtly patricidal image of an angry man dragging his father along the ground, and depicts several conflicts between fathers and their vengeful children, who seek to assert their place in the world by overpowering those who came before them – a theme, too, in *Melanctha*, whose father is furious at his daughter's 'wandering'. After the split with Leo, her work moved away from the subject of families; she scattered details of childhood through her autobiographies, but always avowed, when pressed, that her recollections were scant. But the notebooks, now combined with Leo's accounts, offered fleeting insights into the torment of their teenage years – memories Gertrude seems to have suppressed, but which Leo never could. It's likely that Leo's domination, at home, reminded her of her father; that writing him out of her life was, for Gertrude, a necessary stage in leaving this part of her past behind.

Leo's memories, honed over decades of introspection, are more sustained than Gertrude's. He describes his father's aggression and constant rule-making, and the succour of a fantasy life – which, he claimed, he never shared with Gertrude, despite their constant companionship. In particular, he recalled the casual antisemitism of his classmates in Oakland, which instilled in him a lifelong sense of otherness: Gertrude, he suggested, was oblivious to his suffering. She remembered her school as pleasantly international, and seems to have felt the weight of tradition more keenly in the home than out of it, at this point: 'Jewish parents do not like children's minds to wander beyond their keeping,' she wrote in a notebook, echoing Melanctha's restless quest and Adele's anxiety in *Q.E.D.* that her taboo sexuality will render her an outcast from her middle-class family. Leo, however, credited Gertrude with no such depth of thought or feeling – on matters personal or artistic. Also included in *Journey into the Self* were facsimiles of his supercilious annotations to *Paris France*. Where Gertrude describes her realisation that a painting is always a flat surface – an insight, to her, with profound implications, proving the inherent falsity of representational art – Leo sneered, 'What a clever young person.'

'He must have had a great complex about Baby', Van Vechten wrote to Toklas, 'as he mentions her on nearly every page.' Toklas, by return of post, asked him never to broach the subject of Leo again. Her own feelings towards Leo, Van Vechten reflected, remained mysterious. She had lived with him and Gertrude for three years, had clearly witnessed the schism, but her role in it – despite Leo's griping – had never been fully explained. *Journey into the Self* had detailed the split from Leo's perspective – but Toklas was determined not to rise to its provocation. John Malcolm Brinnin, still working on his putative Stein biography, offered to 'mount the defence of Gertrude against the attack of Leo', but Toklas sternly informed him the subject was of no interest: if he had to write about Gertrude, she reiterated, Brinnin should focus purely on her work. She did, of course, have much more to say on Leo – but, for now, she held back. Gertrude, she recalled, had once met a man who told her he had recently seen her brother in Florence. 'No,' Stein had replied, 'I only have one brother and he lives in California.' When the man left, Toklas asked her why she had denied Leo's existence. 'Oh Leo she answered. I have forgotten him – for years.' Toklas told a friend she had read *Journey into the Self* 'to purge myself of him as Gertrude did in fourteen. Now her complete forgetfulness of him is working for me too.'

//

Toklas was struggling with her finances. Much of 1949 had been taken up with combating the 'cold aggression' she had begun to face from Gertrude's nephew Allan Stein, who had started to pay closer attention to his inheritance. Now in his late fifties, Allan had grown up in the midst of the Parisian art world – Picasso had painted his portrait at eleven – but he had struggled, as an adult, to forge his own identity, free of his parents' bohemian milieu. Stein and Toklas had known Allan all his life: when Michael was impatient with him as a child, Gertrude would chide her brother, reminding him how kind he had always been to her and Leo. They had missed his wedding, in 1939, to avoid seeing Leo and Nina, but they were close enough that Toklas had called him to the hospital when Stein was dying. His oldest son, Daniel, from his brief first marriage to a dancer, had plunged into debts so severe that Allan's mother, Sarah Stein, had sold all her Matisses to pay them off; now, Allan was struggling to provide for his second wife, Roubina, and their two young children, and was beginning to show interest in the cache of invaluable paintings that were blocked from his possession by his late aunt's inconvenient elderly companion.

In January 1949, Roubina had told Toklas that Allan was gravely ill; the following month, she reported that they were separating. Roubina threw herself on an unwilling Toklas for sympathy and advice – 'Forced to listen for hours,' she told Van Vechten, 'I told her to go to a good lawyer.' To hold her complaints at bay, Toklas agreed to act as a witness against Allan in the subsequent divorce trial – a decision which dissolved any possibility of co-operation between them on matters relating to the Stein estate. By the end of the year, Allan – needing money fast – had contacted his lawyer wanting to sell one of Stein's paintings, which he was not legally permitted to do without Toklas's consent, since their capital was protected first for the publication of Stein's manuscripts. Toklas, spooked, instructed her housekeeper, Gabrielle, that Allan was not to be admitted to the apartment at any time, and that in the event of Toklas's sudden death a lawyer must be summoned to seal the flat immediately. Lest Allan somehow make his way into the fortress, she had each paint-ing stamped on the back of the canvas 'From the Estate of Gertrude Stein'. But in January 1950, Roubina telephoned to let her know that Allan had died, their divorce incomplete.

Toklas felt faintly triumphant to have outlived Allan. But Gallup and Van Vechten were deeply concerned about her vulnerable financial position – and wondered, between themselves, why Stein had made her will so complicated. 'I think Baby should have left everything to Alice without strings', wrote Van Vechten to Gallup, 'and I HATE her having difficulties.' The only way to protect her interests, they agreed, was to begin the publication programme as quickly as they could, and at minimal cost to the estate. With this in mind, Gallup approached Yale University Press with a frank proposal. Given Yale's long-standing association with Stein through her archive, would the press consider taking on the publication of Gertrude Stein's complete unpublished work, with any financial losses incurred to be compensated promptly by the Stein estate? There was some pushback within the press – one editor complained that 'publishing Stein was not consistent with the dignity of Yale' – but in October 1950, six months after *Things as They Are* appeared, it was confirmed that Yale would commit to publishing eight volumes over as many years. The press proposed that Van Vechten be appointed series editor, with an advisory committee composed of Gallup, the critic Donald Sutherland and Stein's old friend Thornton Wilder. Over cocktails, Gallup broke the good news to Van Vechten, who dispatched it to Paris via telegram: 'Yale Press accepts but no details yet love and kisses and glory be – Carlo.'

To Toklas, the news came first as a staggering relief. But soon, she was overcome by joy at 'what this would have meant to Baby'. She told Milton Saul that the news 'has the overpowering effect of a miracle lately beheld – everything seems to be bathed in the light of the vision'. To other friends, she described it as 'a dream realised': 'It is so good that it doesn't seem possibly true.' Van Vechten was initially keen that 'EVERYTHING should be published as soon as possible in as few volumes as possible', but Gallup gently persuaded him that it would be best to spread the material over several years, in order to keep Stein's name in front of the public for a longer period. On 1 December 1950, the two men met in New York to make a tentative division of the pieces into eight volumes. Fearing that a strictly chronological approach would 'give the undertaking rather too much of the atmosphere of an inquest', they decided to begin with a book of early portraits. Its title piece, 'Two: Gertrude Stein and Her Brother', written around the time of the schism with Leo, described a gradual shift in relations between three characters each 'very different the one from the other of them', identifiable – if very obliquely – as Gertrude, Leo and Alice. Later volumes would be arranged around specific longer works – *Mrs Reynolds*, *A Novel of Thank You*, *Stanzas in Meditation* – while shorter portraits, poems and plays would be arranged at their discretion. The Yale Edition of the Unpublished Writings of Gertrude Stein was launched.

The press suggested that each volume be prefaced with an introduction by a prominent friend of Stein's, or someone familiar with her work. For the first book, there was an obvious choice to 'start the series off with a bang': Alice B. Toklas herself. The suggestion made Van Vechten's heart sink: he knew exactly how Toklas would react. Shortly after Stein's death, he had written to implore her to write a memoir of

Carl Van Vechten and Alice B. Toklas at
Chartres, 1949 (photo: John Breon)

her own. 'In every letter you write something about Baby I never heard
before,' he had told her. 'You knew her so well; you write it so well. You
are the ONLY one to write about her and you MUST.' But to Gallup,
who had backed up Van Vechten's pleas, Toklas feigned pure bemusement, echoing her insistence that biographers could learn nothing from
her: 'It seems so strange that you should think I could possibly write
anything about Gertrude that would add to what she so completely
so perfectly said herself.' To Van Vechten, whom she knew better, she
gave a little more insight into the paralysing effects of her grief. If the
prospect of writing about Stein crossed her mind, she told him, 'I find
myself in the armchair with my head all swimming.' Whenever he
pressed the question, she shut the prospect down more firmly: 'I can't

tell the casual stranger that I loved Baby and that is all I seem to know now – that I love her and that she is gone.'

Now, under pressure, Van Vechten tried to coax her again: laying on the guilt trip, he suggested that Stein would surely implore her to write a preface if the publication depended on it. Toklas remained 'aghast' at the suggestion that she speak on Stein's behalf, abandoning half a century's habit of making herself invisible. 'The atmosphere of Baby's home', she protested, 'was a private matter . . . if my existence had ever made the slightest difference to her work it was of nothing to equal the effect for example of landscape.' But, reluctantly, she capitulated. 'It is with the sense of Baby's horror of being left in my hands for anything but personal devotion that I say yes to you with a conviction that I am betraying Baby,' she wrote to Van Vechten. 'It will be going against the only moral principle that means anything to me. But if Yale Press is asking it and you insist – what can be managed will or rather must be done for publication is the most important thing left in the world.'

Van Vechten, satisfied, returned to his own work, hoping for no more interruptions. But Toklas was driven into a spiral of panic. The idea of writing the preface had become 'a torment beyond bearing'. Resolute, she wrote to Thornton Wilder, telling him she was in a 'great trouble'. She had accepted the commission, she explained, 'blinded with fear rage and tears' and wanting to please Van Vechten, but knew for certain that Stein would have 'despised and hated the idea'. 'Can you get me out of this hateful thing?' she begged him.

Toklas had not been in touch with Wilder for some time. She and Stein had not heard from him since he joined the army midway through the war, and he hadn't sent condolences to Toklas for several months after Stein's death, eventually explaining that he had been overwhelmed with work and his mother's illness – a delay she had never forgiven. An additional awkwardness had soured their relationship. In *Everybody's Autobiography*, Stein had written that she intended to appoint Wilder as her literary executor. But when he asked Toklas, belatedly, if that responsibility was still his, she coldly replied that the honour had gone to Van Vechten. She knew that Wilder would feel stung to be demoted: she told Gallup that he and Van Vechten had always felt 'a natural antipathy – a natural *mépris* – a jealousy concerning Gertrude'. Stein was not averse to setting her enthusiasts against one another: when asking Wilder for his opinion on a manuscript, she would slyly mention that Van Vechten had 'read it through in one sitting having intended only to look at it and that always does touch an author'. The two were well aware that they were rivals: 'Don't you go calling TW a Woojums!' wrote Van Vechten to Stein in 1934. 'I will bite him!' Now, Wilder was only too glad of the chance to regain some of the favour he had lost – and to mount a challenge to Van Vechten's authority. Within days, he cabled Toklas that she could consider herself absolved: he had telephoned Gallup, who had promised to explain the situation to Van Vechten.

Van Vechten was irritated to lose his preface, and to be played against Wilder like this, though he made efforts to curb his annoyance. But the vehemence with which she had reacted made him think again about the Toklas–Stein relationship. 'Gertrude', he told Gallup, 'invariably told Alice that she could not write. Even a cookbook. When Alice suggested this she ridiculed and tortured her to such an extent that Alice never even wrote a long letter during Gertrude's lifetime.' On one occasion, he recalled, Toklas was so hurt at a barrage of insults that she refused to speak to Stein for several days. 'The result of all this is that Alice is overcome by fear (the most dangerous emotion, because it is treacherous and devious in its effects) at the very idea of touching pen to paper when the subject is GERTRUDE.' The refusal, he considered, was all the more serious because of the book's likely lack of popular appeal. 'She knows she may even be throwing Gertrude to the winds, but she actually *can't* do it.'

With the printing deadline fast approaching, Van Vechten was under pressure to find someone to step in and write the preface to the first volume of Stein's unpublished writings – someone close to Stein, with enough name-recognition to give the book a chance at selling. Eventually Virgil Thomson suggested Janet Flanner, whose weekly column 'A Letter from Paris' had endeared her to *New Yorker* readers since 1925. Flanner – who divided her time between female lovers in Rome and Paris – was one of the only visitors to the salon who cultivated an independent friendship with Toklas: she retained fond memories of the 'ladies' table', where Toklas would mete out gossip as slowly and deliberately 'as if she were detailing the recipe for a fruitcake'. She agreed to write the preface, on condition that Toklas would tell her what to say. Toklas consented to sit for an interview, though warned Flanner she 'would learn nothing from me concerning Gertrude's private life – habits – or tastes'. The women spent six hours together on 3 February 1951, talking about the early portraits. Most of them were dated vaguely (1908–12), but Toklas firmly told Flanner that the first one was 'Ada' – Stein's portrait of Toklas. 'She was like one of the fates, sitting & spinning as she talked to me,' Flanner reported to Van Vechten. 'She said it made her happy to have talked so long of such a happy time as then. The time when G was alive.' Flanner tried to persuade Toklas to allow her to transcribe her comments, edit them and publish them under Toklas's name, but Toklas, to her amusement, was 'adamant'. When Van Vechten wrote to thank her for the preface, Flanner replied she was glad to have been useful – to Stein, to Toklas, and to him. 'It was a pleasure doing the interviews with Alice, a real joy to hear and see her delicate wise thoughtful mind and memory with full function like the inside of a watch, still keeping Gertrude's time.'

//

Toklas's resistance to writing the Yale introduction reflected her lingering desire to stay in the shadows. But at the very same time as she was negotiating with Van Vechten, other events showed just how decisively she could act when she felt her exertions were required. With the Yale Edition finally in the works, Toklas turned her attention to a clandestine matter, unbeknownst to Van Vechten and Gallup. Indicted for his war crimes, Bernard Faÿ had spent the last year of Stein's life in jail. Three days after Stein's funeral, Toklas had written to a friend, lamenting that Faÿ's trial had been postponed so many times, and entreating her to intercede with an influential acquaintance who might be able to get him moved to a nursing home. His imprisonment, Toklas confided, had 'weighed very heavily upon Gertrude's mind' in her final days. 'Gertrude completely disagreed with his political ideas,' she insisted, but 'she never had any doubt as to his complete loyalty to his friends and to his two countries.' Faÿ was, Toklas went on, 'anti-mason – anti-communist . . . a friend of Marshal Pétain – *not* of Vichy or heaven forbid the Germans. If he accepted the directorship of the National Library it was to save its treasures from German spoliation – which he did.' At his trial, which had finally begun in December 1946 (six months after Stein's death), Faÿ had denied all the charges against him. He protested that he had aimed only to defend French culture, citing the case of Stein's art collection, which he now claimed to have protected throughout the war, not just on that one occasion in July 1944 when the Gestapo had tried to seize it. He alleged that he had given information to the Resistance from as early as 1941, and had tried to persuade Pétain to take a stronger stand against the Germans: he branded the prosecution's case 'an outrageous falsehood'. The court heard evidence from Faÿ's friend Denise Aimé-Azam, who claimed that when she had been forced to wear the yellow star identifying herself as Jewish, he had defiantly taken walks with her around Paris. But the jury dismissed his account. On 17 December 1946, he was sentenced to a life of hard labour, and sent to a prison hospital on the Île de Ré.

Now that Stein was powerless to help him, Toklas pledged to take up Faÿ's cause herself. Following the guilty verdict, Toklas told a friend she was 'trying every means to have him pardoned'. She tracked his situation closely, in communication with a group of supporters, including their mutual friend Jean Cocteau, who were seeking a retrial or at least improved prison conditions for Faÿ. She kept this work quiet: she knew that many of her friends were highly sceptical of his claims to innocence. But to her, this work was 'a sacred trust'. Did Toklas truly believe, even after the trial (which presented evidence of his collaboration which Stein, of course, never saw), that his actions had been misconstrued? Toklas's own politics remained mysterious: though she had shared every moment of Stein's war experiences, she spoke of Faÿ – and of Pétain – only by explaining Stein's opinions of them. To her, freeing Faÿ represented a mission on a par with securing the publication of the manuscripts: these two tasks were entwined, in her mind, as Gertrude's last wishes. It was her duty, to Stein, to carry them out – notwithstanding the personal cost.

In August 1950, Faÿ had been moved to Fontevraud in Angers, one of the harshest prisons in France, where his health deteriorated so badly that he was transferred to hospital. On 30 September 1951 – eleven days after the publication of the first Yale volume – he escaped. The previous day, a blonde woman had been spotted lurking in an alleyway under Faÿ's window, dressed in a blue cape with Red Cross insignia. A fellow patient later reported seeing the woman leading an elderly man, disguised in a cassock, through the hospital side-gates, and bundling him into a waiting car. The arrangements for the escape had been made by Denise Aimé-Azam. But the funds came from none other than Alice B. Toklas. Without telling Picasso's gallerist Daniel-Henry Kahnweiler – who should have overseen all sales, but who hated Faÿ and might have scuppered the deal if he had known where the proceeds were going – she had quietly sold two Picasso works, and passed the money to Aimé-Azam.

Did Stein's influence, even in death, compel her actions? Or would Stein have been surprised – even shocked – at Toklas's daring? Donald Sutherland – the scholar whose study of Stein's work was published, also by Yale, that same month – was one of Toklas's closest confidants while the escape was being planned. He later recalled that the mission had been intricate, and that Toklas had grown increasingly paranoid – she was convinced that her elderly housekeeper was informing the police about her 'intrigues against the Republic'. Sutherland claimed Toklas was actually arrested after the escape, and that she insisted on being taken for questioning in a taxi, not a police car, so her neighbours wouldn't talk. Other friends dismissed the idea that Toklas was ever interrogated, though several of her co-conspirators were. In any case, Faÿ was delivered to Switzerland, where he lived under an assumed name, teaching French history at the local university. He was officially pardoned by the French president in 1959. The attendant publicity was double-edged: his students, who had not previously known about his past, began to question why their education had been entrusted to some-one convicted of such reprehensible activity during the war. Faÿ responded to his critics in his 1961 autobiography – now, for the first time, claiming he had protected Jews, including Stein and Toklas, throughout the war.

'The great puzzle', wrote Sutherland, 'was why Alice was so complete in his cause that she put herself in danger, on top of risking the alien-ation of many old friends.' To most of those friends, the answer was clear: loyalty. In part, loyalty to Faÿ himself, in gratitude for his protec-tion of the art collection and, possibly, of Stein and Toklas themselves. But above all, loyalty to Stein, whose wishes she now felt satisfied were fulfilled. Holding a copy of the first Yale book that September, Toklas told Gallup, felt unreal: turning its pages and reading 'the portraits of nearly forty years ago that I haven't seen for many years'. But she was privately reflecting on her other, simultaneous triumph – and imagin-ing, perhaps, Stein's pleasure and pride.

//

Meanwhile, in Vermont, Milton Saul – now in sole charge of the Banyan Press – continued to watch, with decreasing optimism, for reviews of *Things as They Are*. Nearly eighteen months after the book's

publication, his patience was finally rewarded. On 15 September 1951 –
four days before the first Yale volume was published; two weeks before
Faÿ's escape – *Things as They Are* was reviewed in the *New Yorker* by
the influential critic Edmund Wilson, who called the book 'a production of some literary merit and of much psychological interest'. Wilson's
review was not entirely positive – having read all Stein's work chronologically, he considered it marred by a 'vagueness that began to blur it
from about 1910 on'. But he discussed the novel's sexual dynamics in
detail: not with an eye to sensation, but simply to read the book on its
own terms. *Things as They Are*, Wilson wrote, had made him wonder
whether the opacity of Stein's later work was 'due to a need imposed by
the problem of writing about relationships between women of a kind
that the standards of that era would not have allowed her to describe
more explicitly'. The novel, he wrote, 'is a story of the tangled relations
of three Lesbian American girls of the early nineteen-hundreds, told
with complete candor and an astonishing lack of self-consciousness'. He
warned readers not to expect anything explicit, like the sexological case
studies of Havelock Ellis, which had been published around the same
time the novel was written: despite Toklas's worries, the novel contained
'nothing in the least scandalous (unless the subject itself be considered
so)'. Yet he ended his review on a sympathetic note of regret for Stein,
whose 'great iceberg of megalomania', he wrote, 'must have been forming in an emotional solitude'.

The review marked the first time that Stein's work had been discussed in the context of her sexuality. Wilson's speculation that her
dissociative use of language arose from her inability to speak fundamental truths about herself aloud was not a new theory, Van Vechten
told Gallup: 'I have hinted at it more than once, even in her presence, and it was one of Leo's pet ideas tho' I think he never printed
it.' But Wilson's casual mention of the word 'lesbian' marked a turning point in the book's – and Stein's – reception. The Banyan Press
started receiving more than twenty orders a day: 'Orders arrived
from practically every girls' college in the country,' reported Saul

to Fredericks, 'and as Carlo says, I have an unparalleled mailing list of Lesbians by now.' On 1 October – just as Bernard Faÿ crossed the border to his Swiss sanctuary – Van Vechten told Toklas that Saul was spending entire days sending out copies; he noted too that 'Metro-Goldwyn is even talking of a movie, changing one of the women to a man!' Saul and Van Vechten noted to their pleasant surprise that Toklas was 'not displeased with the Wilson review. She takes the broad viewpoint that it will stimulate interest in other writings.' By the end of the year, the edition was officially sold out – and would not, Van Vechten decided, be reprinted.

//

The next few months were quieter for Toklas, exhausted from her efforts. But she was gratified to see Stein's work beginning to take on a life of its own – not only in readers' responses to her newly published texts, but also in performance. Stein's last opera, *The Mother of Us All*, had premiered at Columbia University in May 1947, and was broadcast live on the radio; Van Vechten hosted an afterparty for Virgil Thomson and the cast, where guests were served New Orleans gumbo. The composer Leonard Bernstein, reviewing the libretto in the *New York Times*, suggested that Stein had 'come closer than any other writer except Joyce to the medium of music'; praising her collaboration with Thomson, he concluded that Stein's most lasting legacy might be to other artists. In December 1951, his point was underlined by a spectacular production of Stein's 1938 play *Doctor Faustus Lights the Lights*, mounted at New York's Cherry Lane Theatre by a collaborative anarchist company called the Living Theatre. Its directors, a young couple named Julian Beck and Judith Malina – friends of Claude Fredericks, they were among the first readers of *Things as They Are* – railed against the 'sham' of conventional theatre: the refined banality of Hollywood, the 'sugary realism' of profit-driven Broadway. They saw the theatre as an ideal place to model an ethical

Remy Charlip as 'Viper' in the Living Theatre's *Doctor Faustus Lights the Lights*, Cherry Lane Theatre, 7 December 1951

revolution, to expose the hypocrisies of capitalist society and create an experience that would leave both audience and actors fundamentally changed. In their search for a way to express real feeling, to 'make life on the stage', they had turned to Stein's writing on drama – which they took as a 'manifesto' – and to her plays. 'How can you have a lively civilisation if the language is outmoded and no longer says what anyone can possibly want to mean?' wrote Beck. 'How can you enlarge the limits of consciousness if language atrophies?' Malina, in her diary, answered the question: 'Gertrude Stein has clues,' she wrote. 'Work on this!'

Stein's take on the Faust myth had never been staged; the text had only recently appeared in a volume titled *Last Operas and Plays*, which Van Vechten had persuaded the publisher Liveright to issue in 1949. Its instant adoption by a cutting-edge theatre company – young people, coming fresh to Stein's work – provided neat proof of the value of the posthumous publication programme. A remorseful, isolated Faustus remonstrates with the demon Mephisto, who taught him to invent the electric light – rendering him immortal, but destined to live unhappily in the artificial glare of eternal neon. The central tension lies between Faustus and the compound figure 'Marguerite Ida and Helena Annabel', an enigmatically shifting character who seeks Faustus's help after a viper's bite. While Faustus must simply dream of death, aware that he has forsaken everything that gives life meaning, she has a quest, the chance of a sexual awakening, and hope for renewal. Stein's vision of a godless and hostile world, where humanity is responsible for its own damnation, resonated deeply with Beck and Malina. Faustus's exchange of his humanity for technological advancement recalled the existential threat of the hydrogen bomb, which they protested on the streets daily amid the escalation of armaments for the war in Korea. 'The over-simple words breaking the language to smithereens,' wrote Malina. 'The ideas, too, both dark and radiant.'

Van Vechten was entranced by the performance. The company – including actors portraying a writhing serpent and a barking dog – deftly evoked a hellish vision of instability through a haunting soundscape (written especially for piano and oboe) and a set which, according to the *New York Times*, suggested 'a gigantic, angry pin-ball machine'. The poet John Ashbery, a friend of Beck and Malina, called it 'one of the most beautiful things I've ever seen on the stage'. Van Vechten reported to Toklas that the audience had 'acted as if they were seeing Gielgud in *Hamlet*', and invited Malina to his apartment so he could photograph her in costume. Malina enjoyed his conversation, as they looked over the Central Park skyline by twilight, but felt he 'talks of Gertrude assuming that she is much less understood than she is'. 'She freed the theatre in every dimension,' Malina wrote later. 'She simply plowed everything under and allowed us a wide field to experiment with new forms. And the seeds she planted have continued to grow.'

Toklas was delighted by the reports, though disappointed when the Living Theatre repeatedly failed to pay their royalties – the theatre was eventually shut down by the fire inspector (who was pursued down the street by a troupe of actors wielding bamboo spears), and Beck and Malina were briefly imprisoned for tax arrears. But the following May, 1952, Toklas was able to attend a performance of *Four Saints in Three Acts* in Paris, as part of a festival called Masterpieces of the Twentieth Century. Mounted under the auspices of the Congress for Cultural Freedom, which had been established two years earlier to organise anti-communist action among Western intellectuals, the festival's aim was to showcase work made possible by the climate of freedom in which the artists worked. Among the highlights were a production of Stravinsky's *Rite of Spring* (thirty-nine years after Stein, Toklas and Van Vechten attended its second night), a display of abstract paintings sent by New York's Museum of Modern Art, and the reprisal of *Four Saints*, again with an all-black cast. If the casting choice was designed to counter the widespread notion that America was a racist country, the celebration of Stein's joyfully unconventional libretto was evidently intended to draw a pertinent contrast with Socialist Realism, the Soviet Union's official artistic style. The festival was broadcast to countries behind the Iron Curtain through Radio Free Europe. Many on the French Left were suspicious of the venture, and were not surprised to discover, years later, that it had been covertly funded by the CIA. It was ironic that, in the space of six months, Stein's work had been performed by groups repre-senting both anarchist counterculture and American hegemony. But to Toklas, who served tea, cake and punch to the 'charming' *Four Saints* singers at 5 rue Christine, both productions were testament to her efforts to keep Stein's work alive, and get it into the hands of readers, who would interpret it in their own ways.

The events of the past few years – the publication of *Things as They Are*, the launch of the Yale Edition, the slowly mounting critical

appraisal of Stein through reviews, book-length studies, and now performances – had heartened Toklas, notwithstanding Leo Stein's final
sting. Crucially, the belated interest in *Things as They Are* had marked a
shift in Stein's reception towards a more nuanced understanding of her
identity – not as a distraction from her work, but as an integral aspect
of it. During the debate over the love notes five years earlier, Gallup had
made the case that Stein's life and work were inseparable: that Toklas's
policy of minimising the significance of personal relationships – Leo,
May Bookstaver, their own intimacy – actually limited the scope of
Stein's writing, which always drew its primary inspiration from daily life
and engaged, in myriad subtle ways, with the genre of autobiography.
The opening of the archive had brought Stein's process into focus. But
– as Leon Katz had found out with his study of the notebooks – it had
also engendered questions, rooted in those early years when Gertrude,
Leo and Alice shared 27 rue de Fleurus. Katz had concluded that finishing *The Making of Americans*, and setting up home without Leo, formed
the pivotal moment in Stein's life and work – but only Toklas could
reveal how those years had unfolded. Now, six years after Stein's death,
it was time for a fresh attempt to persuade her to talk.

//

'WHO do you think is here, RIGHT NOW??????' Gallup wrote
to Van Vechten on 27 October 1952. 'LEON KATZ, who leaves for
Europe – for a year – on Wednesday!' Katz had not been seen at the
library since 1948, and the men had assumed he had given up his Stein
work. In fact, Katz had been busily transcribing and annotating the
notebooks over the past four years, in spare moments from his teaching job, and had a detailed chronology of the writing of *The Making
of Americans* almost complete, tracking Stein's progress on the novel
month by month over a decade. Gallup wrote to Toklas to warn her
about the impending arrival of an inquisitive Stein scholar on European
shores. 'Katz is the young man, you remember, who was working on

the notebooks for *The Making of Americans* and the early period in general . . . I hope you will have time to see him.'

Earlier that year, Katz had been awarded a grant from the Ford Foundation to visit Paris for the purpose of research on Gertrude Stein's development as a writer. Daunted, but knowing this was an irresistible opportunity, he wrote directly to Toklas for the first time. Would she, he asked, read through Stein's early notebooks with him, providing explanations for the more recondite names, dates and allusions, and augmenting Stein's anecdotes with any complementary recollections of her own? It was an audacious request, given Toklas's known antipathy to biographers, but Toklas agreed. 'You may take it for granted', she told Katz, 'that anything I can possibly do to help you will be done but you must not suppose that that can be of any great assistance.' Stein had never shown her these notebooks, and she was intrigued – if apprehensive – to discover what lay within. 'Nothing but really nothing could have stopped me,' she told Sutherland. Moreover, she was charmed by the energy of the young man who wrote to her so winningly. At a lacklustre moment, the prospect of revisiting her past stirred in Toklas a twinge of rare excitement. She invited him over to the rue Christine the following Tuesday, at half past eight.

13 : *CHRONIQUE SCANDALEUSE*

L eon Katz rang the bell at 5 rue Christine at the appointed hour, on 11 November 1952. As he waited, Katz listened to muffled barks and frantic clattering from within the apartment, its exterior still streaked with soot from the war years. After a long pause, the door slid open and a 'little gnome of a woman' peered out at him, her face creased with suspicion. Toklas had permanently closed the dining room rather than sell off any paintings to pay for heating ('We ate Madame Cézanne but I don't want – figuratively – to burn a Picasso'). Now, she spent her days huddled with Basket by a single electric radiator, chain-smoking cigarettes. A lone bulb hung precariously from the ceiling, its light occasionally catching the eyes of the portraits on the wall, which gazed sternly down at their shabby custodian from the crumbling plaster.

The meeting got off to an inauspicious start when Basket – blind and arthritic – escaped on to the roof, promptly followed by Toklas, who climbed out of the window into the rain to rescue him. Back in her seat, bedraggled and nervous, Katz recalled that Toklas 'made her dislike of being interviewed about Stein immediately and abundantly clear'. Before they met, she had warned him that she considered most scholars thoroughly misguided. The rival biographer John Malcolm Brinnin had visited her two years earlier, and put her off immediately by being 'visibly moved to be in Baby's home'. Brinnin had lost all her respect, she told Katz, when he asked her first about Guillaume Apollinaire's influence on Stein, which she considered 'nil, absolutely nil', then about Stein's relationship with Ernest Hemingway, whom Toklas hated with a vengeance ('I made Gertrude get rid of him,' she told Sutherland). Determined to thwart his book, she had informed Brinnin she would take legal action if her own name was mentioned outside the context of her role as editor of the Plain Edition. ('What would legal action mean?' she asked Van Vechten. 'It sounded harsh and menacing when it flowed forth.') When Katz mildly protested his admiration for Hemingway, he felt the heat of the Toklas temper: '*The Old Man and the Sea* has the EMPTIEST sea in all of LITERATURE,' she shouted in fury.

But Toklas's interest was piqued by this first encounter, and she invited Katz to return the next day. As soon as Katz brought out his transcriptions of the notebooks, some 400 typed pages, Toklas was astonished to see that they were 'more voluminous than I had any idea of'. She had remembered Stein, in the early years, wearing a purse on a belt containing a pencil, loose coins, and one of these little notebooks; she had seen Stein extract the notebook when a thought came to her, and jot down a word or two – though never, she thought, a full sentence. But the notes Katz produced, she told Gallup, were 'about 80 per cent fuller than I knew'. As Katz began to read them aloud, Toklas's fascination – and her surprise – only deepened. She told Sutherland that Stein's comments on people 'could be of a frankness that makes indiscretion appear pale'. The most pressing question, to her mind, was what Stein had intended to happen to the notebooks. Had she meant to send them to Yale? Did she consider them 'work' to be published? They had been put away in a cabinet for more than thirty years, and Toklas was sure

Leon Katz, *c.*1950s

Stein had never reread them ('she had forgotten them as she had the *Q.E.D.* . . . as she had Leo'). In any case, she told Gallup, 'The notes are wonderful beyond all imagining – they are more important than any one of the manuscripts.'

Through the 'dark dreary dismal and damp' Paris winter, they sat side by side in the dark room ('emptier than ever', Toklas wrote, since the Picasso portrait had left), Toklas shivering in a horsehair chair made to measure in London, Katz – not daring to take Stein's matching seat – on the sofa. Between November 1952 and February 1953, Katz and Toklas met several times a week from around five until midnight, with a short interruption at eight when Toklas went to the kitchen and returned with bowls of hot soup. Amid a cloud of smoke – his Chesterfields, hers Pall Mall – they went through the notebooks 'line by line, word by word', Katz reading passages aloud and pressing Toklas to remember details of people, places, events and impressions. Toklas, Katz recalled, set the rules for their collaboration: 'If I knew to ask, she would tell everything, if I didn't, *tant pis*: her hooded look and her silent tongue would reveal nothing.' She would not hesitate to berate him when he asked a question she considered 'stupid' – which, he soon deduced, was often code for one she did not want to answer. At other times, he caught a glimmer of amusement as she paused, then relented: 'Katz, you're a detective.'

She told Donald Sutherland that Katz was 'sensitive with a sleuth-like gift', and that his subtle enquiries had led her into 'deep water'. He 'treats the least slip as a criminal offence,' she wrote, 'and has his little facts all in the front of his mind'. To other friends, she described Katz as 'extremely intelligent and sympathetic' and the work they were doing 'fascinating'. She remained on her guard towards Katz's more intimate questions – she told Sutherland that 'one answered by refusing to answer very much like an FBI investigation' – but eventually, she admitted, 'my answers and asides (!) became of an indiscretion that will please you . . . My contribution makes it a *chronique scandaleuse*.' Katz knew he was succeeding when, after a particularly salacious anecdote involving an artist friend's affairs with the poet Guillaume Apollinaire and the politician Marcellin Berthelot, Toklas tossed her pillow into the air and cackled, 'Oh, I wish I could be alive to see Marie Laurencin's face when she reads *that*!'

In her previous encounters with biographers, and in her dealings with the archive, Toklas had strained to uphold the charmed narrative she and Stein had spent decades promoting, of perfect domestic unity in service of Stein's unquestioned genius. But her encounter with Katz brought a complicating factor, which upset the balance of power between them. From the notebooks, he possessed first-hand knowledge of Stein's private thoughts in this early period, which both knew had the potential to cause Toklas serious distress. Katz quickly assuaged her fears of exposure by assuring her that once he had completed his thesis on Stein's early writings he would deposit the notes from their conversations at Yale, and nothing would be published without her consent. This stipulation, she told Gallup, meant that 'it has been possible and a pleasure to let myself go'. But Katz was worried about Toklas's potential reaction to that early note he had found, where Stein unleashed vitriol against her in such unpleasant fashion. Afraid that he was tampering cruelly with Toklas's memory by forcing her to confront parts of Stein that her partner never intended her to see, Katz decided not to show this particular note to Toklas until he had gained her trust. Instead, he began with the earliest notes, and soon was regaled with a flow of memories.

//

Toklas vividly remembered her first meeting with Stein: her sunbrowned face, her beautiful voice, the coral brooch she wore and the sense of presence she exuded. At first, however, she thought Stein's attentions were focused squarely on her friend Harriet Levy and her cousin Annette Rosenshine, the anxious girl with 'eyes like a frightened deer's', whom Toklas, meanly, still called 'the Stinker'. Toklas 'loathed' Rosenshine. She considered her miserable and self-centred, and felt she made 'enormous capital' of her various anxieties – the subject of Rosenshine's daily sessions with Stein, her self-appointed guru. Toklas freely told Katz how she relished misleading Rosenshine into missing her appointments with Stein, knowing Stein would 'give Annette merry hell' for it. In the notebooks, Katz delicately pointed out, Stein had suggested Toklas was jealous of Rosenshine: 'From the way Alice acts about the Annette business I may come gradually to think that she cares more about loving than about me, that is she cares more about having completely possession of loving me than of loving me.' But Toklas countered that the jealousy was all Rosenshine's, who 'was very anxious not to let me get close to Gertrude'. Toklas, it seemed, had elbowed out rivals for Stein's attention just as determinedly as Stein had asserted herself in Toklas's Paris life. 'By the time I came to Paris, Gertrude had had about enough of Annette,' she told him. 'The Stinker getting greener and greener was frightful to see.'

Toklas explained to Katz that Stein had read her letters to Rosenshine, become interested, and cross-examined Rosenshine for information about her, all before she arrived in Paris. This, Toklas said, comprised largely of scandalised mutterings from Rosenshine's mother, who disapproved of Toklas's father ('she had such notions as that he was going to marry the servant girl and close the house') and urged her daughter to avoid Toklas when she came to Paris. With her illicitly gained knowledge, Stein met Toklas not only with a preconceived sense of her personality, but with somewhat garbled notions of her prior romantic attachments. In her letters, Toklas had often mentioned her friends Lily Hansen and Nellie Jacot. Rosenshine's mother disapproved of these women: she thought they were 'fast', and had tried to persuade Toklas's father to forbid his daughter associating with them. But the way Toklas spoke about Lily and Nellie caught Stein's attention for other reasons: it sparked the suggestion, to her, that Toklas might be romantically interested in women. Her intrigue at this prospect was tempered, even before they met, by a twinge of jealousy. Stein, Toklas explained to Katz, had jumped to the conclusion that 'my relation with Nellie had more meaning than it had'. In fact, Toklas explained, in her youth she had enjoyed flirting with charming older men. 'Gertrude never actually saw this side of me. There was no one in Paris like that for me.'

In the summer of 1908, during a hill walk in Fiesole, Toklas had finally explained to Stein that she and Nellie Jacot were friends, nothing more. That conversation, Toklas told Katz, was the most crucial one in the development of their intimacy – and resonated through Stein's writing for a decade. A 1922 text called 'Didn't Nelly and Lilly Love You' took its title from the question Stein had asked Toklas that summer. 'Can you decline history,' writes Stein, recasting her anxiety over Toklas's past as a grammatical problem. History, she suggests, is not fixed, but can be revised if a couple so choose. Through dialogue – Stein's questioning, Toklas's resolute affirmation – they establish a shared future, and a marriage, not by a legal ceremony but by the speech act of promises made. 'We may say', writes Stein triumphantly, 'that the history of Didn't Nelly and Lilly love you is the history of wishes guessed expressed and gratified.' The text plays joyfully with storytelling conventions: past and present, truth and fiction blur, as Stein describes their lives in California before meeting one another, merging events from their respective pasts, as if they had always been inseparable. 'Care for me,' Stein wrote. 'I care for you in every possible way.' Stein recalled that hilltop conversation again in her 1928 text 'A Lyrical Opera Made by Two', written for Toklas's birthday, and a celebration of twenty years of partnership. 'Not any Lillie not any Nellie,' Stein wrote there, claiming Toklas as her own.

There was, of course, an irony to Stein's unfounded jealousy. She had not told Toklas about her own attachment to May Bookstaver, nor shown her the novel she had written about her thwarted passion. Katz had, by now, been able to read *Things as They Are*, and made the connection between the love triangle depicted with such raw feeling in the novel, and the story which Emma Lootz Erving and Mabel Weeks had told him. He knew the question of May would have to be broached, but wasn't sure how Toklas would react. Eventually, he decided to bluff, and brought the name up casually. Toklas, assuming he knew far more than he did, began to speak.

From the start, Toklas had known of May Knoblauch as an old friend of Stein's. Toklas remembered opening the door to May and her husband in the summer of 1910, when they arrived for a visit before Stein was out of bed one morning, and noticing that May's gown was studded with gems. Later that year, she and Stein were shopping in Urbino, when Stein found a fifteenth-century pot with signs of the Passion carved on the inside, and told her, 'I'll send it to May Mary because she was very nice about *Three Lives* and I never gave her anything.' She remembered, too, that May had been 'outraged' when Gertrude entrusted the manuscript of *The Making of Americans* not to her, for placing with an American publisher as she had done with *Three Lives*, but to another friend, Alice Woods Ullman. Stein probably didn't intend this as a slight – she didn't discriminate among potential helpers – but Toklas remembered Ullman returning to Paris and telling Stein, 'If you've made a friend of me, you've lost one in May.'

Toklas told Katz she had not realised the historical significance of the relationship until 1932, when Stein had stumbled, by chance, on the old manuscript of *Q.E.D.* As Stein had feared, Toklas saw the discovery of this past entanglement as a betrayal of their shared and fundamental understanding, established in that Florentine hilltop conversation, that there would be no secrets between them. Immediately, May loomed as a spectre recasting their whole relationship in her shadow; Stein's protestations that this manuscript was an ancient relic of long-forgotten feelings for someone she hadn't thought of in years did nothing to quell Toklas's wrath. 'In a passion,' she told Katz, she had destroyed all Knoblauch's letters to Stein. But even after Stein had told Toklas to keep the manuscript – even tear it up if she wanted to – Toklas, now on edge, became 'hypersensitive to signs'. She found a previously innocuous 'M' carved into Stein's writing table, and sanded it off in rage. For a year and a half, Toklas confessed to Katz, she 'tormented' Gertrude. During the American tour, she told any of Stein's old friends who called that Stein was sleeping and could not be disturbed: 'I didn't want her to see any of them.' In Thornton Wilder's apartment in Chicago, Stein told her that if she did not drop the subject once and for all, their life together would be over. Toklas never mentioned May Knoblauch again.

Katz was astonished at the revelations. It was impossible to countenance the idea that Stein and Toklas – the couple synonymous with devotion – could ever have separated. But he now saw that Stein had written the *Autobiography* – her testament to their unity – in the midst of a grave rupture. If 'Didn't Nelly and Lilly Love You' showed Stein light-heartedly suggesting that history can be remade, the *Autobiography* now appeared to be her own effort to do just that. Her adoption of Toklas's voice now took on a rather different meaning. In writing Toklas's autobiography on her behalf, was she trying to guarantee her partner's silence? Katz remembered seeing the newspaper reports of the American tour, where journalists had speculated that Toklas might not even exist, except in Stein's imagination. It was chilling to imagine them travelling around the country in a furious stand-off – to know that Toklas was seething from the sidelines as she watched her partner be feted for the book that bore her own name. For as hard as Stein had tried to rewrite the past, Toklas had clearly not forgotten May Knoblauch. From their sessions, Katz had learned that her memory was sharp as anything – and that she was capable of bearing a grudge for decades.

After this conversation, Toklas wrote to Gallup to register her alarm at the tenor their sessions had begun to take. 'Katz,' she wrote, 'by deduction analysis and imagination has got from the notes a great deal that in a kind of a way was not his affair so to speak.' Above all, Toklas wanted Gallup's reassurance that this 'inspired researcher' would never have access to the private love letters locked in Gallup's safe. 'From a stray line,' she wrote, 'he will base – and correctly – allusions in the portraits.' Gallup assured her that the love notes remained scrupulously under seal. 'I am not surprised that Katz has trespassed on this forbidden territory,' he wrote to Van Vechten, who replied: 'Katz HAS opened Pandora's box, with a bang!'

//

But Toklas and Katz continued their sessions, delving back now to the early months of Toklas and Stein's relationship. She was on firmer ground, here, and showed obvious pleasure in telling stories, her memories stirred by odd references in the notebooks. When Toklas arrived in Paris, she told him, 'all of Gertrude's days were empty'. Stein didn't make plans, Toklas explained, just took distractions as they came; she didn't emerge from bed until lunchtime, and rarely left the house with purpose, but would wander around the arrondissement window-shopping and watching the crowds, or take the train out to the suburbs, shivering her way home on the open-top bus. During the first six months of their acquaintance, Stein bombarded Toklas with questions about her childhood, laughing at Toklas's dry wit and pithy turns of phrase. Toklas already knew that Stein had found her difficult to parse. When they first met, Toklas explained to Katz, Stein – who had 'very high-minded' Puritan values (expressed by Adele in *Q.E.D.*) – was stunned by Toklas's casual attitude to personal ethics ('I believe with Henry James,' she wryly told him, 'not in morals but in manners'). In particular, Stein criticised her ability to continue friendships with people whose values Stein considered beyond the pale. But Toklas mildly retorted that her friendship was not conditional on good behaviour (an idea which clearly stuck with Stein, given their shared loyalty to Bernard Faÿ). 'With my friends,' she told Katz, 'I may be surprised, but I'm never shocked by anything in any way.' During the winter of 1907, while picking wild violets in the gardens of Versailles, Stein told Toklas bluntly where she stood among the 'types' Stein was charting in the 'Diagram Book': she was an 'old maid mermaid'. Over forty years later, Toklas perfectly remembered her tart reply: 'Oh, rats.'

After their exchange of promises on the Fiesole hilltop in the summer of 1908, Toklas told Katz, Stein began to discuss her characterological project with her. She remembered Stein's 'mad enthusiasm' for Otto Weininger's book *Sex and Character*, and how 'frightfully shocked' she had been when she learned that Weininger had killed himself. As they grew closer, Stein enlisted Toklas's help. She would give an example of a type, and ask Toklas to suggest friends who conformed to its description. Stein would listen to people, Toklas remembered, with 'phenomenal and endless' patience – 'listening to the rhythm, the repeating of whoever for as often and for as long a time as she had'. Toklas was fascinated by Stein's work, and took her role in it completely seriously as their intimacy deepened. She also had her own ideas about it. While Stein, privately, analysed Toklas's character in her notebooks, grappling with her attraction

Alice B. Toklas at the rue Christine, 1951 (photo: Ettore Sottsass)

and her fear of surrendering her freedom entirely to another person, Toklas was pondering how to guide her work away from the influences she deemed destructive. Chief among them, she told Katz, was Gertrude's brother.

//

Toklas shared 27 rue de Fleurus with Gertrude and Leo for almost three years. By the time Leo left, in the spring of 1913, relations between them had evidently broken down beyond repair. In the archive, Katz had come across a letter from Leo to Mabel Weeks written in June 1920, in which he described Toklas as 'a person almost entirely without love'. 'What her feeling toward Gertrude is I don't know,' he wrote, 'but I'm quite sure it isn't that.' Behind her apparent willingness to retreat into the shadows, he concluded, was a sinister desire for control.

Toklas informed Katz that the break between the Stein siblings had not been at her behest – but only because she did not have the power to effect such a rupture. If she could have made it happen, she told him bluntly, she would have: Leo had become 'unreasonable and unbearable'. Toklas had come to dislike Leo's quickness to take offence, and his penchant for what she called 'deep-thinking'. Gertrude, she explained, 'always saw the essence of the thing, and was crystal clear, secure, vehement', but Leo was 'a man with nothing to say, and he would elaborate endlessly and maddeningly without making a point'. While others put up with his belligerence, Toklas made her feelings known. After a long evening listening to Gertrude and Leo argue furiously about Californian politics, before it transpired they were basing their opposing positions on one single article in the *Argonaut* they had both read, she told Gertrude – in terms strikingly similar to Helen addressing Adele in *Q.E.D.* – that she was tired of this insistence on thinking in intellectual and moral terms, which seemed to come at the cost of any human connection. She noticed how Leo would criticise others on the flimsiest of grounds – how he would look at a single line of prose and begin to expostulate wildly on the writer's flaws – and would interrupt and correct Gertrude whenever she spoke, until she would inevitably conclude the argument was not worth pursuing.

Toklas revealed that Gertrude had asked for Leo's opinion on *Three Lives*, and been disheartened by his overwhelmingly negative reaction. While she was writing *The Making of Americans*, Toklas remembered, Leo would wander over unbidden and read pages from the unfinished manuscript, then ridicule her writing in front of their friends. Toklas found his disloyalty reprehensible. Gradually, Gertrude pushed back against the rigidity of her brother's ideas – his 'paucity of internal experience', and his inability to 'unconventionalise', which she had come to see as the mark of a truly original thinker. 'Real thinking', she wrote in a notebook, 'is conceptions aiming and aiming again and again always getting fuller, that is the difference between creative thinking and theorising.' She was coming to see the process of creation – the struggle to realise a vision – as the most significant aspect of a work of art; its final form, she thought, marked the culmination of a long, vital battle in the artist's mind. Midway through *The Making of Americans*, Stein describes the 'complete disillusionment' of trying to get others to understand, and the freedom of deciding to give up trying to please someone who cannot be pleased. Leo's response to her writing, she wrote elsewhere, 'destroyed him for me and it destroyed me for him'. While Leo's disdain came as a blow, it was clear that Toklas gave Gertrude not only the strength to continue, but the assurance to challenge him. In the notebooks was a draft reply to a detractor who had questioned the necessity of all her repetition. 'My being an artist', she wrote with confidence, 'is its justification.'

Katz, now, understood the tensions which lay behind the narrator's regretful statement, in *The Making of Americans*, that she doesn't expect her work will find an audience. 'I write for myself and strangers,' Stein explains. 'No one who knows me can like it. At least they mostly do not like it . . . I do this for my own sake . . . This is now a history of my love of it. I hear it and I love it and I write it.' Later, she confesses the toll that disdain has taken, and expresses the 'perfect joy' of finding a reader – even just one person – who really does believe in the work. 'You write a book,' she explains,

and while you write it you are ashamed for every one must think you are a silly or a crazy one and yet you write it and you are ashamed, you know you will be laughed at or pitied by every one and you have a queer feeling and you are not very certain and you go on writing. Then some one says yes to it, to something you are liking, or doing or making and then never again can you have completely such a feeling of being afraid and ashamed that you had then when you were writing or liking the thing and not any one had said yes about the thing.

'Some one says yes to it': the most romantic words Stein ever wrote. She began to attach notes to the pages she left by the typewriter late at night, confessing anxieties and seeking approval. In one, Stein confessed her fear that she was, in her increasing dependence on Toklas, 'beginning to lose [my] liberty'. But the notes showed that she had started to write for Toklas, feeding on her support. 'Dearest,' read one, attached to her short piece 'Rue de Rennes', 'This is a trial, I have no idea what its like and very much doubt if it tells the story. If not I will try it again. Please be all well. Y.D.' Toklas would reply, sometimes offering encouragement, sometimes confirming Stein's avant-garde instincts. ('A question mark', she rejoined on one piece, 'is not admitted by us moderns.') Stein expressed her new-found happiness in the pages of *The Making of Americans*. 'I am filled just now quite full of loving being in myself,' she wrote. 'Loving is to me just now an interesting, a delightful a quite completely realised thing. I have loving being in me more than I knew I could have in me. It was a surprising thing to find it so completely in me.'

By the time Toklas moved into the rue de Fleurus, Stein would discuss her work with her alone. 'Gertrude', Toklas told Katz simply, 'wasn't talking to Leo any more.' And from the trust she had earned, Toklas was able to persuade Stein to channel her intuitive understanding of people in a more empathetic direction, away from abstracted analyses in diagrams and charts. Katz concluded that it was at Toklas's encouragement that Stein finally broke off from *The Making of Americans* and wrote her first series of portraits, focusing on an individual for who they were, rather than to exemplify a character type. After this, Toklas explained, Stein developed a new, more human approach to other people. No longer was she desperate to change people's behaviour and tell them where they were going wrong (as she had with Annette Rosenshine and Harriet Levy); her interest now lay in character itself, and the infinite possible directions it might take. Her success with portraits sent her back to the novel with renewed enthusiasm and widened emotional horizons, ready to explore the 'multitudes' within her characters, and present them as rounded, almost Cubist individuals. 'Toward the last half of the writing of *The Making of Americans*,' Toklas told Katz, 'she was conscious of the certainty that she had genius and that her work was of the first importance.'

Near the end of the novel, a change comes over the narrator, which Katz now understood as reflecting the happiness and security Stein had found in her relationship. Her initial fears about losing her sense of identity had dissolved: she now felt assured in herself for the first time. Commenting later on the shift in her style around this time, Stein had admitted, 'I myself was becoming livelier just then.' This change in Stein, Katz now saw, drove the novel's innovations: its new aesthetic boldness was a product of her growing confidence. *The Making of Americans* had started off as a family saga, animated by questions of inheritance and the way traditions shift and stick as they are passed down between generations. From the clashes between the older and younger generations emerge the enigmatic Brother Singulars – 'misplaced' outsiders with 'a passion to be free': perhaps gay, perhaps

Jewish, striking out alone against the pull of conformity. 'It is sad here for us,' writes Stein early on in the book, including herself in the category, 'there is no place in an adolescent world for anything eccentric like us, machine making does not turn out queer things like us, they can never make a world to let us be free each one inside us.' The Brother Singulars are only mentioned twice in the novel, but represent what becomes, over the process of writing, its abiding theme: how 'vital singularity' may emerge from tradition; how an individual steeped in the past may break out of it, discover themselves, and learn – like Adele in *Q.E.D.* – to see 'things as they are'.

What use is the old, when making the new? Stein was striving to answer this question for herself, but also for literature. She knew that writing *The Making of Americans* would leave her an 'outlaw'. Leo's departure marked a major break with her family of origin, but also released her to pursue her singular ambitions in writing, and to live independently with Toklas – a renunciation of nineteenth-century conventions both literary and social. Near the start of the book, the narrator expresses anxiety about her outsider status: she sees herself as a 'chronicler' skulking on the margins, watching her generation grow up and marry and start families of their own, and worrying that she stands out as different. By the end of the novel, Stein could define herself proudly as a Singular: ready to answer back to anyone who might condemn her work, her sexuality, her Jewishness, and bask in the acceptance of the audience she had found. Living with Toklas, she could write as she wanted, dress unconventionally, stride confidently through the streets of Paris. Otto Weininger's intellectual framework for the potential of a lesbian genius was now supplanted by Toklas's belief in her, which breathed life into theory: Stein's lifelong conception of her writing as a shared enterprise, akin to procreation, emerges from this first moment of recognition. Rereading *The Making of Americans* in light of his interviews, Katz came to see it, anew, as a product of love: Stein's love of people, her love of writing, her love of the sensation of 'looking and comparing and classifying', and her love of Toklas. For the first time, Stein was not only listening, but being heard. As Katz put it: 'Alice had won more than Gertrude's unconditional love. She had also won a place in her creative life.'

//

As the months wore on, Toklas's impressions of Katz only warmed. A few weeks into their interviews, Basket died. 'His going has stunned me,' she wrote to Van Vechten. 'It is the beginning of living for the rest of my days without anyone who is dependent upon me for anything.' Toklas brushed aside Katz's commiserations, but she wrote to Gallup that he had been 'very kind', and that the interviews were keeping her occupied amid her grief for the dog, compounded by the sense of losing one more link to her life with Stein. In December, their sessions were interrupted by the arrival of Roland Duncan, a student who had been sent to interview Toklas by the Oral History Project of the University of Berkeley's Bancroft Library, which had just acquired – from Stein's niece, her sister Bertha's daughter Gertrude Stein Raffel – the diaries of Stein's mother, Amelia Keyser Stein. These charted her delight in the progress of the infant Gertrude, and made clearer than before how ingrained the family were within Oakland's Jewish community, respecting holidays and customs in a way Stein never did as an adult. Toklas told Duncan about her own childhood: she spoke a little more about her beloved mother and her brother Clarence, ten years younger, whom Toklas had practically raised herself, but refused to be drawn on her Jewish roots: 'We never had any feeling of any minority,' she insisted. 'We represented America.' To his and Katz's surprise, Toklas said California was still 'God's own country' to her; she would have gone back there, she said, but it seemed right to stay in Stein's home. When Duncan complimented Toklas on her memory, she snapped back that he should have known what it used to be: she could have told him everything that happened every single day until Stein died. 'I lost my memory then,' she told him.

As Toklas relaxed, her indiscretions about other people multiplied. It's clear, from her answers to Katz, that nothing escaped her in her years of 'sitting with the wives': she kept tabs on which of her friends had neuroses about diet, who had incestuous feelings towards their fathers, who faked their tarot readings. Her fond accounts of witty remarks made by Stein recall the teasing tone of the *Autobiography*: sternly telling Toklas not to use slang as she always got it 'crooked'; demanding that Toklas join her at a portrait-sitting with a talkative acquaintance because 'four ears would make me have to hear less'; poking fun at Toklas for loving perfume yet complaining at the stench of cow dung ('You're fond of smells, aren't you? You should want to know all smells'). Picasso featured prominently in her memories, sitting across from Stein in his studio, their knees knocking on tiny children's chairs, talking. 'They talked to each other each for their own good, not for the other's, and so they cleared their own minds as they spoke.'

During his time in Paris, Katz was eager to make contact with more of Stein's friends, to gather a wider range of perspectives on his subject. But he soon saw that Toklas considered him her own. When she heard that Katz intended to interview the 'ungracefully ageing' painter Francis Rose, she phoned him in the morning, 'alert lest Francis's tongue in a fit of irrepressible inventiveness permanently soil Gertrude's posthumous reputation', and pleaded with him to report back everything Rose told him for her own verification. (Rose proceeded to lead Katz on a tour of Paris's gay bars, regaling him with tales of Stein dancing tipsy on a grand piano which Toklas, the next day, coolly stripped of Rose's embellishments.) In February 1953, Katz left Paris – which was plunged into a smothering fog – and travelled to Italy to interview Bernard Berenson, who still lived at I Tatti in Fiesole. He found Berenson jovial, chuckling as he recalled Stein standing over him waving her arms as she poured out her (negative) analysis of his character, to his total bemusement. When Katz returned to Paris, he found Toklas eager to hear about the visit, in particular the state of the I Tatti gardens. Among her memories of Berenson was his abiding terror that the single safety pin which held together Gertrude's usual monk's garment might burst at any moment.

From this point, Katz was treated as a dear friend. Toklas took him out with her to the opera; she brought him to Natalie Barney's Friday evening salon and to jovial lunch parties frequented by 'left-over Surrealists from the Thirties'. For the first time in their acquaintance, Katz sensed that Toklas had decided to 'live again'. No longer was she the retiring wife, silent and watchful and concerned only with her partner's comfort. Now, she appeared to enjoy her role as host, attuned to the flow of conversation and ready to fill silences with piquant anecdotes of her own. And, she confessed, she had begun to write a cookbook.

As their conversations continued, Katz noticed that some of Toklas's most animated memories were those of her own childhood, not to do with Stein at all. She contradicted the impression, given in Stein's portrait 'Ada', that her family life had been unhappy – Stein, she explained, had been surprised, and a little envious, to hear that Toklas had experienced none of the teenage angst that she had. When they returned during the lecture tour to California, where they had both spent their adolescence, Toklas had been excited to take Stein into the Yosemite, and show her all the places she remembered. But Stein, to her disappointment, was hesitant to visit old stomping grounds, worried about the memories that might flood back. ('There is no there there,' she wrote, famously, of Oakland: it brought back nothing.) In San Francisco, Toklas remembered, Stein went down alone to the beach at night, saying she wanted to look at the ocean. When they reached the Algonquin Hotel in New York a week later, there was an envelope waiting for them containing a teaspoon of sand from the beach, addressed to Stein in her own handwriting. Toklas attributed Stein's ambivalence to the difficult years after her mother's death, when she dropped out of school and retreated completely into books. 'Gertrude hated her own past,' said Toklas. 'She referred to it as little as possible.'

Katz would regularly stay with Toklas until past midnight, leaning forward in his chair to catch her animated outpourings. When he left one night, he borrowed her portable typewriter to log his notes over-night. In exchange for her time, they had agreed that he would also type up pages from the cookbook she was writing: to her amusement, Toklas was now the writer with a devoted secretary of her own. As she handed it to him, Toklas sighed and said, 'Sometimes I look at that machine and hate every key on it.' Glancing at Picasso's painting of a nude girl with a basket of flowers on the wall, and beyond to the gallery of Cubist heads arrayed in the corridor, she added, 'Sometimes I hate all of these pictures, each separately and all together.' But when Katz asked her what she meant, she retreated, replying only, 'It's a long story,' as she hastily showed him out into the cold night. Walking home in the snow, having missed the last metro, Katz reflected that this was the first time she had hinted at any lingering resentment towards the life of self-sacrificial devotion she had led. Looking back over the notebooks, he remembered – with a shudder – the early entry in which Stein had attacked Toklas with a torrent of insults. Katz resolved that now their sessions were drawing to a natural close, he would show her the page with the cruel note at last.

The next evening, he warned her that this fragment was 'written with considerable animus toward her, and that it would be well for her to be prepared for its contents'. The following morning, she phoned him to admit that she had hardly slept, and asked him to come over early. She snatched the paper from his hands on the doorstep, and went into the bedroom to read it alone. After a few minutes, she came back into the living room with a look of 'indescribable relief' on her face. 'Oh, that's all right,' she said. 'I thought it was quite different.' Astonished, Katz asked her what she had feared. 'I was afraid', Toklas replied, 'that Gertrude had accused me of disloyalty. That's the only thing that would matter.'

What toll, Katz wondered, had this life taken on Toklas? In a note written shortly after their return from a holiday in Italy, Stein described Toklas as 'the St Thérèse type'. Katz had also noticed a letter, signed Y.D., addressed to 'Thérèse' – clearly an affectionate nickname for

Alice. When he asked Toklas who Thérèse was, Toklas replied that 'St Thérèse didn't know herself apart from the Christ, if there was anything apart'. In what way, Katz asked, did Stein think of Toklas as that type? Pained, hesitant, Toklas replied: 'Because I felt toward Gertrude as St Thérèse felt toward the Christ. For me, it was the same experience and the same relation.' After a long pause, she added in anger, 'It was stupid of you to ask.' But another note quickly cheered her. Referring to Alice, Stein casually wrote, 'I love her.' When Katz read this aloud, Toklas started. 'She says it? Just like that?' Katz confirmed, and Toklas sat back in deep satisfaction. 'Well then, *c'est ça.*'

Was Stein's love ever in doubt? As the interviews concluded, Katz found Toklas as hard to fathom as when they started. Toklas had strongly suggested she did not see herself apart from Stein and, it seemed, did not want to. Her identity, for forty years, had rested on her role in Stein's life and work – and the idea that Stein might ever have questioned her loyalty was, he understood, more than she could have borne. Toklas had always been complicit in the mythology of their relationship: that Stein was the writer, the genius, the husband, while Toklas's role was to serve and enable that genius to flourish. But in her conversations with Katz, Toklas had recalled her youthful talents as a pianist – she had given public recitals and considered turning professional – and had intimated, even, that she was held in high regard among San Francisco's eligible bachelors. Yet ever since they met, Stein had been her work: they had made, undoubtedly, a rich, stimulating and joyful life together, but one not without sacrifices, almost entirely falling to Toklas. The flashes of discomfort Katz had noticed in their conversations – her momentary vehemence towards the typewriter and the paintings; the story of the bitter feud after the discovery of *Q.E.D.* – seemed to complicate the public image of mutual devotion. But Toklas had remained adamant that she had no desire to be recast or rehabilitated from her position in the shadows. If she was to emerge, it would be on her own terms.

At the end of their final session, Toklas handed back to Katz his typescripts of the notebooks, which she had read through in their entirety the previous night. At the door, Toklas told him how moving it had been to hear Stein's voice again, 'describing mutual friends with such deadly precision', just as Toklas remembered them. As Katz was about to leave, she stopped him.

'During all the interviews,' Katz wrote fifty years later,

one could tell from her eyes when she was concealing, when she was open, when plainly lying, but it never happened that one saw her entirely vulnerable, never. Now suddenly her face changed and became almost a child's face. And she said, 'You see, when Gertrude came into this room, the room would light up, the day would light up, the year would light up – and my life would light up.' There was indeed no more to be said but 'Goodbye, Miss Toklas.' And I left.

14 : PARADES AND FIREWORKS

In March 1952, a few months before Katz arrived, Toklas sat for a portrait by Dora Maar, a former partner of Picasso. Maar painted her at home, a tea tray on the table in front of her and Basket at her side. It was, in some ways, a mirror – or an echo – of Picasso's portrait of Stein. Maar had spent eight years in Picasso's shadow, her own talents sidelined by his numerous depictions of her as the 'Weeping Woman'. Since Stein's death, Maar and Toklas had grown close: it's tempting to wonder if they felt a certain recognition, both defined by their partner's image. 'All portraits of me are lies,' Maar insisted. 'They're Picassos. Not one is Dora Maar.' Katz's interviews had made clear how much the *Autobiography* was Gertrude Stein's story, not Alice B. Toklas's. But, as Katz had intuited, something in Toklas was beginning to shift. She was no longer Stein's invention: she was beginning to talk.

Dora Maar with her portrait of Alice B. Toklas, 1952 (photo: Michel Sima)

After the intensive sessions with Katz ended, Toklas succumbed to a serious bout of jaundice and stayed in bed for several weeks. But she had found their conversations so stimulating that she wanted to continue. She wrote to Katz, suggesting he return the next summer and they could travel together to Majorca 'where there is wonderful food and summer living to be had': she teased him with the possibility that she would 'recount for you my life together with Gertrude almost day by day'. She even tried to intercede with the director of the Ford Foundation to extend Katz's funding, but to no avail: Katz had a teaching job and a family to return to in America. As autumn 1953 turned to winter, she was surprised and somewhat hurt not to hear from Katz again: 'Through the notes,' she told Gallup, 'he got to know more about me than practically any one.' More time passed, and her hurt turned to anger. Katz, she complained, 'has behaved shockingly . . . I don't like to think of the material I gave him floating about and falling into unknown hands'. She was somewhat mollified when a young man, Katz's former college roommate, dropped in to see the art collection and deliver some news: Katz and his wife had separated, he was living in Poughkeepsie, and despite a period of great stress he remained 'enthralled' with his work on Stein. Toklas wrote again to tell him she forgave his long silence, but felt their long winter together entitled her to some news of him: 'Though you were once mistaken for an assassin,' she added, 'you showed yourself a friendly comrade.'

Toklas now seemed to enjoy holding court at 5 rue Christine. Seven years had passed since Stein's death, and most dutiful visits from her former friends had ceased, but new visitors, sometimes famous ones, often stopped by to admire the paintings – Georgia O'Keeffe, John Cage, Greta Garbo – and Toklas had made some friends of her own, who knew her as herself, not as Stein's companion. Lunch with Alice Toklas was a ritual experience. She would lead visitors down the narrow hallway and into the salon, where she would sit by the fireplace, next to an antique table on which stood a silver donkey wagon – a gift from Van Vechten – filled with cigarettes, a large box of kitchen matches poised at its side. Toklas served meals herself, leaping up and vanishing to the kitchen, then returning laden with innumerable jugs and platters bearing dainty sauces and desserts. There was a sense among Toklas's friends that her self-effacement was, by now, as one put it, 'a form of publicity in itself'. Some worried that she was lonely, and regretted that Stein had quarrelled with so many people who might now have provided welcome friendship. Others, like Donald Sutherland, suspected that despite her helpless demeanour, Toklas was an 'essentially militant' character, and 'may well have enjoyed having enemies as much as having friends, if not more'.

Though most still assumed her life was a pale shadow of what it once was, Toklas was by no means incapable of making her own entertainment. She went often to the opera and the ballet, while their old friend the designer Pierre Balmain – now one of Paris's leading couturiers – sent a car for her whenever he had a show, and his models waved at her from the catwalk as they turned. She travelled: she visited Bernard Faÿ in Switzerland, and retraced old routes through Perpignan and Granada ('The landscape is more exciting than I can remember,' she wrote. 'Everything is filled with the memory of Gertrude.'). Through Gallup's work soliciting extra letters for the Stein archive, she reconnected with a couple, Ethel Mars and Maud Hunt Squire, whom Stein had immortalised in an early portrait, 'Miss Furr and Miss Skeene' (perhaps the first text to use 'gay' in its contemporary meaning), and visited them in Vence. She took on young artists and writers as protégés of her own, just as Stein had done: the journalist Otto Friedrich, the painter Nejad Devrim, the poet James Merrill, with whom she kept up long after his affair with Claude Fredericks had ended. And she stayed in touch with friends around the world through her industrious letter-writing, which she referred to as 'my work'. During Stein's lifetime, Toklas had corresponded on her own behalf with only a handful of friends. But now, with no more manuscripts to type or proofs to correct, her letters – written in tiny longhand, with her fountain pen often bleeding through the thin airmail stationery – became an outlet for

Toklas's dry wit, piercing scepticism and poignant memories. Gallup, Van Vechten and others had long since given up asking her to write about her life with Stein: they had grudgingly accepted that 'there was no real hope of being able to overcome some forty years of Gertrude Stein's influence to the effect that she can't write'. So it came as something of a surprise to her friends when Toklas announced that she had written her cookbook at last.

//

Over the years, Toklas had amassed a store of recipes as extensive as any professional chef's. For decades, she had collected rare eighteenth- and nineteenth-century recipes, copying them religiously from the manuscript cookbooks of ancient French chateaux in the region around Bilignin. She pored over cookbooks – classical French ones, or her favourites, American investigations of foreign food (*Can the Greeks Cook?*) – as avidly as Stein read her detective novels, and would often discuss the merits and flaws of newfangled kitchen gadgets in letters: 'The weenie eggbeater with the long handle created a version of mayonnaise that is rapid and economical.' She was a skilled and discerning cook; her food tended to be simple (a lot of meat, cream and butter) but of exquisite quality. 'What did we have for dinner', wrote Stein in a text called 'Advertisements', 'we had a melon lobster chicken then beet salad and fruit.' Toklas sized up each cut of meat at the butcher's, knew how to select the ripest produce at market, and was familiar with an encyclopaedic range of herbs and spices with which to season it, including international influences from curry powder to soy sauce. Their closest friends knew that cooking was Toklas's art form, the kitchen as much her domain as the writing studio was Stein's.

In the 1930s, the two of them had even discussed collaborating on a cookbook. Among the papers at Yale is a green notebook, with its title scrawled on the front cover: 'We Eat: A Cookbook by Alice B. Toklas and Gertrude Stein'. Apart from one cake recipe in Toklas's writing, the book is entirely in Stein's hand, but begins – as if she was dictating – with Toklas's first memory of a kitchen: the enormous coffee boiler, the black stove, the cook Katy who brought homemade Yorkshire puddings to the small Alice as she sat at the table engrossed in picture books. The notebook quickly trails off, but in her letters Stein occasionally referred, usually in jest, to the book Toklas would one day write. In *Everybody's Autobiography*, she described the hilarity when a woman on their boat back from America read their palms and claimed to see that Stein was a surgeon and Toklas was a writer. She does not seem to have noticed the irony that, for each of them, this was a path they might well have followed, had circumstances not intervened.

Instead, Toklas's creative outlets were cooking and sewing, both of which she dismissed as purely domestic hobbies. Yet in June 1946, just weeks before Stein's death, two footstools Toklas had embroidered to designs by Picasso (he sketched directly on to her canvas, and she fitted her designs usually to old chairs) had been shown in an enormous exhibition of French tapestry, organised by the Louvre. Toklas would certainly not have called herself an artist – yet she could have rightfully claimed to be a collaborator of Picasso, even one-upping Stein, who had merely sat for him. In 1950 Van Vechten had obtained her a commission to write an article on cookery for *Vogue*, but she had to be placed under serious pressure to complete the assignment, insisting she had nothing to say. 'She began to repair dish towels in order to put off the evil day,' her friend Joseph Barry reported from Paris. 'We bought her new ones. Then she said she had to answer 53 letters. She stayed with us a month and got the number down to 6. Finally she did it.' She continually demurred when cajoled to expand the article into a book – 'It would only be adding to the unprofessional women cooks who rush into advising their victims to dubious results,' she repeated – but the handsome payment she received for the article made her think again. She claimed the project was undertaken 'solely to earn some pennies' – but it was a chance, too, to find her own voice, so long submerged.

Van Vechten was thrilled to hear she was finally writing. 'PLEASE ORGANISE YOUR COOK BOOK,' he had entreated her some years earlier. 'Put it together and send it to me and I WILL GET IT PUBLISHED FOR YOU.' Katz, too, had encouraged her. As well as typing her work in progress, he had helped her draw up possible chapter structures; at Yale he had seen the notebook titled 'We Eat', and suggested asking Gallup to create a transcript so that it might be included as an appendix. Whether it slipped her mind, or she did not want Stein to encroach on her own first volume, Toklas did not take up the idea. Instead, she decided to ask friends for their own favourite recipes, to bulk out the page-count: among those who complied were Natalie Barney (stuffed eggplant), Virgil Thomson (gnocchi alla piemontese), Fania Marinoff (lamb curry) and Carl Van Vechten (garlic ice cream). As well as a recipe for Chinese eggs, the artist Francis Rose presented her with a charming sequence of illustrations for the book, from Toklas peeling pears in the living room at Bilignin to Stein in a Red Cross ambulance, driving merrily through the hills.

Toklas lamented that her friends' contributions would be 'undoubtedly the only thing of merit in the deadly dull offering'. She played down her talents outrageously. Toklas's personality shines through her prose: matter-of-fact, witty, acute. Her recipes, full of wise recommendations (cream should be added to sauces at the last moment, with the saucepan tilted not stirred; lobster cooks best when 'boiled furiously') are interspersed with opinionated discursions into the history and culture of French food, the differences between French and American eating habits, the effects of war on food distribution. But the book's chief delights are the stories of life with Gertrude Stein, who appears here as a doughty sidekick in Toklas's culinary adventures. The book is full of memories of notable meals they shared: the varieties of gazpacho Toklas studied in Spain while Stein was writing *Tender Buttons*; the long country drives from Bilignin, stopping at every restaurant to check the menu for the rare salmon carp from their local lake; the 'gastronomic orgies' of the American tour. Toklas's book also told the history of the succession of international chefs they had hired at home: the 'enchanting' Austrian who made ice cream in individual moulds and introduced them to Sachertorte; Trac, whom Toklas taught to make desserts; and Nguyen, his successor, who astonished their more traditional French visitors with his subtly flavoured noodles and rice. Eventually, Stein took up a low-salt diet, which tested Toklas's ingenuity, while the privations of the war years forced further economising and invention. By its end, the cookbook had told the story of their life together, movingly and fully, through food. And it had established Alice B. Toklas as a writer. When she told Thornton Wilder she was planning a cookbook, she reported to Van Vechten with amusement, 'He looked at me surprised and said reprovingly – But Alice have you ever tried to write.' She quoted his shocked reaction on the last page of her book, self-deprecating to the end: 'As if a cookbook had anything to do with writing.'

Toklas told friends she was sure no one would read *The Alice B. Toklas Cook Book*. She preferred to direct their attention to the latest instalment in the Yale Edition of Stein's work – *As Fine as Melanctha*, published in September 1954, two months before the cookbook. It was the fourth volume in the series, and its preparation had not been smooth. The lawyer for the Stein estate, Edgar Allan Poe, had asked Van Vechten to sign an attestation that he would not require any more funds for the publication programme. Toklas begged him just to sign whatever they asked for – she wanted to avoid dealings with Allan's widow Roubina as far as possible – but with the price of paper rising rapidly, Van Vechten was concerned that he would be powerless to proceed if existing funds ran out before the series was complete. To assuage his fears, Toklas assured him that she would sell a painting, as was her right according to the terms of Stein's will. She wouldn't reveal what she sold, but she reported that she had obtained an extra $10,000, to be kept secret from Poe. The series could proceed. But the publication was dwarfed by anticipation for Toklas's cookbook – spurred by a contro-versy she had not anticipated.

Among the recipes contributed by friends was one sent in by

Brion Gysin, a Morocco-based artist whom Toklas had recently met via Van Vechten. Its name was Haschich Fudge, and its ingredients included fruit, nuts, spices and *Cannabis sativa*. 'This is the food of Paradise,' proclaimed Gysin's accompanying text. 'Euphoria and brilliant storms of laughter; ecstatic reveries and extension of one's personality on several simultaneous planes are to be complacently expected.' Toklas's American publisher, surprised to see the recipe among the extra pages Toklas submitted to them months late (her customary procrastination having already wreaked havoc with their publication schedule), telegraphed to the Attorney General at Washington to check if it was permissible to print: he responded that it was a criminal offence to buy, sell, smoke or indeed cook with marijuana leaves, but not to write about them. Erring on the side of caution, they decided to quietly cut the recipe – but the British publisher let it through. When *Time* magazine drew attention to the incongruous inclusion – suggesting the recipe provided new insight into Gertrude Stein's writing method – Toklas at first insisted she was being libelled, then blamed her ignorance of the Latin name for marijuana: she claimed she had not had time to proofread the book before it was published, which accounted also for some of the measurement errors which rendered certain recipes dangerously misleading. 'Thornton said that no one would believe in my innocence,' wrote Toklas, 'as I had pulled the best publicity stunt of the year.' (Gysin claimed he had submitted the recipe suspecting it would bring in sales, knowing Toklas needed the money badly; he claimed, too, that he later furnished her with her first taste of the fudge, feeling she ought to try it.) The book became one of the bestselling cookbooks of all time, thanks in large part to the notorious 'hash brownies', but also to the captivating charm of Toklas's voice. 'She is doing what I begged her to do in the first introduction,' wrote Van Vechten to Gallup: 'gossiping about Gertrude.'

//

At the age of seventy-eight, Toklas now had every claim to her own celebrity. But while she was glad of the royalties that flooded in – she finally heated the apartment, for the first time since the war – she bridled at any suggestion that her personal success was in any way comparable to her partner's. When a new would-be Stein biographer, a theatrical British aristocrat named Elizabeth Sprigge, asked Toklas to sit for an interview, Toklas leapt at the chance to turn the focus back to Gertrude Stein and her work. She had almost given up on hearing from Leon Katz, and hoped that Sprigge would write the book destined to secure Stein's legacy. Before their first meeting, she sent flowers to Sprigge's hotel. But when Sprigge turned up at the rue Christine, Toklas was dismayed to discover that she found Stein's work hard going, and was planning to write a pacy narrative of bohemian Paris – in which she expected Toklas to play a leading role.

Sprigge found Toklas's stern injunctions quaint and funny rather than threatening. 'I am not allowed to call Gertrude Stein "short",' she wrote in her diary. '"Not tall", "broad", "sturdy", even "heavy" Alice allows, but "short", she says, gives the wrong impression.' Finding Toklas 'prickly as a hedgehog', Sprigge began to look for other ways to immerse herself in her project. She walked to the rue de Fleurus, where she was showered with dust from building work, and was soon exchanging cigarettes and tales of Picasso with the workmen. She talked to Maria Jolas of *transition* magazine, who told her how Stein had cut her off for championing Joyce. 'Her life was made up of battles,' Jolas told Sprigge. 'A rather rowdy character – Red Queen – off with their heads! But she didn't bear a grudge and she could be kind. When I lost a child, she and Alice were round at once with flowers.' And she took a bus down to Belley, where the patron of the local brasserie told her Stein used to visit every day, stuffing groceries into the pockets of her wide skirt, and waiters at the Hôtel Pernollet described the wind whistling as Stein sailed past in the Ford. 'What emerges strongly', wrote Sprigge in her journal, 'is that while in Paris Gertrude Stein is a subject of controversy and curiosity, in Belley she is a subject of affection and interest.' Madame

Roux, the mother of Stein's gardener, was shocked when Sprigge innocently asked if Stein had enjoyed gardening herself. 'No, madame. She only wrote her books. She was a genius.'

Sprigge gathered a wealth of material from her travels: she found Stein's old friends excited to gossip, share theories, settle old scores. But if she had assumed that she would eventually win Toklas over, she soon came to realise that she had underestimated her stubbornness. Sprigge shared her concerns with Thornton Wilder: she did not want to upset Toklas, she told him, but knew she had to write about her if she was to tell the truth about Stein. Wilder replied that Toklas was bound to be proprietorial: 'You're dealing with a very old lady,' he reminded her, 'and one who has led a very peculiar life which has always been entangled in *histoires* – scandal, gossip.' Toklas's main frustration, however, was Sprigge's lack of interest in Stein's writing. 'In her heart of hearts,' she complained, 'she despises Gertrude's method and does not understand.' She lost her final shred of respect when Sylvia Beach told her that Sprigge had asked whether she agreed that Toklas had probably written Stein's work. When Toklas read Sprigge's manuscript, in March 1956, she told friends it was 'worse than I feared'. Sprigge portrayed Stein, once again, as a figure of interest primarily because of her eccentricity and her famous friends.

It's possible there was a touch of guilt here. Toklas had maintained that she would never encroach on Stein's territory by writing a memoir – but through the cookbook, she had found an intriguing and subversive way to write autobiography while maintaining her position in the background. But by focusing on the kitchen, she had drawn attention to the area in which she was indisputably in charge, subtly asserting authority even as she protested that she was not an author. It was, in a way, an experiment comparable to the *Autobiography* in its formal playfulness: blending history, memoir, even detective story (one memorable chapter, featuring carp and pigeons, is titled 'Murder in the Kitchen'). Despite her continued insistence that it was a mere triviality knocked off quickly for money – a crass commodity, not a work of art – the cookbook's success had inadvertently eclipsed Stein's at a crucial moment. While the fifth Yale volume, *Painted Lace*, was printed in half as many copies as the first due to dwindling interest in the series, Toklas's book was being translated and reprinted; she was regularly invited to contribute recipes and columns to popular magazines, to be interviewed, to travel. But she found she could not fully enjoy the success: not only was Stein not there to share it, she was wracked by remorse that it should have been Stein's all along.

//

Stung by Sprigge's 'vulgarities and insinuations', and still bewildered by Katz's silence, Toklas retreated into herself. She refused to lend paintings to a New York gallery that had hoped to display the rue Christine collection with 'parades and fireworks and general rejoicing', and rejected its offer to pay her plane fare if she would attend the opening: 'Does she think the pictures are vegetables and I am a market woman?' she exclaimed bad-temperedly, when the gallerist asked under what conditions she might be persuaded to sell the artworks. But she was cheered by a retrospective of Picasso's early work in Paris, for which the Metropolitan Museum sent over his portrait of Stein, its first trip abroad since it left the rue Christine eight years earlier. 'It was a joy and a pain to see it again,' she wrote.

In many ways, Toklas felt like a living relic of a bygone past. Paris, as the 1950s dwindled, was again full of young Americans, from James Baldwin to William Burroughs, eager to peruse the old haunts of Hemingway, Fitzgerald and Gertrude Stein: to pursue a romantic ideal of freedom, and soak up the literary inheritance – the now-booming myth of the Lost Generation – that seemed to imbue the very streets of the Left Bank. To this new generation, Paris was a talisman, its cobbled streets and smoky cafés a refuge from McCarthy-era America's strict conformist censure. And it was a place to create culture anew: international, multiracial, political, avant-garde. There, the Olympia Press published books that couldn't pass the US censor; a new English-language book-shop, named Shakespeare and Company in homage to Sylvia Beach's, provided stray writers with books and beds; poets were experimenting with cutting up texts at the so-called Beat Hotel, a couple of blocks from the rue Christine; small magazines – *Les temps modernes*, *Zero*, the *Paris Review* – offered platforms to new voices as *transition* once had to Stein. Her legendary salon now appeared frozen in aspic: a historical artefact, no longer a vital force. In the spring of 1959, Beach lent her personal archive, including photographs of Stein and the typescript of a poem she had written to encourage friends to subscribe to Shakespeare and Company, to an exhibition called The American Writers of Paris and Their Friends. One entire wall was plastered with a photo montage showing the façade of the old Dingo café in Montparnasse, with original chairs and tables from the café placed in front of it. There, wrote Janet Flanner in her *New Yorker* report of the show, Alice B. Toklas sat with friends against the fake backdrop of her past, while the tones of George Anteuil's *Ballet mécanique* wafted from a nostalgic pianola.

But rather than contemplate mortality, Toklas was preoccupied with her own rebirth. On Christmas Day of 1957, she joyfully told Van Vechten that she had, a few weeks earlier, been admitted to the Catholic Church, confessed, and received Holy Communion. Dora Maar, who lived a block away and whom Toklas saw regularly, had laid the ground-work, assuring Toklas that Stein was such a great figure – 'like Moses' – that she was undoubtedly in heaven, and that Toklas would be able to see her again, if she joined the Catholic Church. Denise Aimé-Azam – who had orchestrated Bernard Faÿ's escape from prison – recommended an English priest, Father Edward Taylor, to whom Toklas talked at great length before deciding to convert. (Taylor expressed some discomfort taking confession in a room decorated with paintings of naked women; Toklas made some small skirts and bodices from cloth and paper, and attached them to the Picassos before he arrived.) She told Van Vechten she was informing only a few people of her 'new life', but that she would write to Gallup. 'It is wonderful to be part of the great Catholic Church,' she told another friend, 'where I should have been long ago.'

It was an astonishing statement. Toklas was Jewish by birth – her Polish grandfather had been a rabbi – and though she had never practised, the conversion seemed a drastic and incongruous step. Her friend Donald Sutherland was one of few who understood. The previous summer, Sutherland and his wife had taken Toklas on a road trip from Paris to Albi, diverting from their route to visit notable churches along the way, including one at Germigny-des-Prés. Toklas, Sutherland remembered, was entranced by the small church, the oldest in France: its tranquillity and light, its Byzantine mosaic showing angels and the Ark of the Covenant. As they left, she pointed out a series of blue enamel plaques set along the walls of the nave, and asked if he remembered a blue brooch Stein used to wear of exactly that colour. Months later, Toklas told him that her conversion had occurred in that church. Stein loved blue: 'Every bit of blue is precious,' she once wrote. Seeing that colour in the church, Sutherland imagined, helped Toklas 'remember the beatific side of Gertrude, not her angry or vengeful or desperate moments'. What's more, he felt she needed to 'devote herself completely to something': without Stein in person, Catholicism was her choice.

But the conclusive factor, for Toklas, was the prospect of reuniting with Stein after death. She explained to Van Vechten that she had talked at length with Bernard Faÿ, a devout Catholic, 'about the church and Baby's Judaism – which was a kind of ethical conception – a modern version of the Mosaic law which of course included no future life'. Toklas dreaded the idea that Stein was stuck permanently in Limbo. But Faÿ and Taylor had made the case to her that with enough prayers and penitence, Stein could be rescued and settled in Purgatory to await Toklas, before they went on together to Heaven. 'That is what is such a comfort to me now,' wrote Toklas, 'the peopled heaven – not only God and Jesus but the angels and saints.' It was a risky conclusion to draw. Stein's penchant for Catholic saints and paraphernalia was no substitute for baptism and confession. But Toklas was convinced – or chose to convince herself. 'You were her dearest friend during her life,' Toklas wrote to Faÿ, 'and now you have given her that eternal life.' Whether Faÿ's assurances represent a charlatan act on a vulnerable woman or a kindness done for her comfort, Toklas was resolute and radiant in her new-found faith. 'The past is not gone,' she wrote, 'nor is Gertrude.'

But while Toklas's spiritual needs were satisfied, her financial situation was concerning. She drew a monthly allowance of $400 from the Stein estate, with which she paid her personal expenses, but her dealings with the estate's various lawyers and administrators were erratic, and her allowance was occasionally withheld without warning. 'Gertrude Stein – in her generosity to me – did not foresee that such an occasion could arise,' she wrote frostily to her lawyer. Van Vechten couldn't understand why she didn't sell another painting if she needed money; he concluded that it was a matter of pride for her not to cost Stein's estate a cent for her personal welfare. She refused the help of friends, too: she sternly upbraided one who had dared to suggest 'coming to my rescue by having a subscription taken for my benefit or turning the flat into a tourist centre'. In September 1957, she reluctantly sold Picasso's landscape *Paysage Vert*, for $18,750; a fresh appraisal of the collection the following year valued it at 204,500 francs, a fourfold increase on a decade earlier.

'I wish to God Gertrude had drawn up a better will,' wrote Joseph Barry to Van Vechten. It was frustrating to see Toklas surrounded by Picassos yet struggling to feed herself: why, they asked, had Stein let this happen? Surely she could have foreseen difficulties with a complicated will which set the interests of one executor so directly against the other? The tragedy, of course, was that Stein and Toklas could not be legally married: if they had been, none of these problems would have been likely to arise. In making Allan her heir, Stein had condemned Toklas to the role of temporary custodian, living among possessions that were not ultimately hers. Perhaps there were tax advantages to this arrangement; perhaps they agreed she should honour her kinship responsibilities to Allan, towards whom she felt fondly – she saved all his solemn childhood letters to 'Aunty Gertrude' (signed 'with heaps of love to Uncle Leo and Miss Toklas'). 'Is it best to support Allan,' Stein had asked in her 1927 poem *Patriarchal Poetry*, connecting the dilemma of will-writing with her ambivalent feelings about her family and male tradition more broadly. But the compromise she had reached now seemed, to everyone, to have been bungled. It had started to look uncomfortably as though Stein's determination to assure her literary legacy had only prolonged her partner's dependence. Had she not imagined Toklas surviving so long without her?

15 : WHAT IS THE QUESTION?

Now approaching her eightieth birthday, Toklas was painfully aware that her fading memory was unreliable. A few days after Stein's death, Toklas had reported to Van Vechten her last words. 'What is the question?' Stein had asked, then after a pause, 'What is the answer?' Toklas told friends she thought often of those words, which gave her comfort: 'Were they not a summing up of her life and perhaps a vision of the future?' But years later, Van Vechten wrote to ask for clarification, since other versions were circulating, using slightly different formulations. In some, Stein's second retort had elaborated into, 'If there is no question then there is no answer.' In others, the order of the comments was reversed: 'What is the answer?' Stein had asked, and receiving no reply, 'In that case, what is the question?' Each alternative, it seemed, could be traced back to a single source: Toklas herself. Confronted with her own inconsistency, Toklas was plunged into despair. It was a stark demonstration of the difficulties of biography. Toklas saw clearly how the slippery nature of memory could easily lead to falsehoods being crystallised on paper and passed down as truth. Again, she contemplated the idea of writing about Stein more fully than she had in the cookbook. She could not rely on biographers – slapdash like Sprigge, liable to disappear like Katz – to act as her mouthpiece. If she wanted to maintain control of the Stein legend, she would have to do it herself.

In January 1958, Toklas wrote to Max White, a writer they had met during the American tour, who had stayed in touch with Toklas since Stein's death. The author of several works of historical fiction, which Stein had praised, White was a diffident, somewhat reclusive character who had developed the uncanny ability to say the right thing to Toklas whenever she needed it. Detecting her displeasure at its indiscretions, he had written scornfully of W. G. Rogers's 1948 memoir about his friendship with Stein ('a very thin broth . . . a book of mistaken devotion'), and he had warmly praised *Things as They Are* when none of her other friends seemed interested in reading it. She knew that he admired Stein's work, and he had got on well with both of them. Now, she explained, an editor named Robert Lescher had suggested that

Toklas might work alongside a more established author on a book of her own memoirs – and she was minded to agree. She asked White to be her ghostwriter.

White responded with enthusiasm, and Toklas was soon making plans to visit him in Rome. 'My only luxuries are cigarettes and bath,' she wrote, '– and my dear dear Max seeing you!' On 18 April, she sent him a contract setting out terms for 'the book that we shall jointly write concerning my life, my memories and experiences': he was to receive 50 per cent of all proceeds, but Toklas would retain 'full authority' over the book's content and style. There was only one stumbling block: Toklas was under contract with Harper for a second cookbook, which needed to be completed before she was free to work with Lescher's publisher, Henry Holt and Company. To discharge her duty, she arranged to supply recipes for a book to be titled *Aromas and Flavors of Past and Present*, which would be edited by a well-known food writer named Poppy Cannon. This book contained no anecdotes on life with Stein, just brisk recipes prefaced by a firm injunction from Toklas to waste nothing and use only the best of everything: 'If the budget is restricted, restrict the menu to what the budget affords.' Cannon provided chatty annotations above each recipe, often offering short cuts or cheaper adaptations bound to rouse Toklas's ire (a stock cube here, a tinned ingredient there). Nonetheless, Toklas was pleased enough with the book to send a copy to Eleanor Roosevelt, 'en souvenir of a memorable meeting in 1934'.

By the end of May, she was reporting that 'the work with Max White is advancing rapidly'. She told Van Vechten that they had 'agreed that the reminiscences should be centered on Baby and her work' and that her own memories should be discarded, except where they might throw light on Stein's methods. 'You agree – don't you? I am nothing but the memory of her.' But a few weeks later, she reported 'very strange news'. On 14 June, White had written to her announcing 'quite inexplicably' that he was destroying all his notes and abandoning the collaboration. White, she complained, had 'just disappeared into thin air': he had left a dinner party at midnight without mentioning anything, but the following morning had checked out of his hotel and left behind no forwarding address. On 29 June he wrote to the publishers from a hotel in Madrid, informing them that the project was doomed. Toklas, he declared, 'is too old and too ill to remember. All she can do is lie and deny it and contradict herself.'

In a later statement, which he delivered to the Gertrude Stein archive at Yale, White explained the situation further. The work, he wrote, was impossible. Toklas told stories he knew could not be true, but refused to admit it. He felt uncomfortable that she was paying his travel expenses, which left him entirely beholden to what she wanted, and he had begun to sense her 'deep animosity' when he questioned some of her more outlandish claims. It was clear from the beginning, White wrote, that 'the many years of their oddly-lit *gloire* were going to give Alice trouble in separating fact from fiction' – but her determination that this book would contain no real self-reflection, but would once again tell the story of 'forty years of devotion to Gertrude and her growing fame', left him complicit in what he believed to be a highly partial narrative – an affront to his honesty as a writer. To White, biography ought to aspire to a rounded truth: mere hagiography, he thought, served no purpose except to Toklas's twisted sense of subservience. Stein, he thought, was a complex and fascinating subject – and Toklas's reticence actually diminished her. He had torn his notebooks into confetti, stuffed them into a mail-sack and dumped them in a public rubbish bin a block away from the rue Christine. He wrote later that he considered Toklas's life with Stein to be one of 'incredible heroism', yet also 'one of the saddest of human stories'. 'A more enslaved woman would be hard to find among contemporaries,' he said. 'And when Gertrude was dead, she continued as the slave to a legend.'

Toklas, of course, saw things differently. When the initial indignation at White's betrayal subsided, she decided to write the book alone. 'The memories do not frighten me,' she wrote. The publisher offered her the services of a secretary and a further advance, but she refused.

She was prepared to sequester herself and, finally, do as so many friends had long urged her to do: write her autobiography of Gertrude Stein. 'Alice has invariably been inconsistent in her behaviour,' wrote Van Vechten to Gallup, 'but this, I believe, is the most inconsistent step she has taken.' Toklas worked on the book gradually for the next five years; Robert Lescher spent an annual week with her, editing the fifty pages she had written during the previous year. She was given an extra spurt of motivation by the conclusion of the Yale publication programme in November 1958, with *A Novel of Thank You*, introduced by the outgoing series editor, Carl Van Vechten. In his preface, he recalled his surprise at reading, in the *New York Times*, that Stein had appointed him her literary executor, and remembered how his heart had sunk when he saw the pile of manuscripts awaiting his attention. But, he wrote, the prospects had brightened: now, her operas were heard on the radio, the Banyan Press's *Things as They Are* had sold out after Edmund Wilson's 'flaming review'; just recently a dramatic version of *Brewsie and Willie* was presented on television. Stein, he proclaimed, remained a vital force in contemporary culture.

It was an optimistic assessment. A Yale volume had appeared every year between 1951 and 1958, with introductions of variable quality. The series had accomplished its basic aim: the full expanse of Stein's work was now available to the public in printed form. The university press imprimatur had given a certain stamp of respectability, and each new volume had provided an annual occasion for reviews and reassessments. But these tended to rehash old jibes – this was nonsense; automatic writing; the manic outpourings of an inflated ego. By the time the series was complete, the first instalments were already out of print. 'Baby is talked about,' a sanguine Toklas wrote to Van Vechten, 'written about even – quoted frequently – but only the young and often poor read her books. It isn't so different from what it always was. She is still years ahead of today and that is wonderful.' But among Stein's admirers lingered a sense that her reputation was floundering just at the point when they had done all that they could to establish it.

Thirty years after the *transition* wars, Stein remained controversial enough to inspire heated critical debate. That same year, 1958, the professor Benjamin Lawrence Reid published a book titled *Art by Subtraction: A Dissenting Opinion of Gertrude Stein*, which he described as 'an essay in decapitation'. Reid lambasted Stein's work for its opacity, maintaining that in stripping away all associations from words she was eliminating the possibilities of beauty, emotion and imagination, and – iconoclastically – rejecting the rich history of human knowledge. The takedown occasioned an impassioned response in *Accent* magazine by the young writer William H. Gass – later to become a major postmodern novelist and essayist – who dismissed it as 'a muddled and angry piece of journalese'. Reid, Gass pointed out, was trying simultaneously to destroy Stein's 'overinflated reputation' and to claim she was hardly read: he couldn't have it both ways. Most egregiously, his argument failed to engage with her writing at all. Stein's work, wrote Gass, mounted 'a challenge to criticism': 'it requires us to consider again the aesthetic significance of style, to examine again the ontological status of the artist's vision, his medium, and his effect'. None of Stein's contemporaries, Gass added, 'attempted anything like the revolution she proposed': in using language not 'merely to communicate' but to 'make a vital thing of words', he concluded that she had 'unsettled the whole of prose'. While Reid had argued Stein's work was important only to those who knew and admired her, and was nothing without her personality, Gass's response proved that a new generation of readers was starting to find her, and even see her marginality as heroic: he later located Stein in the 'permanent avant-garde'. Stein had always wanted her work to be wildly popular. But it was becoming clearer, as Toklas had acknowledged, that her influence lay outside the mainstream – where it was, as Gass's essay demonstrated, beginning to take root.

But the bad reviews still stung, and Toklas remained indignant, on Stein's behalf, at the wilful misreadings that continued to plague her reception. Meanwhile, Stein's peers – the writers whose success, in many cases, she had envied in her lifetime – were posthumously achieving the canonical status that eluded her. The Yale Edition appeared over a decade in which modernism was the subject of numerous studies, anthologies and scholarly debates, which sought to assess the period with authority as the number of its living practitioners dwindled. The term itself was highly contested – Ezra Pound wrote that he and T. S. Eliot had launched a movement 'to which no name has ever been given' – but Wyndham Lewis's description, in his 1937 memoir, of himself, Pound, Eliot and Joyce as the 'Men of 1914' set the boundaries for subsequent decades of criticism. Stein, of course, had claimed she 'started the whole thing' with *The Making of Americans*. But over the 1950s and 1960s, as modernism entered the academy, few scholars accepted Stein's centrality to the movement: she was regularly dismissed, pushed to the margins, or simply ignored.

Old rivalries compounded the frustrations. While she was dealing, incredulously, with Elizabeth Sprigge, Toklas fielded a visit from the scholar Richard Ellmann, who was at work on his monumental biography of James Joyce, whom Stein, Toklas remembered bitterly, had considered 'a grievous thorn in her side'. (She held grudges even longer than Stein: she told Van Vechten that the only suggestion she made towards the *Autobiography* was to include a quote from Picasso describing his main rival, Georges Braque, and James Joyce as 'the incomprehensibles whom anybody can understand'.) Ellmann's meticulously researched book cemented Joyce's position as a major figure in the primary aesthetic movement of the century, and was credited with making his work intelligible to a wider public. Hugh Kenner, meanwhile, was hard at work on his behemoth *The Pound Era*, which placed Pound at the centre of modernist history alongside Joyce, Eliot and Lewis. His hugely influential study not only transformed Pound's reputation – floundering after his support of Mussolini and pronounced antisemitism – but shored up the prominence of the 'Men of 1914', naming the entire epoch in their honour while denigrating the work of most women modernists.

Meanwhile, reviewers had largely taken Sprigge's book (published in

1957) as another opportunity to attack Stein, now critiquing not her work but her outsized image. Sprigge's text barely conceals her bemusement at her subject; her efforts to be discreet for Toklas's sake, ironically, led to some serious interpretative contortions, and her research journal (which she sent to the Stein archive at Yale) is far more revealing than the finished book, which largely regurgitates Stein's autobiographical writings. John Malcolm Brinnin's biography of Stein – which had been in the works since 1946, and finally appeared in 1959, the same year as Ellmann's *James Joyce* – was more psychologically acute and analytical, though still weakened by Toklas's lack of co-operation. While Sprigge drew primarily on Stein's memoirs, not daring to print the indiscretions her friends had so willingly confided, Brinnin delved deeper into her work, recalling Thornton Wilder's injunction to him, delivered with a knuckle-cracking handshake and a piercing stare: 'Don't talk *about* Gertrude. She did that. *Do* her.' Neither book discussed Stein's relationship with May Bookstaver (Brinnin called her a 'literary agent'), or read *Things as They Are* as autobiographical: neither had been allowed to see the 'Diagram Book', which remained sealed to all researchers except for the still-vanished Leon Katz. He was the only scholar Toklas had trusted enough to speak to openly – and his ongoing silence prolonged her wait for an assessment of Stein's early writing grounded in a study of her notebooks, which Toklas told friends formed the most revealing material the archive held. Van Vechten considered Brinnin's book far superior to Sprigge's, but Toklas seethed at both of them. She did not recognise Stein in either writer's effort to conjure her. She took the only recourse left to her: she annotated copies of Brinnin's and Sprigge's books, and sent them both to Yale. The margins are full of derision: 'no no no'; 'nonsense'; 'never'. The only story she would now accept was her own.

The writing of her memoir, however, was interrupted by a bitter dispute. Multiple high-profile art robberies had hit the headlines in recent years, which had heightened the anxiety of Allan Stein's widow, Roubina, that her children's inheritance remained in the care of a frail, possibly erratic old woman, protected only by ancient wooden shutters which could easily be breached. Over the years the estate's lawyer, Edgar Allan Poe, had often recommended re-evaluating the paintings, since their value had increased so greatly that the current insurance was no longer adequate; he also urged Toklas to consider placing them in a safer location than the apartment, which she staunchly refused to do. In 1960, Roubina Stein was alerted that a Picasso drawing, labelled as once belonging to the Stein collection, had sold at auction for around $10,000. Picasso's fame was booming: his 1905 painting *La Belle Hollandaise* had recently garnered the highest price ever commanded by a living artist, while his retrospective that year at London's Tate Gallery had opened to enormous fanfare, with a party featuring flamenco dancers and a special after-hours viewing attended by the Queen. Shocked to discover one of the Steins' works on the secondary market, Roubina demanded a new inventory be made of the collection, which revealed that it had depleted since Stein's death: a portfolio of Picasso's drawings and an oil painting, *Man in Top Hat*, had vanished without a trace.

Toklas calmly explained to Roubina's personal lawyer, Bernard Dupré, that she had sold these works to Daniel-Henry Kahnweiler back in 1953, when Van Vechten needed funds to guarantee the Yale Edition. Roubina was furious that Toklas had made a sale without consulting her, and at a fee (set, Toklas retorted, by Picasso himself) she considered far below market rate. She brought a legal action against Toklas, complaining that she left the collection unguarded for prolonged periods when she was away from home on her regular trips to the baths at Acqui in Italy (which helped with her arthritis), and that even when she was in residence, the apartment was vulnerable to intruders. Roubina demanded that the collection be declared 'endangered', and that all the artworks should be removed at once to a safe, dry, guarded place: the Chase Manhattan bank vault in Paris.

Toklas was kept aware of proceedings through her own lawyer, Russell Porter, but still left for Rome in the autumn of 1960 to avoid the chill of a French winter, staying at a convent in Monteverde. The nuns were Canadian, and after an inauspicious start – a copy of *Lolita* fell out of her handbag – Toklas enjoyed their company, music and food. Writing to friends, she lamented that she had had to (temporarily) give up smoking, her only luxury, but that she found Rome 'ravishing': 'Spring green peas from the hills are incredible. And the ices are unequaled.' She funded the trip by agreeing to read from *The Autobiography of Alice B. Toklas* for a record label ('I was born in San Francisco, California,' she uncannily intones in her deep, regal drawl: Toklas performing Stein performing Toklas). While there, she was thrilled to attend a papal audience at the Vatican ('momentous and moving'), and gorged on garlic artichokes bathed in olive oil at the local trattoria. But she returned to 5 rue Christine at the end of April 1961 to find the apartment ransacked. The paintings were gone from the walls; faint grubby outlines marked where they had once hung. They had been removed by court order the day before Toklas returned.

Gallup visited her in October – she gave him Stein's inkwell as a parting gift – and reported that she had 'become reconciled to the absence of the pictures'. Her lawyer had advised her not to sue for their

Mlle Toklas fait le marché rue Christine by Sir Francis Rose, *c.*1960

return. Toklas assured worried friends that she was sanguine about the loss: 'My memory', she wrote to Sutherland, 'is more vivid than my sight.' The writer Otto Friedrich visited the following year, 1962, and found her much aged: the 'iron vitality' of a decade ago was gone, and her back, he wrote, 'was hunched like that of someone being crushed'. For Sutherland, the gaps on the walls, which Toklas refused to cover, were 'pale and ghostly reminders of departed richnesses': the loss of the paintings a harsh emblem of Toklas's alienation from her former life. She was furious at Roubina Stein, and had started to go through everything in the flat, sending items of value to Yale before they could be sequestered. Janet Flanner devoted several *New Yorker* columns to her friend's plight, pointing out that Stein's work had been published in eight Yale volumes thanks only to Toklas's determination and self-denial. The art collection was not just property but a memorial to Stein and to their life together: Toklas and Stein had shared their home with these paintings, she wrote, 'in the civilised intimacy that relates certain human beings and objects when they have long lived together. It was a collection with its own kind of private life.' Another friend, the critic Fanny Butcher – a committed champion of Stein's work, who had hosted Stein and Toklas in Chicago in 1934 – shuddered to see the dreary apartment, its walls adorned only by mirrors which seemed to multiply the emptiness. 'The glaring squares of white against the dusty walls', she wrote, 'were almost like a graveyard of white tombstones marking where the Picassos and Matisses and Braques and Picabias and the whole gay assemblage had once lived. Alice was a shrunken and sad little figure to look at, but strangely at last she was Alice B. Toklas, famous herself, not, as she had been all of her life, Gertrude's shadow.'

But Toklas's travails were not over. In May 1963, she confessed to Sutherland that she was once again 'in a devil of a mess'. Five years earlier, 5 rue Christine had been sold to a new company, who offered tenants the opportunity to buy their apartments. Toklas decided against it: 'The French law protects aged ladies,' she wrote confidently, 'so I can stay on for the rest of my days.' But the law stated that an apartment could not be vacant for more than four months a year, and the new owner sued for possession. Toklas received her eviction order, demanding she leave within twenty-four hours, from her bed. The sheriff who served it to her noted her response: 'I was born in 1877. If I leave this apartment it will be to go to Père-Lachaise.'

Friends rushed to help her. Janet Flanner cabled to André Malraux, the minister of cultural affairs, who briefly stayed the eviction. The designer Pierre Balmain offered to donate as much money as was needed, and suggested moving Toklas to the Trianon Palace in Versailles: 'I am ready to kill all these crooked lawyers,' he raged to Daniel Joseph, a Baltimore lawyer newly appointed (following Edgar Allan Poe's retirement, aged ninety) as administrator of the Stein estate. Toklas wrote to Gallup asking him to dig out from the archive the certificate for the Médaille de la Reconnaissance Française awarded to her after their work for the wounded in the First World War, which she wanted to present at her trial (ironically, he could only find Stein's). While her case was considered, she spent three months at the American Hospital – where Stein had died – following a broken hip and leg from a fall. But before she could be discharged, the owner of 5 rue Christine sent an ultimatum ordering her expulsion. Friends secured a lease for her on a modern fourth-floor flat at 16 rue de la Convention, five kilometres west of the rue Christine, which Toklas described as 'down near the Seine at the end of the world'. The apartment was lacking character, she could hear her neighbours sneeze, and she was forbidden to drive nails into the walls ('in a country of painting!'). She had only one artwork left to take with her, a Seine landscape by Dora Maar which her house-keeper, Madeleine Charrière, placed on the floor, leaning against the wall. 'I miss the old flat', Toklas wrote frankly, 'that was filled with memories of Gertrude Stein.'

Her book, *What Is Remembered*, was published in 1963, and greeted with bemusement by both critics and friends. They had hoped for a late insight into Toklas's psychology, even if they didn't expect a revisionary counter-narrative to Stein's *Autobiography*. Instead, Toklas appeared to be missing from her own memoir. 'Did she never wish for a life of her own, for anything of her own?' asked the *Saturday Review*. *Time* wrote that Toklas seemed to have 'disappeared virtually without a trace into Gertrude Stein's life', and called it 'the sad, slight book of a woman who all her life has looked in a mirror and seen somebody else'. 'What would Alice have been without Gertrude?' wrote the *New York Post*. 'It is as empty a question as what is a Rockefeller without money.' Even Donald Gallup described *What Is Remembered* as 'a mere ghost of the book that she would have written sixteen years earlier', but expressed his relief that she had, at last, completed the task. He knew Toklas could not win her long battle against Stein's biographers without setting down her own story. With *What Is Remembered*, she had achieved this on her own terms: she managed somehow both to speak and to remain invisible.

The passive voice of the title even excised Toklas's authorial agency. What was remembered were the stories cemented in the course of their marriage, formed and honed through endless repetition and subtle negotiation. Friends remembered Toklas quietly correcting Stein when in full flow with wild anecdotes – Virgil Thomson suggested that 'every story that ever came into the house eventually got told in Alice's way' – but even with Toklas shaping the material, Stein ultimately remained the storyteller. Toklas borrowed her structure and many of her set-pieces from the *Autobiography* – implicitly endorsing Stein's telling as the 'original', and hers the copy – and closed her narrative where she felt her real life had ended: at Stein's death. She had written a final chapter covering the years she had stayed on alone – 'I picked up my life as I could,' it began, 'not expecting in the least that I should live' – but decided to cut it, since it had turned into a diatribe against the Stein heirs. Her book certainly doesn't mention May Knoblauch, though she does tartly describe an awkward lunch with Etta Cone – whose friends had told Sprigge that Stein had initially 'wanted Etta to be her Alice' – where she and Cone had argued over who would pay the bill. Just a couple of enigmatic passages hinted at the darker memories stirred by her sessions with Katz. The first winter, she wrote, 'Gertrude diagnosed me as an old maid mermaid which I resented . . . I cannot remember how this wore thin and finally blew away entirely.' During a freezing winter in Saint-Rémy, she wrote, Toklas found herself bursting into tears and telling Stein she wanted to go home – 'but Gertrude had written so well there, and so happily and so much, that I made up my mind I would behave and not complain'. Most conspicuously of all, Toklas only once mentions the *Autobiography* by name, even when describing the American tour and Stein's attendant celebrity. Perhaps she resented her name being made so public; perhaps it brought back difficult memories of the tensions which precipitated the book's writing and waged on during the tour. Toklas's evasiveness, much like Stein's, was far from inadvertent.

Memory is an act of creation. To most readers, the main disappointment of *What Is Remembered* – an otherwise absorbing account of two rich and exciting lives – was its failure to answer the questions so many had about life with Stein, to speak frankly of their life together. But in a way, her refusal to reveal more was Toklas's assertion of autonomy. Every Stein biographer, from Rogers to Katz to Sprigge, had noted what she refused to admit: that she was indispensable to Stein's work – but the memoir marked her final rebuttal of their attempts to elevate her status. She remained elusive by choice. 'Gertrude did my autobiography,' she claimed, 'and it's done.' As often with Toklas, this statement – apparently so self-denigrating – is actually a boundary being firmly set. One review lamented that *What Is Remembered* contained no 'confessions of the heart'. But Toklas felt no desire to invite the reader into her private life: the 'truth' of her autobiography lay, paradoxically, in the way she remained hidden. What she shows us is, perhaps, artfully self-referential after all: herself and Stein annotating each other's stories endlessly, until it's impossible to tell them apart.

//

A very different memoir, published the following year, took a final swipe at Stein and Toklas. In 1956, Ernest Hemingway had found a Louis Vuitton trunk he had stored, thirty years earlier, in the basement of the Hôtel Ritz. It contained the notebooks he had filled, in the 1920s, with observations of the people he had watched, from behind his beer glass or mug of café crème, in neighbourhood bars around Paris. Now living in Cuba, Hemingway worked up the notebooks into a nostalgic memoir titled *A Moveable Feast*, which his widow saw to publication three years after his suicide in July 1961. It tells the story of an aspiring writer living cheaply in hotels, scribbling in cafés over rum and oysters, teaching Ezra Pound to box and plying F. Scott Fitzgerald with whisky sours. Stein figures prominently in the memoir's first chapters, chatting away to Hemingway while 'her companion' – never named – sews silently. She tells him he 'might be some new sort of writer', and counsels him to economise on clothes and buy art instead; she dismisses Aldous Huxley and D. H. Lawrence, presses on him a novel about Jack the Ripper, and describes him and his friends as a 'lost generation'. But Hemingway's portrait of Stein, initially friendly, takes a dark turn when he describes the end of their friendship – an elaboration of the story he had hinted at, years earlier, to Donald Gallup. One afternoon, he claims, he visited the rue de Fleurus and was shown in by the housekeeper. From upstairs, he heard 'someone speaking to Miss Stein as I had never heard one person speak to another . . . Then Miss Stein's voice came pleading and begging, saying, "Don't, pussy. Don't. Don't, please don't. I'll do anything, pussy, but please don't do it."'

Hemingway's mock-discretion leaves it to the reader to imagine what Toklas may have been threatening. His tone of titillated disgust is designed both to expose the sadomasochistic dynamic he detected in Stein and Toklas's relationship, and to prove his own repulsion. There were complex psychological motives at play here. Stein reminded Hemingway of his mother, who was only two years her senior; in 1948, he told W. G. Rogers (speaking of Stein) that 'I always wanted to fuck her and she knew it'. Toklas evidently saw Hemingway as a would-be rival: 'Don't you come home with Hemingway on your arm,' she told Stein when she went out for a walk – one of the few lines in the *Autobiography* authentically delivered in Toklas's voice. After reading the *Autobiography* he railed to friends at Stein's description of him as 'yellow' – an innuendo implying queerness, or even femininity, which the macho Hemingway was desperate to disavow. He swore he would get his revenge on Stein when he wrote his own memoirs (she was 'a fine woman,' he declared, 'until she went professionally patriotically goofily complete lack of judgement and stoppage of all sense lesbian with the old menopause') – and concludes his account of Stein with an image of her as a haughty, power-crazed Roman emperor, quarrelling with everyone and diluting her great art collection with worthless paintings. 'I liked her better before she cut her hair,' he told Rogers, with an implied scoff at both her sexuality and her success – betraying, of course, his own insecurities.

Hemingway told his readers they were welcome to take *A Moveable Feast* as fiction. Whether or not this scene between Stein and Toklas actually occurred – and it's certainly tinged with homophobia and score-settling bravado, as well as possibly some sexual envy – it's a psychologically plausible reading of the subtext to their relationship: Toklas silent in public but privately dominating; Stein outwardly imperious but compliant behind closed doors. 'You will give me orders will you not,' she wrote in a 1916 text titled 'Water Pipe'. 'I will never question. Your lightest wish shall be my law.' But it reduces the relationship to a caricature, and reimposes a hierarchy that their complex dynamic defies. The notebooks, *The Making of Americans*, *Lifting Belly*, the *Autobiography*, the cookbook, *What Is Remembered*: all, cumulatively, are testament to a collaboration, a dialogue, that extended across decades, in the home and on the page. Toklas, her own account of history complete, felt no need to respond to Hemingway's blustering attack. Once a week, a student came to read aloud to her. During one session, he picked up *A Moveable Feast* from her table and settled into its narrative, but faltered, horrified, when he reached this passage, unsure whether to continue. To his surprise, Toklas appeared not the least disconcerted. 'I wonder what all that was about,' was her only remark.

//

The death of Carl Van Vechten, on 21 December 1964, came as a 'great shock' to Toklas, who considered him her 'rock and mainstay'. Her band of friends was dwindling. Each departure, now, was an echo of Stein's; each funeral made Toklas question her own extended survival. There were practical implications, too: Toklas was now nearly blind, confined to her bed, and besieged by bills, demands and admonishments from belligerent lawyers. During the crisis of her final years, Toklas's primary champion was a young Polish opera singer named Doda Conrad, whom she had met in a cinema queue when he stepped in to solve a confusion over her ticket. The *New York Times*, some years earlier, had praised him as a 'sincere, sensitive and imaginative artist': he employed all these qualities in his tireless work for Toklas's comfort.

Shocked that Janet Flanner seemed to be the only one of her friends doing anything to protest her mistreatment by the Steins, Conrad stepped in, determined to overhaul Toklas's financial affairs. He sought assurances from the lawyers that Toklas's expenses would be met by the Stein estate – when she was in hospital, Picasso had sent a cheque for $1,000 to cover her bills – but was told that there was nothing to be done: the paintings were sequestered so could not be sold, and lawyers could draw only on the cash capital that remained in Baltimore. Conrad retorted that the $400 a month Toklas was receiving from the estate – most of which went straight to bills and lawyer's fees – was far from adequate, but the lawyers continued to equivocate. Madeleine Charrière, her housekeeper, had not been paid for over a year, and was footing many of Toklas's bills herself. 'I feel that Gertrude's primary concern in setting up the will was that her companion of many, many years' standing should be properly looked after in her old age,' wrote

Conrad, 'and it is thoroughly immoral for Roubina or anyone else to interfere with this explicit wish.'

In the spring of 1965, Flanner and Conrad established a committee of friends who were willing to support Toklas. Its members – including Virgil Thomson, Pierre Balmain, Thornton Wilder, and Van Vechten's widow Fania Marinoff – contributed approximately $550 a month to cover expenses – salaries, pharmacy bills, monthly visits from a priest – with an extra $100 per month sent by Donald Sutherland for luxuries, which Toklas spent on airmail stamps, sherry for visitors, cigarettes and eau de cologne. Charrière came over each morning to help her bathe and dress (Toklas reported that her housekeeper had 'become without any reason a roaring Communist, but remains a good Catholic'), while her old GI friend Joseph Barry visited regularly to read letters aloud to her and answer them. Many of her late letters are in his handwriting; those written in her own large spidery hand tend to trail off where she loses concentration. But she continued to revel in gossip, though by now, reports from friends tended to involve illness and death: 'I pray for *everybody* twice a day,' she wrote.

In June, the American Cultural Centre in Paris organised a celebration – Hommage à Gertrude Stein – and invited Toklas to be guest of honour. An actor, Nancy Cole, transformed herself into Stein for a virtuoso one-woman performance of several of her works, while tributes were read from numerous friends and acquaintances. The director of the Metropolitan Museum revealed that a pointed comment of Stein's during the American tour ('Whenever I go into a museum, I look out of the window') had inspired him to install several new windows in his buildings, while Thornton Wilder, with perennial optimism, announced that 'the day is not far off when Gertrude Stein's insights will be acknowledged as one of the great achievements of the century'. In the event, Toklas was too ill to attend, but a French translator of Stein's work visited to interview her for *Le Monde* to mark the occasion. She found Toklas wizened and numinous, like a sibyl, and sensed that she had told all her stories a hundred times and was no longer able to say anything spontaneous. Did she remember her life in Paris like Stein had told it in the *Autobiography*? Toklas looked disgruntled. Yes, she answered. *'Pourquoi pas?'*

That summer, she had a cataract removed from her right eye: Thomson, who accompanied her to the hospital (having long since forgiven her for her role in the infamous 1930 falling-out), speculated that she was making sure she could see Gertrude clearly when the time came. Toklas's tastes remained extravagant: Charrière would buy fruit at the local market and carry it back in bags from luxury shops, to give Toklas the illusion that she continued to eat the best in Paris. Conrad, meanwhile, ramped up negotiations with the lawyers for the estate, travelling to Baltimore to petition for the eighty-nine-year-old Toklas to receive an adequate pension for the rest of her life. He proposed a compromise: that Toklas would renounce her right to life interest in the estate in exchange for an allowance of $1,000 a month, with the paintings to become property of the heirs (Roubina's children Michael and Gabrielle, both in their early twenties, and their older half-brother Daniel from Allan Stein's first marriage). Finally, a judgement was made in her favour: the Steins had agreed to Conrad's proposal, and Toklas was out of financial danger. But before Conrad could pick up the phone to tell her, it rang. It was Janet Flanner, whispering that Alice B. Toklas was about to take her last breath. She died in the early hours of 7 March 1967.

//

Toklas's will, written in 1959, began with an injunction that surprised no one: 'I wish to be buried in the same tomb as Gertrude Stein in the Père-Lachaise Cemetery.' Her original will left her money to Father Edward Taylor of Saint-Pierre-de-Chaillot Church, but a codicil dated 30 January 1963 split the royalties from *What Is Remembered* between her housekeeper Madeleine Charrière and another friend, Virginia Knapik, and asked that news of her death should be wired to

Donald Gallup. Her last years had been difficult: she had told a nurse she was ready to die. With her memoir, she had discharged her final act of devotion to Gertrude Stein. Her *New York Times* obituary, printed the day after her death, described the two of them as 'inseparable companions, faces in the mirror to each other, and conductors of probably the most renowned cultural salon in the world'. Although Toklas was 'mainly content to let Miss Stein scintillate in public,' the obituary portrayed her as a complex, almost tragic, almost heroic figure: 'one of the really great cooks of all time', a small but steely woman whose sad end should not overshadow a life of extraordinary vigour.

The funeral service was short and sparsely attended. A handful of friends proceeded to Père-Lachaise, where Stein's tomb was opened and Toklas's tiny coffin lowered inside to sit beside Stein's. The front of the stone still bore Stein's name alone; Toklas's date of death was added to her name on the back. 'There they lie together now,' wrote Toklas's friend James Lord, 'united forever in fact and in memory, each having served in her own indomitable and creative way the human hunger for art and the artist's craving for immortality.' Janet Flanner, leaning on the tombstone, introduced a note of levity when she remarked, 'God knows the gossip these two are going to make after so long!' Conrad had insisted that the funeral costs should be paid by the Stein estate, so that the balance of the Paris bank account he had opened for Toklas could be returned to her generous friends. He was stunned to discover, through the lawyers wrapping up her affairs, that Toklas had her own, apparently forgotten account in Boston, where the royalties from the cookbook had, in fact, accumulated nicely. 'The scoundrel!' exclaimed Flanner, when Conrad, crestfallen, reported the news. 'She did us well!'

16 : THE BRANCHES

The news, which broke in January 1968, that Gertrude Stein's collection was up for sale set the New York art world abuzz with excitement. A bevy of French and American lawyers, acting on behalf of Allan Stein's three children, worked around the clock to remove the paintings from Paris before the French government could prevent their export. The Museum of Modern Art was eager to acquire six of the best Picassos, but the Steins had set the condition that the works – thirty-eight by Picasso and nine by Juan Gris – must be sold together as a single collection, independently valued at $6.8 million. The museum's trustee David Rockefeller made a proposition to four of his colleagues on the board: that they club together to purchase the collection in its entirety, and pledge to donate six paintings to MoMA, with the rest to be shared among themselves. The syndicate prevailed, and on the afternoon of 14 December 1968, the five men met in a back room of the museum, leaned the paintings along the walls, and drew lots from an old felt hat to determine the order in which they would select works for their private collections. Rockefeller went first, and chose *Young Girl with a Flower Basket*, which (despite Gertrude's dislike of the legs) she and Leo had bought in 1905 for $30. It was now valued at almost a million dollars.

Before the collection was dispersed, the group decided that the forty-seven works should be displayed together, at MoMA, for a final time. In 1970, the museum announced that the planned exhibition was expanding: curators were working to reassemble as many of the works originally owned by Gertrude, Leo, Michael and Sarah Stein as they could, in an inspired effort to recreate the salons of 27 rue de Fleurus and 58 rue Madame in the years before the First World War. Since Gertrude and Leo had bought their first painting, the Stein collection had evolved many times over: paintings had been sold for contingency reasons (to raise funds for the Plain Edition, or for wartime food supplies), and traded unsentimentally with dealers, friends or relatives for money or alternative works. The curators pored over old photographs of the apartment interiors, identifying pictures and sleuthing to discover their current whereabouts. Eventually they gathered more than 200 artworks from ninety collections across the world, from Melbourne, Zurich, Oslo and – despite Cold War tensions requiring lengthy diplomatic negotiations between government emissaries – Saint Petersburg. The Baltimore Museum of Art lent several pieces from the collection of Claribel and Etta Cone, who had regularly bought paintings when the Steins needed money. A couple in Oklahoma lent Matisse's *Nude Before a Screen*, one of the paintings Michael and Sarah had taken to San Francisco in 1906 and shown to Alice Toklas and Annette Rosenshine, setting both women's imaginations on a course to Paris. And the New York owners lent Cézanne's still life of a bowl of apples, the work Gertrude was most disappointed to lose to Leo in the split. For the first time, it was united with *Pomme (Apple)*, by then the property of David Rockefeller, which Picasso had painted to console Gertrude for the absence of her favourite Cézanne. An inscription on the back of this canvas read 'Souvenir pour Gertrude et Alice. Picasso Noel 1914.'

Toklas's chairs

Toklas wrote that Stein 'absolutely used the pictures every minute of the day'. These works had hung on Stein's walls for decades; they were part of her – and part of Toklas, who had lived alone with them for almost twenty years. Their public display marked a new era: the Stein–Toklas salon had survived both its originators, and passed into the realm of legend. Janet Flanner's review struck a mournful note: 'In their new, sleek museum showcase,' she wrote, 'the major value that seemed lacking was private love.' At the heart of the exhibition, borrowed from Yale, were two eighteenth-century chairs featuring needlepoint lovingly stitched by Toklas after Picasso's designs. They stood, empty, against a blown-up photograph of the atelier's interior, as if waiting for Stein and Toklas to emerge from a hidden doorway and take up their familiar seats once more.

//

Without Toklas alive to steward her legacy, Stein's future rested on her readers: the 'strangers' for whom she had always claimed to write. As her personality faded beyond living memory, her work would have to stand on its own terms. The exhibition's enormous popularity with new audiences, who had never visited the Stein salon and had no vested interest in her, boded well. Stein had always had a small but devoted band of readers, even when her work was being rejected by publishers and derided by critics: since her death, Toklas had fielded numerous fan letters from people who wanted to tell Toklas, as her proxy, what Stein's work had meant to them. Some had even established their own Stein collections, clamouring for relics of the rue de Fleurus: scraps of paper bearing Stein's signature, horsehairs from the sofa, frayed envelopes stamped with Toklas's personalised wax seal, emblazoned with the immortal line 'rose is a rose is a rose'. In many ways, these collectors – often young gay men, who looked to Stein as a mother figure and an example – helped carry her memory forward and give fresh impetus to her legacy: their efforts hunting down rare copies of early works, compiling bibliographies, and tracking her posthumous life by saving reviews, playbills, posters and other ephemera formed a DIY counterpart to Donald Gallup's official archival stewardship. And this, in turn, fed and fed off a wave of interest from a new generation of readers, artists and writers who looked to Stein's path-breaking work as they forged their own.

'Again', wrote the poet John Ashbery in his review of the MoMA show, 'we are reminded that the twentieth century, whatever else it may be, is the century of *Matisse, Picasso and Gertrude Stein*.' Ashbery was part of a group of young New York artists – musicians, painters, actors, poets – who congregated in Greenwich Village dive bars (the Cedar Tavern; the San Remo). In this circle, Stein's books were read avidly, tattered copies passed around and discussed between friends over cheap beer and Martinis. One of Ashbery's closest friends was the poet Frank O'Hara, who as an undergraduate at Harvard had written a term paper on *The Autobiography of Alice B. Toklas*, which he described as 'one of the most interesting things I've ever read by anyone'. In his poem 'Memorial Day 1950' – his announcement of himself as an artist, which features an image of Picasso chopping through dead art with an axe – O'Hara described his intention to complete 'several last things / Gertrude Stein hadn't had time for'. He took her as a model of immediacy and directness, drawing on her multiplicity of meaning and her American idiom, which he inflected with a cool contemporary lyricism.

To Ashbery, O'Hara and their peers, Stein offered a model of a life devoted entirely to art – an uncompromising commitment to her vision in the face of mockery, rejection and misunderstanding. They admired the way she turned her home into a crucible of artistic innovation; they read her lectures not as self-aggrandisement but as multifaceted works of aesthetic theory. Above all, they were interested in her writing, and the possibilities it offered to theirs. To many poets, of the New York School and beyond, the way Stein took language apart, violating all the rules of grammar, offered a blueprint for their own probings of form, memory and voice. To artists pioneering new varieties of pop art or abstraction, her repetition and her non-representational use of words offered a literary equivalent to the freedom they sought in painting, sculpture or collage. And to theatre directors, actors, dancers and musicians, her exploration of words' sonic quality lent itself perfectly to cross-disciplinary performance, the form perhaps most on the ascendance in post-war New York. Stein was part of more than one revolution: after her death, across an ocean, she found readers who would take her work utterly seriously, and build on its foundations with an explosion of creativity that would reshape every notion of twentieth-century art.

Three elements, in particular, cemented Stein's position as the forerunner to a revolution in aesthetics which reverberated down the decades. The first was the enormous influence of John Cage, composer and polymath, whose radical experiments with sound and silence – from household objects to radio static – reformed ideas of what music was. Cage had engaged with Stein's work since his student days, and some of his first compositions set her poems to music; when asked to list the ten books that had influenced him most, he began with Stein: 'any title'. His most famous composition, *4' 33"*, consists of whatever sounds happen to fill the time – the rustling and breathing of audience members; distant drilling or conversation; protests outside the performance venue – heightening listeners' attention to what's around them, leaving proceedings ungoverned by the composer, and the effects undetermined. Cage used sounds like Stein used words: not for the purpose of melody, illustration or narrative development, but for themselves. Both saw experience as something impressionistic and cumulative, not linear: their work was intimately bound up with time, demanding close attention to, and in, the present moment. The function of art, Cage suggested – echoing Stein – is 'to draw us nearer to the process which is the world we live in'. Just like Stein, Cage set out to create compositions that would reflect experience, disavowing any preconceived intentions, and laying emphasis less on the finished piece than the process of its making, the environment of its performance, and the audience's perceptual awareness.

Cage's efforts to blur distinctions between art and life had far-reaching implications for artists working across media. He was a crucial instigator in spreading Stein's ideas to his collaborators – the Living Theatre, with whom he shared a studio, whose performances of Stein in the 1950s had become legendary; his partner Merce Cunningham, whose modern dance incorporated impressionistic, everyday movements, freeing the body from the structures of formal choreography just as Stein liberated words from the constraints of grammar. And among those who took up Stein's work most enthusiastically were Cage's students. His Experimental Composition class at New York's New School was attended, in the late 1950s, by a cluster of artists – including Jackson Mac Low, Allan Kaprow and George Brecht – looking to explode boundaries between artistic disciplines. With like-minded contemporaries, including Yoko Ono and Nam June Paik, they gathered downtown in lofts and studios and made experimental, multimedia art under the loose umbrella of 'Fluxus'. Stein's importance to this group was cemented by the republication of several of her books, in cheap and attractive editions, by the Something Else Press – a Chelsea-based publishing house founded in 1963 by another of Cage's students, a moustached film-maker in his early twenties named Dick Higgins.

Determined that his generation should know the history on which they were building, Higgins established the press to set avant-garde texts by his peers alongside classics from the past (which he described as 'love letters to the future'). 'Our Patron is Gertrude Stein and we're republishing everything she wrote,' declared Higgins in an early manifesto. 'She's the mother of us all and satisfies all our needs for roots. We're the branches.' Higgins described Stein's work as 'an entire cosmology of the arts', and was determined to 'steal her back from the rare book freaks and collectors who had appropriated her', by making her work available to the readers who needed her most: artists who might recognise her as a precursor or seek her as a reference point. The press's first Stein book, in 1966, was a facsimile of the 1925 Contact Edition of *The Making of Americans* (the first time the novel had been published in the US unabridged); four more reissues followed over the 1970s, including *Lucy Church Amiably* and *G.M.P.*, both of which had originally appeared through Stein's own Plain Edition. The ultimate aim was clearly defined: for 'Stein the poet to emerge from Stein the legend'. 'Where oh where is the man to publish me in series?' Stein had asked Van Vechten in 1916. In Higgins, half a century later, Stein found him. At a time when the Yale Editions were almost impossible to come by, the Something Else Press project heralded a significant revival of her work in print, forming a crucial bridge between the Yale series and the 'Classic' editions that would, eventually, follow on.

Since the Living Theatre's celebrated productions, Stein's plays had become a touchstone for directors bent on transforming the tradition of European avant-garde theatre into a specifically American art. Her work found an unlikely posthumous home at the Judson Memorial Church, an imposing nineteenth-century building on New York's Washington Square. Since the mid-1950s, thanks to a forward-thinking pastor eager to use this vast space to serve local artists (whom he considered 'secular prophets'), the church had become a hub of radical performance in downtown New York: a pioneering troupe of postmodern dancers practised and performed there, while its basement hosted some of the earliest Happenings, a kind of event – inspired by Cage, and very much in Stein's tradition – without plot or conventional staging, emphasising space and duration over dramatic action. During the 1960s, the church's resident directors, Al Carmines and Lawrence Kornfeld (who had trained with Julian Beck and Judith Malina at the Living Theatre), mounted several hugely acclaimed productions of Stein's plays, devising spontaneous stagings fusing dance, music and theatre which allowed performers to respond organically, with their bodies and voices, to the text and the space. They rehearsed collaboratively, reading Stein's plays over and over to discern their logic; Carmines, at the piano, layered sequences into harmonies that would complement the words' emotional timbre, while the dancers – among them Lucinda Childs and Yvonne Rainer, both of whom became leading choreographers – came up with a stream of ordinary yet unexpected movements to emulate the word games of each text. Kornfeld, as director, wanted his productions to explore unspoken feelings and 'Steinian ways of looking at people': his actors were not pretending to be characters who already existed in a creator's mind, but were creating something fresh, unpredictable and real. 'What is happening up there is them,' he wrote. 'It's not a story.'

'The Judson Poets' Theater performs Gertrude Stein the way the Moscow Art Theatre does Chekhov,' wrote *Newsweek* in response to their version of her 1920 play *In Circles*, which toured America over 1967–9, and came to London in the autumn of 1968. Kornfeld remembered his satisfaction that *In Circles* had proven Stein could be popular, and – above all – that her work felt current, and consequential. 'She wasn't some kind of joke,' he said, 'this lady who collected writers and painters and wrote these strange things . . . We weren't interested in her celebrity, her kookiness, the way the world perceived her. We saw her as an avant-garde artist, and deadly serious.' To celebrate the theatre's tenth anniversary, in 1972, Kornfeld teamed up with a close friend of his, with whom he had long shared his passion for Stein. It was none other than Leon Katz, who was now teaching drama at Carnegie Mellon University in Pittsburgh, not far from where Stein was born. Katz deeply admired Kornfeld's approach to Stein's work: 'His productions of Stein do what her plays do,' he wrote: 'open doors on many meanings.' At Kornfeld's suggestion, Katz adapted *The Making of Americans* into a libretto: it featured Stein as the omniscient writer-narrator, serenely directing the characters who move around her.

//

Leon Katz never did return to see Alice B. Toklas. But he continued to work on Stein's notebooks for the rest of his life, hesitant to release his material until his studies were complete. His PhD dissertation, 'The First Making of *The Making of Americans*: A Study Based on Gertrude Stein's Notebooks and Early Versions of Her Novel (1902–1908)', was approved in 1963 – a ten-year delay which was to prove characteristic. By that point, the story of his months with Toklas had acquired mythical status. His dissertation – there's no indication Toklas ever read it – revealed, for the first time, Stein's 'hopeless love affair' with May Bookstaver, which Katz argued marked the start of Stein's 'sombre psychological wisdom'. The thesis is peppered with intriguing footnotes citing information Toklas had personally given him, but the full story of their interviews, Katz hinted, would emerge only when the notebooks were published in full. With Gallup's blessing, Katz then signed a contract with Liveright for an edition of Stein's notebooks, annotated with his and Toklas's comments, timed to coincide with her centenary in 1974. Writing in the *New York Review of Books* in 1971, Virgil Thomson described the promise of Katz's fresh material as 'a new pinnacle . . . like a partly exposed iceberg' for Stein studies, certain to shine 'a sudden searchlight' on its subject. But deadlines passed, and Katz's major publication never appeared.

The most obvious reason was that he was busy. Stein had to be fitted around his teaching career – by all accounts, he was a charismatic and inspirational professor – and his own work as a playwright and a dramaturg. Another factor was the depth of his continued research: he spent decades ordering and re-ordering his chronology of the notebooks, noticing new elements in *The Making of Americans* that warranted deeper analysis, pinpointing obscure references and conducting further interviews. In 1968, he finally tracked down Annette Rosenshine, now living in California, where she ran art therapy sessions for children. She had never forgotten her early experience in Paris, and always wondered if she was something of an embarrassing secret in Stein's mythology – a 'false note' in the legend that Stein and Toklas had designed together. Rosenshine had written to Stein daily after leaving Paris, and received only short and sporadic replies; on a visit to Paris years later, she had taken some of her own plasticine sculptures to show Stein, only for Toklas to pointedly – bizarrely – switch off the lights. Having been excised from the *Autobiography*,

Rosenshine was satisfied to learn, from Katz, that she had played a brief but formative role in the creation of *The Making of Americans*. A long process of analysis with Jung had confirmed the inadequacies of Stein's aggressive course of therapy, yet she credited Stein, gratefully, with setting her on the path to self-knowledge. As for Toklas's conversion to Catholicism in the hope of reuniting with Stein after death, Rosenshine was scornful. 'Alice had an unconscious resentment of Gertrude,' she told Katz, 'and the whole life of living through another . . . One knew she hadn't lived her own life.'

But the longer Katz's silence continued, the more it frustrated other Stein scholars – in what was now a crowded field. Throughout the 1970s, a spate of projects reignited interest in her life and work: Perry Miller Adato's documentary film *When This You See Remember Me* (1970), Edward Burns's edition of Toklas's letters *Staying On Alone* (1973), James Mellow's biography *Charmed Circle* (1974), Linda Simon's biography of Toklas (1977), and Richard Bridgman's watershed critical study *Gertrude Stein in Pieces* (1970), the first to reassemble the full sweep of her work in chronological order, and to pay frank attention to its erotics. Her one-time correspondent Robert Bartlett Haas achieved his long-awaited dream of a Stein anthology with three volumes of selections from her work (including her final interview), published between 1971 and 1974. And in 1978, the new magazine *L=A=N=G=U=A=G=E* invited a constellation of poets to respond to selections from *Tender Buttons*, celebrating Stein as a major forerunner to a cluster of writers whose work 'recognises language itself as the crucial human experience'. Several responders pointed to the poem's opening line, 'A CARAFE, THAT IS A BLIND GLASS', suggesting something simultaneously transparent and opaque: they heralded Stein's use of language not for the goal of expressing meaning, but as something 'valued for itself, in itself, and as itself'. In the Language poets, particularly Charles Bernstein and Lyn Hejinian, and the critics associated with this school, Stein found readers who saw and communicated the possibilities her 'real' texts contained. Stein's work, they argued, suggested generative new logics, new ways of connecting, new relations between writing and the world – new realities, as vital as science. 'Thirty years from now I shall be accepted,' insisted Stein in 1935. 'The followers are always accepted before the person who made the revolution.' Her words were, finally, beginning to sound prescient.

While Katz's work slowly progressed, the end of Toklas's formidable gatekeeping had opened up new avenues for biographers. Most critics, in her lifetime, had followed Toklas's reticence on Stein's sexuality: apart from Edmund Wilson, only one article, published in 1959 in a journal called *Homophile Studies*, questioned the fact that Stein had never been publicly acknowledged as a lesbian, even though *Things as They Are* could be considered the 'most completely homosexual novel ever written' ('of what other novel can it be said that a heterosexual does not even appear?'). And in June 1957, the inaugural issue of *The Ladder*, a magazine published by the first lesbian civil rights organisation in the US, had picked out *Things as They Are* as a significant item of 'lesbiana', regretting that 'few or no copies of this book are available'. Indeed, Donald Gallup had declined many requests to reprint *Things as They Are* – including one, in 1961, from the editor of an anthology of lesbian literature, which Toklas had absolutely refused to countenance. But in 1970 he allowed Liveright to print a new edition, accompanied by Stein's early novella *Fernhurst* (which she had incorporated, in revised form, into *The Making of Americans*), and the five surviving chapters of *The Making of Americans'* first draft. The original title, *Q.E.D.*, was restored, as were the small details that were changed in order to mask the novel's autobiographical roots. Gallup warned the lawyer representing Alice B. Toklas's estate that Leon Katz's introduction would inevitably name the real people who inspired the novel: 'I think that Miss Stein's own sexual interests are now well enough known and accepted so that Mr Katz's references should cause no sensation.'

In the atmosphere of cultural openness fostered in the wake of the Stonewall uprisings of 1968, Stein and Toklas were now held up as lesbian icons, pioneering foremothers whose radical marriage had made lesbian sexuality visible. The Alice B. Toklas LGBTQ Democratic Club was founded in San Francisco in 1971 to train queer activists and advocate for civil rights; a Gertrude Stein equivalent launched in Washington, DC, a few years later. In 1992, Jo Davidson's statue of Stein was unveiled in New York's Bryant Park (the first statue of an American woman in one of the city's public parks); the following year, on Valentine's Day, a group called the Lesbian Avengers installed, next to her, a six-foot plaster statue of Toklas, to protest her erasure from the record, make lesbian love visible, and celebrate both 'butch genius' and 'forgotten femmes'. Extracts from *Lifting Belly* were read aloud to cheers and whistles, before the crowd broke into a spontaneous waltz – one couple embracing on the snowy lawn.

This activist energy was matched by an explosion of new scholarship, as well as an overhaul in biographers' tendencies to elide their subjects' sexual lives. The first generation of Stein scholars had been predominantly male, but now a wave of feminist and post-structuralist critics began to examine Stein's work, extolling its joyous exploration of sexuality, its anarchic, anti-patriarchal forms, and its openness to

Flyer for the Lesbian Avengers
Valentine's Day Action, 1993

psychoanalytical readings. Some readers argued that Stein's liberating language anticipated the French theory of *écriture féminine*, a mode of writing grounded in the female body and experience; she was increasingly read as a philosophical poet, the head of a complex lineage of experimental writing, no mad eccentric but a literary theorist of profound originality who knew – as she always avowed – exactly what she was doing. Stein, wrote the Marxist critic Fredric Jameson, was an 'astonishing genealogical precursor' to postmodern literature, a 'postmodernist *avant la lettre*'. Despite the 'passionate repudiation' of her work some decades earlier, he argued, 'a mutation in the sphere of culture has rendered such attitudes archaic'. Every time she was labelled 'ahead of her time', Stein's determination to keep writing, to preserve her legacy through the posthumous publication programme, seemed to be vindicated.

Over the 1970s and 1980s, restagings and recordings of *The Mother of Us All* layered Stein's text with contemporary resonance – one cartoonist merged her features with those of the second-wave feminist activist Gloria Steinem – while a drive to recover lost foremothers fostered a radical reappraisal of literary history. Shari Benstock's *Women of the Left Bank* (1986) offered a counter-narrative to the macho stories of *A Moveable Feast*, highlighting the rich cultural life of Paris's lesbian denizens, while Stein featured prominently in Bonnie Kime Scott's 1990 anthology *The Gender of Modernism*, a corrective to the many mid-century studies which had neglected women and writers of colour. New anthologies of Stein's own writing followed, and in 1998 her work achieved the status of a two-volume Library of America edition, incorporating her into an explicitly canon-building project.

And these decades saw her work reprinted by new publishing houses, launched with a mission to recover women's histories and to revitalise work which mainstream presses still avoided. In 1989, Naiad Press published *Lifting Belly* in a stand-alone edition, presenting Stein's work directly to a lesbian audience for the first time. In her introduction, the editor Rebecca Mark described reading the poem in the Yale volume *Bee Time Vine*, and becoming 'so excited that I told everyone I knew about this erotic, lesbian poem' – before discovering that few of her lesbian friends had heard of it, since reviewers had carefully skimmed over the poem's obviously celebratory sexuality, and the book had quickly gone out of print. A decade later, another publication demonstrated just how significantly attitudes had changed. After Gallup's retirement in 1980, librarians at Yale unlocked the safe containing the love notes between Stein and Toklas he had loyally guarded for decades; they were added officially to the collection's public catalogue in 1995. With the permission of Calman A. Levin, the Baltimore attorney now representing the estate of Gertrude Stein, the Stein–Toklas correspondence was published in 1999 as *Baby Precious Always Shines*. In her illuminating introduction, positioning the letters as documents of desire in the tradition of Sappho's love poems, the editor, Kay Turner, made the persuasive case that the enigmatic 'cows' – which scholars had only recently begun to discuss as code for orgasms – also, incontrovertibly, indicate faeces. 'Splash goes the cow now, splash splash splash,' writes Stein. 'Sweetly and slowly out from she will splash from her little behind just nicely plop into the water . . . out comes a cow.' Turner, ingeniously, reads these notes as expressing an ongoing concern for Toklas's digestive health: Stein's training as a doctor, her love for Toklas, and the talismanic powers of her writing all combine in an attention Turner reads as 'the hallmark of married intimacy'.

//

What would Stein and Toklas have made of this? To have her sex life, let alone her bowel movements, scrutinised feels like the worst nightmare Toklas could have imagined when she begged Gallup to destroy those notes, in 1947. After two decades wrangling for control over her past and Stein's, the last vestiges of privacy had been swept away. Even a biographer must sympathise with her plight: what right does a reader have to anyone else's story? It had long been acknowledged that this question was particularly fraught for writers, who usually become public figures by dint of work done in paramount solitude. Tennyson compared biographers to 'carrion vultures', Oscar Wilde called them 'bodysnatchers', Margaret Oliphant lamented the ransacking of 'private drawers'. And for writers' families, who had not chosen this exposure, the intrusion feels all the more acute. But no one had broken into 16 rue de la Convention or Père-Lachaise: Stein had sent the notes to the archive, and Toklas – reluctantly – had allowed them to stay there, on the implicit understanding that after she was dead, anyone might read them. Fifty years had passed since she had burned the bulk of these notes. And as Turner argued, echoing Gallup's entreaties of half a century earlier, the texts contained nothing which Stein had not, if obliquely, revealed in her public writing: 'No truth exposed here concerns anything except the power of love.'

Would Stein have felt differently to Toklas? How far did her desire for posthumous recognition extend – and how much of this interest could she, in 1946, have anticipated? The celebrity she had experienced in her lifetime had, largely, been a positive experience: autograph-hunters approaching her at restaurants, strutting around Paris with an entourage of handsome young men. By the 1990s, the very nature of celebrity had changed, and the taboos which still governed in Stein's day – the American reporters solemnly acknowledging her 'secretary' as they filed their copy – now appeared quaint. Ironically, Stein's most direct comment on future curiosity about her private life comes from a source who specialised in fabulation. Samuel Steward spent two fortnights with Stein and Toklas at Bilignin in the 1930s, and visited Toklas devotedly each Christmas after Stein's death, while running a tattoo shop in Chicago, archiving his sexual conquests in a document he called 'The Stud File', and writing a series of pulp erotic novels chronicling the adventures of a leather-jacketed hustler named Phil Andros. In a memoir of his friendship with Stein and Toklas, published in 1977, he recalled Stein mentioning a long-ago novel, very restrained, but still 'too outspoken' to be published yet. In the car, on the way to pick up milk in Belley, Steward remembered Stein grabbing his knee and asking if he knew she and Alice were lesbians. With a 'hot curl of fire' up the back of his spine, Steward stammered that he did, but it was nobody's business – until Stein interrupted briskly to explain that most of their good friends understood. Still, she went on, 'it would be better not to talk about it, say for twenty years after I die, unless it's found out sooner or times change'. Writing decades after her death, Steward often has Stein confide first in him ideas which cropped up in her later writing or subsequent scholarship – but Stein's comments ring true in substance, if not quite in tone: exasperation at the necessary privacies of lesbian life in a homophobic culture, and an eager hope that times would change, and that she, and her work, might find a place – an afterlife – in this imagined future.

These were the impulses which drove Stein to send her effects to Yale, to conceive of the posthumous publication project and appoint Van Vechten to carry it out. But it's impossible to be sure how consciously Stein made her archive: whether she remembered exactly what indiscreet scrawls lay in every notebook she threw into the suitcase for Yale, whether she and Toklas discussed, seriously, where the boundaries lay for each of them between work and life, public and private. According to Katz, Toklas – alarmed to see Stein bundling dentist's bills and rent slips into boxes – had urged her to be more selective in what she sent to Yale, but Stein had replied that it wasn't for her to dictate what future readers might find useful: 'You can never tell whether some laundry list might not be the most important thing.' The love notes, the laundry lists, the notebooks Katz discovered – all are thrilling prospects, for a biographer, because of the unmediated insight into the writer's way of life, the material conditions from which her work arose. The love notes are traces of the fleeting transitional moments at the end of Stein's working day, as she slowly emerged from a concentrated writing session, laid a text aside for typing, and let her surroundings swim back into focus. They offer candid glimpses into the relationship which made all Stein's work possible. The case against biography – or the publication of letters, diaries, notebooks – would see the work of art as something pure, separate from the maker, not to be corrupted by prurient poking around in closets or washbaskets. But for Stein, such separation was impossible. 'Facts of life make literature,' she once wrote. Her earlier work explored the process of shaping everyday experience into language; her later writing dwelt at length on the relationship between author, text and audience. The love notes and Stein's writing – the life and the art – are inextricable.

//

Ulla Dydo was the scholar whose meticulous work demonstrated most powerfully the relationship between Stein's writing and her daily life – and unearthed one of the most stunning posthumous discoveries in the process. Dydo had been a fixture in the Yale reading room since the 1970s, commuting several days a week from New York to examine Stein's manuscripts. An obsessive researcher – she often drafted letters to fellow Stein scholars in the middle of the night, unable to sleep as she mulled over archival inconsistencies – Dydo's scholarship broke new ground precisely because of how seriously she took Stein's writing. She began from the assumption that Stein's methods were deliberate, her words carefully chosen, and the material circumstances of her work's composition significant. Dydo read Stein's work not as a series of separate texts but as a single, continuous project, each text engendering the next. The distinction between texts, she realised, was often more nebulous than had been previously supposed: Stein rarely had multiple pieces on the go, but worked at one idea until she felt it held no more possibilities. The Yale series had printed Stein's pieces haphazardly, grouped according to length and theme rather than chronology; the project, Dydo argued, was set up in a way that precluded coherence. Only by reading her systematically, in order, could Stein's work be understood in context: 'not only as a series of separate texts but also, in a sense, as a single spiritual autobiography whose vocabulary is generated by the daily life but whose voice is uniquely hers'. Few scholars had ever examined Stein's manuscripts in detail, relying instead on the printed texts; Dydo went back to the originals, and was soon rewarded with a trove of insights.

'I do all my work in my head and only write down what it is my head finally accepts,' Stein once wrote to a student who had enquired about her process. Like many of her statements about herself, this was far from the full story. Stein did cross out, make false starts, correct and edit – and her sentences were not usually planned before she sat down to write. Instead, Dydo noticed that Stein's texts often took their starting points from the illustrations on the covers of her notebooks, French children's exercise books she bought in bulk from the stationer Beauvais on the rue du Lac. A poem titled 'A Bouquet' began in a book with a cover showing long-skirted women arranging flowers, while 'Natural Phenomena' was composed in one from a series featuring volcanoes, lightning and high tides. In other cases, texts that appeared entirely non-specific in their final printed form were revealed to start from sustained observation of a person, whose name was silently erased in a subsequent draft ('Picasso' replaced with 'him'), rendering the final text apparently abstract. Dydo saw how the events occupying Stein at the moment of composition – as charted in a separate series of smaller notebooks, filled with apparently ephemeral jottings – seeped into her texts: a chimney fire, a car accident, the birth of a friend's grandchild, the first strawberries of the season. These preparatory notebooks were filled with private ritual – the coded initials, the talismanic dedications – whereas Stein's printed books, Dydo wrote, were 'stripped of the process that gave them being'. In the archive, Dydo concluded, were the vestiges of the private life which she saw as 'the central context for Stein's capacity to meditate and to write'. Only through a close study of the notebooks and manuscripts, she argued, could Stein's work be read as it was written. 'It is the work, not the much touted and falsely dramatised personality,' she wrote, 'that is the legacy of Gertrude Stein.'

Among the notebooks Dydo examined in the late 1970s were those in which Stein had composed *Stanzas in Meditation* in the summer of 1932 – the fateful months in which she discovered the *Q.E.D.* manuscript, and began to write the *Autobiography*. The poem began in a brown notebook, its front cover decorated with a crowing rooster, wings outstretched against a blazing sun. Inside, in looping italics slanting at a 45-degree angle to the neat square grid, are lines of poetry – just four to a sheet, swathes of white space between each. Turning the pages, Dydo noticed a strange pattern of corrections. Each time the word 'may' occurred, it had been crossed out and replaced with a different word – 'to-day', 'day', or 'can' – even where such replacements rendered the sentences incomprehensible. In the typed version, too, every appearance of the word 'may' – as a month, or a verb, or as part of the compound 'maybe' – had been obliterated with a black scribble, sometimes almost cutting through the thin paper, and replaced, in handwriting, with a near-equivalent that entirely disrupts the text's sense, rhyme and rhythm. In the second, clean typescript, all evidence of 'may' had been

One of the notebooks for *Stanzas in Meditation*, 1932

removed; the text is silent, the disruption of its previous draft smoothed over. The 1956 Yale edition printed the text in its later form, without a single 'may': Dydo concluded that the editors had taken the nonsensical sentences as Steinian idiosyncrasy, and not questioned them. 'This is her autobiography one of two,' Stein had written in *Stanzas*, as if dropping a clue to its far-from-obvious personal origins. The discovery opened up what Dydo called a 'biographical detective story'.

Following Leon Katz's revelation, in his dissertation, of Toklas's fury at discovering the old intimacy between Stein and May Bookstaver that summer, Dydo proposed that the alterations, more than 400 of them, were made at Toklas's behest, when she was given *Stanzas* to type shortly after reading the manuscript of *Q.E.D.* (The realisation that 'may' might represent a person as well as a verb had come to Dydo in a dream, during the summer of 1980, when she and Katz were examining the notebooks together.) The recurrence of the word 'may' in *Stanzas* was a betrayal even beyond the secret of *Q.E.D.*, Dydo argued. It marked Bookstaver's intrusion into the most intimate space of their marriage – Stein's writing. As Dydo worked, she found more evidence in short texts written around the same time, showing both how the rediscovery of *Q.E.D.* had played on Stein's mind, and how violently Toklas had reacted to it. In 'A Manoir', a character named May Maiden in the manuscript is changed, in the typed text, to 'May Maiden Hoar'; in 'Short Sentences', every May, Mary and 'may' is underlined reprovingly in Toklas's purple pencil. Another character is called Babette, Toklas's middle name; Toklas has pointedly changed her name to Anne, while an Alice and an Alice Babette are crossed out entirely, leaving blanks in the typescript. If Toklas was being supplanted by May, she was making her own threat: she would erase herself from Stein's life in return – but register her betrayal within the very words of the text. It was an extraordinary intervention. The integrity of Stein's writing relied on Toklas's accurate transcription of her handwritten drafts: if Toklas asserted her power to make changes to the work, the routine they had established would crumble. Within the bizarre textual mystery of the *Stanzas*,

Dydo concluded, lay a quarrel between Stein and Toklas that spilled from life to the page and back again. 'Who is winning', wrote Stein in *Stanzas*, 'why the answer of course is she is.'

//

Only one living person had heard Alice Toklas talk about that strained summer which precipitated a confrontation of Stein's past, a crisis in their relationship, and a swerve in Stein's writing which entirely transformed her career. The question which nagged at Dydo, and other Stein scholars, was simple: what exactly had Alice Toklas told Leon Katz about these tensions? Over the years, Katz's apparent inability to complete and publish his work on the notebooks had started to bother other scholars. The original notebooks, and his typescripts, were now available at Yale, but – although he had willingly answered questions, and scattered information in conversations, letters and articles over the years – Katz had never shown anyone the transcripts of his interviews with Toklas, and their contents remained the subject of much speculation. It wasn't just that scholars were hungry for the juicy details of the Gertrude–Alice–May or Gertrude–Alice–Leo dramas. Toklas's first-hand account of the writing of *The Making of Americans* would, they believed, spur a surge of popular and academic interest in the novel Stein always considered her greatest achievement. Katz alone possessed the clues that would enable a fuller understanding of *The Making of Americans*; his annotations, and Toklas's commentary, would make it possible – as he himself had promised – for 'life and work to be read as one'.

Katz continued to work on the annotated notebooks all his life, with an extra push in his final few years; he pronounced himself satisfied with his text just days before his death, at the age of ninety-seven, in January 2017. His papers, now held alongside Stein's at Yale, are the repository of half a century's devoted scholarship; the final manuscript of Stein's annotated notebooks – the culmination of his life's work – is represented by multiple drafts, in varying states of completion. A single notebook contains Katz's scrawls from his sessions with Toklas. Back in America, Katz typed Toklas's remarks out on index cards; over the years, he re-typed his material on to now-yellowed typewriter paper, eventually replaced by printouts of Microsoft Word documents, important sections overlaid with pink highlighter pen. Katz painstakingly cross-referenced passages from Stein's notebooks with Toklas's comments on each snippet, and amalgamated the texts in ring binders: white paper for Stein's writings, blue for Toklas's remarks, and yellow for Katz's own annotations. The result is a blockbuster volume with the notebooks' full contents arranged in chronological sequence, interspersed with contextualisation and analysis from Toklas and Katz, two experts with different stakes in their shared subject.

In that ring binder with its colour-coded sections lie three alternative forms of biographical evidence, all valuable, all troubling. Stein's unfiltered notes, written to herself, show her working out thoughts in progress, many of which she would later revise or renounce entirely: although she sent them to Yale, it seems unlikely they were intended for posterity. Toklas's comments serve as a reminder that memory mutates in strange ways: these are fragments of experience shaped over decades into an accepted narrative, its stability threatened by the arrival of Katz, the biographer who knows too much. And finally, there's Katz himself, who never met Stein, but whose intervention in Toklas's memories resurrected and recast a long-ago drama between two remarkable women.

It's possible that one reason Katz's publication stalled was that the complexities of the Stein–Toklas relationship proved overwhelming: too thorny, too personal, to be contained within a work of pure literary scholarship. Instead, he turned to a medium more suited to reproaches and recriminations: theatre. In Katz's archive is the script for a play he devised, which presents Stein and Toklas in conversation with each other, with the audience, and with Katz himself. Here, the 'drama' between them plays out as a slow tussle between competing worldviews: Stein 'struggling' to assimilate this new influence on her life and work, Toklas 'waiting' for Stein to surrender, until finally, with slightly sinister satisfaction, she can pronounce that Stein is 'not talking to Leo any more, only to me'. In a note for the director, labelled 'The Story of Alice Winning Gertrude Entirely', Katz suggested that this scene should culminate in 'a genuine at-one-ness', but the actors should convey a certain ambivalence towards their truce. 'It was not yet clear – as it very probably never was – which one really "won".'

In part, the fictional framework served as a disclaimer when his reconstructions of conversations became speculative. Yet it also allowed Katz to respond emotionally to his encounter with Toklas: to express the human truths he had discerned (according to Stein's own methods) through many hours of careful listening. Another short play in his archive is a fantasised monologue in which the dying Toklas, rocking in her wicker chair, remembers the visits of a young man armed with pencil, paper and a tranche of Stein's own notebooks, innocently asking what she recalled of May Bookstaver. 'I knew what I was doing,' he has Toklas declare. 'The pleasure of looking into a stranger's face and betraying Gertrude as she had betrayed me . . . I told him how I screamed, Damn you, Gertrude, damn you . . . even in the pages of her scribbling, every "may" became "can", every page captured in my typewriter cleansed of May.'

Katz had not mentioned the changes to *Stanzas* in his dissertation, and Dydo – who detailed her discoveries in her 2003 book *The Language that Rises* – was never quite sure whether or not Toklas had said anything to Katz that confirmed her theory that Toklas herself demanded these changes, or even carried them out herself. Katz, for his part, stated that he had told Dydo the story 'reported whole' from the interviews, and her dream must have postdated this conversation. In an essay about his interviews published in the *Yale Review* in 2012, Katz described this scene in further detail, apparently quoting at length from Toklas: 'I went almost mad. I destroyed every sign, every letter, of the recollection of May . . . I went through manuscripts Gertrude was writing then, and changed every mention of the word "may" to "can".'

But in the handwritten notes from his interviews with Toklas, and in the subsequent index cards recording the encounters, I could find no record of this sensational statement. It's impossible to know what to make of this apparent discrepancy: whether those remarks were made off the record, imprinted only in Katz's memory to be resurrected some fifty years later, or are the product of later embellishment, retrospectively added to corroborate a plausible reconstruction of events at which neither Katz nor Dydo was present. There are no tape recordings of the interviews; Toklas never approved her spoken comments, and there is no way now to confirm exactly what was said between her and Katz in those intense months of conversation. Biography, like detective fiction, is a precarious structure; some mysteries must remain unresolved.

//

Janet Malcolm – caustic dissector of scholarly intrigues, and author of brilliant books on biographical and journalistic ethics – told the story of Dydo's dream and Katz's silence in a 2005 *New Yorker* article. After hearing out the scholars' frustrations at his book's non-appearance, Malcolm attempted to arrange an interview with Katz. He turned up a day early, and declined to rearrange their encounter, resenting Malcolm's insinuations that he was somehow shifty and secretive about his work, and wary that she was not really interested in Stein's writing, but was seeking a good story. Instead, Malcolm's interest was drawn to another element in Stein's life: her friendship with Bernard Faÿ, and her survival of the war in Vichy France. In 1996, a doctoral student named Wanda Van Dusen had published Stein's introduction to the Pétain translations (notably, the one piece of writing Stein had actively decided not to publish) in an academic journal, speculating that Faÿ had encouraged Stein to undertake the project, either to curry favour with Pétain or in return for his protection. While Malcolm was trying to pin down Leon Katz, Edward Burns, another long-standing Stein expert, was in Paris, examining a freshly released trove of papers at the national archives, which laid bare the extent of Faÿ's vicious campaign against Freemasons. Among the documents he found there was an official report of Faÿ's denunciations of library employees, and the damning journal of Faÿ's lover and secretary William Gueydan de Roussel.

In another *New Yorker* essay, published in 2006, Malcolm reported on Burns's discoveries, bringing the question of how these two elderly Jewish lesbians had survived the war in Vichy France into the popular consciousness. Five years later, an academic book by Barbara Will offered a detailed account of Faÿ's intellectual ties to the far right, and proposed that Stein's continued friendship with him was symptomatic of her uncomfortable attraction to reactionary thought. Her decision to consider translating Pétain, Will argued, displays a deeply flawed moral judgement at odds with her 'radically antiauthoritarian, antipatriarchal poetics'.

Will's assessment of Stein's politics and wartime actions passes quickly over a wealth of contradictory material (Stein's work for Resistance magazines, her expressions of disillusionment with Pétain in *Wars I Have Seen*, her reflections on vulnerability in *Mrs Reynolds*). But her book – or a sensationalised abbreviation of its argument – attracted a lot of attention. Its 2011 publication coincided with two major travelling exhibitions designed to foreground Stein's central position in European modernism, one of which – The Steins Collect at the San Francisco Museum of Modern Art, continuing at Paris's Grand Palais and the Metropolitan Museum of Art in New York – reunited the Stein collection forty years after the MoMA show. With the spotlight on Stein, articles in the mainstream press began to condemn her, often taking Will's research out of context and exaggerating both its claims and its conclusions, transmogrifying Stein from a complex and contradictory figure into an outright monster. The *New Yorker* cited Stein's 'pro-Fascist ideology' and called for the Met to acknowledge that Stein's collection was saved from the Gestapo thanks to her 'collaborationist activities'. The *Washington Post* argued that Stein 'is essentially in the same category as Ezra Pound (fascist-sympathizing poet), Louis-Ferdinand Céline (collaborationist writer) and Paul de Man (anti-Semitic literary critic)', while the polarising commentator Alan Dershowitz, in the *Huffington Post*, went furthest of all: Stein, he claimed, was 'a major collaborator with the Vichy regime', who had 'publicly proclaimed her admiration for Hitler during the 1930s, proposing him for a Nobel Peace Prize'. The smears escalated, the claims reverberated: the museum adjusted its wall texts, and even the White House removed Stein's name from a celebration of Jewish Heritage Month.

The Nobel nomination would indeed be seriously shocking – if it were true. In a 1934 interview with the *New York Times* magazine, Stein had sarcastically suggested Hitler ought to receive the prize because 'by driving out the Jews and the democratic and Left elements', he was 'removing all elements of contest and of struggle from Germany'. It's clear from her full statement that Stein was being heavily (and characteristically) ironic – and the article plainly states she spoke with an 'impish' look on her face. She goes on to criticise America's stringent immigration laws, in contrast to France's more open policies, arguing that a world without the 'constant stimulation' of competition and activity leads only to 'dullness and stagnation'. The poet Charles Bernstein compiled a dossier of essays by Stein experts to provide context and counterbalance to the insinuations and falsehoods spreading fast about Stein's war years. He noted that the source of the Nobel myth could be traced back to a claim made in a Zionist magazine, in an article rebuking Jews who weren't sufficiently supportive of Israel: Stein's alleged endorsement of Hitler was invoked as part of a tirade against Jews who fail to recognise their own interests, after the Nobel Prize was given to the Palestinian leader Yasser Arafat in 1994. The author, Gustav Hendrikssen, claimed he was on the Nobel committee which rejected Stein's proposal: the fact that the committee had officially denied receiving any contact from Stein appeared not to have quelled the slander.

Why, asked Bernstein, were readers so easily persuaded to take these attacks on Stein as gospel, when the facts were easily available to refute them? Why must Stein be black or white, when the inconsistencies in her political views, the desperation of her wartime circumstances, the shifts in her position across time, all call out for a far more nuanced viewpoint? Stein repeatedly spoke of her hatred of fascism; she championed the Maquis and consistently criticised Hitler in unequivocal terms. She was not one of the war's heroes – but nor was she an outright villain. Should Stein have 'bravely and publicly denounced' both Faÿ and Pétain, asked Leon Katz, thus inviting her own deportation? One of the only certainties in this episode is the utter, bewildering horror of the circumstances under which Stein made her decisions.

Stein has always made people uncomfortable. Her detractors have consistently focused on her friendships, her looks, clichéd ideas of her style; anything but her writing. Her excesses – linguistic and bodily – have been seen as suspect, 'ominous', as though she must have something to hide. Discussions of artists with unsavoury politics or personal histories tend to hinge on how and whether art can be divorced from its maker, how enjoyment of a work can or should change if its creator is disgraced. But Stein's work is usually considered dispensable in these conversations: derided, caricatured, flattened, as if it's a relief to have a concrete reason to dismiss her. Most responses to Janet Malcolm's book *Two Lives* – which brought together her two *New Yorker* articles – approvingly echoed her description of *The Making of Americans* as 'impenetrable'; a *New York Review of Books* critic suggested that Stein's 'language of equivocation' in that novel might even imply a fundamental 'evasiveness about the truth'. Stein's work is employed to impugn her life, her life invoked to discredit her work. Both have far more to offer curious readers than these reductive approaches allow.

//

'I'll be happy, damn happy, if people come back to my writing every twenty-five years', Stein told a friend, 'because they will slowly begin to understand what I'm trying to say.' In recent years, scholars and artists have worked to shift the conversation back to Stein's writing, in its fullest and richest scope. Studies have read Stein's work in relation to transmasculinity, celebrity, Dada aesthetics, Surrealism, while notions of her influence have expanded to encompass movements including New Narrative, Oulipo and other global avant-gardes. Imaginative responses to Stein, meanwhile, have offered intriguing counter-narratives to the archive, probing its gaps and silences. The artist Faith Ringgold's epic quilt *Dinner at Gertrude Stein's* (1991) portrays a stitched Stein hosting a crowd including Zora Neale Hurston, James Baldwin, Langston Hughes and Ringgold's protagonist/alter ego, Willia Marie Simone, while Monique Truong's 2003 novel *The Book of Salt* presents Stein through the eyes of Binh, a Vietnamese cook employed at 27 rue de Fleurus. In the steamy setting of the Toklas kitchen, Truong makes a fascinating, multilayered exploration of race, class, power and authorship, subtly asking the question: who has the right to anyone else's story?

An exhaustive study of Stein's cultural afterlife would take another book: this is a very selective snapshot. Stein has played a cameo in a Disney film (introducing Anastasia to Paris with a brandished rose); she featured in a long-running cult cartoon strip in the 1970s, and has spawned a surprising expanse of merchandise, from dolls to beer mugs (steins, of course) to a rather terrifying pillow, now in the collection of Johns Hopkins' Sheridan Libraries. The poet Eileen Myles has called her 'the world's biggest influence'. She has inspired one of the most generative afterlives of any writer – whether responses arise in the form of interpretation, critique, homage or simply, as the poet Kenneth Koch put it, in the feeling that 'one is suddenly free to write something almost entirely unlike her but that wouldn't be possible if her work weren't there'. Re-reading Stein through others' eyes expands the pleasure of reading her for oneself: her vibrant afterlife has cast her work afresh as new voices come into dialogue with it, drawing out different meanings and possibilities. 'I suppose some day I will be the acknowledged grandmother of the modern movement,' Stein wrote in 1921 after a string of disappointing rejections. A century on, her rueful joke reads more like a prophecy.

One more example of Stein's enduring legacy. On 30 December 1973, the Paula Cooper Gallery in New York threw open its doors for a marathon reading of *The Making of Americans*, which concluded in the evening of New Year's Day. Over more than fifty hours, dozens of readers – artists, writers, scholars, passers-by – took turns to read the novel aloud. The wooden floors were strewn with foam cushions, and artworks removed from the white walls so people could lean against them; a coffee urn was kept topped up, and some brought sleeping bags, primed to keep the reading going through the early hours. Many, even those who just stopped in on their way somewhere else, stayed for hours. The event, organised by Fluxus artist Alison Knowles, became an annual tradition, taking place at the gallery every year until 2000, and still periodically revived. As the novel is read aloud, the beguiling flow of its rhythms is revealed, the repetitions first maddening, then profound. The humour of Stein's writing shines through, and – above all – the beautiful moments of clarity, the emphasis on life, on living. As the hours pass, the novel 'beginning again and again', readers bear witness to the narrator's growing excitement in her work, her flashes of understanding, her loneliness, her desperation to be understood, and her questing insight into human nature, charting the inevitable passage from birth towards death. Like a DJ, Stein blurs and distorts language, sampling, looping, the pulse of her insistent beat building up through emphasis, varying through subtle shifts. In her 'continuous present', time passes and stands still, until the novel slows and fades with its ponderous, heartbreaking final dirge – 'Dead is dead'. I can't imagine a greater tribute to Stein than people gathering together to read her work: vindication, just as she longed for, of her writing's enduring vitality.

EPILOGUE EPILOGUE EPILOGUE EPILOGUE EPILOGUE EPILOGUE EPILOGUE EPILOGUE

I arrived in Belley on a sweltering July afternoon. The market stalls lining the narrow high street were starting to deflate their cheerful awnings, though a few tables were still laden with cheeses, pastries, apricots and peaches. Rush-hour traffic was beginning to encircle the town's tiny roundabout, while the cafés around the central fountain were laying tables – crisp white napkins, green carafes of icy water – for evening service. The Hôtel Pernollet, tucked on a side street a few steps from the roundabout, was no more – demolished in 2013 – but the sandstone houses, the bustling shopfronts, the imposing cathedral remained, just as Stein and Toklas would have known them. I could easily see how they'd fallen in love with this place. On the drive down from Lyon station, watching the scenery unfold in panorama from the window – sheep grazing on huge swathes of verdant pastureland, punctuated by clusters of farmhouses and church spires, with cloud-topped mountains in the distance, and the occasional staggering waterfall as the road passed between cliffs – I understood how this landscape had fostered in Stein the idea of a text as an expanse of space. Cresting a hill with the valley laid out below, the scenery appeared still, yet full of life. As I took in the view, time seemed to collapse: ancient ruins lingered beside working farms, natural beauty alongside man-made structures. My rental car felt like an allusion, now, to Stein's beloved Ford, as I hurtled, like so many of Stein's friends and biographers before me, towards her country home.

That first day, I struck out on foot from Belley in the direction of Bilignin: a half-hour stroll past fields of sunflowers and vineyards. The hamlet stretches along a single, sleepy street, now signposted as 'rue Gertrude Stein'; her house – marked by a discreet bronze plaque – stands behind a high stone wall, and the wrought-iron gate was locked. I wandered down to the bottom of the road, where a dirt track swooped down to the valley and led back along the winding river behind the houses, a path Stein took almost daily with her dogs, swatting at weeds with the leash as she went. From the back, Stein's home was instantly recognisable: I could see the low wall with the two tiny turreted cupolas where she so often sat, and the sedate manor rising behind it, its façade covered with ivy. I climbed back up the hill to rue Gertrude Stein, and left a note in the mailbox, explaining that I was writing about Stein, that I was in the area for the week, that I didn't want to disturb but – just in case the present owner might be willing to show me behind the gates – I would return.

Over the following days, I immersed myself in Stein's countryside. I visited the imposing Abbaye d'Hautecombe, nestled on the banks of the Lac du Bourget, where Stein used to visit the monks; I peered through the gate at the ornate chateau in Béon where Stein would often dine with her friend the Baroness Pierlot, spying the garden where Stein's plays were performed during the war by local children. At Izieu, I visited the Jewish children's home raided by Nazis in April 1944, now a museum offering powerful testimony to these atrocities. I went to the market town of Virieu-le-Grand, where Stein was photographed

The gates to Stein and Toklas's house at Bilignin

shooting a bullseye at a country fair, to Artemare, where their favourite restaurant (Hôtel Berrard) was still in operation, and to the tiny Lucey Church, where her description of its 'steeple that looks like a pagoda' proved entirely accurate. At Culoz, after locating the hilltop manor where she and Toklas saw out the war, and the bust of Stein now standing serenely in its formal gardens, I entered the tiny museum to find Stein venerated as a local hero: a volunteer proudly showed me a blackened stove that once belonged in Stein's home (I learned its name: Le Clos Poncet), and the transcription of a speech by the French president François Mitterrand – an admirer of Stein's writing, who had visited them at Culoz – inaugurating a 1987 exhibition in her honour. At Vieu-en-Valromey, I stalked the fields looking for the Roman ruins where Stein often posed for photographs with guests, in what seems to have been a rite of passage for her visitors. In one, Paul Bowles stands on top of the column (it's tempting to imagine Stein and Toklas giving him a leg-up); in another, Stein and Basket flank the monument while Pépé, confused, perches next to Stein's head. I found the column, a solitary landmark on the bucolic horizon, ducked under the barbed wire enclosing a flock of interested cows, and took a hasty selfie, exactly where Stein had stood.

The next time I passed through Bilignin, I glimpsed an elderly woman grappling with a garden hose behind the iron gates. Seeing my chance, I caught her attention, and explained in halting French that I had left her a note a few days earlier. She sighed. 'I never let anyone inside,' she told me, 'but you're here, and I'm tired of gardening . . . What would you like to see?' I must have looked stunned, because she laughed as she unlocked the gate, and suggested 'Les jardins?' We walked around the side of the house to the back, and suddenly there were the flower beds, set within the perfectly manicured box hedges which were Toklas's great pride. There was the wall, and the valley sloping down to the river, and rising again in the distance to the misty Ain hills. The garden was exactly as I'd seen it in so many old photographs, but vibrant with life and colour.

She was ninety-eight, she told me, and the house had belonged to her family for generations. As a teenager during the war, she was living with her mother and brother down in Belley – her father was away fighting – until her parents decided to reclaim the Bilignin manor from their long-standing tenants. She remembered coming up with her mother to negotiate with Stein for the ending of her lease. 'She was not happy,' she told me, with a wry eyebrow raised. 'She did not want to leave.' I didn't want to pressure her to invite me into the house, but I decided to test the waters with a leading question – 'Is it the same inside, as it was when she was here?' 'Oui,' she nodded. 'Exactly the same.' Unable to resist, I asked if I could just step beyond the French windows, which were open next to us, offering a tantalising glimpse of the panels I was sure belonged to Stein's old study. She agreed, and I gasped: here was the room so familiar from Cecil Beaton's photographs of Stein at her writing desk, the walls painted with Italianate frescoes showing elegant corbeilles of fruit, flowers and hunting horns. The plasma TV was the only indication that any time had passed since Stein sat here writing, with Toklas gathering strawberries outside, the dogs frolicking in the maze of hedges, and Mont Blanc glistening in the distance.

Over the course of writing this book, I've spent many months in archives: at the New York Public Library, where I'd walk past Stein's statue in Bryant Park on my way to the subway; at the Addison M. Metcalf Collection of Steiniana in California, where I marvelled at the reach of Stein's legacy and the passion she inspired in her admirers; and at Yale, where I gingerly handled the manuscripts touched first by Stein, then by Toklas, then Gallup, Katz and so many others. But visiting Bilignin, the place she perhaps felt most herself, brought Stein to life in a new way altogether. While I was there, I read a detective novel written, in 1985, by Stein's friend Samuel Steward: a somewhat farcical romp starring Stein and Toklas as unlikely sleuths. I found I could instantly imagine the conversations Steward describes, based on his observations of them at their most relaxed: could feel Stein blundering cheerfully around the house while Toklas cooks an elaborate meal 'just to show I love you', hear Toklas dryly correcting Stein on every point of detail in the flow of a wildly embellished anecdote, and smell the cigarette smoke wafting over the box hedges as Stein's beefsteak laugh booms out over the valley. The novel opens with Stein and Toklas reminiscing conspiratorially, expressing mock horror at the length of their relationship (thirty years!) as they placidly contemplate ageing. They roll their eyes at each other's foibles, tease one another (jokes about flirting with the handsome young gardener elicit protestations of jealousy), and comfort and care for each other in ways that are as touching as they are understated. 'Eating's one of the two pleasures left,' complains Stein, when Toklas warns her she'd better start watching her weight. 'And the other?' asks Toklas. Stein looks at her with a twinkle: 'Writing, of course.' In pointed contrast to Hemingway's salacious insinuation of perversity, Steward's testimony simply shows two women who were – as Toklas puts it here – 'still in love with loving'.

Stein argued that detective stories are satisfying because they conclude with clean-cut solutions: all loose ends tied up, the significance of every clue revealed. In real life, by contrast, 'it is more interesting if you do not know the answer at all'. There is no one answer to the enduring enigma of Gertrude Stein: her life, like her work, defies any single meaning. This is how I've come to see Stein, and Toklas too: as complex, flawed, confounding, funny, fascinating people. Above all, I know I'll never stop returning to her writing: finding in it new pleasures, new questions, new ways of seeing the world. Stein's piece 'Sentences' begins 'A sentence is made by coupling', inscribing Toklas, as always, in her work. She carries on, invoking cars and candelabras, an hourglass and a Christmas tree as she hits her stride, wrestling with fugitive adjectives and plaintive verbs. As she writes, Toklas stirs. 'In looking up from her embroidery', writes Stein, 'she looks at me.' It's an example, I think, of the reward of reading Stein: of persevering through the haze of words until something piercing – something real and human – comes into focus. In the midst of an arcane examination of grammar, we're suddenly with the two women in their living room, Toklas sewing, Stein writing, the paintings surrounding them, Basket lolling at their feet. In that glance shot between them is the love that sustained Stein's writing and her being. 'She is my wife,' writes Stein. 'That is what a paragraph is. Always at home.'

NOTES

Abbreviations of Works Cited

Works by Gertrude Stein

AABT – *The Autobiography of Alice B. Toklas* (1933; Penguin Modern Classics, 2001)
A&B – *Alphabets and Birthdays* (Yale University Press, 1957)
AFAM – *As Fine as Melanctha* (Yale University Press, 1954)
BTV – *Bee Time Vine* (Yale University Press, 1953)
CE – *Composition as Explanation* (Hogarth Press, 1926)
EA – *Everybody's Autobiography* (1938; Virago, 1985)
FIA – *Four in America* (Yale University Press, 1947)
G.M.P. – *Matisse Picasso and Gertrude Stein with Two Shorter Stories* (1932; Something Else Press, 1972)
G&P – *Geography and Plays* (Four Seas Company, 1922)
HTW – *How to Write* (1931; Dover Press, 2018)
HWW – *How Writing Is Written: Volume II of the Previously Uncollected Writings of Gertrude Stein*, ed. Robert Bartlett Haas (Black Sparrow Press, 1974)
I – *Ida: A Novel*, ed. Logan Esdale (Yale University Press, 2012)
LA – *Gertrude Stein: Writings 1932–1946*, ed. Catharine R. Stimpson and Harriet Chessman (Library of America, 1998)
MA – *The Making of Americans* (1925; Dalkey Archive Press, 1995)
N – *Narration: Four Lectures* (University of Chicago Press, 1935)
NB – *The Notebooks of Gertrude Stein for 'The Making of Americans' 1903–1912*, ed. Leon Katz (Éditions rue de Fleurus, 2021)
O&P – *Operas and Plays* (Plain Edition, 1932)
P&P – *Portraits and Prayers* (Random House, 1934)
PF – *Paris France* (B. T. Batsford, 1940)
PL – *Painted Lace* (Yale University Press, 1955)
Q.E.D. – *Fernhurst, Q.E.D. and Other Early Writings* (Liveright, 1971)
SM – *Stanzas in Meditation: The Corrected Edition*, ed. Emily Setina and Susannah Hollister (Yale University Press, 2012)
SW – *Selected Writings of Gertrude Stein*, ed. Carl Van Vechten (Random House, 1946)
TB – *Tender Buttons* (1914; City Lights Books, 2014)
'TI' – 'Transatlantic Interview', in Robert Bartlett Haas (ed.), *A Primer for the Gradual Understanding of Gertrude Stein* (Black Sparrow Press, 1973)
TL – *Three Lives* (1909; Penguin Modern Classics, 1979)
'TWL' – 'The Winner Loses, a Picture of Occupied France', *Atlantic Monthly*, November 1940.
Two – *Two: Gertrude Stein and Her Brother, and Other Early Portraits*, 1908–1912 (Yale University Press, 1951)
UK – *Useful Knowledge* (Payson & Clarke, 1928)
WIHS – *Wars I Have Seen* (Random House, 1945)

Letters

BP – *Baby Precious Always Shines: Selected Love Notes Between Gertrude Stein and Alice B. Toklas*, ed. Kay Turner (St Martin's Press, 1999)

CVV – *The Letters of Gertrude Stein and Carl Van Vechten, 1913–1946*, ed. Edward Burns (Columbia University Press, 2013)

DA – *A Description of Acquaintance: The Letters of Laura Riding and Gertrude Stein*, ed. Logan Esdale and Jane Malcolm (University of New Mexico Press, 2023)

ES – 'Gertrude Stein and *The Atlantic*', *Yale University Library Gazette*, 28/3 (1954), pp. 109–28

FF – *The Flowers of Friendship: Letters Written to Gertrude Stein*, ed. Donald Gallup (Knopf, 1953)

MD – *A History of Having a Great Many Times Not Continued to Be Friends: The Correspondence Between Mabel Dodge and Gertrude Stein, 1911–1934*, ed. Patricia R. Everett (University of New Mexico Press, 1996)

PP – *Correspondence: Pablo Picasso and Gertrude Stein*, ed. Laurence Madeline, tr. Lorna Scott-Fox (Seagull Books, 2018)

SA – *Sherwood Anderson/Gertrude Stein: Correspondence and Personal Essays*, ed. Ray Lewis White (University of North Carolina Press, 1972)

SOA – *Staying On Alone: Letters of Alice B. Toklas*, ed. Edward Burns (Liveright, 1973)

TW – *The Letters of Gertrude Stein and Thornton Wilder*, ed. Edward Burns, Ulla Dydo and Bill Rice (Yale University Press, 1996)

VT – *The Letters of Gertrude Stein and Virgil Thomson*, ed. Susan Holbrook and Thomas Dilworth (Oxford University Press, 2010)

Other

ABTCB – *The Alice B. Toklas Cook Book* (1954; Anchor, 1960)

JS – *Journey into the Self: Being the Letters, Papers and Journals of Leo Stein*, ed. Edmund Fuller (Crown, 1950)

WIR – Alice B. Toklas, *What Is Remembered* (Holt, Rinehart and Winston, 1963)

Archives

Bancroft – Annette Rosenshine Papers, Bancroft Library, UC Berkeley

Columbia – Random House Records, 1925–1999. Rare Book and Manuscript Library, Columbia University, MS#1048

Getty – The Banyan Press archive, 1946–1986. The Getty Research Institute, Los Angeles, 900230A

HRC – The Carlton Lake Collection of Gertrude Stein, Harry Ransom Center, the University of Texas at Austin, MS-04960

NYPL – The Carl Van Vechten Papers, Manuscripts and Archives Division, the New York Public Library, MSS Col 3142

Princeton – Charles William White Papers, Princeton University Library, C1484

YCAL MSS 76 – The Gertrude Stein and Alice B. Toklas Papers, Yale Collection of American Literature, Beinecke Rare Book and Manuscript Library, Yale University

YCAL MSS 77 – The Gertrude Stein and Alice B. Toklas Collection, Beinecke

YCAL MSS 78 – The Leo Stein Collection, Beinecke

YCAL MSS 792 – The Dorothy Norman Papers, Beinecke

YCAL MSS 833 – The Robert Bartlett Haas Collection on Gertrude Stein and the Conference Press, Beinecke

YCAL MSS 838 – The Donald Clifford Gallup Papers, Beinecke

YCAL MSS 935 – The Janet Malcolm Papers, Beinecke

YCAL MSS 1050 – The Carl Van Vechten Papers, Beinecke

YCAL MSS 1409 – The Leon Katz Papers, Beinecke

YCAL MSS 1610 – The Edward Burns Collection of Alice B. Toklas and Gertrude Stein Papers, Beinecke

Prologue

vii 'Controversial Figure' – All quotes taken from newspaper articles about Stein, found among her papers at YCAL MSS 76 and YCAL MSS 77.

3 'a hooting owl' – See *Everybody's Autobiography* for the hooting owl, 'A Lyrical Opera Made by Two' for pansies and *Lifting Belly* for salmon-pink.

'like a beefsteak' – Mabel Dodge, *European Experiences*, p. 324.

'creative literary mind' – *EA*, p. 12.

'think of the Bible' – *The Geographical History of America*, in *LA*, p. 407.

'with such conviction' – Thornton Wilder, introduction to *FIA*, p. v.

5 'are naturally only' – *CE*, pp. 8–9.

'I am working' – Gertrude Stein biography, in Peter Neagoe (ed.), *Americans Abroad: An Anthology* (Servire Press, 1932), p. 418.

'one of the least read' – *Washington Post*, 28 July 1946.

'everyone who ever' – *MA*, p. 175.

'business of an artist' – *HWW*, p. 157.

'What is a noun' – 'Sentences', in *HTW*, p. 123.

6 'Prepositions' – 'Sentences', in *HTW*, p. 120.

'My sentences' – *AABT*, p. 78.

'I write to write' – 'Praises', in *PL*, p. 123.

'the intensity of the fight' – 'How Writing is Written', in *HWW*, p. 154.

7 'There's good' – Richard Wright to Dorothy Norman, 23 July 1946. YCAL MSS 792.

'I love my love' – *N*, p. 37.

8 'The private life' – *A Long Gay Book* in *G.M.P.*, p. 107.

'fake intellectual' – Leo Stein to Hiram Haydn, 21 July 1947. YCAL MSS 78.

9 'Katz's notes' – Janet Malcolm, *Two Lives*, p. 143.

10 'the witnesses' – *The Geographical History of America*, in *LA*, p. 389.

'Witnesses corroborate' – *Saints and Singing*, in *O&P*, p. 86.

1: Out of the Old World

15 run-down – Fernande Olivier, Picasso's partner, offers a pungent description of the studio in her 1933 memoir *Picasso and His Friends*.
    'meditated' – *AABT*, p. 56.
    'For me' – *Picasso*, in *LA*, p. 502.

16 'long struggle' – *AABT*, p. 61.
    Weickersgrüben – Annie Cohen-Solal, in *Picasso the Foreigner*, pinpoints the Steins' place of origin, which most previous biographers had wrongly called 'Weigersgruben'.
    'out of the old' – *MA*, p. 36.

17 haunted Gertrude – See *EA*, p. 97, among other places: 'there were to be five children and if two little ones had not died there would be no Gertrude Stein.'
    'round little pudding' – Leo Stein to GS (quoting their aunt Rachel), 8 October 1917. *FF*, p. 119.
    'It is better' – *EA*, p. 55.

18 'dark and dreadful days' – *WIHS*, p. 14.
    'nothing is clear' – *WIHS*, p. 27.
    'They never knew' – *MA*, p. 135.

19 'accomplished young miss' – *San Francisco Examiner*, 11 July 1887. The article is accompanied by a drawing of Stein: her first official portrait.
    stalking the streets – In her notebooks, Stein describes her schoolfriend Cora Moore, whose mother held seances, and who took Gertrude walking around East Oakland in the evenings, Moore talking to men they met and making appointments to see them later. It's likely that these experiences fed into the urban 'wanderings' of Melanctha.
    'Our life without' – *EA*, p. 121. For more detailed descriptions of the Steins' family and childhood, see Brenda Wineapple, *Sister Brother*, and Linda Wagner-Martin, *Favored Strangers*.

20 'extraordinary sympathy' – ABT to CVV, 14 May 1947. YCAL MSS 1050.
    'internal and solitary' – 'Portraits and Repetition', in *LA*, p. 289.

21 infectious chuckle – Mabel Weeks, interview with Leon Katz, 23 April 1949. YCAL MSS 1409, and 'In Memoriam', *Radcliffe Quarterly*, August 1946.

22 'Her first real influence' – ABT to William Clifford, 16 November 1947. YCAL MSS 77.
    précis – Leon M. Solomons and Gertrude Stein, 'Normal Motor Automatism', *Psychological Review*, 3/5 (1896).

23 'I was supposed' – 'The Gradual Making of *The Making of Americans*', in *LA*, p. 271.
    'It is very interesting' – *AABT*, p. 86.

24 'bitter and often tyrannical' – 'Only a Question of Rent', in Rosalind Miller, *Gertrude Stein: Form and Intelligibility*, p. 111. Miller had first visited Stein's archive at Yale in 1944, and managed to send a telegram to Culoz asking Stein's permission to examine her earliest writings; her thesis advisor, Lionel Trilling, encouraged her to seek publication. Her expanded dissertation, with the pieces

Stein wrote at Radcliffe as an appendix (which Trilling called 'a remarkable document'), was published in 1949. Miller noted several correspondences between these short pieces and Stein's later work.

24 'fiendish yells' – 'In a Psychological Laboratory', in Miller, *Gertrude Stein: Form and Intelligibility*, p. 121.
'a scientist of force' – 'In a Psychological Laboratory', p. 146.
'intense emotions' – 'In the Red Deeps', in Miller, *Gertrude Stein: Form and Intelligibility*, p. 108.

25 wouldn't recognise him – *EA*, pp. 55–6.
'a toss up' – Quoted in Barbara Pollack, *The Collectors*, p. 110. See Carolyn Burke, 'Gertrude Stein, the Cone Sisters, and the Puzzle of Female Friendship' for an intriguing exploration of the Cone–Stein relationship.
'A sheltered life' – Margaret Sterling Snyder to GS, 29 April 1896. *FF*, p. 8.
'efficiency of the college woman' – 'The Value of College Education for Women', 1899. Claribel Cone and Etta Cone Papers, Baltimore Museum of Art, CP5.20.1.

26 Lewellys Barker – In his autobiography, Barker remembered Stein as one of his first pupils, and 'often wondered whether my attempts to teach her the intricacies of the medulla oblongata had anything to do with the strange literary forms with which she was later to perplex the world.' Lewellys Barker, *Time and the Physician*, p. 60.
one of her professors – John Whitridge Williams.

27 'I am going abroad' – GS to Lewellys Barker, 1902. Reproduced in Steven Meyer, *Irresistible Dictation*, pp. 94–5. See Meyer for an extended discussion of Stein's relationship with Barker, and his efforts to support her scientific career, thwarted by Stein's repeated (sometimes catastrophic) failures to complete the work he gave her.
'openly bored' – *AABT*, p. 90.
'her pet subject' – Etta Cone, diary, 14 September 1901. Claribel Cone and Etta Cone Papers, Baltimore Museum of Art, CP5.20.1.
May Bookstaver – Their relationship can only be reconstructed, now, from Stein's novel *Q.E.D.* In his PhD thesis, Leon Katz cites Toklas telling him the novel was 'simply rapportage', its dialogue based on Stein's correspondence with Bookstaver – which Toklas destroyed.

28 'sexual desires' – 'Degeneration in American Women', in Wineapple, *Sister Brother*, p. 412.
'neither the inclination' – *Q.E.D.*, p. 97.
'Degeneration' – Brenda Wineapple found the essay in the papers of Mary Mackall Gwinn Hodder, and it appears as an appendix to Wineapple's excellent book *Sister Brother*, pp. 409–14.

30 'everybody talks to everybody' – *NB*, p. 58.
'Maggie being the history' – *NB*, pp. 63–4.
'strain and stress' – *MA*, pp. 436–7.

31 'the dead weight' – *Q.E.D.*, pp. 99–100.
   'Yeishin' – *NB*, p. 61. She was probably drawing on an article by Ernest
   Fenollosa, 'An Outline of Japanese Art', *Century*, 56/1–2 (May/June 1898): the
   first to bring a comprehensive survey of Japanese art to American readers.
   'a hopeless coward' – *Q.E.D.*, p. 80.

2: *Vita Nuova*

33 'creative seeing' – *JS*, p. 195.
34 'never-satisfied question mark' – David Edstrom, *Testament of Caliban*, p. 239.
35 'Good God no' – Note within the manuscript of *Q.E.D.* YCAL MSS 76.
36 'succeeded in rendering' – Leo Stein to Mabel Weeks, undated. *JS*, p. 16.
   'incredible place' – *AABT*, p. 34.
37 'nastiest smear' – Leo Stein, *Appreciation*, p. 158.
   'perfectly natural' – *AABT*, p. 40.
38 Sarah joined – Matisse called her 'the really intelligent one of the family'.
   'a genius' – Leo Stein to Mabel Weeks, 29 November 1905. YCAL MSS 78.
   'repelled and shocked' – *AABT*, p. 49.
39 'Cézanne gave me' – 'TI', p. 15.
40 'arduous and troubled' – *TL*, p. 9.
   'inborn intense wisdom' – *TL*, p. 86.
   'something that would move' – *TL*, p. 98.
41 'afraid to let himself' – *TL*, p. 118.
   'did not know' – *TL*, p. 118.
   'It was a struggle' – *TL*, p. 139.
   'Every day now' – *TL*, p. 141.
42 She had been reminded – The first version of *The Making of Americans* drew freely
   on the travails of Stein's older cousin Bird. She had separated eight years earlier
   from her husband, Louis Sternberger, who had promptly brought action against
   his father-in-law, Stein's uncle Solomon, for 'alienation of his wife's affections'.
   Stein was close to Bird, who kept her apprised of the saga, but their relationship
   soured after a quarrel in April 1906. Stein was furious when Bird suddenly
   announced her engagement to Howard Gans, her divorce lawyer: she could not
   countenance the fact that she had been replaced as Bird's chief confidante, and
   that Bird had not told her about this developing relationship – an unprecedented
   disruption in their established dynamic. 'She admired and depended on me,'
   wrote Stein, outraged (and somewhat outrageously) in her notebook. 'As anything
   but a superficial relation it is over . . . she has never been one bit influenced.' She
   drafted a series of acerbic letters, condemning 'damn fool' Howard and Bird's
   'thick-skinned stupidity'. But in her fiction, if not in life, Stein retained control
   of Bird. She drew on her feelings of usurpation for David Hersland's regret at his
   'failure of influence' over Julia: the 'final split' between David and Julia, Stein
   wrote in her notebooks, would be 'like mine with Bird'.

42 'history of a family's progress' – She retained this phrase as the completed novel's subtitle.
'I began' – 'The Gradual Making of *The Making of Americans*', in *LA*, p. 272.

43 'everybody always' – *MA*, p. 139.
'dynamic magnetism' – Annette Rosenshine, 'Life's Not a Paragraph' (undated manuscript). Bancroft.

44 'the kind of being' – *MA*, p. 136.
'The Bazarofians' – *NB*, p. 307.

45 'The free soul' – *NB*, p. 310.
'passionate women' – *NB*, p. 77.

3: Man of Letters

47 'Do get up' – *WIR*, p. 13.

48 coral brooch – This brooch, which Stein is wearing in Picasso's portrait, was given by Toklas's friend Louise Taylor to the Fitzwilliam Museum in Cambridge, along with other jewellery and ornaments owned by Stein and Toklas. It may have been made by Michael Stein, who designed jewellery.

49 'It was Gertrude' – *WIR*, p. 23.
'vengeful goddess' – *WIR*, p. 23.

50 'one of the most' – *AABT*, p. 20.

51 destructive influence – Rosenshine's unpublished memoir, 'Life's Not a Paragraph' (Bancroft), and interviews conducted towards the end of her life, offer her perspective on this episode.

52 philandering Swedish American sculptor – Edstrom is an intriguing character who figures significantly in Stein's notebooks; he is the subject of one of her first portraits, titled 'A Man'. The would-be biographer was Hutchins Hapgood; Harriet Levy tells the story in *Paris Portraits*.
'You are the only' – Fernande Olivier to GS, 19 September 1907. YCAL MSS 76.

53 'Writing books' – *NB*, p. 114.
'Begin this new thing' – *NB*, p. 203.

54 'a new gospel' – Ford Madox Ford, 'Women and Men', *Little Review*, 4 (1918), pp. 40–1.
'broad and deep characterology' – Otto Weininger, *Sex and Character*, p. 83.
See Leon Katz, 'Weininger and *The Making of Americans*', for detailed analysis.

55 'any special tendency' – Leon Solomons to GS, 4 January 1898. YCAL MSS 76.
'the instant' – 'The Modern Jew Who Has Given Up the Faith of His Fathers Can Reasonably and Consistently Believe in Isolation', 1896. Published, with an introduction by Amy Feinstein, in *PMLA*, 116/2 (March 2001), p. 423. See Feinstein, *Gertrude Stein and the Making of Jewish Modernism* for a compelling demonstration of the links between Stein's Jewishness and her formal modernism.

55 'I don't like' – Gertrude's PS in a letter from Leo Stein to Fred Stein, 20 July 1896. YCAL MSS 78.
'deep-seated craving' – Weininger, p. 65.
56 'a higher form' – Weininger, p. 66.
'Pablo & Matisse' – *NB*, p. 415. In her book, Feinstein argues that Stein 'specifically associates modern artistic production with Jewish character' – the 'earthy' and 'resisting' types into which she places herself, Picasso and other artists.
57 'clad in nothing'– Mary Berenson to her family, 21 June 1908. Quoted in Berenson, *A Self-Portrait from Her Letters and Diaries*, p. 146.
climbed a mountain – Probably the one on which the Convento dell'Incontro is sited. See *WIR*, p. 50.
58 'like sheet lightning' – *NB*, p. 257.
'like living history' – *WIR*, p. 54.
'deep humanity' – Hutchins Hapgood to GS, 22 April 1906. *FF*, p. 31.
'too unconventional' – Pitts Duffield to GS, 14 August 1906. *FF*, p. 34.
'noble combination' – GS to Mabel Weeks, May 1906. YCAL MSS 76.
'running amuck' – Emma Lootz Erving to GS, 4 May 1906. YCAL MSS 76.
59 'May has invested' – Emma Lootz Erving to GS, 10 March 1908. YCAL MSS 76.
'I want to say' – F. H. Hitchcock to GS, 16 January 1909. *FF*, p. 44.
'a very masterpiece' – *Kansas City Star*, 18 December 1909.
'quite extraordinary' – *The Nation*, 20 January 1910.
'something really new' – *Boston Morning Herald*, 8 January 1910.
'the pages devoted' – *Rochester NY Post*, 24 December 1909.
'Eccentric Authoress' – Reprinted in *New York City Press*, 13 February 1910.
60 'discussion of pairs of people' – *A Long Gay Book* in *G.M.P.*, p. 17.
'Any one knowing' – *A Long Gay Book* in *G.M.P.*, p. 25.
'Please tell the artichoke' – *A Long Gay Book* in *G.M.P.*, p. 105.
'Spice the same' – *A Long Gay Book* in *G.M.P.*, p. 105.
'A lovely love' – *A Long Gay Book* in *G.M.P.*, p. 101.
'the new love' – Levy, p. 85.
61 'feel their pulses' – *MA*, p. 202. Stein saw Levy as possessed by 'total vanity yet no self-belief'. 'Harriet owns herself,' wrote Stein in her notebook, 'she has put herself in a triple-lined double back action automatic safe, has put the key away in another and hired 16 policemen to guard them day and night.' She concluded that Levy should take more risks in order to 'face herself', and told her frankly that the alternative was suicide: that night, Levy told Toklas she had seen God.
leave Paris – Stein composed a snide portrait that summer titled 'Harriet', beginning with the line 'She said she did not have any plans for the summer.' In another text, 'Harriet Fear', she contrasted Levy's indecision with someone else – clearly Toklas – who was 'completely satisfying some one'.

61 'came to be happier' – 'Ada', in *G&P*, p. 16. Stein had previously used the name Ada as a pseudonym for Etta Cone, a previous 'aider' whom Toklas had displaced as Stein's typist.

63 'everybody who came' – *AABT*, p. 125.
'any one being' – *A Long Gay Book* in G.M.P., p. 22.
'one feeling light' – 'Nadelman', in *P&P*, pp. 51ff.
'one dancing' – 'Orta or One Dancing', in *Two*, p. 301.
'I like it' – *MA*, p. 539.
'I had the existence' – 'Portraits and Repetition', in *LA*, p. 307.

64 'whom some were' – 'Picasso', in *P&P*, p. 17.
'You will be very careful' – GS to Alfred Stieglitz, 6 March 1912. YCAL MSS 76.
'the Post-Impressionist spirit' – Editorial to *Camera Work*, August 1912, p. 3.
'There was one' – *MA*, p. 313.
'I am all unhappy' – *MA*, p. 348.

65 'It makes it simple to be certain' – *MA*, p. 581.
'comforting to me' – *MA*, p. 581.
'Dead is dead' – *MA*, p. 498.
'I have a flush' – *MA*, p. 729.
'Don't understand others' – *NB*, p. 565.

66 'the new people' – *MA*, p. 3.
'real experience' – *MA*, p. 19.
'a master' – *MA*, p. 21.
'This that I write' – *MA*, p. 33.
'Soon there will be' – *MA*, p. 176.
'different from all' – *MA*, p. 115.

67 'everybody always is' – *MA*, p. 139.
'complete understanding' – *MA*, p. 283.
'Repeating is' – *MA*, p. 221.
'Each one slowly' – *MA*, pp. 300, 302, 327.
'Perhaps no one' – *MA*, p. 454.
'complete desolation' – *MA*, p. 729.
'Sometimes it is' – *MA*, p. 574.

4: Extreme Cubist Literature

69 'but truly' – *MA*, p. 33.
'myself and strangers' – *MA*, p. 289.
'I want readers' – *MA*, p. 289.
'worked terrifically' – *AABT*, p. 130.
'people, their character' – *AABT*, p. 130.
'first felt' – *AABT*, p. 130.

70 'more important than' – 'TI', p. 17.

70 'intellectual passion' – *AABT*, p. 228.
'The more exactly' – *EA*, p. 232.
'I was alone' – *Picasso*, in *LA*, p. 508.
'intellectual recreation' – 'Poetry and Grammar', in *LA*, p. 331.
71 'a dinner set' – *TB*, p. 17.
'Sausages in between' – *TB*, p. 53.
'Cold coffee' – *TB*, p. 49.
'Act so that' – *TB*, p. 63.
'In the inside' – *TB*, p. 35.
'Why is a feel' – *TB*, p. 58.
'associational emotion' – *AABT*, p. 228.
72 'I took individual words' – 'TI', p. 18.
'Writing may be made' – 'Finally George a Vocabulary of Thinking', in *HTW*,
p. 269. See Steven Meyer, *Irresistible Dictation*, ch. 2, for a discussion of Stein's
work at Johns Hopkins: he points out that in 1897, the year Stein entered
medical school, Charles Sherrington had introduced the idea of the synapse
as 'an anatomical and functional explanation for the mechanism by which
the individual neuronal units could communicate with each other' – a major
paradigm shift.
'Give known or pin ware' – 'Guillaume Apollinaire', in *P&P*, p. 20.
'Toasted susie' – 'Preciosilla', in *CE*, p. 32.
73 'one of the most remarkable' – Mabel Dodge to GS, April 1911. *FF*, p. 52.
'On account of' – Mabel Dodge to GS, 27 January 1913. MD, p. 163.
74 'the most important' – Mabel Dodge to GS, 24 January 1913. MD, p. 157.
'not at *all*' – Mabel Dodge to GS, 24 January 1913. MD, pp. 159–60.
'You have made' – GS to Mabel Dodge, May–June 1913. MD, p. 189.
'is doing with words' – Mabel Dodge, 'Speculations, or Post-Impressionism in
Prose', *Arts and Decoration*, March 1913. MD, p. 269.
75 'the name of Gertrude Stein' – Mabel Dodge to GS, March 1913. MD, p. 175.
'Hurrah for gloire' – Quoted in Mabel Dodge, *Movers and Shakers*, p. 35.
'damned nonsense' – Leo Stein to Mabel Weeks, 7 February 1913. *JS*, p. 53.
'Gertrude Stein's latest' – Mary Berenson to her family, 21 November 1912.
Quoted in MD, p. 77.
'I am working' – Mabel Dodge to GS, March 1913. MD, p. 177.
'It takes lots of shoving' – GS to Mabel Dodge, February 1913. MD, p. 169.
'This is post-impressionist' – CVV, 'Cubist of Letters Writes New Book', *New
York Times*, 24 February 1913.
76 'He wants me' – GS to Mabel Dodge, May 1913. MD, p. 195.
'a wonderful personality' – CVV to Fania Marinoff, 2 June 1913. *CVV*, p. 16.
'one must only' – CVV to GS, 17 May 1916. *CVV*, p. 54.
'I tried to' – Quoted in Bruce Kellner, 'Baby Woojums in Iowa', p. 8.
'absolutely third-rate' – Mabel Dodge to GS, 29 March 1914. MD, p. 220.
77 'I really believe' – Mabel Dodge to GS, April 1914. MD, p. 223.

77 'Officer' – *Detroit News*, June 1914.
'a scramble' – *Pittsburgh Dispatch*, 5 June 1914.
'can be read' – George Cram Cook, 'New York Letter', *Chicago Post*, 12 June 1914.
'one of the most unique' – 'Claire Marie's New Books for Exotic Tastes', spring 1914. YCAL MSS 76.
'an entirely new' – 'Gertrude Stein Plagiary', *New York Evening Sun*, 13 June 1914.
78 'extreme Cubist literature' – *Chicago Tribune*, 5 June 1914.
'It will not do' – Richard Burton, 'Posing', *Minneapolis Bellman*, 17 October 1914.
'Gertrude Stein has provided' – Alfred Kreymborg, 'Gertrude Stein: Hoax and Hoaxtress', *New York Morning Telegraph*, 7 March 1915.
'Miss Stein has' – CVV, 'How to Read Gertrude Stein', *The Trend* (August 1914).
'There was a doubt' – Dodge, *Movers and Shakers*, p. 38.
79 honeymoon – A note from GS to ABT, on Garland's Hotel stationery, begins, 'My dear wife, here we are in London on our honeymoon.' YCAL MSS 76.
'perfect whirlpool' – *JS*, p. 23.
'tommyrot' – Leo Stein to Mabel Weeks, 4 February 1913. *JS*, p. 48.
'one of the greatest changes' – Leo Stein to Mabel Weeks, 7 February 1913. *JS*, p. 52.
80 'During the winter' – *AABT*, p. 153.
'grossly disproportionate' – Leo Stein to GS, undated (1913). *JS*, pp. 56–7.
'Alice's final' – Dodge, *European Experiences*, p. 333.
'everything to save' – Dodge, *European Experiences*, p. 327.
'such a strong look' – Dodge, *European Experiences*, p. 332. Dodge omitted to mention that she had done her best to provoke strife between Stein and Toklas by teasingly concocting a non-existent flirtation between Toklas and her friend Constance Fletcher, which may well have alerted the couple to her own questionable intentions.
'so self-obliterating' – Dodge, *European Experiences*, p. 326.
'all-important second fiddle' – Leo Stein to Mabel Weeks, 1 June 1920. YCAL MSS 78.
81 'manifestation of homosexuality' – Kellner, 'Baby Woojums in Iowa', p. 6.
'cook an egg' – Kellner, 'Baby Woojums in Iowa', p. 6.

5: A Puzzle Picture

84 'because it was' – ABT to Donald Gallup, 31 July 1950. YCAL MSS 838.
'ten days in Cambridge' – they stayed with the family of the poet Hope Mirrlees, whom they had met in Paris, and had dinner at Newnham College with the classicist Jane Ellen Harrison.
Alfred North Whitehead – In the *Autobiography*, Toklas lists him alongside Stein and Picasso as the three geniuses she has known. Stein's growing conception of her own work as mathematical – the 'intellectual passion for exactitude' – was

shaped in part by her intense encounter with Whitehead, whose work, like her own, explored the progression of time and its relationship to human perception. See Kate Fullbrook, 'Gertrude Stein and Alfred North Whitehead', and Steven Meyer, *Irresistible Dictation*, for more on Stein and Whitehead.

85 'The search for food' – 'Painted Lace', in *PL*, p. 1. See Rosalind Moad, '1914–1916', for a detailed study of Stein's war writing and reconstruction of her movements over these years.
'I'll make literature' – 'Gentle Julia', in *BTV*, p. 178.
'I was determined' – 'No', in *AFAM*, p. 33.
'We are examples' – 'Let Us Be Easily Careful', in *PL*, p. 35.

86 'furs, a hat' – 'Farragut or a Husband's Recompense', in *UK*, p. 15.
'That is Cubism!' – *Picasso*, in *LA*, p. 504.
'the war doesn't' – William Cook to GS, 6 January 1915. YCAL MSS 76.
'very content and peaceful' – GS to Harry Phelan Gibb, 11 April 1915. YCAL MSS 76.

87 'In my portraits' – 'Plays', in *LA*, p. 262.
'I love cherish' – *Lifting Belly*, in *BTV*, pp. 61ff.
'permanent caress' – *Lifting Belly*, in *BTV*, p. 37.

88 'a continuous Christmas' – *AABT*, p. 192. Their work is reported in regular AFFW bulletins, held in YCAL MSS 76.

89 'began to work' – *AABT*, p. 206.
'absorbing literature' – GS to CVV, 18 April 1916. *CVV*, p. 53.
'Your name pops up' – CVV to GS, March 1916. *CVV*, p. 50.
'genuinely interesting figures' – 'New Poems by Gertrude Stein', *Vanity Fair*, March 1919. The June 1917 issue had prefaced her portrait 'Have They Attacked Mary. He Giggled' with the description 'Miss Stein, who is immensely famous in France, is a Jewess, once of San Francisco, but now of Paris.'
'Your poems' – Ellery Sedgwick to GS, 25 October 1919. YCAL MSS 77. This amusing correspondence – starting with Stein's assumption that she is addressing a woman – has been published in the *Yale University Library Gazette*. ES, p. 110.

90 'I may say' – GS to Ellery Sedgwick, October 1919. YCAL MSS 77. ES, p. 111.
'judge and jury' – Ellery Sedgwick to GS, 4 December 1919. YCAL MSS 77. ES, p. 111.
'My work is' – GS to Ellery Sedgwick, December 1919. YCAL MSS 77. ES, p. 112.
'There is a public' – Henry McBride to GS, 13 November 1920. *FF*, p. 137. Stein met McBride, an art critic for the *New York Sun*, in 1913: in the *Autobiography*, she notes that he 'used to keep Gertrude Stein's name before the public all those tormented years', by urging his readers to 'laugh with and not at her'.

91 'almost ecclesiastical' – John Glassco, *Memoirs of Montparnasse*, p. 79.
'The paintings' – James Lord, 'Where the Pictures Were', p. 6.

91 'Being only one' – Arthur C. Fifield to GS, 19 April 1912. *FF*, p. 58.
'the amount of' – Benjamin Huebsch, quoted in Donald Gallup, 'The Making of *The Making of Americans*', appendix to *Q.E.D.*, p. 178.
'Nobody knows' – 'As Fine as Melanctha', in *AFAM*, p. xv.

92 Four Seas – Stein was introduced to the publisher by Kate Buss, an American journalist who hoped, at one point, to write Stein's biography. Stein sent the editor a copy of *Three Lives*, inscribed 'to Edmund R. Brown, who has been called a really honest publisher from Gtde Stein who hopes to find it out'.
'brilliant work' – Autobiographical notes for *Geography and Plays*. YCAL MSS 76.
'consists in a rebuilding' – *G&P*, p. 8.
'Miss Stein Applies' – *Baltimore Sun*, 25 August 1923.
'a garish collection' – *Bookman*, September 1923.
'419 pages of drivel' – H. L. Mencken in *Smart Set*, October 1923.
'Gertrude Stein is' – 'Medals for Miss Stein', *New York Herald Tribune*, 13 May 1923.

93 'the world broke in two' – Willa Cather, *Not Under Forty* (Knopf, 1936), p. v.
'Year One' – In the *Little Review* (Spring 1922), Pound published a calendar with the heading 'Year 1 p.s.U. (*post scriptum Ulysses*)'.
'seems to us' – *Chicago Tribune*, 4 February 1923.

94 'the beginning' – *AABT*, p. 233.
'village explainer' – *AABT*, p. 217.
'After all these years' – ABT to Donald Sutherland, 30 November 1947. YCAL MSS 77. *SOA*, p. 92.
'I want to be included' – Autobiographical notes for *Geography and Plays*. YCAL MSS 76.

95 'talking' – 'What Are Masterpieces and Why Are There So Few of Them', in *LA*, p. 355.
'I know I am' – GS to Mabel Weeks, 1922. YCAL MSS 76.
'a very big thing' – CVV to GS, 16 April 1923. *CVV*, p. 73.

96 'creating the contemporary' – GS to F. Scott Fitzgerald, 22 May 1925. Quoted in *Correspondence of F. Scott Fitzgerald*, p. 164.
'like brothers' – Ernest Hemingway to Sherwood Anderson, 9 March 1922. *Selected Letters 1917–1961*, p. 62.
'devote their lives' – *AABT*, p. 234.
'I made it clear' – Ernest Hemingway to GS, 17 February 1924. *FF*, p. 159.
'There seems no doubt' – GS to CVV, 23 June 1924. *CVV*, p. 101.

97 'zip of intelligence' – Robert McAlmon to GS, August 1924. *FF*, p. 162.
'It is a bit monumental' – GS to Sherwood Anderson, summer 1925. *SA*, p. 47.
'You know I want' – GS to Robert McAlmon, quoted in Gallup, 'The Making of *The Making of Americans*', appendix to *Q.E.D.*, p. 206.
'philanthropic enterprise' – Robert McAlmon to GS, spring 1926. *FF*, p. 189.

98 'a truly psychological' – Marianne Moore, 'The Spare American Emotion', *The Dial*, February 1926.

98 'a very necessary book' – Katherine Anne Porter, 'Everybody is a Real One', *New York Herald Tribune*, 16 January 1927.

100 in *Vogue* – The magazine was edited by the flamboyant lesbian Dorothy Todd, who (until she was fired) broadened its scope significantly to embrace modernist writing and art.

'We are lying crushed' – Virginia Woolf to Roger Fry, 16 September 1925. *The Letters of Virginia Woolf, 3: 1923–1928*, p. 209.

'an anxious, exacerbating affair' – Virginia Woolf to Vanessa Bell, 2 June 1926. *Letters, 3*, p. 269.

'a pretty good address' – GS to CVV, 3 February 1926. *CVV*, p. 126. Stein expresses her anxiety about the occasion in her text *A Novel of Thank You*, written earlier that year; she claimed she wrote the lecture while waiting at the garage for her car to be repaired.

'Beauty is beauty' – *CE*, p. 11.

101 'It is really too bad' – *CE*, p. 9.

'went off very well' – *AABT*, p. 253. The Cambridge lecture took place at Trinity College on 4 June 1926, and the Oxford version at Christ Church on 7 June.

'a squat Aztec figure' – Harold Acton, *Memoirs of an Aesthete*, p. 161.

'For a very long time' – *CE*, p. 10.

6: Shoving the Unshoveable

103 'really began to make' – GS to Robert Bartlett Haas, June 1937. YCAL MSS 833.

'complete actual present' – 'Plays', in *LA*, p. 251.

'light and air' – 'Portraits and Repetition', in *LA*, p. 307.

'always in relation' – 'Plays', in *LA*, p. 265.

'In Saint Remy' – 'Talks to Saints', in *PL*, p. 108.

'A girl with' – 'A Saint in Seven', in *CE*, p. 33.

104 'to really completely' – 'Portraits and Repetition', in *LA*, p. 307.

'quantities of portraits' – 'Portraits and Repetition', in *LA*, p. 307.

'Gertice. Altrude' – Manuscript notebook for *Lend a Hand*. YCAL MSS 76.

'There is a key' – *A Book Concluding With As a Wife Has a Cow A Love Story*, Éditions de la Galerie Simon, 1926. This text was published by Daniel-Henry Kahnweiler's gallery, with original lithographs by Juan Gris.

105 'My wife is my life' – 'A Lyrical Opera Made by Two', in *O&P*, p. 49.

106 'the working artist's working life' – Virgil Thomson, *An Autobiography*, p. 90.

'pear trees' – *Four Saints in Three Acts*, in *O&P*, p. 21.

'How many acts' – *Four Saints in Three Acts*, in *O&P*, p. 45.

'Scene One' – *Four Saints in Three Acts*, in *O&P*, p. 35.

'Neither you nor I' – GS to Virgil Thomson, 11 February 1938. *VT*, p. 254.

group of artists – Known as the Neo-Romantics, these included Kristians

Tonny, Christian Bérard and Eugène Berman. Stein's play 'At Present' (subtitled 'Nothing But Contemporaries Allowed') features them all as characters, along with 'P. Picasso', 'Alice B.' and Basket. Shortly after the French translation of *The Making of Americans*, Stein and Hugnet collaborated on *Dix Portraits* (1930), a selection of ten of Stein's portraits, printed in both Stein's English and Hugnet and Thomson's French, illustrated with original lithographs by the artists featured. For more on this group and Stein's relationship with them, see Patrick Mauries, *Theatres of Melancholy*.

107 'Young France' – GS to Henry McBride, 28 February 1928. YCAL MSS 76. A few of her portraits had been translated into German by the artist Arnold Rönnebeck, and Jean Cocteau quoted her work in *Le Potomak* (1919), but this was the first sustained engagement with her work in another language.
'internal troubles' – 'TI', p. 19. She also describes the difficulties of this translation in *Four in America* (in the 'Henry James' section).
'I dunno' – GS to Virgil Thomson, 12 July 1930. *VT*, p. 161.
'declines further acquaintance' – GS to Virgil Thomson, 21 January 1931. *VT*, p. 169.

108 'the Executioner' – Janet Flanner, interviewed by Perry Miller Adato, 30 May 1970. YCAL MSS 77.
'a lot of confidence' – Françoise Gilot and Carlton Lake, *Life with Picasso*, pp. 60–3.

109 'for some time' – Bravig Imbs's *Confessions of Another Young Man* offers a detailed account of his own and other friends' ostracisms.
'lighted kerosene lamp' – Elliot Paul, 'Gertrude, Alas, Alas', *Esquire*, July 1946.
'The geniuses came' – *AABT*, p. 95.

110 'her pronounced moustache' – M. F. K. Fisher's foreword to the 1984 Harper & Row edition of *The Alice B. Toklas Cook Book*.
'I am a husband' – 'Didn't Nelly and Lilly Love You', in *AFAM*, p. 245.
'Psychologically and emotionally' – ABT to William Clifford, 20 January 1948. YCAL MSS 77.
'Play, play' – 'Play', in *P&P*, p. 160.

111 'The world is' – *AABT*, p. 19.

112 'Alice Toklas's conscience' – *EA*, p. 15. Stein tells several versions of this story, in the *Autobiography*, in *Everybody's Autobiography*, and (more obliquely) in *Lucy Church Amiably*. The friends who helped her were Georges Maratier and Bernard Faÿ, and the lieutenant's name was Ferdinand Bonhomme.

113 'we love him' – *EA*, p. 106.
'I like ordinary' – *New York Herald Tribune*, 7 April 1935.

114 'making you richer' – Julian Stein to GS, 13 April 1927. YCAL MSS 76.
'We sign our checks' – 'Mildred's Thoughts', *The American Caravan* (Macaulay Company, 1927), p. 648.
'born in wedlock' – 'Finally George', in *HTW*, p. 317.

115 'model to every one' – *A Sonatina Followed by Another*, in *BTV*, p. 8.

115 'Alice is making tapestry' – GS to Virgil Thomson, 2 January 1929. *VT*, p. 98.
'new conception of prose' – GS to Harry Phelan Gibb, December 1927. YCAL
MSS 76. Stein had met Gibb in London and wrote often to him; he suggested
the idea of the Plain Edition to Toklas.
'making a desperate effort' – GS to Sherwood Anderson, February 1929. *SA*,
p. 68.
'intensive study' – GS to Virgil Thomson, 23 February 1929. *VT*, p. 107.
'paragraphs were emotional' – 'What Is English Literature', in *LA*, p. 218.
'Think in stitches' – 'Sentences', in *HTW*, p. 130.
'Grammar. Fills me with delight.' – 'A Grammarian', in *HTW*, p. 98.
'I am a grammarian' – 'A Grammarian', in *HTW*, p. 101.
'I return to sentences' – 'Sentences and Paragraphs', in *HTW*, p. 18.
'Grammar if complicated' – 'Arthur a Grammar', in *HTW*, p. 47.
116 'Forget grammar' – 'A Grammarian', in *HTW*, p. 101.
'Realism in America' – 'Suggestions for a New Magic', *transition* (June 1927).
'Stein and the *steinizing*', 'highbrow clown', 'arch-fraud' – Wyndham Lewis,
'The Diabolical Principle', *The Enemy*, 1/3 (first quarter, 1929), pp. 11, 13.
117 'gargantuan mental stutter' – Wyndham Lewis, *The Art of Being Ruled*, p. 346.
'a cold, black suet-pudding' – Wyndham Lewis, *Time and Western Man*, p. 77.
'at opposite poles' – 'Work in Progress', *transition* (December 1927).
'that eyebold' – James Joyce, *Finnegans Wake*, p. 91.
'something precisely ominous' – T. S. Eliot, 'Charleston, Hey! Hey!', *Nation
and Athenaeum*, 40/17 (29 January 1927).
118 'whale out of water' – Lewis, 'The Diabolical Principle', p. 11.
'old tub of guts' – Quoted in Humphrey Carpenter, *A Serious Character*,
p. 401.
'Gertie Stein' – Ezra Pound to Archibald MacLeish, 13 February 1927.
Carpenter, *A Serious Character*, p. 400.
'are no older' – Laura Riding, 'The New Barbarism and Gertrude Stein',
transition, 3 (June 1927). A version of this essay was published in *A Survey
of Modernist Poetry*, edited by Riding and Robert Graves. For the full and
intriguing story of Riding's mounting obsession with Stein, see *DA*.
'fresh significance' – Mina Loy, 'Gertrude Stein', in *The Last Lunar Baedeker*
(FSG, 1996), p. 26.
'I don't like attacks' – GS to Laura Riding (draft), June 1928. *DA*, p. 29.
119 'We have decided' – GS to CVV, 17 January 1931. *CVV*, p. 233.
'an edition of first editions' – *Lucy Church Amiably* press release. YCAL MSS
76.
'Here we are' – GS to Henry McBride, 17 January 1931. YCAL MSS 76.
120 'It is interesting' – GS to Ellen Daniel, July 1932. YCAL MSS 76.
'a literary personality' – Edmund Wilson, *Axel's Castle*, pp. 253, 238.
121 'as hard to read' – Dorothy Chamberlain, 'Gertrude Stein, Amiably', *New
Republic*, 7 April 1931.

121 'a long dull poem' – GS to Louis Bromfield, summer 1932. YCAL MSS 76. She used this phrase in several letters to other correspondents, too.

'A sentence' – 'Sentences and Paragraphs', in *HTW*, p. 158.

'exactness' – GS to Leonard B. Gandalac (draft), 27 May 1932. YCAL MSS 76.

122 'hidden with intention' – 'Here. Actualities', in *PL*, p. 12.

'The first recognition' – *Q.E.D.*, pp. 65, 66, 95.

123 *Well of Loneliness* – The book was selling 100 copies a day in Paris by the time it was banned in Britain, in November 1928. Hall and Una Troubridge visited Stein at the rue de Fleurus and (according to Troubridge) both 'fell for her in one heap'.

'History is made' – 'We Came. A History', in *Readies for Bob Brown's Machine* (Roving Eye Press, 1931), p. 99. This text was composed for Brown, a Paris-based writer who conceived the idea of a 'reading machine' which would print texts on ticker tape and flash them before the eye to speed up the reading process; he asked several writers including Stein to contribute 'readies' for his prototype, which was never made.

7: Knockout and a Wow

125 'I was a little scared' – GS to Lindley Hubbell, 22 August 1933. YCAL MSS 77. Hubbell, who worked at the New York Public Library, was 'a nice young man', in Toklas's words, who had been writing to Stein about her work since the 1920s, when he told her he had tried to have *Tender Buttons* recategorised from 'eccentric literature', but it had only been moved to 'Rare Books'.

'I am not interested' – Notebook for *Tous Que Je Sais*. YCAL MSS 76.

'beautiful and unusually' – *EA*, p. 1.

126 'pretty good housekeeper' – *AABT*, p. 272.

'I like a view' – *AABT*, p. 7.

'and this is it' – *AABT*, p. 272.

127 'With a little clever handling' – William Bradley to Alfred Harcourt, 28 December 1932. Quoted in Ulla E. Dydo, *The Language that Rises*, p. 544.

'It is an extraordinary' – Alfred Harcourt to William Bradley, 18 January 1933. YCAL MSS 76.

'After these years' – 'The Story of a Book', in *HWW*, p. 62.

'Affirmation' – GS to Lindley Hubbell, 17 December 1932. YCAL MSS 77.

128 'our long correspondence' – Ellery Sedgwick to GS, 11 February 1933. *FF*, p. 261.

'As you read her' – Maslin Marshall, 'All of Us', *Clinton Herald*, 8 July 1933.

'clear as a comic strip' – *Newsweek*, 9 September 1933.

'may begin to understand' – *Time*, 11 September 1933.

129 'I am as happy' – GS to Lindley Hubbell, June 1933. YCAL MSS 77.

'Has Gertrude Stein a Secret?' – *Atlantic Monthly*, January 1934.

'Everything I write' – Gertrude Stein biography, in Peter Neagoe (ed.), *Americans Abroad: An Anthology* (Servire Press, 1932), p. 418.

129 'There are no real cases' – GS to Lindley Hubbell, 17 December 1932. YCAL MSS 77.

130 'The idea is not to think' – *New York City Call*, 7 June 1914.
'NO, it is not so automatic' – GS to Ellery Sedgwick, February 1934. YCAL MSS 77.
'There is no pleasure' – 'And Now', in *HWW*, p. 64.

131 'I began to think' – 'And Now', in *HWW*, p. 63.
was worth money – *EA*, p. 67.

132 'If you are a genius' – *EA*, p. 68.
'what happened' – 'And Now', in *HWW*, p. 63.
'The other book was gay' – 'And Now', in *HWW*, p. 63.
'only really modern' – 'What Are Masterpieces and Why Are There So Few of Them', in *LA*, p. 358.

133 'It always did bother' – *EA*, p. 37.
'a great deal puzzled' – Donald Brace to William Bradley, 11 May 1934. Quoted in Dydo, p. 601.

134 'Do try to make' – GS to William Bradley, 25 May 1934. YCAL MSS 76.
'The readers of the autobiography' – 'The Story of a Book', in *HWW*, p. 62.

135 'American retrospective' – See Steven Watson, *Prepare for Saints*, for the full story of the *Four Saints* production.
'I do not wish' – Quoted in William Bradley to Virgil Thomson, 15 May 1933. *VT*, p. 200.
'the commercial value' – GS to Virgil Thomson, 6 June 1933. *VT*, p. 210.

137 'it begins to look' – Joseph Alsop, *New York Herald Tribune*, January 1934.

138 'Since the Whisky Rebellion' – Lucius Beebe, *New York Herald Tribune*, 9 February 1934.
'a gasp of astonishment' – Henry McBride, *New York Sun*, 9 February 1934.
'a knockout and a wow' – CVV to GS, 8 February 1934. *CVV*, p. 295.

139 'a child's dream' – Gilbert Seldes, 'Delight in the Theatre', *Modern Music* (March–April 1934).
'the most interesting' – John Martin, *New York Times*, 25 February 1934.
'come to America' – CVV to GS, 8 September 1933. *CVV*, p. 274.

140 'read eagerly' – Bernard Faÿ to GS, 25 May 1926. YCAL MSS 76.
'I always did say' – GS to Bernard Faÿ, 1926. Quoted in Barbara Will, *Unlikely Collaboration*, p. 55.
'Interesting if true' – *EA*, p. 37.
'Jo Davidson always said' – *EA*, p. 37.

141 seek invitations – An appendix to *TW* gives the full tour itinerary.
'I am so pleased' – GS to CVV, 25 August 1934. *CVV*, p. 332.
'My dearest Carl' – GS to CVV, 16 August 1934. *CVV*, p. 329.
House guests at Bilignin – Among them was the young James Laughlin, founder of the publishing house New Directions: Stein didn't think much of his press releases, but took him around with her to change her tyres, which

went flat daily. He wrote in September 1934 that 'I have learned more about writing in these few days than ever I have known before'. He planned to write a book about the work, but abandoned the project. See Ian S. MacNiven, *'Literchoor Is My Beat'*.

142 'the only ones' – GS to Julian and Rose Ellen Stein, October 1934. YCAL MSS 76. Julian (Stein's 'favourite cousin') was the son of Stein's uncle Samuel, and worked for the Baltimore banking firm Stein Brothers & Boyce, founded in 1853 by Samuel and Meyer. Rose Ellen, his wife, translated the *Autobiography* into Braille.
'What will I say to them' – 'Meditations on Being About to Visit My Native Land', in *PL*, p. 254.
'most talked-about' – 'Gertrude Stein: Her Words "Do Get Under Their Skin"', *Newsweek*, 27 October 1934.
'the French poodle' – *Des Moines Register*, 2 December 1934.

143 'Robin Hood's forest' – *New York Times*, 25 October 1934.
'secretary-stooge' – *Des Moines Register*, 2 December 1934.
'inseparable as ham and eggs' – *Des Moines Register*, 2 December 1934.
'a microscopic person' – Marguerite Steedman, *Atlanta Journal*, February 1935. Stein noted on this clipping, 'Keep this one for one.'
'Pussy' and 'Lovey' – *New York Telegraph*, 21 November 1934.

144 'If you enjoy it' – GS, interviewed by William Lundell, 12 November 1934. Recordings of Stein reading and talking during the tour can be heard on the PennSound website.
'undoubtedly the most' – Ralph E. Renaud, 'Matinee Idols Find Spotlight Is Boring', *Washington Post*, 1 December 1934.
'You people' – Quoted in Roy Morris, Jr, *Gertrude Stein Has Arrived*, p. 111.
'Miss Toklas always' – *EA*, p. 188.
'She scolds me' – Isabelle Keating, 'Gertrude Stein, Stein is Back, Back, and It's all still Black, Black', clipping from unidentified newspaper, 24 October 1934.
'How do you do, Miss Stein' – *EA*, p. 150.

145 'The twentieth century' – *Picasso*, in *LA*, p. 533.
'perfectly extraordinary' – Quoted in John Malcolm Brinnin, *The Third Rose*, p. 346.
'Government is the least' – *EA*, pp. 177–8. She was at dinner with the philosopher Mortimer Adler and University of Chicago President Robert Maynard Hutchins, at the home of Elizabeth Fuller Chapman, an arts patron and president of the Arts Club of Chicago (known to Stein and Toklas as Bobsy Goodspeed); the police car experience was arranged by Chapman and Fanny Butcher, the literary editor of the *Chicago Tribune*.

146 Dashiell Hammett – This dinner was arranged by Lillian Ehrman, a friend of Van Vechten. Hammett received the invitation on April Fool's Day and nearly didn't turn up.

146 'It is very nice' – *EA*, p. xxi.
　　ten talks – Six were published together as *Lectures in America*; during the tour Stein
　　wrote a four-part series titled *Narration* to deliver at the University of Chicago.
147 'long complicated sentences' – *N*, p. vi.
　　'the thing that' – 'Portraits and Repetition', in *LA*, p. 298.
　　'vitality of movement' – 'Portraits and Repetition', in *LA*, p. 292.
　　'Nothing could bother' – 'What Are Masterpieces And Why Are There So
　　Few of Them', in *LA*, p. 361.
　　'trying in every' – 'How Writing is Written', in *HWW*, p. 156.
　　'The business of Art' – 'Plays', in *LA*, p. 251.
　　'You all have seen' – Thornton Wilder, introduction to *FIA*, p. vi.
149 'I am delighted' – GS to W. G. Rogers, November 1934. YCAL MSS 76.
　　'the precise babbling' – 'Aloft with Miss Stein in Verbal Fog', *San Francisco
　　Chronicle*, November 1934.
　　palilalia – *Journal of Medical Associations*, 29 November 1934.
150 'world's biggest faker' – *Chicago Daily News*, 11 December 1935.
　　'I can't get over it' – GS to Julian and Rose Ellen Stein, undated (1935). YCAL
　　MSS 76.
　　'We are public figures' – *NB*, p. 244.
151 'both a little proud' – *AABT*, p. 233.
　　'Things belong to you' – *EA*, p. 6. Frank O'Hara later riffed on these lines in a
　　letter to the artist Larry Rivers.
　　'God what a liar' – Leo Stein to Mabel Weeks, 28 December 1933. *JS*, p. 134.
　　'As I read' – Albert Barnes to Leo Stein, 2 November 1934. YCAL MSS 1409.
　　Barnes, the famed Philadelphia art collector, had been one of the first to try
　　to persuade the Steins to sell their works, offering $5,000 for a Picasso nude:
　　Michael had sternly told him they were collectors, not dealers. Leo did sell
　　him two Matisse paintings shortly after the split with Gertrude.
　　'hungers and thirsts' – Leo Stein to Mabel Weeks, 7 February 1913. *JS*, p. 52.
152 'Cone sternly' – Edward T. Cone, 'The Miss Etta Cones, the Steins, and
　　M'sieu Matisse', p. 456.
　　'hollow, tinsel bohemianism' – Georges Braque et al., *Testimony Against
　　Gertrude Stein* (Servire Press, 1935).
153 'My French publishers' – GS to CVV, 7 March 1935. *CVV*, p. 407.

8: Publicity Saint

155 'We are moving' – GS to Sherwood Anderson, January 1938. *SA*, p. 106.
　　'the apartment of our dreams' – GS to Elizabeth Fuller Chapman, 16
　　December 1937. YCAL MSS 76.
　　'a detective story' – *The Geographical History of America*, in *LA*, p. 409.
　　'nothing whatever' – *The Geographical History of America*, in *LA*, p. 423.
156 'I am I' – *FIA* p. 119.

156 'errand boy-companion' – Thornton Wilder to C. Leslie Glenn, March 1935.
Quoted in *The Selected Letters of Thornton Wilder*, p. 292.
'I am resolved' – Thornton Wilder to GS, 12 April 1936, *TW*, p. 98.
'only a bundle' – Thornton Wilder to Alexander Woollcott, 16 September
1933. Quoted in *TW*, p. 142.
'I am not leading' – *EA*, p. 262.
157 Norman Holmes Pearson – Pearson was also an agent, recruiting students to the
CIA. See Greg Barnhisel, *Cold War Modernists* and *Code Name Puritan*, Annette
Debo, 'Norman Holmes Pearson: Canon-Maker' and Michael Holtzman, 'The
Ideological Origins of American Studies at Yale' for more, especially on his
work with American Studies at Yale: his archive-building was part of a broader
concerted effort, at Yale, of cultural diplomacy amid the Cold War.
'If it is not printed' – *EA*, p. 90.
158 'No doubt' – *The Autobiography of William Carlos Williams*, p. 254.
159 'chicken made of glass' – 'Mildred's Thoughts', *The American Caravan* (Macaulay
Company, 1927), p. 664. It also recalls 'alas a dirty bird', a line from *Tender Buttons*.
The process of archiving – See Logan Esdale's introduction to his edition
of *Ida* for more on the way Stein's archiving process fed into the novel. *Ida*
borrowed from a story which Stein had written as a Radcliffe student, as well
as an old movie scenario originally composed in French ('Two Sisters Who
Are Not Sisters'), short texts titled 'My Life with Dogs' and 'Superstitions',
and a 1934 novelette titled *The Superstitions of Fred Anneday, Annday, Anday A
Novel of Real Life*, which follows a man who moves to Europe and becomes a
celebrity, and is saved from uncertainty by the steadfastness of his partner.
'who achieves publicity' – GS to Bennett Cerf, April 1941. Columbia.
'a person is so publicised' – GS to W. G. Rogers, 1937. Quoted in Rogers,
When This You See Remember Me, p. 130.
160 'There is no use' – *EA*, p. 3.
'There is so little' – GS to Thornton Wilder, 1 October 1939. *TW*, p. 245.
161 'and they know me' – *PF*, p. 42. See Dominique Saint-Pierre, *Gertrude Stein:
Le Bugey, la guerre*, for much more information on Stein's extensive Bugey
community and the way the region's geography, culture and social life imbued
her writing from the mid-1920s onwards.
'entirely new' – GS to Thornton Wilder, 1 October 1939. *TW*, p. 245.
'Really it is xtraordinary' – GS to Daniel-Henry Kahnweiler, 16 July 1940.
YCAL MSS 76.
162 'a thing based on reality' – *PF*, p. 38.
'terribly frightened' – 'TWL'.
'There are enough' – *WIHS*, p. 75.
163 'They all agree' – GS to William P. Sears, 14 November 1940. YCAL MSS 76.
'No one alive' – *New Yorker*, 2 February 1939. Janet Flanner, *Paris Was
Yesterday*, p. 242.
164 'So many points' – *WIHS*, p. 82.

164 'he had saved France' – 'TWL'.
165 'What I cannot understand' – VV to W. G. Rogers, 11 September 1940.
YCAL MSS 1050.
'the calm and peace' – Thérèse Bonney, 'Gertrude Stein in France', *Vogue*, 1
July 1942.
'a country' – 'Why I Do Not Live in America', *transition*, 14 (Fall 1928). In
Everybody's Autobiography she wrote, 'I am an American and I have lived half my
life in Paris, not the half that made me but the half in which I made what I made.'
'Everybody knows you' – 'TWL'.
166 'Here in this' – 'TWL'.
'Dear me' – 'TWL'.
'familiar because' – 'TWL'.
'filled with sorrow' – *WIHS*, p. 57.
'a kind of history' – GS to William P. Sears, 23 December 1940. YCAL MSS 76.
'It takes courage' – *Mrs Reynolds* (Yale University Press, 1952), p. 1.
Mrs Reynolds – In early 1943 Stein passed the manuscript to the
photojournalist Thérèse Bonney, who took it to Bennett Cerf, but wartime
paper shortages meant it was not published. Its arrival in New York was,
however, reported: the *New Yorker*'s 'Talk of the Town' column claimed that
customs officers had suspected Bonney of smuggling out coded messages, 'but
she told them no, it was a novel by Gertrude Stein and they all said oh'.
'Eighty percent' – *Mrs Reynolds*, p. 74.
167 'death, bombs' – CVV to Hutchins Hapgood, 1941. YCAL MSS 1050.
'*kept safely*' – CVV to GS, 11 September 1940. *CVV*, p. 681.
'Let's write' – CVV to GS, 24 January 1941. *CVV*, p. 698.
'a guide to your ideas' – Robert Bartlett Haas to GS, June 1937. YCAL MSS
76. He confessed, too, that his fiancée – who had initially been bemused to
discover that 'the walls of my room are seething with framed Steiniana' –
was now a devoted fan too; delighted, Stein wrote a short poem celebrating
their engagement ('Prothalemium for Bobolink and His Louisa'), which they
printed on tinsel paper and hung on their Christmas tree.
168 'beauty and wit' – Thornton Wilder to GS, 1 April 1941. *TW*, p. 285.
169 At this point – See Robert O. Paxton, *Vichy France*, Renée Poznanski, *Jews in
France During World War II*, and Annette Wieviorka, *The Era of the Witness*
for accounts of what French people knew when about the deportations.
'We hear stories' – *WIHS*, p. 145.
170 'when the persecutions' – *WIHS*, p. 243.
'Most of the French' – *WIHS*, p. 244.
'You are obviously' – Stein reported Rey's words to Eric Sevareid, quoted in
Not So Wild a Dream, p. 459.
171 one local Resistance fighter – Romain Godet told Edward Burns that he and
his friends were aware of Stein and planned to protect her if the need arose.
See appendix to *TW* for a detailed reconstruction of Stein's war years.

171 Many survivors – See especially recent scholarship by Jacques Sémelin and Renée Poznanski on the experiences of Jews in Vichy France, drawing on a wide range of personal testimonies.

'Of approximately 320,000' – In Belgium, by comparison, 60 per cent of Jews survived the war; in the Netherlands, the figure was 25 per cent.

172 'rather favoured strangers' – *WIHS*, p. 114.

Neighbours loaned – In *WIHS* she singles out the generosity of Paul Genin, who gave them a monthly allowance for six months when they were unable to draw on US funds. The Parisian dealer was César de Hauke.

173 'Nowhere in the world' – *WIHS*, p. 157.

'otherwise they will' – *WIHS*, p. 50.

'where nobody can' – *WIHS*, p. 50.

'They are always' – *WIHS*, p. 50.

174 'The literary magazines' – Pierre Drieu la Rochelle, 'La Fin des Haricots', *La Nouvelle Revue Française* (December 1942).

'the terror of' – *WIHS*, p. 145.

175 'bombed to bits' – *WIHS*, p. 188.

Years later – Joan Chapman, daughter of Paul Genin, quoted in Janet Malcolm, *Two Lives*.

'a plunge' – *WIHS*, p. 122.

'the first thing' – *WIHS*, p. 55.

176 'We who lived' – *WIHS*, p. 234.

177 'a faint tone of sorrow' – Sevareid, p. 458.

178 'I can tell you' – 'Broadcast at Voiron', quoted in Sevareid, p. 462.

'Joyous Days Endless Love' – GS to CVV, 25 November 1944. *CVV*, p. 760.

'Now that it is all over' – GS to Rose Ellen Stein, undated (1945). YCAL MSS 76. There's no record in the archive of any communication between Gertrude and Leo before or during the war.

179 'We were very moved' – 'We Are Back in Paris', in Stefan Schimanski and Henry Treece (eds), *Transformation Three* (Lindsay Drummond, 1945), p. 5.

two German agencies – Edward Burns's extensive research notes on Faÿ and his trial – including Stein's correspondence with Faÿ's lawyer Georges Chresteil, and Chresteil's deposition to the court – are in Janet Malcolm's archive at Yale. Faÿ's statement titled 'On My Activities from September 1939 to 1944', at Princeton University Library, claims that he protected Stein's collection from August 1940 to August 1944. He elaborates on the measures he took to save the collection in July 1944 in his memoir, *Les Precieux*, pp. 165–6.

9: To Be Historical

181 perpetrated – Robert O. Paxton's 1972 book *Vichy France* was the first to lay bare the collaboration and repressive policies of the Vichy regime, and to argue that the regime's antisemitic measures were not solely the result of German pressure:

his argument was met with widespread backlash by French readers who were still unwilling to confront this past. See Julian Jackson, *France on Trial* for a nuanced history of France's feelings about Pétain and the Vichy years.

182 'It's a miracle' – GS, statement for Bernard Faÿ, 14 March 1946. YCAL MSS 76.
'We held rather' – Statement for Bernard Faÿ.
'certainly did certain' – GS to Francis Rose, undated. HRC.

183 'communist conspiracy' – Bernard Faÿ, memo, 18 September 1942. Quoted in Barbara Will, *Unlikely Collaboration*, p. 164. See Will for a detailed reading of Faÿ's politics and wartime activities.
Gueydan de Roussel – The scant evidence suggests their relationship was marked by jealousy: Gueydan de Roussel denounced Faÿ's friends and lovers, including their library colleague Philippe Poirson, with whom Faÿ was also romantically involved, and his close friend and loyal supporter Denise Aimé-Azam. It's likely that Faÿ's sexuality, which he kept hidden, contributed to Stein's sympathy towards him.
'I spend a week' – Bernard Faÿ to GS, September 1941. YCAL MSS 76.
'My responsibilities are growing' – Bernard Faÿ to GS, early 1942. YCAL MSS 76.

184 'Nobody else' – Malcolm Cowley, 'Gertrude Stein for the Plain Reader', *New York Times*, 11 March 1945.
'almost unbelievable' – Jean Wahl, *New Republic*, 19 March 1945.
'I always thought' – *WIHS*, p. 87.
'Pétain then did save' – *WIHS*, p. 92.
'I found the book' – GS to Bennett Cerf, undated (December 1941). Columbia.
'fascinating occupation' – GS to W. G. Rogers, quoted in *When This You See Remember Me*, p. 164.

185 'held them together' – 'Introduction to Pétain's *Paroles aux francais*'. The introduction is printed in *TW*, pp. 406ff. For a detailed analysis of the unpublished translations, see Václav Paris, 'Gertrude Stein's Translations of Speeches by Philippe Pétain', *Jacket2*, 6 May 2013.
'duty was' – Faÿ, *Les Precieux*, p. 162.

186 'During this horrible' – Faÿ, *Les Precieux*, p. 162.

187 'appeaser, collaborator, Fascist' – Bennett Cerf to GS, February 1946. Columbia.
'KEEP YOUR SHIRT ON' – GS to Bennett Cerf, February 1946. Columbia.
'Baby believed' – ABT to CVV, 4 April 1947. YCAL MSS 1050.
'as cowards and traitors' – Quoted in Jackson, *France on Trial*, p. xxxi.

188 'My point of view' – GS to W. G. Rogers, 17 April 1946. YCAL MSS 76.
'all shades of opinion' – *PF*, p. 77. When her friend W. G. Rogers enclosed a note with some corn seeds, jokingly warning her not to share his corn with any fascists – referring to her neighbours, including Henri Daniel-Rops, who were

members of the Croix de Feu – Stein retorted, 'Why not if the fascists like it, and we liked the fascists.' In the last year of the war, she told him the corn was ready for harvest, adding 'And it is allied corn you may be sure.' Her comment 'We liked the fascists,' quoted in *Everybody's Autobiography*, has often been taken out of context.

189 'singular seductiveness' – 'People', *Time*, 15 January 1934.
'worse than fascism' – GS to W. G. Rogers, December 1936. YCAL MSS 76.
'individual liberty' – See particularly *Four in America*. 'I don't envisage collectivism,' she wrote in *transition*, 21 March 1932. 'There is no such animal, it is always individualism, sometimes the rest vote and sometimes they do not, and if they do they do and if they do not they do not.' By 1946, her stance seems to have shifted towards a more capacious idea of democratic involvement: see *Yes Is for a Very Young Man*, *Brewsie and Willie* and 'TI'.
'thinking for us' – 'My Last About Money', *Saturday Evening Post*, 10 October 1936.
'father Mussolini' – *EA*, p. 113.

190 'She did not seem' – Memo from Stein's 11-page FBI file, quoted in Natalie Robins, *Alien Ink*, p. 207.
'generally always wrong' – *EA*, p. 27.
'Writers only think' – 'The Situation in American Writing', *Partisan Review*, 6/4 (Summer 1939).
'I cannot write' – *PF*, p. 38. She had already paraphrased the line in a similar way in the *Autobiography*: 'If you are way ahead with your head you naturally are old fashioned and regular in your daily life.' Flaubert's phrase comes from an 1876 letter to Gertrude Tennant.
'a long war' – *WIHS*, p. 161.

191 'the divided families' – Programme notes for *Yes Is for a Very Young Man*, Pasadena Playhouse, March 1946. YCAL MSS 76. The production was directed by Lamont Johnson, who had met Stein in Paris and discussed the play with her at length. On 25 July he sent a telegram informing her the production would transfer to New York (this fell through, but Toklas recalled Stein's delight at receiving the news, so soon before her death).
'My patriotism is fundamental' – Interview with Eleanor Wakefield, *New York World*, 18 May 1930.
'I have lived' – *WIHS*, p. 132.

192 'All the boys' – CVV to George Edward George, 9 July 1945. *Letters*, ed. Bruce Kellner, p. 217.
'Hello, Gertrude' – Quoted in Donald Sutherland, 'Alice and Gertrude and Others', p. 298.
'for some reason' – Cecil Beaton, *Self Portrait with Friends*, p. 164.
'To think' – GS to W. G. Rogers, 3 December 1945. YCAL MSS 76.

193 his grandmother's voice – Richard Wright, 'Gertrude Stein's Story Is Drenched in Hitler's Horrors', *PM*, 11 March 1945.

193 'You'd tell them' – Richard Wright to GS, 29 October 1945. YCAL MSS 76.
194 'the best American' – Ben Burns, 'Double-Talk Prose, Common-Sense Talk',
Chicago Defender, 27 October 1945.
'his meditations' – 'TI', p. 32.
'Goodness' – 'Off We All Went to See Germany', *Life*, 6 August 1945.
'persecution' – 'The New Hope in Our "Sad Young Men"', *New York Times*
magazine, 3 June 1945. In November 1945 the editor of *Negro Digest* wrote to
Stein, asking her for an essay on the subject 'If I Were a Negro'; he reminded
her that he had asked that question when they met at the rue Christine, and
'you indicated that if you were a Negro you would do exactly as you are doing
now'.
'When the war' – Virgil Thomson to GS, 5 December 1941. *VT*, p. 268.
195 'all the literature of the period' – GS to Virgil Thomson, 24 September 1945.
VT, p. 272.
'sensationally handsome' – Virgil Thomson to GS, April 1946. Quoted in
Richard Kostelanetz (ed.), *Gertrude Stein Advanced*, p. 154.
Constance Fletcher – A friend of Mabel Dodge whom Stein met at the
Villa Curonia: 'Portrait of Constance Fletcher' marks a defining shift from
the early portrait style to that of *Tender Buttons*. She was the author of
Kismet under the pseudonym George Fleming, and Henry James's *Aspern
Papers* was allegedly inspired by her love affair with Lord Lovelace, Byron's
grandson.
'in this epoch' – *The Geographical History of America*, in *LA*, p. 472.
196 'father of his country' – *FIA*, p. 162.
'Fathers are depressing' – *EA*, p. 113. See *Paris France* for a connection of
personal and political outrage at paternalism: 'Every adolescent has that dream
every century has that dream every revolutionary has that dream, to destroy
the family.'
'Patriarchal poetry' – *Patriarchal Poetry*, in *BTV*, p. 264.
equal opportunities – In a way Stein was coming full circle, to the feminism
of her Radcliffe and Baltimore days. In *What Is Remembered* Toklas notes
Stein's jealousy that she had actually met Anthony in her youth. In May
1947 Anthony's niece wrote to Toklas of her pleasure at the opera: 'Miss
Stein caught the essence of the struggle Aunt Susan led – and its pathos – the
constant betrayal by the politicians who used her when she was useful – but
would not vote for her laws.'
'I think some' – GS to Bennett Cerf, undated (September 1945). Columbia.
'Keep your pants on' – Bennett Cerf to GS, 11 December 1945. YCAL MSS
76.
'I always wanted' – *SW*, p. vii.
197 'I was not at all' – 'TI', p. 16.
'has a stake' – 'TI', p. 17.
'You see it is' – 'TI', p. 29.

197 'eternal vanity of the mind' – 'TI', p. 35.
198 'a lot of mice' – GS to Donald Gallup, 19 February 1946. YCAL MSS 76.
'I hope they' – GS to Donald Gallup, 11 July 1946. YCAL MSS 76.
'the occupation' – ABT to CVV, 31 July 1946. YCAL MSS 1050. *SOA*, p. 4.
'it was necessary' – ABT to Donald Sutherland, 13 February 1947. YCAL
MSS 76.
'adopted nephew' – Joseph Barry, *French Lovers*, p. xiii.
In the car – Barry, p. 250.
'all confidence' – ABT to CVV, 3 September 1946. YCAL MSS 1050. *SOA*,
p. 13.
'She was furious' – ABT to CVV, 31 July 1946. YCAL MSS 1050. *SOA*,
p. 4.

Reckoning

202 'Gertrude Stein, famed woman writer' – All quotes are from obituaries,
contained in box 146. YCAL MSS 76.
205 'the most widowed' – Quoted in Alice T. Friedman, 'Queer Old Things'.
'Please remember' – Sam Edwards to ABT, August 1946. YCAL MSS 76.
One folder in the archive is filled with such condolence letters.
'I wish to God' – ABT to W. G. Rogers, 28 October 1947. YCAL MSS 77.
SOA, p. 88.
206 'to pay' – Last will and testament. YCAL MSS 76.
'Identity always worries' – *EA*, p. 97.
'passionate and urgent' – Otto Weininger, *Sex and Character*, p. 136.
'most intensely alive' – 'Portraits and Repetition', in *LA*, p. 290.
'a future life feeling' – *NB*, p. 479.
207 'Nobody listens' – *FIA*, p. 127.
'the most important' – *MA*, p. 221.
208 'Is Gertrude Stein' – *WIR*, p. 150. The novelist was James Branch Cabell.
'That puts a different light on it,' he replied; Toklas responded, 'For you. Not
for me.'
209 'Dead is dead' – ABT to Elizabeth Hansen, 14 April 1949. *SOA*, p. 156.
210 'authoress' – *San Francisco Chronicle*, 24 August 1937.
'Gertrude never left' – James Lord, 'Where the Pictures Were', p. 38.
211 'She was surprisingly modern' – Richard Wright to Dorothy Norman, 31
July 1946. YCAL MSS 792. Stein had told Wright to ask Christopher Blake
for anything he needed; his only request was an icebox to keep a supply of
penicillin essential for his daughter. Blake promised to have it stored at a
nearby bar where he knew the manager, but some weeks later, Wright went
to the bar to retrieve the medicine, and was told by the barman that it was
gone. A friend from the French security service told Wright that Blake and his
boyfriend were well-known members of a criminal gang dealing on the black

market, who were constantly seeking food and medicine from the US that they could sell on for francs. But when Wright called Stein to remonstrate that she had told him to place his trust in someone so unreliable, he was shocked to find that her response was not sympathy or contrition, but anger. He was responsible for himself in Paris, she told him in clipped tones, and hung up the phone. Blake tells his side of the story in a letter to Janet Malcolm (YCAL MSS 935) and in an unpublished novel and play, held in the Addison Metcalf Collection of Steiniana at Scripps College, Claremont.

211 'permits the writing' – Waverley Lewis Root, 'Season's Most Brilliant Book is Stein's Biography', *Paris Tribune*, 9 October 1933.

10: Poisoned Wheat

213 'He stood alone' – ABT to CVV, 24 February 1947. YCAL MSS 1050.
He had called – The Metropolitan Museum of Art historical clippings and ephemera files – Pablo Picasso's Portrait of Gertrude Stein, Box 43/Folder 6.
'Good God' – ABT to W. G. Rogers, 17 February 1947. *SOA*, p. 52. This was not the end of Toklas's annoyance with the Met. Six weeks after it arrived there, the painting was transferred to the Museum of Modern Art, following an agreement between three New York institutions to redistribute their collections chronologically. Toklas spent many months battling for its return to the Met, since Stein disapproved of MoMA ('You can be a museum or you can be modern', she wrote to its director Alfred Barr, 'but you can't be both.') She was eventually triumphant: the painting returned to the Met in 1950.
'Baby is going' – ABT to CVV, 21 February 1947. YCAL MSS 1050.
'The rue de Fleurus' – CVV to ABT, 24 January 1947. YCAL MSS 76.
214 'like another parting' – ABT to William Cook, 14 October 1947. YCAL MSS 77.
'so much' – ABT to Louise Taylor, 20 February 1947. YCAL MSS 1610.
'Without Baby' – ABT to Fania Marinoff, 21 February 1948. *SOA*, p. 104.
215 all this was a blur – Toklas was not interested in Sartre, and told a friend she was sceptical of 'existentialist propaganda'.
'a veritable invasion' – ABT to Annette Rosenshine, 30 June 1948. Bancroft.
'he hasn't been' – ABT to CVV, 8 December 1946. YCAL MSS 1050.
'who is sad' – ABT to CVV, 25 October 1946. *SOA*, p. 28.
'as a deity' – James Lord, *Picasso and Dora*, p. 272.
'Welcome to' – John Malcolm Brinnin, *Sextet*, p. 239.
'gossip fest' – M. Cameron Grey, 'Miss Toklas Alone', *Virginia Quarterly Review*, 52/4 (Autumn 1976), p. 693. Otto Friedrich has a similar account of Toklas's verbatim quotation from the *Autobiography*.
216 'didn't write about' – ABT to Donald Gallup, 29 November 1946. YCAL MSS 838. *SOA*, p. 36.
'prodded Gertrude' – ABT to Donald Gallup, 2 December 1947. YCAL MSS 838. *SOA*, p. 93.

216 'deeply touched' – CVV to ABT, 4 August 1946. YCAL MSS 76.
217 'she certainly meant' – ABT to CVV, 3 September 1946. YCAL MSS
1050. *SOA*, p. 13. Only a few manuscripts were deemed to be excluded from
this injunction. 'The manuscript translation of Pétain's speeches with its
introduction is one that comes to mind at once,' wrote Gallup to Van Vechten
on 5 March 1947. 'I doubt, however, if interest in this and desirability of
publishing either here or in France would be great at the present moment. I
think Gertrude had finished the labour of translating while she had still the
lingering belief and hope that "Papa Pétain" was really a sly hero and not just a
weak old man.'
'wastepaper collection centre' – Donald Gallup, 'The Gertrude Stein
Collection', p. 26.
'Very good news' – Fortune reading, undated. YCAL MSS 76.
'almost every communication' – Gallup, 'The Gertrude Stein Collection', p. 27.
218 'poisoned wheat' – The *New York World Telegram* of 15 April 1947 ran an
article under the headline 'Yale Separates Stein Papers from Poisoned Wheat':
'Miss Stein put the lethal grain into the boxes and bureau drawers in which
she stuffed manuscripts, letters, photographs and rejection slips to keep the
rats from gnawing on the literary fare. Despite this, said the Yale authorities,
the rats chewed some of the papers and some of the poisoned wheat. There is
no one to say which caused the greater gastric upset.'
'remarkable personality' – Gallup, 'The Gertrude Stein Collection', p. 27.
'friendships and feuds' – Gallup, 'The Gertrude Stein Collection', p. 27.
'I am sure' – Donald Gallup to CVV, 23 May 1948. NYPL.
'How wonderful you are!' – CVV to ABT, 21 March 1947. YCAL MSS 76.
219 'We have found' – *New York World Telegram*, 20 March 1932.
'the Donalds' – One was Donald Evans, publisher of *Tender Buttons*, Two was
his friend Donald Angus.
'It is very nice' – 'Saving the Sentence', in *HTW*, p. 12.
'splendid drunken twenties' – CVV, 'How I Remember Joseph Hergesheimer',
Yale University Library Gazette, 22/3 (January 1948), p. 87.
220 'consummate artistry' – Quoted in CVV to GS, 23 October 1933. *CVV*, p. 281.
'a truly great story' – Nella Larsen to GS, 1 February 1928. *FF*, p. 216.
221 'an affront' – W. E. B. Du Bois, *The Crisis*, 33/2, 1926. See Emily Bernard,
Carl Van Vechten and the Harlem Renaissance for a nuanced discussion of
Van Vechten and race, the novel and the fallout, and his position within the
Harlem Renaissance.
222 'to insure' – CVV to Claude McKay, 22 October 1941. *Letters*, ed. Bruce
Kellner, p. 179.
'The tax man' – CVV to ABT, 21 March 1947. YCAL MSS 76.
'To know that' – ABT to Donald Gallup, 12 October 1948. YCAL MSS 838.
'You realise surely' – ABT to Donald Gallup, 11 March 1947. YCAL MSS
838. *SOA*, p. 54.

223 'sorrow and shame' – Quoted in Donald Gallup, *What Mad Pursuits!*, p. 144.
'more courteous than sincere' – Gallup, *What Mad Pursuits!*, p. 117.
'make the letter' – Ernest Hemingway to Donald Gallup, 22 September 1952.
Selected Letters 1917–1961, p. 781. Gallup's selection of letters written to Stein
was published in 1953 as *The Flowers of Friendship*.
'she completely forgot' – *AABT*, p. 93.

224 'the interesting good fortune' – Louis Bromfield, 'Gertrude Stein:
Experimenter with Words', *New York Herald Tribune*, 3 September 1933.
'I have finished' – Louis Bromfield to GS, summer 1932. YCAL MSS 76.
'It is a subject' – ABT to Donald Gallup, 19 April 1947. YCAL MSS 838.
SOA, p. 63.

225 'as much as I can' – ABT to CVV, 19 April 1947. YCAL MSS 1050.

226 'The trouble' – ABT to CVV, 9 May 1947. YCAL MSS 1050.
'heart breaking' – ABT to CVV, 28 April 1947. YCAL MSS 1050.

227 'It's not easy' – *Q.E.D.*, p. 85.
'pulses were differently timed' – *Q.E.D.*, p. 104.
'Haven't you ever' – *Q.E.D.*, p. 66.
'Don't you ever' – *TL*, p. 120.

228 'college bred' – *Q.E.D.*, p. 54.
'a kiss' – *Q.E.D.*, p. 102.
'In the telling' – Claude McKay, *A Long Way From Home* (Lee Furman, 1937),
p. 248.
'Gertrude was' – Leo Stein to Mabel Weeks, 6 February 1934. Quoted in *JS*,
p. 137. See Michael North, *The Dialect of Modernism*, Yeonsik Jung, 'Why
Is Melanctha Black?', and essays in Marianne DeKoven (ed.), *Three Lives
and Q.E.D.*, for discussion of *Melanctha*, *Q.E.D.* and race; and Feinstein,
Gertrude Stein and the Making of Jewish Modernism (ch. 2) for an examination
of Adele's Jewish roots, and the way Stein associates her Jewish characters in
Q.E.D. with elements of blackness.

229 'You must realise' – CVV to ABT, 16 May 1947. YCAL MSS 76.
'The characters were' – ABT to CVV, 21 May 1947. YCAL MSS 1050.
'Between us' – CVV to Donald Gallup, June 1947. NYPL.

230 'puzzled at finding' – Donald Gallup to ABT, 31 August 1947. YCAL MSS 838.
'Mrs Knoblauch's letters' – ABT to Donald Gallup, 5 September 1947. YCAL
MSS 838.
'make a scandal' – ABT to CVV, 21 May 1947. YCAL MSS 1050.

231 'high collars and monocles' – Sylvia Beach, *Shakespeare and Company*, p. 115.

232 'She is very lovely' – 'Bundles for Them', *Little Review*, 9 (Spring 1923).
'Gertrude showed no' – Mabel Weeks, interview with Leon Katz, 23 April
1949. YCAL MSS 1409.
'I was overcome' – 'Sentences and Paragraphs', in *HTW*, p. 17.
'This must not' – 'Bonne Annee', in *G&P*, p. 302.
'if it has' – *EA*, p. xxi.

233 'Little Alice B.' – *A Sonatina Followed by Another*, in *BTV*, p. 12.
'To-day there is' – *BTV*, p. 12.
'Do you feel satisfied' – *BTV*, p. 29.
'A little new book' – Notebook for *A Novel of Thank You*. YCAL MSS 76.
The love notes are now filed, at the Beinecke, under the intriguing title
'autrespondence', as if Stein and Toklas are a single entity.
'What are you' – 'All Sunday', in *A&B*, pp. 100, 102.
234 'By loving her' – *BP*, p. 152.
'Precious baby' – *BP*, p. 15.
'Sweet pinky' – *BP*, p. 161.
'complete devotion' – *BP*, p. 10.
'I love her' – *BP*, p. 123.
'My darling wifey' – *BP*, p. 24.
235 'little hubby' – *BP*, p. 56.
'She wants' – VV to Donald Gallup, 21 May 1947. YCAL MSS 838.
'they were *not*' – ABT to CVV, 21 May 1947. YCAL MSS 1050.
236 'The DD' – ABT to Donald Gallup, 25 May 1947. YCAL MSS 838. The
initials quickly became a source of intrigue and speculation: Virgil Thomson,
writing the preface to *Bee Time Vine*, noted the subtitle of *A Sonatina Followed
by Another*: 'dedicated by request to D.D.' He asked Toklas, who told him that
'D.D.' didn't exist and was 'one of Gertrude's fantasies'. Gallup was alarmed when
Thomson subsequently addressed a letter to 'D.D.', meaning 'Dear Donald' –
'you can imagine,' he wrote to Van Vechten, 'that it gave me quite a turn.'
237 'before the biography' – CVV to Donald Gallup, 29 May 1947. NYPL.
238 'these notes contain' – Donald Gallup to CVV, 31 May 1947. NYPL.
'Notes are' – *BP*, p. 163.
'The notes make clear' – Donald Gallup to ABT, 31 May 1947. YCAL MSS 838.
'Surely there will be' – CVV to ABT, 1 June 1947. YCAL MSS 76.
'I'm not being' – ABT to CVV, 21 May 1947. YCAL MSS 1050.
239 'These letters' – CVV to ABT, 1 June 1947. YCAL MSS 76.
'Eureka and blessed' – CVV to Donald Gallup, 11 June 1947. NYPL.
'Three cheers' – Donald Gallup to CVV, 12 June 1947. NYPL.

11: 'Diagram Book'

241 'Everything just went blank' – ABT to CVV, 28 April 1947. YCAL MSS
1050. The photograph, by William Chapman, is in the Yale collection.
Henry James – In her notes for *Q.E.D.* Stein copied out several passages of
James's 1902 novel *The Wings of the Dove*, and Adele compares Helen to his
character Kate Croy.
242 'frustrate' – quoted in Leon Edel, *Henry James*, p. 556.
243 John Malcolm Brinnin – Toklas had admired a poem about Stein he had written
in *Harper's* ('Pass gently, pigeons on the grass') and sent him a wood carving of

an octopus astride a horse belonging to Stein as thanks. Brinnin was director of the YMCA poetry centre in New York – now known as the 92nd Street Y – and brought Dylan Thomas to the US in 1955. Brinnin described his meetings with Toklas in his essay 'Mushroom Pie in the Rue Christine' in *Sextet*.

244 'I hope he isn't' – Donald Gallup to CVV, 9 February 1947. NYPL. Sawyer's admiration for Stein is detailed at length in his eccentric unpublished memoir, 'My Life Without Gertrude Stein', held at the McFarlin Library, University of Tulsa. He is mentioned briefly in James Atlas's biography of Delmore Schwartz; he compiled a bibliography of Stein's work and was working on an 'all-inclusive critical work', which never materialised. He vanished in the 1950s and was rumoured to have committed suicide, but wrote to Gallup again in 1981, as if no time had passed, asking him to update him with a list of Stein-related publications since 1958.

'repeated references' – ABT to Julian Sawyer, 12 June 1947. *SOA*, p. 69.

'ignorant – unintelligent' – ABT to Donald Sutherland, 8 October 1947. YCAL MSS 77.

Fernanda Pivano – Former partner of Cesare Pavese, who had translated *The Autobiography of Alice B. Toklas* into Italian. She was an important translator of Hemingway and the Beat poets. Pivano and her husband Ettore Sottsass visited Toklas several times: Pivano describes their meetings in *America Rossa e Nera* (1964).

'dry as a bone' – ABT to CVV, 31 January 1947. YCAL MSS 1050.

245 'intellectual and secular' – Donald Sutherland, *Gertrude Stein*, p. 14.

'Knowing that' – ABT to Donald Sutherland, 18 March 1948. YCAL MSS 77.

'He would write' – CVV to ABT, 29 December 1946. YCAL MSS 76.

'Miss Stein was' – Rogers, *When This You See Remember Me*, p. 169.

246 'There were so many' – W. G. Rogers to ABT, 6 July 1948. YCAL MSS 76.

'all the correspondence' – Donald Gallup to CVV, 3 October 1947. NYPL.

'nothing inflammable' – Donald Gallup to CVV, 3 October 1947. NYPL.

'unimportant biographers' – CVV to Donald Gallup, undated (October 1947). NYPL.

'first-rate' – application for a Ford Foundation grant. Ford Foundation Collection, Fund for the Advancement of Education, FFP 1952–3, box 8 folder on Leon Katz.

'She will stand' – application for a Ford Foundation grant. Ford Foundation Collection.

247 'peculiar difficulties' – Leon Katz to CVV, 25 October 1947. YCAL MSS 1050.

'absolutely nothing' – CVV to Leon Katz, 29 October 1947. YCAL MSS 1050.

'the latest' – CVV to ABT, 29 October 1947. YCAL MSS 76.

248 'as much a diary' – 'Why Publish?' Among the submissions Katz made to publishers, proposing a biographical-critical study of Stein based on the notebooks. YCAL MSS 1409.

248 'a liar' – *NB*, pp. 336–7. See Barbara Will, *Gertrude Stein, Modernism, and the Problem of 'Genius'* for an analysis of Stein's classification of Toklas as a 'prostitute type' (a Weininger term) – an ideal match for the masculine 'genius'.
249 'I am convinced' – CVV to Donald Gallup, October 1948. YCAL MSS 1050.
250 'under the spell' – *AABT*, p. 64.
    'a period of' – Katz introduction to *Q.E.D.*, p. 32.
251 'been glad' – All quotes from Mabel Weeks, interview with Leon Katz, 23 April 1949. YCAL MSS 1409.
    'Make Jane Sandys' – *NB*, p. 124. In another note, she describes the two of them lying down in a field at night: 'Platonic because neither care to do more.'
252 'outrageously unfeminine' – All quotes from Emma Lootz Erving, interview with Leon Katz, May 1949. YCAL MSS 1409.
253 'emotional sexual aristocrat' – *NB*, p. 360.
    'monumental aesthetic awakening' – Book proposal. YCAL MSS 1409.
254 'Our initiative' – *NB*, p. 273.
    'the great master' – *NB*, p. 381.
    'his laziness' – *NB*, p. 532.
    'Pablo is never' – *NB*, p. 533.
255 'By the way' – Marion Walker to GS, 11 June 1909. *FF*, p. 45.
    'minor writing talent' – Leon Katz, Guggenheim Fellowship proposal, 1970. YCAL MSS 1409.
256 'lack of imagination' – *NB*, p. 191.
    'blind mind' – *NB*, p. 237.
    'every conceivable kind' – *NB*, p. 344.
    'Have to do miracle' – *NB*, p. 237.
    'Work out the drama' – *NB*, p. 520.
    'To know surely' – *NB*, p. 375.
258 'The friends' – ABT to CVV, 12 September 1946. YCAL MSS 1050.
259 'huge woman' – Alfred Stieglitz, 'Six Happenings', *Twice a Year* (Fall/Winter 1946–7).

12: A Sacred Trust

261 'the blackest villainy' – ABT to CVV, 3 September 1946. YCAL MSS 1050. *SOA*, p. 14.
    'Bennett' – CVV to ABT, 18 January 1948. YCAL MSS 76. The jacket of *The Geographical History of America* (1936) carried a statement from Cerf: 'I do not know what Miss Stein is talking about. I do not even understand the title. I admire Miss Stein tremendously, and I like to publish her books, although most of the time I do not know what she is driving at. That, Miss Stein tells me, is because I am dumb.'
262 'cute looking and alert' – CVV to ABT, 31 July 1947. YCAL MSS 76.
    Claude Fredericks went on to teach classics at Bennington College, where his

pupils included the novelist Donna Tartt. His diary, spanning his life from the age of eight to his death at eighty-nine in 2013, was the subject of a *New Yorker* essay in 2021, titled 'The Most Ambitious Diary in History'.

262 'C van V sent me' – ABT to Claude Fredericks, 27 December 1947. Getty.

263 'guided to the public' – CVV to ABT, 4 January 1948. YCAL MSS 76.
'just slipping' – ABT to CVV, January 1948. YCAL MSS 1050.
'really stupendous' – CVV to Claude Fredericks and Milton Saul, 23 January 1948. Getty.
'complete hysteria' – Milton Saul to CVV, 26 January 1948. YCAL MSS 1050.
'my new belt' – CVV to Milton Saul and Claude Fredericks, 30 December 1947. Getty.
'utter secret' – CVV to Claude Fredericks and Milton Saul, 5 February 1949. Getty.
'should be considered' – Claude Fredericks to ABT, 10 May 1949. YCAL MSS 76.

264 'special publisher' – CVV to Claude Fredericks, January 1950. Getty.

265 'make it seem' – Claude Fredericks to CVV, 12 April 1948. Getty.
Things as They Are – The phrase is borrowed from Matthew Arnold's *Culture and Anarchy*. Amy Feinstein argues that Stein's thought was deeply influenced by Arnold's view of religion, particularly his opposition of the forces of Hebraism and Hellenism.
'must never see' – ABT to CVV, 15 March 1948. YCAL MSS 1050.
'told of her friendship' – *Collection of the Société Anonyme: Museum of Modern Art 1920* (Yale University Art Gallery, 1950), p. 21.
'I burn to see' – CVV to Donald Gallup, 14 May 1950. NYPL.
'No one seems' – Milton Saul to ABT, 1 June 1950. Getty.

266 'You will understand' – ABT to Donald Gallup, 1 July 1950. YCAL MSS 838.
'the most famous animal' – James Merrill to Helen Ingram Plummer, 5 May 1951. Merrill later regularly used a Ouija board, summoning Toklas to preside as medium, ushering visitors in and out as she used to do at the rue de Fleurus. Stein and Toklas appear in his poem *The Book of Ephraim*.
'fabulously opinionated' – Claude Fredericks to James Merrill, 2 June 1950. Collection of Marc Harrington.

267 'I can't say' – Leo Stein to Howard Gans, 8 July 1946. *JS*, p. 276.
'ghastly twaddle' – Leo Stein to Fred Stein, September 1945. YCAL MSS 78.
Neither had collected – Among the artists Gertrude did collect independently were Juan Gris, Francis Picabia and Francis Rose.

268 'Leo, Known as Gertrude's Brother' – Lloyd Morris, *New York Herald Tribune*, 20 July 1947.
'Gertrude Stein's Feud' – Quoted in Leo Stein to Fred Stein, 2 July 1947. *JS*, p. 291. In May 1935 Leo had written to the *New Yorker* to correct an 'outrageous' article which quoted Leo, overheard in a Florence café, saying of Gertrude, 'I hate her.' Leo's letter, published under the heading 'We Stand Corrected', stated

that 'the phrase attributed to me falsely and foully poisons the atmosphere'.

268 'A year and two days' – ABT to W. G. Rogers, 10 August 1947. YCAL MSS 77.
'The differences' – *JS*, p. 298.
'such a sweet' – GS to Louis and Mary Bromfield, undated. Quoted in Brenda Wineapple, *Sister Brother*, p. 362.
'When I wrote' – *LA Times Sunday Magazine*, 14 April 1935.

269 'The only thing' – *EA*, p. 61.
'many things' – Nina Stein to Hiram Haydn, undated (early 1948). YCAL MSS 78.
'with one goal' – *JS*, p. vi.

270 'the antagonism' – *JS*, p. 77.
'the family romance' – *JS*, p. 78.
'an utter failure' – *JS*, p. 87.
'Nothing could have' – *NB*, p. 151. The phrase is quoted from Toklas's memory. Gertrude claimed to remember – See *EA*, p. 59: 'About an unhappy childhood well I never had an unhappy anything.'

271 'preferred nephews' – Gertrude Stein Raffel, 'There Once Was a Family Called Stein', in Robert Bartlett Haas (ed.), *A Primer for the Gradual Understanding of Gertrude Stein*, p. 127.
'disagreeable condition' – *NB*, p. 132.
'angry the way' – *NB*, p. 132.
'It was not easy' – *MA*, p. 45.
'keep him warm' – *NB*, p. 491.

272 'Jewish parents' – Quoted in Linda Wagner-Martin, *Favored Strangers*, p. 62.
'a great complex' – CVV to ABT, 30 June 1950. YCAL MSS 76.
'mount the defence' – ABT to Donald Gallup, 29 September 1950. YCAL MSS 838.

273 'I only have' – ABT to CVV, 4 July 1950. YCAL MSS 1050.
'to purge myself' – ABT to Donald Sutherland, 4 August 1950. YCAL MSS 77.
'cold aggression' – ABT to Donald Gallup, 23 March 1948. YCAL MSS 838.
Allan Stein – Matthew Stadler's 1999 novel *Allan Stein* portrays a curator in search of Allan's lost drawings. Allan was more successful than Gertrude in prevailing upon the generosity of Etta Cone: her last purchase, in 1949, was a Picasso portrait of Allan as a child, which Allan sold her to cover his debts.

274 'Forced to listen' – ABT to CVV, 14 February 1949. YCAL MSS 1050.
'I think Baby' – CVV to Donald Gallup, 30 March 1948. NYPL.
'publishing Stein' – Donald Gallup, *Pigeons on the Granite*, p. 149.

275 'Yale Press accepts' – CVV to ABT, 2 October 1950. YCAL MSS 76.
'what this would' – ABT to CVV, 9 October 1950. YCAL MSS 1050.
'overpowering effect' – ABT to Milton Saul, 15 October 1950. Getty.
'a dream realised' – ABT to William Cook, 22 September 1951. YCAL MSS 77.
'It is so good' – ABT to William Cook, 15 October 1950. YCAL MSS 77.
'EVERYTHING' – CVV to Donald Gallup, undated (March 1947). NYPL.
'give the undertaking' – Donald Gallup to CVV, 11 March 1947. NYPL.

275 'start the series' – CVV to ABT, 5 November 1950. YCAL MSS 76.
276 'In every letter' – CVV to ABT, 24 September 1946. YCAL MSS 76.
'It seems so strange' – ABT to Donald Gallup, 15 November 1946. YCAL MSS 838.
'I find myself' – ABT to CVV, Easter Monday 1947. YCAL MSS 1050.
'I can't tell' – ABT to CVV, 28 September 1946. YCAL MSS 1050.
277 'The atmosphere' – ABT to CVV, 27 September 1950. YCAL MSS 1050. *SOA*, p. 205.
'Baby's horror' – ABT to CVV, 9 November 1950. YCAL MSS 1050.
'torment beyond bearing' – ABT to Donald Gallup, 31 December 1950. YCAL MSS 838.
'great trouble' – ABT to Thornton Wilder, 20 November 1950. YCAL MSS 76. *SOA*, p. 215.
278 'a natural antipathy' – ABT to Donald Gallup, 21 December 1946. YCAL MSS 838. *SOA*, p. 40.
'read it through' – GS to Thornton Wilder, 23 November 1935. *TW*, p. 67.
'Don't you go' – CVV to GS, 1 December 1934. CVV, p. 352.
'invariably told Alice' – CVV to Donald Gallup, 20 December 1950. NYPL.
279 'recipe for a fruitcake' – Janet Flanner, 'Memory Is All: Alice B. Toklas', in *Janet Flanner's World*, p. 335.
'would learn nothing' – ABT to Donald Sutherland, 10 March 1951. YCAL MSS 77.
'one of the fates' – Janet Flanner to CVV, 6 February 1951. YCAL MSS 1050.
'It was a pleasure' – Janet Flanner to CVV, 15 April 1951. YCAL MSS 1050.
280 'weighed very heavily' – ABT to Elizabeth Fuller Chapman, 25 October 1946. *SOA*, pp. 25–6.
'an outrageous falsehood' – Bernard Faÿ, 'On My Activities from September 1939 to August 1944'. Princeton University Library Special Collections, 0683.698.34.
'trying every means' – ABT to Elizabeth Fuller Chapman, 19 December 1946. YCAL MSS 442.
'a sacred trust' – ABT to Elizabeth Fuller Chapman, 25 October 1946. *SOA*, p. 26.
281 The arrangements – Author's correspondence with Edward Burns, who met Faÿ, Aimé-Azam and others in Toklas's circle. Faÿ confirmed to Burns that Toklas had put up funds for his escape. Aimé-Azam lived on the Right Bank; she had a wonderful art collection, including some works by Géricault, about whom she wrote a book. She converted to Catholicism, probably influenced by Faÿ. She was denounced by Gueydan de Roussel and investigated by the Gestapo in December 1942, who searched her apartment hoping to find documents that would compromise Faÿ. Despite this, she always remained loyal to Faÿ.
282 'intrigues against the Republic' – Donald Sutherland, 'The Conversion of Alice B. Toklas', p. 137.
'The great puzzle' – Sutherland, 'Conversion', p. 138.
'the portraits' – ABT to Donald Gallup, 19 September 1951. YCAL MSS 838.

283 'I have hinted' – CVV to Donald Gallup, 29 September 1951. NYPL.
'Orders arrived' – Milton Saul to Claude Fredericks, 10 November 1951. Getty.

284 'Metro-Goldwyn' – CVV to Donald Gallup, 29 September 1951. NYPL.
'not displeased' – Milton Saul to Claude Fredericks, 10 November 1951. Getty.
'come closer' – Leonard Bernstein, 'Music and Miss Stein', *New York Times*, 22 May 1949. The libretto was published by Liveright in a collection called *Last Operas and Plays*.
'sugary realism' – Judith Malina, *Diaries, 1947–1957*, 19 July 1948. The theatre's first performance, held in Beck and Malina's living room in the summer of 1951, was a version of Stein's *Ladies' Voices*. Van Vechten had refused their suggestion that John Cage should compose the music for *Dr Faustus* on the grounds that 'he'd probably score it all for drums'. They reprised *Ladies' Voices* at the Cherry Lane in March 1952.

285 'make life on the stage' – Julian Beck, 'An Essay on the Living Theatre', p. 11.
'How can you' – Beck, 'An Essay on the Living Theatre', p. 8.
'Gertrude Stein has clues' – Malina, 29 May 1951.

286 'The over-simple words' – Malina, 31 August 1951.
'pin-ball machine' – *New York Times*, 3 December 1951.
'one of the most' – Interview with John Ashbery, *Performing Arts Journal*, 3/3 (Winter 1979).
'Gielgud in *Hamlet*' – CVV to ABT, 3 December 1951. YCAL MSS 76.
'talks of Gertrude' – Malina, 16 August 1951.
'She freed the theatre' – Malina quoted in Steven Watson, *Prepare for Saints*, p. 304.

288 'WHO do you think' – Donald Gallup to CVV, 27 October 1952. NYPL.
'Katz is the young man' – Donald Gallup to ABT, 30 October 1952. YCAL MSS 838.

289 'You may take it' – ABT to Leon Katz, 8 November 1952. YCAL MSS 1409.
'Nothing but really' – ABT to Donald Sutherland, 8 January 1953. YCAL MSS 77.

13: *Chronique Scandaleuse*

291 'little gnome' – Leon Katz, 'A Year with Alice B. Toklas', p. 2.
'We ate Madame Cézanne' – ABT to CVV, 25 December 1946. YCAL MSS 1050. *SOA*, p. 41.
'made her indifference' – Katz, 'A Year', p. 3.
'visibly moved' – ABT to CVV, 27 September 1950. YCAL MSS 1050. *SOA*, p. 204.
'nil, absolutely nil', Katz, 'A Year', p. 3.
'I made Gertrude' – Donald Sutherland, 'Alice and Gertrude and Others', p. 297.
'What would legal' – ABT to CVV, 21 September 1950. YCAL MSS 1050.
'The Old Man' – Katz, 'A Year', p. 4.

292 'more voluminous' – ABT to William Whitehead, 7 December 1952. YCAL MSS 77.

292 '80 per cent' – ABT to Donald Gallup, 24 November 1952. YCAL MSS 838.
'of a frankness' – ABT to Donald Sutherland, 8 January 1953. YCAL MSS
77. *SOA*, p. 273.

293 'she had forgotten' – ABT to Donald Sutherland, 8 January 1953. YCAL
MSS 77. *SOA*, p. 273.
'The notes are wonderful' – ABT to Donald Gallup, 11 February 1953. YCAL
MSS 838.
'dark dreary dismal' – ABT to Mark Lutz, 17 December 1952. YCAL MSS 77.
'line by line' – ABT to Donald Sutherland, 8 January 1953. YCAL MSS 77.
'If I knew' – Katz, 'A Year', p. 5.
'sleuth-like gift' – ABT to Donald Sutherland, 8 January 1953. YCAL MSS
77. *SOA*, p. 272.
'treats the least slip' – ABT to Donald Sutherland, 8 July 1953. YCAL MSS
77.
'extremely intelligent' – ABT to William Whitehead, 7 December 1952.
YCAL MSS 77.
'one answered' – ABT to Donald Sutherland, 8 January 1953. YCAL MSS
77. *SOA*, p. 273.
'my answers' – ABT to CVV, 24 November 1952. YCAL MSS 1050. *SOA*,
p. 268.
'My contribution' – ABT to William Whitehead, 7 December 1952. YCAL
MSS 77.

294 'Oh, I wish' – Katz, 'A Year', p. 6.
'let myself go' – ABT to Donald Gallup, 24 November 1952. YCAL MSS
838.
'eyes like a frightened deer's' – *NB*, p. 513.

295 'From the way' – *NB*, p. 512.
'was very anxious' – *NB*, p. 341.
'By the time' – *NB*, p. 379.
'she had such notions' – *NB*, p. 341.

296 'my relation with Nellie' – *NB*, p. 339.
'Gertrude never actually' – *NB*, p. 341. There's a hint at this in *What Is
Remembered*: on the ship over, Toklas gets talking to a commodore, who sends
her a 'compromising' letter soon after her arrival in Paris. After her first walk
with Stein, Toklas tears up the letter, implicitly renouncing all other suitors –
and men.
'most crucial one' – *NB*, p. 339.
'Can you decline history' – 'Didn't Nelly and Lilly Love You', in *AFAM*,
pp. 227, 230.

297 'I'll send it to May' – *NB*, p. 259. After meeting Nellie Jacot, interestingly,
Stein told Toklas that Nellie reminded her of May – 'she was sensationally
beautiful and alluring,' according to Toklas, 'looked like a Borgia'.
'If you've made' – Ullman, in an unpublished memoir, describes her friendship

with the Steins; she remembered Stein giving her a 'ruthless trampling' until Toklas set down her knitting and told Stein, 'This happens too often. You can't always be right.'

297 'In a passion' – Leon Katz, 'The First Making of *The Making of Americans*', p. 16.

'hypersensitive to signs' – *NB*, p. 369.

298 'I didn't' – Katz, 'A Year', p. 16.

'Katz, by deduction' – ABT to Donald Gallup, 22 January 1953. YCAL MSS 838.

299 'I am not surprised' – Donald Gallup to CVV, 26 January 1953. NYPL.

'Katz HAS opened' – CVV to Donald Gallup, 29 January 1953. NYPL.

'all of Gertrude's' – *NB*, p. 257.

'very high-minded' – *NB*, p. 121.

'with Henry James' – *NB*, p. 339.

'With my friends' – *NB*, p. 342.

300 'Oh, rats' – *NB*, p. 271. In the manuscript of 'Ada', the protagonist is named Alice. One line reads: 'And the daughter coming to be an old maid mermaid then' – 'old maid mermaid' is crossed out, and changed to 'that one'. I suspect that, by the time Toklas moved in, this original designation was a joke between them.

'mad enthusiasm' – *NB*, p. 335.

'listening to the rhythm' – *NB*, pp. 294–5.

301 'a person' – Leo Stein to Mabel Weeks, 1 June 1920. YCAL MSS 78.

'deep-thinking' – *NB*, p. 338.

'always saw the essence' – *NB*, p. 378.

'a man' – *NB*, p. 526.

302 'paucity of internal' – *NB*, p. 553.

'Real thinking' – *NB*, p. 557.

'complete disillusionment' – *MA*, p. 484.

'destroyed him for me' – *EA*, p. 60.

'My being an artist' – *NB*, p. 159.

'I write for myself' – *MA*, p. 289.

303 'and while you' – *MA*, p. 485.

'beginning to lose' – *NB*, p. 483. Elsewhere, Stein writes that her own group 'have too intimate an acquaintance with fear to wish it; they love freedom, they wish to be conquered only by themselves for that is to conquer fear.'

'This is a trial' – *NB*, p. 642.

'a question mark' – Notebook, *c*.1912. YCAL MSS 76.

'I am filled' – *MA*, p. 604.

304 'talking to Leo' – *NB*, p. 498. Some years later, Gertrude and Alice were stuck in traffic when they saw Leo crossing the road; the incident inspired Stein's 1931 piece 'She Bowed to Her Brother'. Samuel Steward told Brenda Wineapple Toklas had seen that bow, and told him Gertrude's expression was

'compounded of something sardonic yet affectionate, and containing some regret . . . and a little love'. Wineapple, *Sister Brother*, p. 1.

304 'Toward the last half ' – *NB*, p. 385.
'I myself was' – 'The Gradual Making of *The Making of Americans*', in *LA*, p. 280.
'passion to be free' – *MA*, p. 47.

305 'It is sad – *MA*, p. 47.
'looking and comparing' – *MA*, p. 289.

306 'Alice had won' – Leon Katz, book proposal. YCAL MSS 1409.
'His going' – ABT to CVV, 24 November 1952. *SOA*, p. 268.
'very kind' – ABT to Donald Gallup, 5 December 1952. YCAL MSS 838.
'We never had' – ABT, interview with Roland Duncan. Duncan's interview can be read online, though the text is unreliable.

307 'crooked' – *NB*, pp. 403, 439.
'They talked' – *NB*, p. 392.
'ungracefully ageing' – Katz, 'A Year', p. 11. Rose was enduringly loyal to Stein and Toklas. But others found him erratic, even unstable. His autobiography, *Saying Life*, which he dedicated to Stein, is replete with unverifiable stories, many patently invented. See also Samuel Steward's novel *Parisian Lives*, a veiled portrait of Rose drawing on their own friendship and stories told to Steward by Stein and Toklas.

308 'left-over Surrealists' – Katz, 'A Year', p. 20.
'no there there' – *EA*, p. 251. The phrase has become ubiquitous: in January 2023 President Joe Biden used it in reference to some classified documents found at his home.
'Gertrude hated' – *NB*, p. 177.

309 'Sometimes I look' – Katz, 'A Year', p. 7.
'written with considerable' – *NB*, p. 335.
'I was afraid' – Katz, 'A Year', p. 10.
'St Thérèse type' – *NB*, pp. 436–7. Katz recounts the conversation in his commentary.

310 'I love her' – *NB*, p. 298.

311 'During all the interviews' – Katz, 'A Year', p. 22.

14: Parades and Fireworks

313 'All portraits of me' – James Lord, *Picasso and Dora*, p. 123. When Lord protested that she was recognised internationally through those portraits, she retorted, 'Does Madame Cézanne care? Does Saskia Rembrandt care? Remember that I, too, am an artist.' The portrait of Toklas now hangs in the Beinecke Library.

314 'where there is' – Katz, 'A Year with Alice B. Toklas', p. 21.
'Through the notes' – ABT to Donald Gallup, 10 December 1953. YCAL MSS 838.

314 'has behaved shockingly' – ABT to Donald Gallup, 20 September 1954. YCAL MSS 838.

'Though you were' – ABT to Leon Katz, 25 August 1954. YCAL MSS 1409.

315 'a form of publicity' – Donald Sutherland, 'Alice and Gertrude and Others', p. 288. He remembers handing Toklas a bunch of flowers for Stein, and Toklas showing them to Stein saying 'Look what Donald has brought me' – which he took as a subtle rebuke.

'essentially militant' – Sutherland, 'Alice', p. 295.

'The landscape' – ABT to Donald Gallup, 11 July 1952.

316 'no real hope' – Donald Sutherland to CVV, 8 August 1951. YCAL MSS 1050.

'The weenie eggbeater' – ABT to Samuel Steward, 24 October 1952. Bancroft. *SOA*, p. 266.

'What did we have' – 'Advertisements', in *G&P*, p. 343.

317 two footstools – In her review of the exhibition (*New Yorker*, 26 June 1946), Janet Flanner described Toklas's work as showing 'new possibilities in tapestry'.

'She began' – Joseph Barry to CVV, 2 June 1950. YCAL MSS 1050.

'unprofessional women cooks' – ABT to William Whitehead, 1 March 1952. YCAL MSS 77.

'solely to earn' – ABT to William Cook, 13 March 1953. YCAL MSS 77. She did some other writing in these years, for money: a translation of *The Blue Dog*, a book of folk tales by a Belgian teenager named Anne Bogart; an article on furniture for *House Beautiful*, an article on French fashion for the *Atlantic Monthly*, a review of F. Scott Fitzgerald's stories for the *New York Times* (she called him 'the most gifted of his generation').

318 'PLEASE ORGANISE' – CVV to ABT, 27 May 1947. YCAL MSS 76.

'undoubtedly the only' – ABT to Louise Taylor, 14 March 1953. YCAL MSS 77. *SOA*, p. 275.

319 'He looked at me' – ABT to CVV, 1 November 1946. YCAL MSS 1050. *SOA*, p. 30.

320 'This is' – *ABTCB*, p. 273.

'Thornton said' – ABT to Donald Gallup, October 1954. YCAL MSS 838. *SOA*, p. 310. The 1968 Peter Sellars film *I Love You, Alice B. Toklas* features this recipe – now ubiquitously known not as Brion Gysin's fudge but Alice B. Toklas's brownies. Toklas probably met Gysin while he was staying with William Burroughs at the Beat Hotel, 9 rue Gît-le-Cœur.

'She is doing' – CVV to Donald Gallup, 29 October 1954. NYPL.

321 'I am not allowed' – Elizabeth Sprigge, 'Journal in Search of Gertrude Stein, 1954–1955'. YCAL MSS 77.

'Her life was' – Sprigge, 'Journal'.

322 'You're dealing with' – Sprigge, 'Journal'.

'heart of hearts' – ABT to Annette Rosenshine, 9 September 1955. Bancroft.

322 'worse than I feared' – ABT to Virginia Knapik, 23 March 1956. YCAL MSS 77. Knapik and her husband Harold became close friends of Toklas in these years; Toklas did not know that both were CIA agents.

323 'vulgarities and insinuations' – ABT to Isabel Wilder, 8 April 1956. YCAL MSS 77.
'parades and fireworks' – CVV to Bruce Kellner, 31 October 1955. NYPL.
'Does she think' – ABT to CVV, 16 March 1956. YCAL MSS 1050. *SOA*, p. 336.
'joy and a pain' – ABT to Dilkusha Rohan, 13 June 1955. HRC.

324 'like Moses' – My source for Dora Maar's role in Toklas's conversion is an email from Edward Burns, who was told about it by Maar herself, and confirmed by Harold and Virginia Knapik. Burns also told me the story of Edward Taylor's discomfort: Taylor told him this himself, and the Knapiks again confirmed.
'It is wonderful' – ABT to Virginia Knapik, 9 January 1958. *SOA*, p. 356.
'Every bit of blue' – *G.M.P.* in *G.M.P.*, p. 275. The brooch is in the collection of the Fitzwilliam Museum.

325 'remember the beatific' – Donald Sutherland, 'The Conversion of Alice B. Toklas', p. 135.
'about the church' – ABT to CVV, 25 December 1957. YCAL MSS 1050. *SOA*, p. 355.
'You were her dearest' – ABT to Bernard Faÿ, June 1960. *SOA*, p. 383.

326 'The past' – ABT to Samuel Steward, 7 August 1958. YCAL MSS 76.
'Gertrude Stein' – ABT to Russell Porter, 28 December 1961. *SOA*, p. 409.
'coming to my rescue' – ABT to Dilkusha de Rohan, 1 February 1954. HRC.
'I wish to God' – Joseph Barry to CVV, 23 March 1950. YCAL MSS 1050.

15: What Is the Question?

329 'Were they not' – ABT to CVV, 24 April 1953. YCAL MSS 1050. *SOA*, p. 277. She reported variant versions of the last words to Van Vechten on 2 August 1947 and 24 April 1953, and uses another alternative in *What Is Remembered*.
'very thin broth' – Max White to ABT, 6 June 1949. YCAL MSS 76.

330 'My only luxuries' – ABT to Max White, 25 February 1958. Princeton.
'the book that' – ABT to Max White, 18 April 1958. Princeton.
'en souvenir' – At time of writing, the inscribed copy is listed and pictured on charlesagvent.com.
'the work with' – ABT to John Schaffner, 29 May 1958. *SOA*, p. 360.
'agreed that the reminiscences' – ABT to CVV, 21 May 1958. YCAL MSS 1050. *SOA*, p. 358.
'very strange news' – ABT to John Schaffner, 17 June 1958. *SOA*, p. 361.
'just disappeared' – ABT to Samuel Steward, 7 August 1958. *SOA*, p. 364.

331 'is too old' – Max White to Arthur Bullows, 29 June 1958. Princeton.

331 'deep animosity' – Max White to Liveright, November 1974 (draft). YCAL MSS 77.
'incredible heroism' – Max White to Linda Simon, 13 May 1975. Princeton University Library, General Manuscripts Collection C0140.
'The memories' – ABT to John Schaffner, 17 August 1958. *SOA*, p. 366.

332 'Alice has invariably' – CVV to Donald Gallup, 11 July 1958. NYPL.
In his preface – He also announced his resignation as Stein's literary executor, passing the mantle to Donald Gallup. An editor at Yale University Press returned Van Vechten's preface with a query on the last page: 'We are a little worried that the tone as well as the phrasing of this material may create the impression that you are washing your hands of a wearying task rather than introducing your successor in a job that brings its own rewards.'
'Baby is talked about' – ABT to CVV, 24 June 1952. YCAL MSS 1050.

333 'an essay in decapitation' – B. L. Reid, *Art by Subtraction*, p. vii.
'muddled and angry' – William H. Gass, 'Gertrude Stein: Her Escape from Protective Language', *Accent* (Autumn 1958). Gass wrote several more essays on Stein; he's one of her astutest and most stylish critics.
'permanent avant-garde' – William H. Gass, *Finding a Form*, p.205.

334 'to which no name' – Quoted in Sean Latham and Gayle Rogers (eds), *Modernism: Evolution of an Idea*, p. 1.
'started the whole thing' – Latham and Rogers (eds), p. 1.
'a grievous thorn' – ABT to Donald Sutherland, 30 November 1947. YCAL MSS 77. *SOA*, p. 91.
'the incomprehensibles' – *AABT*, p. 229.

335 'Don't talk *about*' – John Malcolm Brinnin, *Sextet*, p. 247.
'no no no' – Her corrections tended to represent points of detail: Basket, for example, was not purchased 'at a department store' but came from 'a kennel near Bordeaux'.

336 personal lawyer – Roubina remarried a Bernard Dupré; it seems more than likely that this is the same person.

337 'Spring green peas' – Otto Friedrich, *The Grave of Alice B. Toklas*, p. 37.
'momentous and moving' – ABT to Dilkusha de Rohan, 2 December 1960. HRC.
garlic artichokes – She ate garlic artichokes and oysters, followed by two Pall Malls smoked one after the other, at lunch with two friends of Van Vechten's, Donald Windham and Sandy Campbell. With her eyesight failing, she told them she navigated by smell; she remembered those artichokes for the rest of her life, and often recalled them in letters to Windham and Campbell, a young gay couple who reminded her, perhaps, of herself and Stein. Windham recalls their visits in *The Roman Spring of Alice Toklas*.
'become reconciled' – Donald Gallup to CVV, 1 October 1961.

338 'My memory' – ABT to Donald Sutherland, 6 December 1961. YCAL MSS 77.
'iron vitality' – Friedrich, p. 39.
'pale and ghostly' – Sutherland, 'Alice', p. 284.

338 'the civilised intimacy' – Janet Flanner, 'Paris Journal', *New Yorker*, 5 December 1961.
'The glaring squares' – Fanny Butcher, *Many Lives – One Love*, p. 424.
'in a devil' – ABT to Donald Sutherland, 16 May 1963. YCAL MSS 77. *SOA*, p. 413.
'The French law' – ABT to W. G. Rogers, 26 May 1958. *SOA*, p. 359.

339 'I was born in 1877' – Quoted in Joseph Barry, 'Alice B. Toklas', *Village Voice*, 16 March 1967.
'I am ready to kill' – Quoted in Doda Conrad to Janet Flanner, 20 July 1964. YCAL MSS 77.
'down near the Seine' – ABT to Harold and Virginia Knapik, 6 December 1964. YCAL MSS 77.
'I miss the old flat' – ABT to Benjamin Benno, 2 March 1965. YCAL MSS 77. *SOA*, p. 417.

340 'Did she never' – *Saturday Review*, 13 April 1963.
'disappeared virtually' – *Time*, 22 March 1963.
'What would Alice' – *New York Post*, 7 April 1963.
'a mere ghost' – Donald Gallup, *Pigeons on the Granite*, p. 127.
'every story' – Virgil Thomson, *An Autobiography*, p. 177.
'I picked up' – Draft for *What Is Remembered*, HRC.
'wanted Etta to' – Sprigge, 'Journal'.

341 'diagnosed me' – *WIR*, p. 44.
'but Gertrude' – *WIR*, p. 122.
'Gertrude did' – Simon Michael Bessie, introductory note to the 1984 edition of *The Alice B. Toklas Cook Book*.
'confessions of the heart' – Paul Carroll, 'Alice and Gertrude: A Memoir', *Chicago Daily News*, 27 March 1963.

342 'might be some' – Hemingway, *A Moveable Feast*, p. 20.
'someone speaking' – Hemingway, *A Moveable Feast*, pp. 103–4.
'I always wanted' – Ernest Hemingway to W. G. Rogers, 29 July 1948. *Selected Letters 1917–1961*, p. 650.

343 'Don't you come' – *AABT*, p. 238. In Hemingway's archive is a six-page diatribe titled 'The Autobiography of Alice B. Hemingway', mocking Toklas's Polish origins and parodying the relationship.
'a fine woman' – Ernest Hemingway to Arnold Gingrich, 3 April 1933. *Selected Letters 1917–1961*, p. 384.
'I liked her better' – Ernest Hemingway to W. G. Rogers, 29 July 1948. *Selected Letters 1917–1961*, p. 650.
'You will give' – 'Water Pipe', *Larus*, 1 (February 1927).

344 'I wonder what' – Philip Pendered to Janet Malcolm, 16 July 2005. YCAL MSS 935.
'great shock' – ABT to Donald Windham and Sandy Campbell, 13 July 1965. YCAL MSS 77. Some years earlier, Van Vechten's archival impulses

had turned to his own life. He spent years annotating his own letters with explanatory footnotes for future readers; he kept everything from dried flowers to receipts, with a zest for immortality not so different from Stein's. Like hers, his archives contained some secrets. In 1962, Van Vechten had bequeathed to Yale several large boxes which he asked to remain sealed until twenty-five years after his death. When Gallup duly opened them in December 1989, he found a collection of scrapbooks filled with newspaper clippings, photographs and comics, comprising an archive of gay erotica.

344 'sincere, sensitive' – *New York Times*, 30 November 1941.
'I feel that' – Doda Conrad to Russell Porter, 16 April 1965. YCAL MSS 1610.

345 'roaring Communist' – ABT to William Whitehead, 19 May 1965. YCAL MSS 77.
'I pray for' – ABT to Dilkusha de Rohan, 20 March 1963. HRC.
'Whenever I go' – James J. Rorimer to the organisers of Hommage à Gertrude Stein, 8 May 1965. HRC.
'the day is not' – Thornton Wilder to the organisers of Hommage à Gertrude Stein, 10 May 1965. HRC.

346 '*Pourquoi pas?*' – Marie-Claire Pasquier, interview with Alice B. Toklas, *Le Monde*, 22 March 1967.
'I wish' – Alice B. Toklas, last will and testament. YCAL MSS 77. According to Edward Burns, Edward Taylor was surprised Toklas had remembered him and refused to exercise any rights under the will; Toklas's estate passed to her childhood friend Louise Taylor, who appointed Burns her successor as trustee.

347 'There they lie' – James Lord, 'Where the Pictures Were', p. 39.
'God knows' – Doda Conrad, *Dodascieles*, p. 426.
'The scoundrel!' – Conrad, *Dodascieles*, p. 426.

16: The Branches

349 David Rockefeller – He tells the story in his memoirs, pp. 443ff.
a million dollars – The painting last sold in 2018, for $115 million.

351 'absolutely used' – ABT to Louise Taylor, 7 January 1947. YCAL MSS 1610. *SOA*, p. 45.
'In their new' – *Janet Flanner's World*, p. 342.
collectors – Chief among them was Addison M. Metcalf, whose collection of 'Steiniana' at the Ella Strong Denison Library, Scripps College, Claremont, is a repository rivalling Yale's in its depth. Metcalf's archive details his efforts to engage Van Vechten and Gallup: he sent them parcels of 'Stein Cookies', baked in a rose-shaped mould; owned a parakeet named 'Carlo', which he taught to say 'pigeons on the grass alas'; and corresponded with many of Stein's friends and fellow admirers. See also the memoir of Robert Wilson, proprietor of New York's famous Phoenix Bookshop: his collection is at the Johns Hopkins University Libraries.

352 'Again we are' – John Ashbery, *ArtNews*, February 1971. Ashbery had reviewed Stein's *Stanzas in Meditation* in 1954, and compared its bursts of vivid language amid a stream of connecting words ('where', 'which', 'these') to 'certain monochrome de Kooning paintings in which isolated strokes of color take on a deliciousness they never could have had out of context'. Willem de Kooning, in turn, told an interviewer he was thinking about Stein's portraits when he painted his *Woman* series – begun in 1950, the same year as Bradley Walker Tomlin's abstract painting *In Praise of Gertrude Stein*, in which letters dance unmoored across the canvas. De Kooning and O'Hara shared a close friend, the dance critic Edwin Denby, who was a major champion of Stein's work among this set: in a 1936 essay on librettos for *Modern Music*, he had described Stein as 'our greatest poet'.

'one of the most interesting' – O'Hara to his family, 12 November 1946, quoted in Brad Gooch, *City Poet*, p. 99. O'Hara died during a trip to Fire Island with Virgil Thomson and J. J. Mitchell; his last meal before the accident was cooked by Thomson from the *Alice B. Toklas Cook Book*. Another of his best-loved poems is titled 'À la recherche d' Gertrude Stein'.

'artists pioneering new varieties' – Among the artists who played most interestingly with Stein's image in these years are Robert Rauschenberg, Jasper Johns, Andy Warhol, Willem de Kooning and Ray Johnson.

353 'any title' – Cage, in Richard Kostelanetz (ed.), *John Cage*, p. 138. *Three Songs* (1932) set to music her texts 'Twenty Years After', 'If it Was to Be', and 'At East and Ingredients', while his 1940 quartet *Living Room Music* – one of his first to experiment with chance, instructing performers to use household objects of their choice as instruments – includes a movement in which performers speak or sing passages from her children's book *The World Is Round*. In the 1940s, Cage had been mentored by Virgil Thomson, who called him 'the most original composer in America, if not in the world' in a recommendation letter for a 1949 Guggenheim Fellowship; during a trip to Paris in June 1949, Cage visited Alice B. Toklas, and wrote to his parents that he had seen 'all the paintings of Gertrude Stein and heard conversation about all the famous people she has known'. See Arnold Aronson, *American Avant-Garde Theatre* on Cage's connection to Stein, and their mutual influence on later performance art: 'For the postwar avant-garde, the wellspring was Marcel Duchamp and its pillars were Gertrude Stein and John Cage.' (p. 20.)

'to draw us nearer' – John Cage, *For the Birds*, p. 81.

354 Nam June Paik – His 1990 work *Gertrude Stein* is a modern addition to her collection of likenesses: a robot body formed of video monitors placed within antique casings.

'Our Patron' – Something Else Press advertising blurb. Quoted in Alice Centamore et al., *Call it Something Else*, p. 21. The press was going to be called Shirtsleeves Press, until Higgins's wife Alison Knowles asked, 'Why don't you call it something else?' See also Higgins's essay 'Why Do We Publish So Much Gertrude Stein' in the *Something Else Press Newsletter*; the conclusion reads 'Why not?'

355 'Where oh where' – GS to CVV, 18 April 1916. YCAL MSS 1050. *CVV*, p. 53.
Stein's plays – Stein has attracted the attention of actors, from Jeff Weiss, who played Faustus at Judson and whose midnight performances of *As A Wife Has a Cow: A Love Story* in the Caffe Cino bar were legendary in the 1960s, to David Greenspan, whose 2022 one-man rendition of *Four Saints in Three Acts* is one of the most astounding feats I've seen on stage. Among the directors who have taken up Stein's work are Robert Wilson, who mounted acclaimed productions of *Dr Faustus Lights the Lights*, *Four Saints in Three Acts* and *Saints and Singing*, creating complex soundscapes replete with stunning lighting effects, and Richard Foreman, an early patron of the Living Theatre and Judson and a participant in Fluxus and the underground cinema movement of the 1960s, who has called Stein 'the major literary figure of the twentieth century'. Philip Glass's hypnotic, plotless five-hour opera *Einstein on the Beach* (1975) took its formal cue from her idea of the landscape play, structured not around narrative but around space; it was choreographed by Lucinda Childs – a participant in *What Happened* at Judson – who performed a solo dance along a single diagonal line for almost an hour, repeating a series of movements in a changing sequence evocative of Stein's cadence. Other choreographers who have engaged with Stein include Andy de Groat, whose *Red Notes* (1977) combined a score by Glass with texts by Stein, and James Waring, whose *Tender Buttons* (1976) was devised by John Herbert McDowell and danced by Arlene Rothlein. See also work by Mark Morris, Charles Stanley, Michael Townsend Smith, the Wooster Group, La Mama, Target Margin Theater Company, Complicité, Ned Rorem, Morton Feldman and Heiner Goebbels, whose haunting musical composition *Songs of Wars I Have Seen* has toured internationally. See Sarah Bay-Cheng, *Mama Dada* for a list of productions of Stein works up to 2004.
a forward-thinking pastor – Howard Moody.
earliest Happenings – One notable event, by Al Hansen, was titled 'The Hamlet of Gertrude Stein'.
hugely acclaimed – The first was *What Happened* (1963), performed by Yvonne Rainer, Lucinda Childs, Aileen Passloff, Arlene Rothlein and Joan Baker. It was produced in a double bill with poet John Weiners' play *Asphodel*, with stage design by Andy Warhol evoking a multimedia version of hell, yet reviewers reported that this experience was 'blotted out by the sheer exuberance of the Stein work' which followed it. Thornton Wilder told Kornfeld afterwards that Stein would have enjoyed it. Its concluding sequence involved the cast pushing the piano across the stage while Carmines continued to play as he walked: the lights gradually faded as the performers left the stage, with the piano. Jill Johnston's *Village Voice* criticism drew welcome attention to Judson and to Stein in these years.

356 'What is happening' – Lawrence Kornfeld, interview, 30 August 1978. Quoted in Robert Joseph Cioffi, 'Al Carmines and the Judson Poets' Theater Musicals', p. 92.
'The Judson Poets' Theater' – Jack Kroll, *Newsweek*, 27 November 1968.
'She wasn't' – Author's interview with Lawrence Kornfeld, 9 December 2022.
'His productions' – Advertisement for theatre workshops by Lawrence Kornfeld. The *New Yorker* of 2 December 1972 commented on 'the extraordinary affinity' between Stein and Carmines, while a letter to the *Village Voice* of 7 December described the production of *The Making of Americans* as 'an increasingly intensive probing of the human existence and subconscious by means of a language so revitalised that we are constantly forced to react in new ways which are both beautiful and terrifying'.

357 'hopeless love affair' – Leon Katz, 'The First Making of *The Making of Americans*', p. 16.
'a new pinnacle' – Virgil Thomson, 'A Very Difficult Author', *New York Review of Books*, 8 April 1971.

358 'Alice had' – Leon Katz, interview with Annette Rosenshine, 1968. YCAL MSS 1409.
'recognises language itself' – Ron Silliman to Bruce Andrews, 6 December 1971, in Bruce Andrews, Charles Bernstein and Ron Silliman, *The Language Letters*, p. 33. The magazine took its typography from Stein's poem 'We Came a History', which places an equals sign between each word; this was actually the idea of Bob Brown, who commissioned the work. Poetry critics who have engaged particularly with Stein include Marjorie Perloff, whose *Poetics of Indeterminacy* was a crucial book in the expansion of modernist criticism. Richard Kostelanetz, as well as devising important Stein anthologies, has done major work to place her among a new avant-garde.
'valued for itself' – Bernstein, 'Gertrude Stein', p. 256.
Lyn Hejinian – Her father, as a college student desperate to get out of Oakland, had written to Stein in 1933; Hejinian treasured the reply, signed 'A. B. Toklas, Secty', thanking him for his appreciation of Stein's writing and wishing him good luck with his own. See especially her 'Two Stein Talks' in *The Language of Inquiry*. Among the many other poets who have engaged with Stein's work are Robert Duncan (see his delightful pamphlet *Stein Imitations*), Rosemarie Waldrop, David Antin, Carla Harryman, Eileen Myles, Anne Waldman, Diane di Prima, bpNichol, Susan Howe, and Bernadette Mayer, who featured Stein's poem 'In' in the second issue of *o to 9* (1967), a staple-bound magazine for conceptual poetry. In 1965 concrete poet Emmett Williams, an editor at the Something Else Press, created the text-art piece *13 variations on 6 words of Gertrude Stein*, in which the words 'when this you see remember me' – a regular phrase of hers – were stamped over and over, each word a different colour, covering the page in an explosion of words set free from their position in Stein's sentence. In the early 1990s, Harryette Mullen's

brilliant responses to *Tender Buttons* – at once critique and homage – were among the first publications of Lee Ann Brown's Tender Buttons Press, devoted to experimental work by women poets.

359 'Thirty years' – 'How Writing is Written', in *HWW*, p. 152.
'most completely homosexual' – A. E. Smith, 'On Gertrude Stein', *Homophile Studies* (Summer 1959).
'I think that' – Donald Gallup to Calvin Levin, 17 April 1970. YCAL MSS 838.

360 the first generation – A notable exception was Allegra Stewart, whose *Gertrude Stein and the Present* (1967) was one of the first to read Stein through a phenomenological lens.
'feminist and post-structuralist critics' – Among the most important critics were Catharine R. Stimpson, Marianne DeKoven, Harriet Scott Chessman, Wendy Steiner and Lisa Ruddick. Later, Diana Souhami's work in lesbian biography showed there is indeed 'no modernism without lesbians'.

361 'astonishing genealogical precursor' – Fredric Jameson, *Postmodernism*, p. 56.
mid-century studies – There was no reference to Stein in Cleanth Brooks's *Modern Poetry and the Tradition* (1939), in John Crowe Ransom's *The New Criticism* (1941), in Frank Kermode's *Romantic Image* (1957) or in the enormous 1965 anthology *The Modern Tradition*, edited by Richard Ellmann and Charles Feidelson (which devoted only nine of its 948 pages to women). In Randell Jarrell's influential 1963 essay *Fifty Years of American Poetry* Stein is cited only for unfairly expelling Ezra Pound from the rue de Fleurus; Alfred Kazin, in his survey of American poetry *On Native Grounds* (1942), mentions her salon only as a site of pilgrimage for male writers, while Cyril Connolly, in *100 Key Books 1880–1950*, declares Stein a blind spot, lamenting that 'I cannot stomach the torrent of her automatic writing nor the greedy show-biz of the autobiographies'.

362 'so excited' – *Lifting Belly* (Naiad Press, 1989), p. xi.
'Splash goes the cow' – *BP*, p. 26.

363 'No truth exposed' – *BP*, p. 4.
specialised in fabulation – See Justin Spring's fascinating biography of Steward, and Steward's own *Lost Autobiography*.

364 'too outspoken' – Samuel Steward, *Dear Sammy*, p. 57.
'hot curl' – Steward, *Dear Sammy*, p. 55.
'You can never' – Leon Katz, 'A Year with Alice B. Toklas', p. 1.

365 'Facts of life' – 'Tourty or Tourtebattre', in *G&P*, p. 403.

366 'not only as' – Ulla E. Dydo, *The Language that Rises*, p. 7.
'I do all' – GS to Clarence Andrews, 1926 (draft). YCAL MSS 76.

367 'stripped of the process' – Dydo, p. 23.

368 'This is' – *SM*, p. 152.
'biographical detective story' – Dydo, p. 491. See *SM* for the original text.

369 'Who is winning' – *SM*, p. 169.
'life and work' – 'Why Publish?' YCAL MSS 1409.

370 The result – In 2021, Katz's sons Fred and Elia published their father's magnum opus: an 800-page volume including Stein's notebooks with Toklas and Katz's commentary.

371 'The Story of Alice' – Leon Katz, 'The Fragmentation of Alfred Hersland' (ms, 2002). YCAL MSS 1409.
'I knew what' – Leon Katz, 'Nurturing Alice' (1998). YCAL MSS 1409.
'reported whole' – Leon Katz to Janet Malcolm, 9 June 2003. Private collection.
'I went almost' – Katz, 'A Year', p. 15.

372 'a 2005' – Janet Malcolm, 'Someone Says Yes to It', *New Yorker*, 5 June 2005.
Wanda Van Dusen – *Modernism/modernity*, 3/3, September 1996. That same year it appeared as the appendix to *TW*.

373 'In another' – Janet Malcolm, 'How Gertrude Stein and Alice B. Toklas Got to Heaven', *New Yorker*, 6 November 2006.
'radically antiauthoritarian' – Barbara Will, *Unlikely Collaboration*, p. 12.
'pro-Fascist ideology' – Emily Greenhouse, 'Gertrude Stein and Vichy', *New Yorker*, 4 May 2012.
'is essentially' – Philip Kennicott, 'Gertrude Stein in full form at Portrait Gallery', *Washington Post*, 21 October 2011.

374 'a major collaborator' – Alan Dershowitz, 'Suppressing Ugly Truth for Beautiful Art', *Huffington Post*, 1 May 2012.
'by driving out' – Lansing Warren, 'Gertrude Stein Views Life and Politics', *New York Times* magazine, 6 May 1934.
'He noted that' – See Charles Bernstein, 'Gertrude and Alice in Vichyland', *Jacket2*, 30 May 2017, and 'Gertrude Stein Taunts Hitler in 1934 and 1945', *Jacket2*, 9 May 2012. 'Saying that Stein endorsed Hitler for the Nobel Prize . . . is like saying that Mel Brooks includes a tribute to Hitler in *The Producers*.'

375 in unequivocal terms – See *Mrs Reynolds, Everybody's Autobiography, A Political Series*.
'bravely and publicly' – Leon Katz, 'A response to "Gertrude Stein's Translations of Speeches by Philippe Pétain"', *Jacket2*, 10 May 2013.
'language of equivocation' – Michael Kimmelman, 'Gertrude Stein and Fascism', *New York Review of Books*, 12 July 2012.
'I'll be happy' – *Dear Sammy*, p. 25.

376 Studies have read – See, for example, Janet Boyd and Sharon J. Kirsch (eds), *Primary Stein*, and Sarah Posman and Laura Luise Schultz (eds), *Gertrude Stein in Europe*.
Faith Ringgold – Other contemporary artists who have engaged with Stein include Lubaina Himid, Eve Fowler, Glenn Ligon, Beatrice Gibson and Hilary Harkness, while between 1992 and 2014 a full-scale reconstruction of her salon existed in Spring Street, Manhattan, a project called *Salon de Fleurus*.
The Book of Salt – Another Stein-inspired novel, which rings somewhat less true than Truong's, is Hassan Najmi's *Gertrude* (Interlink World Fiction,

2013). See also Filip Noterdaeme, *The Autobiography of Daniel J. Isengart* (Outpost19, 2013).

376 cartoon strip – Tom Hachtman, *Gertrude's Follies*, in the *Soho Weekly News*.

terrifying pillow – From the collection of Robert Wilson, Johns Hopkins University Libraries.

'the world's biggest' – Eileen Myles with Amy Kellner, *Index* magazine, 1998.

'one is suddenly' – Kenneth Koch, 'Gertrude Stein Talk'. Kenneth Koch Collection of Papers 1932–2007, Berg Collection of English and American Literature, NYPL.

'I suppose' – GS to Harry Phelan Gibbs, 27 December 1921. YCAL MSS 76.

like a DJ – The electronic music pioneer Pauline Oliveros's 1966 piece *Participle Dangling in Honor of Gertrude Stein* pays tribute to Stein's repetition; Jill Johnston in the *Village Voice* called her 'a musical Gertrude Stein'.

Epilogue

383 'just to show' – Steward, *Murder Is Murder*, p. 8. See Karen Leick, 'The Mysteries of Samuel Steward and Gertrude Stein, Private Eyes' for a discussion of these novels in context of Stein's love of and formal engagement with detective fiction.

'it is more interesting' – 'American Crimes and How They Matter', *New York Herald Tribune*, 30 March 1934.

'A sentence is made' – 'Sentences', in *HTW*, p. 1.

384 'She is my wife' – 'Pay Me', in *PL*, p. 137.

SELECT BIBLIOGRAPHY

See also Abbreviations of Works Cited on p. 387.

Harold Acton, *Memoirs of an Aesthete* (Methuen, 1948)

Bruce Andrews, Charles Bernstein and Ron Silliman, *The Language Letters: Selected 1970s Correspondence*, ed. Matthew Hofer and Michael Golston (University of New Mexico Press, 2019)

Arnold Aronson, *American Avant-Garde Theatre: A History* (Routledge, 2000)

John Ashbery, 'The Impossible' (review of *Stanzas in Meditation*), *Poetry*, 90/4 (July 1957), pp. 250–4

Jennifer Ashton, 'Gertrude Stein for Anyone', *ELH*, 64/1 (Spring 1997), pp. 189–331

Lewellys Barker, *Time and the Physician* (G. P. Putnam's Sons, 1942)

Greg Barnhisel, *Code Name Puritan: Norman Holmes Pearson at the Nexus of Poetry, Espionage and American Power* (University of Chicago Press, 2024)

———, *Cold War Modernists* (Columbia University Press, 2015)

Joseph Barry, *French Lovers: From Heloise and Abelard to Beauvoir and Sartre* (Arbor House, 1987)

Robert Bartlett Haas (ed.), *A Primer for the Gradual Understanding of Gertrude Stein* (Black Sparrow Press, 1973)

Sarah Bay-Cheng, *Mama Dada: Gertrude Stein's Avant-Garde Theater* (Routledge, 2004)

Sylvia Beach, *Shakespeare and Company* (Harcourt, Brace, 1959)

Cecil Beaton, *Self Portrait with Friends: The Selected Diaries of Cecil Beaton* (Weidenfeld and Nicolson, 1979)

Julian Beck, 'An Essay on the Living Theatre', in Kenneth H. Brown, *The Brig: A Concept for Theatre or Film* (Hill & Wang, 1965)

———, *The Life of the Theatre* (City Lights, 1972)

Shari Benstock, *Women of the Left Bank: Paris 1900–1940* (Virago, 1987)

Mary Berenson, *A Self-Portrait from Her Letters and Diaries*, ed. Barbara Strachey and Jayne Samuels (Victor Gollancz, 1983)

Emily Bernard, *Carl Van Vechten and the Harlem Renaissance: A Portrait in Black and White* (Yale University Press, 2012)

Charles Bernstein, 'Gertrude Stein', in Alex Davis and Lee M. Jenkins (eds), *A History of Modernist Poetry* (Cambridge University Press, 2015), pp. 255–74

——— (ed.), *Gertrude Stein's War Years: Setting the Record Straight: A Dossier, Jacket2*, 2012, https://jacket2.org/feature/gertrude-steins-war-years-setting-record-straight

Erica Bilder and Judith Malina (eds), *Theandric: Julian Beck's Last Notebooks* (Harwood Academic Publishers, 1992)

Janet Bishop, Cécile Debray and Rebecca Rabinow (eds), *The Steins Collect: Matisse, Picasso and the Parisian Avant-Garde* (San Francisco Museum of Modern Art/ Yale University Press, 2011)

Lynn Z. Bloom, 'Gertrude Is Alice Is Everybody: Innovation and Point of View in Gertrude Stein's Autobiographies', *Twentieth Century Literature*, 24/1 (Spring 1978), pp. 81–93

Stephen J. Bottoms, *Playing Underground: A Critical History of the 1960s Off-Off-Broadway Movement* (University of Michigan Press, 2006)

Janet Boyd and Sharon J. Kirsch (eds), *Primary Stein: Returning to the Writing of Gertrude Stein* (Lexington Books, 2014)

Jerome Boyd Maunsell, *Portraits from Life: Modernist Novelists and Autobiography* (Oxford University Press, 2018)

Kay Boyle and Robert McAlmon, *Being Geniuses Together* (Hogarth, 1984)

Robert Boynton Helm, 'The Rev. Al Carmines and the Development of the Judson Poets' Theatre', PhD thesis, West Virginia University, 1979

Jeremy Braddock, *Collecting as Modernist Practice* (Johns Hopkins University Press, 2013)

Richard Bridgman, *Gertrude Stein in Pieces* (Oxford University Press, 1970)

John Malcolm Brinnin, *Sextet* (Andre Deutsch, 1981)

———, *The Third Rose: Gertrude Stein and Her World* (Grove, 1959)

William S. Brockman, 'Learning to be James Joyce's Contemporary? Richard Ellmann's Discovery and Transformation of Joyce's Letters and Manuscripts', *Journal of Modern Literature*, 22/2 (Winter 1998–9), pp. 253–63

Joseph Brooker, *Joyce and His Critics* (University of Wisconsin Press, 2004)

Carolyn Burke, 'Gertrude Stein, the Cone Sisters, and the Puzzle of Female Friendship', *Critical Inquiry*, 8/3 (1 April 1982), pp. 543–64

Edward Burns (ed.), *Gertrude Stein on Picasso* (Liveright, 1970)

Fanny Butcher, *Many Lives – One Love* (Harper and Row, 1972)

John Cage, *For the Birds: John Cage in Conversation with Daniel Charles* (Marion Boyers, 1981)

———, *The Selected Letters of John Cage*, ed. Laura Kuhn (Wesleyan University Press, 2016)

———, *Silence: Lectures and Writings* (Wesleyan University Press, 1961)

——— and Kathleen O'Donnell Hoover, *Virgil Thomson: His Life and Music* (Thomas Yoseloff, 1959)

Jamie Callison, Matthew Feldman, Anna Svendsen and Erik Tonning (eds), *The Bloomsbury Handbook of Modernist Archives* (Bloomsbury, 2024)

M. Cameron Grey, 'Miss Toklas Alone', *Virginia Quarterly Review*, 52/4 (Autumn 1976), pp. 687–96

Humphrey Carpenter, *A Serious Character: The Life of Ezra Pound* (Faber, 1988)

Terry Castle, *The Literature of Lesbianism: A Historical Anthology from Ariosto to Stonewall* (Columbia University Press, 2003)

Natalie Cecire, 'Ways of Not Reading Gertrude Stein', *ELH*, 82/1 (2015), pp. 281–312

Alice Centamore et al., *Call it Something Else* (Museo Reina Sofia, 2023)

Amy Hildreth Chen, *Placing Papers: The American Literary Archives Market* (University of Massachusetts Press, 2020)

Harriet Scott Chessman, *The Public Is Invited to Dance: Representation, the Body and Dialogue in Gertrude Stein* (Stanford University Press, 1989)

Robert Joseph Cioffi, 'Al Carmines and the Judson Poets' Theater Musicals', PhD thesis, New York University, 1979

Steve Clay and Ken Friedman, *Intermedia, Fluxus and the Something Else Press* (Siglio Press, 2018)

Chris Coffman, *Gertrude Stein's Transmasculinity* (Edinburgh University Press, 2018)

Annie Cohen-Solal, *Picasso the Foreigner: An Artist in France, 1900–1973*, tr. Sam Taylor (FSG, 2023)

Edward T. Cone, 'The Miss Etta Cones, the Steins, and M'sieu Matisse: A Memoir', *The American Scholar*, 42/3 (Summer 1973), pp. 441–60

Doda Conrad, *Dodascieles* (Actes Sud, 1997)

Wanda M. Corn and Tirza True Latimer, *Seeing Gertrude Stein: Five Stories* (University of California Press, 2011)

Claire A. Culleton and Karen Leick (eds), *Modernism on File: Writers, Artists, and the FBI 1920–1950* (Palgrave Macmillan, 2008)

Kirk Curnutt, 'Inside and Outside: Gertrude Stein on Identity, Celebrity, and Authenticity', *Journal of Modern Literature*, 23/2 (Winter 1999–2000), pp. 291–308

———— (ed.), *The Critical Response to Gertrude Stein* (Greenwood Press, 2000)

Solveig Daugaard, 'Collaborating with Gertrude Stein: Media Ecologies, Reception, Poetics', PhD thesis, Linköping University, 2018

Annette Debo, 'Norman Holmes Pearson: Canon-Maker', *Modernism/modernity*, 23/2 (April 2016), pp. 443–62

Cécile Debray and Assia Quesnel, *Gertrude Stein and Pablo Picasso: Inventing Language* (Éditions de la Réunion des Musées Nationaux, Grand Palais, 2024)

Marianne DeKoven, *A Different Language: Gertrude Stein's Experimental Language* (University of Wisconsin Press, 1983)

———— (ed.), *Three Lives and Q.E.D.: A Norton Critical Edition* (W.W. Norton, 2006)

Laura Doan, *Fashioning Sapphism: The Origins of a Modern English Lesbian Culture* (Columbia University Press, 2001)

Mabel Dodge, *European Experiences* (Harcourt, Brace, 1935)

————, *Movers and Shakers* (Harcourt, Brace, 1936)

Ulla E. Dydo, *Gertrude Stein: The Language that Rises 1923–1934* (Northwestern University Press, 2003)

————, '*Stanzas in Meditation*: The Other Autobiography', *Chicago Review*, 35/2 (Winter 1985), pp. 4–20

———— (ed.), *A Stein Reader* (Northwestern University Press, 1993)

Leon Edel, *Henry James: A Life* (HarperCollins, 1962)

David Edstrom, *Testament of Caliban* (Funk and Wagnalls, 1937)

Logan Esdale and Deborah M. Mix (eds), *Approaches to Teaching the Works of Gertrude Stein* (The Modern Language Association of America, 2018)

Bernard Faÿ, *Les Précieux* (Perrin, 1966)

Amy Feinstein, *Gertrude Stein and the Making of Jewish Modernism* (Florida University Press, 2020)

Elizabeth Fifer, 'Is Flesh Advisable? The Interior Theater of Gertrude Stein', *Signs: Journal of Women in Culture and Society*, 4/3 (Spring 1979), pp. 472–83

F. Scott Fitzgerald, *Correspondence of F. Scott Fitzgerald*, ed. Matthew Bruccoli, Margaret M. Duggan and Susan Walker (Random House, 1980)

Janet Flanner, *An American in Paris* (Hamish Hamilton, 1940)

———, *Janet Flanner's World: Uncollected Writings 1932–1975*, ed. Irving Drutman (Houghton Mifflin, 1979)

———, *Paris Was Yesterday: 1925–1939* (Virago Modern Classics, 2003)

Alice T. Friedman, 'Queer Old Things', *Places Journal* (February 2015)

Otto Friedrich, *The Grave of Alice B. Toklas and Other Reports from the Past* (Henry Holt, 1989)

Kate Fullbrook, 'Gertrude Stein and Alfred North Whitehead', in Janet Beer and Bridget Bennett (eds), *Special Relationships: Anglo-American Affinities and Antagonisms 1854–1936* (Manchester University Press, 2018)

Donald Gallup, *A Curator's Responsibilities*, Rutgers University Occasional Papers no. 76-1 (September 1976)

——— (ed.), *The Flowers of Friendship: Letters Written to Gertrude Stein* (Knopf, 1953)

———, 'The Gertrude Stein Collection', *Yale University Library Gazette*, 22/2 (October 1947), pp. 21–32

———, *Pigeons on the Granite: Memories of a Yale Librarian* (Beinecke Rare Book and Manuscript Library, 1988)

———, *What Mad Pursuits! More Memories of a Yale Librarian* (Beinecke Rare Book and Manuscript Library, 1998)

William H. Gass, *Finding a Form* (Knopf, 1996)

———, *A Temple of Texts* (Knopf, 2006)

Françoise Gilot and Carlton Lake, *Life with Picasso* (NYRB, 2019)

Charles Glass, *Americans in Paris: Life and Death Under Nazi Occupation* (Penguin, 2010)

John Glassco, *Memoirs of Montparnasse* (NYRB Classics, 2007)

Richard J. Golsan, *French Writers and the Politics of Complicity* (Johns Hopkins University Press, 2006)

Brad Gooch, *City Poet* (Harper Perennial, 1993)

Serge Guilbaut, *How New York Stole the Idea of Modern Art*, tr. Arthur Goldhammer (University of Chicago Press, 1983)

Lyn Hejinian, *The Language of Inquiry* (University of California Press, 2000)

Ernest Hemingway, *A Moveable Feast* (Jonathan Cape, 1964)

———, *Selected Letters 1917–1961*, ed. Carlos Baker (Scribner's, 1981)

Michael J. Hoffman (ed.), *Critical Essays on Gertrude Stein* (G. K. Hall and Co., 1986)

Michael Holtzman, 'The Ideological Origins of American Studies at Yale', *American Studies*, 40/2 (Summer 1991), pp. 71–99

Irving Howe, *The Idea of the Modern In Literature and the Arts* (Horizon Press, 1967)

Braving Imbs, *Confessions of Another Young Man* (Henkle-Yewdale House, 1936)

Julian Jackson, *France: The Dark Years 1940–1944* (Oxford University Press, 2001)

———, *France on Trial: The Case of Marshal Pétain* (Allen Lane, 2023)

Lise Jaillant, '*Shucks, we've got glamour girls too!* Gertrude Stein, Bennett Cerf and the Culture of Celebrity', *Journal of Modern Literature*, 39/1 (Fall 2015), pp. 149–69

Fredric Jameson, *The Modernist Papers* (Verso, 2007)
——, *Postmodernism: Or the Cultural Logic of Late Capitalism* (Verso, 1992)
James Joyce, *Finnegans Wake* (Oxford World's Classics, 2012)
Yeonsik Jung, 'Why Is Melanctha Black? Gertrude Stein, Physiognomy, and the
    Jewish Question', *Canadian Review of American Studies*, 49/2 (2019), pp. 139–59
Allan Kaprow, *Essays on the Blurring of Art and Life* (University of California Press, 1993)
Daniel Katz, *American Modernism's Expatriate Scene* (Edinburgh University Press, 2012)
Leon Katz, 'The First Making of *The Making of Americans*: A Study Based on
    Gertrude Stein's Notebooks and Early Versions of Her Novel (1902–1908)', PhD
    thesis, Columbia University, 1963
——, 'Weininger and *The Making of Americans*', *Twentieth Century Literature*,
    24/1 (Spring 1978), pp. 8–26
——, 'A Year with Alice B. Toklas', *Yale Review*, 11 June 2012
Bruce Kellner, *A Gertrude Stein Companion* (Greenwood Press, 1988)
——, 'Baby Woojums in Iowa', *Books at Iowa*, 26 (April 1977), pp. 3–18
——, *Carl Van Vechten and the Irreverent Decades* (University of Oklahoma Press, 1968)
Friedrich Kittler, *Discourse Networks 1800/1900*, tr. Michael Metteer with Chris
    Cullens (Stanford University Press, 1990)
Lawrence Kornfeld, 'Conflict and Change: The Theatre of Gertrude Stein',
    American Journal of Psychoanalysis, 37 (1977), pp. 73–82
Richard Kostelanetz, *The Avant-garde Tradition in Literature* (Prometheus, 1982)
——, *Conversing with Cage* (Limelight, 1988)
—— (ed.), *Gertrude Stein Advanced* (McFarland & Company, 1990)
—— (ed.), *The Gertrude Stein Reader* (Cooper Square Press, 2002)
—— (ed.) *John Cage* (Allen Lane, 1974)
—— (ed.), *The Yale Gertrude Stein* (Yale University Press, 1980)
Sean Latham and Gayle Rogers (eds), *Modernism: Evolution of an Idea* (Bloomsbury,
    2015)
Gwendolyn Leick, *Gertrude, Mabel, May: An ABC of Gertrude Stein's Love Triangle*
    (Grey Suit Editions, 2019)
Karen Leick, *Gertrude Stein and the Making of an American Celebrity* (Routledge, 2009)
——, 'The Mysteries of Samuel Steward and Gertrude Stein, Private Eyes', in
    Debra A. Moddelmog and Martin Joseph Ponce (eds), *Samuel Steward and the
    Pursuit of the Erotic* (Ohio State University Press, 2017), pp. 105–21
Harriet Lane Levy, *Paris Portraits: Stories of Picasso, Matisse, Gertrude Stein, and
    Their Circle* (Heyday, 2011)
Wyndham Lewis, *The Art of Being Ruled* (Black Sparrow, 1989)
——, *Time and Western Man* (Chatto and Windus, 1927)
Anna Linzie, *The True Story of Alice B. Toklas: A Study of Three Autobiographies*
    (University of Iowa Press, 2006)
Astrid Lorange, *How Reading Is Written* (Wesleyan University Press, 2014)
James Lord, *Picasso and Dora: A Personal Memoir* (FSG, 1994)
——, 'Where the Pictures Were', in *Six Exceptional Women* (FSG, 1994), pp. 3–39

Ian S. MacNiven, *'Literchoor Is My Beat': A Life of James Laughlin* (FSG, 2014)

Robin Maconie, *Avant Garde: An American Odyssey from Gertrude Stein to Pierre Boulez* (Scarecrow Press, 2012)

Janet Malcolm, *Two Lives* (Yale University Press, 2007)

Judith Malina, *The Diaries of Judith Malina, 1947–1957* (Grove Press, 1984)

Sharon Marcus, *The Drama of Celebrity* (Princeton University Press, 2019)

Bonnie Marranca, 'Presence of Mind', *Performing Arts Journal*, 16/3 (September 1994), pp. 1–17

Michael Marrus and Robert O. Paxton, *Vichy France and the Jews* (second edition, Stanford University Press, 2019)

Patrick Mauries, *Theatres of Melancholy* (Thames and Hudson, 2023)

Kali McKay, *Gertrude Stein and her Audience: Small Presses, Little Magazines, and the Reconfiguration of Modern Authorship* (University of Lethbridge, 2006)

James Mellow, *Charmed Circle: Gertrude Stein and Company* (Praeger Publishers, 1974)

Steven Meyer, *Irresistible Dictation: Gertrude Stein and the Correlations of Writing and Science* (Stanford University Press, 2002)

Melanie Micir, *The Passion Projects: Modernist Women, Intimate Archives, Unfinished Lives* (Princeton, 2019)

Rosalind Miller, *Gertrude Stein: Form and Intelligibility* (Exposition Press, 1949)

Rosalind Moad, '1914–1916: Years of Innovation in Gertrude Stein's Writing', PhD thesis, University of York, 1993

Howard Moody, *A Voice in the Village* (XLibris, 2009)

Roy Morris, Jr, *Gertrude Stein Has Arrived* (Johns Hopkins University Press, 2019)

Maggie Nelson, *Women, The New York School, and Other True Abstractions* (University of Iowa Press, 2007)

Shirley Neuman and Ira B. Nadel (eds), *Gertrude Stein and the Making of Literature* (Macmillan Press, 1988)

Michael North, *The Dialect of Modernism: Race, Language and Twentieth-Century Literature* (Oxford University Press, 1994)

Fernande Olivier, *Picasso and His Friends*, tr. Jane Miller (Appleton Century, 1963)

Jane Palatini Bowers, *They Watch Me As They Watch This: Gertrude Stein's Metadrama* (University of Pennsylvania Press, 1991)

Isabelle Parkinson, *Gertrude Stein and the Politics of Participation* (Edinburgh University Press, 2023)

Marie-Claire Pasquier, 'Gertrude Stein, théâtre et théâtralité', PhD thesis, Université Paris-Sorbonne, 1991

Robert O. Paxton, *Vichy France: Old Guard and New Order, 1940–1944* (Knopf, 1972)

Marjorie Perloff, *The Poetics of Indeterminacy: Rimbaud to Cage* (Princeton, 1981)

———, *Twenty-First Century Modernism: The New Poetics* (Wiley-Blackwell, 2002)

———, *Wittgenstein's Ladder: Poetic Language and the Strangeness of the Ordinary* (University of Chicago Press, 1999)

Fritz Peters, *Boyhood with Gurdjieff* (Penguin, 1972)

Fernanda Pivano, *America Rossa e Nera* (Vallecchi, 1964)

Agnes Poirier, *Left Bank: Art, Passion and the Rebirth of Paris 1940–1950* (Bloomsbury, 2018)

Barbara Pollack, *The Collectors: Dr Claribel and Miss Etta Cone* (Bobbs-Merrill, 1962)

Sarah Posman, *Vital Stein* (Edinburgh University Press, 2022)

Sarah Posman and Laura Luise Schultz (eds), *Gertrude Stein in Europe: Reconfigurations across Media, Disciplines and Traditions* (Bloomsbury, 2015)

Renée Poznanski, *Jews in France During World War II* (Brandeis University Press, 2001)

Lawrence Rainey, *Institutions of Modernism* (Yale University Press, 1998)

B. L. Reid, *Art by Subtraction: A Dissenting Opinion of Gertrude Stein* (University of Oklahoma Press, 1958)

Joan Retallack (ed.), *Gertrude Stein Selections* (University of California Press, 2008)

John Richardson, *A Life of Picasso*, vols 1–4 (Jonathan Cape, 1991–2022)

Natalie Robins, *Alien Ink: The FBI's War on Freedom of Expression* (Morrow, 1992)

Hannah Roche, *The Outside Thing: Modernist Lesbian Romance* (Columbia University Press, 2019)

David Rockefeller, *Memoirs* (Random House, 2002)

Suzanne Rodriguez, *Wild Heart: A Life: Natalie Clifford Barney's Journey from Victorian America to the Literary Salons of Paris* (Harper Collins, 2002)

Karin Roffman, '"Sitting at the Table" with Stein and Ashbery', *Yale Review* (April 2019)

———, *The Songs We Know Best: John Ashbery's Early Life* (FSG, 2017)

William Garland Rogers, *When This You See Remember Me* (Rinehart, 1948)

Francis Rose, *Saying Life* (Cassell, 1961)

Aldo Rostagno with Julian Beck and Judith Malina, *We, the Living Theatre* (Ballantine Books, 1970)

Hazel Rowley, *Richard Wright: The Life and Times* (Henry Holt, 2001)

Lisa Ruddick, *Reading Gertrude Stein* (Cornell University Press, 1990)

Aline B. Saarinen, 'The Steins in Paris', *American Scholar*, 27/4 (Autumn 1958), pp. 437–48

Dominique Saint-Pierre, *Gertrude Stein: Le Bugey, la guerre* (Musnier-Gilbert Éditions, 2009)

Julian Sawyer, *Gertrude Stein: A Bibliography* (Arrow Editions, 1941)

Adrian Sayre Harris, 'The Judson Poet's Theatre: 1960–1973', PhD thesis, Florida State University, 1978

Jacques Sémelin, *The Survival of the Jews in France, 1940–1944*, tr. Natasha Lehrer and Cynthia Schoch (Hurst Publishers, 2018)

Urmila Seshagiri, *Race and the Modernist Imagination* (Cornell University Press, 2010)

Emily Setina, 'From "Impossible" Writing to a Poetics of Intimacy: John Ashbery's Reading of Gertrude Stein', *Genre*, 45/1 (March 2012), pp. 143–66

Eric Sevareid, *Not So Wild a Dream* (Atheneum, 1976)

Ery Shin, *Gertrude Stein's Surrealist Years* (University of Alabama Press, 2020)

Kenneth Silverman, *Begin Again: A Biography of John Cage* (Knopf, 2010)

Linda Simon, *The Biography of Alice B. Toklas* (Doubleday, 1977)

——— (ed.), *Gertrude Stein Remembered* (University of Nebraska Press, 1994)

Edith Sitwell, *Taken Care Of* (Hutchinson, 1966)

Kathryn S. Smaller, 'Some Letters from Gertrude Stein to Louis Bromfield', PhD thesis, Ohio State University, 1975

Jeff Solomon, *So Famous and So Gay: The Fabulous Potency of Truman Capote and Gertrude Stein* (University of Minnesota Press, 2017)

Diana Souhami, *Gertrude and Alice* (Harper Collins, 1991)

Juliana Spahr, *Everybody's Autonomy* (University of Alabama Press, 2001)

Elizabeth Sprigge, *Gertrude Stein: Her Life and Work* (Hamish Hamilton, 1957)

Justin Spring, *Secret Historian: The Life and Times of Samuel Steward, Professor, Tattoo Artist, and Sexual Renegade* (FSG, 2010)

Leo Stein, *Appreciation: Painting, Poetry and Prose* (Crown, 1947)

Wendy Steiner, *Exact Resemblance to Exact Resemblance* (Yale University Press, 1978)

Paul Stephens, *The Poetics of Information Overload: From Gertrude Stein to Conceptual Writing* (University of Minnesota Press, 2015)

Samuel Steward, *Dear Sammy: Letters from Gertrude Stein and Alice B. Toklas* (Houghton Mifflin, 1977)

———, *The Lost Autobiography of Samuel Steward* (University of Chicago Press, 2018)

———, *Murder Is Murder* (Alyson Publications, 1995)

———, *Parisian Lives* (St Martin's Press, 1984)

Allegra Stewart, *Gertrude Stein and the Present* (Harvard University Press), 1967

Catharine R. Stimpson, 'Gertrice/Altrude: Stein, Toklas and the Paradox of the Happy Marriage', in Ruth Perry (ed.), *Mothering the Mind: Twelve Studies of Writers and their Silent Partners* (Holmes & Meier, 1984)

———, 'Gertrude Stein: Humanism and Its Freaks', *Boundary 2*, 12/3 and 13/1 (Spring/Autumn 1984), pp. 301–19

———, 'Gertrude Stein and the Transposition of Gender', in Nancy K. Miller (ed.), *The Poetics of Gender* (Columbia University Press, 1986)

———, 'The Mind, the Body, and Gertrude Stein', *Critical Inquiry*, 3/3 (Spring 1977), pp. 489–506

———, 'The Somagrams of Gertrude Stein', in *Poetics Today*, 6/1–2 (1985), pp. 67–80

Donald Sutherland, 'Alice and Gertrude and Others', *Prairie Schooner* (Winter 1971–2), pp. 284–99

———, 'The Conversion of Alice B. Toklas', *Colorado Quarterly*, 17/2 (Autumn 1968), pp. 129–41

———, *Gertrude Stein: A Biography of Her Work* (Yale University Press, 1951)

Virgil Thomson, *An Autobiography* (E.P. Dutton, 1985)

Anthony Tommasini, *Virgil Thomson: Composer on the Aisle* (Norton, 1997)

Tirza True-Latimer, *Eccentric Modernisms* (University of California Press, 2017)

John Tytell, *The Living Theatre: Art, Exile, and Outrage* (Grove Press, 1995)

Janine Utell, *Literary Couples and Twentieth-Century Life Writing* (Bloomsbury, 2020)

Wanda Van Dusen, 'Portrait of a National Fetish: Gertrude Stein's Introduction to the Speeches of Maréchal Pétain', *Modernism/modernity*, 3/3 (September 1996), pp. 69–96

Carl Van Vechten, *Fragments of an Unfinished Autobiography* (Yale University Library, 1955)

———, *Letters of Carl Van Vechten*, ed. Bruce Kellner (Yale University Press, 1987)

Ambroise Vollard, *Recollections of a Picture Dealer*, tr. Violet M. Macdonald (Constable, 1936)

Linda Voris, *The Composition of Sense in Gertrude Stein's Landscape Writing* (Macmillan, 2016)

Linda Wagner-Martin, *Favored Strangers: Gertrude Stein and Her Family* (Rutgers University Press, 1995)

Steven Watson, *Prepare for Saints: Gertrude Stein, Virgil Thomson, and the Mainstreaming of American Modernism* (University of California Press, 1998)

Otto Weininger, *Sex and Character* (A. L. Burt, 1906)

Andrea Weiss, *Paris Was a Woman: Portraits from the Left Bank* (Counterpoint Press, 2013)

M. Lynn Weiss, *Gertrude Stein and Richard Wright; the Poetics and Politics of Modernism* (University Press of Mississippi, 1998)

S. M. Wenrick, 'Gertrude Stein Reads Dashiell Hammett: Autobiography and Detective Fiction', PhD thesis, Claremont Graduate University, 1998

Edward White, *The Tastemaker: Carl Van Vechten and the Birth of Modern America* (FSG, 2014)

Annette Wieviorka, *The Era of the Witness*, tr. Jared Stark (Cornell University Press, 2006)

Thornton Wilder, *The Selected Letters of Thornton Wilder*, ed. Robin G. Wilder and Jackson R. Bryer (Harper Perennial, 2008)

Barbara Will, *Gertrude Stein, Modernism, and the Problem of 'Genius'* (Edinburgh University Press, 2000)

———, *Unlikely Collaboration: Gertrude Stein, Bernard Faÿ, and the Vichy Dilemma* (Columbia University Press, 2011)

William Carlos Williams, *The Autobiography of William Carlos Williams* (Random House, 1948)

Edmund Wilson, *Axel's Castle* (Scribner, 1931)

Robert A. Wilson, *Gertrude Stein: A Bibliography* (Phoenix Bookshop, 1974)

———, *Seeing Shelley Plain: Memories of New York's Legendary Phoenix Bookshop* (Oak Knoll Press, 2001)

Donald Windham, *The Roman Spring of Alice Toklas* (Sandy Campbell, 1987)

Brenda Wineapple, *Genêt: A Biography of Janet Flanner* (Pandora, 1994)

———, *Sister Brother: Gertrude and Leo Stein* (Putnam, 1996)

Virginia Woolf, *The Letters of Virginia Woolf, 3: 1923–1928*, ed. Nigel Nicolson and Joanne Trautman (Harcourt, Brace, 1977)

Mia You, 'An Exercise in Analysis as Enjoyment', *Textual Practice*, 36/12 (2022), pp. 1984–2015

LIST OF ILLUSTRATIONS

ACKNOWLEDGEMENTS

T his book began with a quick trip to New Haven in September 2019 to see the Leon Katz papers at the Beinecke Library. To maximise my time in the archive, I spent three days there taking an almost continuous stream of photos to sift through at home; six months later, Covid-19 hit and the library closed to external researchers for two years. That lucky tranche of photos became the bedrock of this project while libraries and archives were off limits. I'm so grateful to Michael Rush of the Beinecke Rare Books and Manuscripts Library for making the Leon Katz papers available to me before they were processed, and to the London Library for their enormous generosity in sending out books during the pandemic, which enabled me to make headway in those years of isolation.

The Beinecke reopened in the summer of 2022, and I spent four months there examining its rich collections: first the hundreds of boxes comprising the Stein and Toklas papers, then the papers of Donald Gallup, Carl Van Vechten, Leo Stein, Leon Katz, Janet Malcolm, Florine Stettheimer, Virgil Thomson, Thornton Wilder, John Breon, Bruce Kellner, Elizabeth Fuller Chapman, Samuel Steward, the Living Theatre and more. Thank you to every member of the wonderful Beinecke staff for their daily support and encouragement, and for sending so many scans of extra material before and after my stint on-site. A special thank you to John Monahan for showing me Toklas's chairs, and to Matthew Rowe for heroic kindness in photo scanning. Thank you to Nancy Kuhl and Timothy Young for their insights into the Stein collection, and to all at the library for the honour of a Donald Gallup Fellowship for that summer. Huge thanks to Alice Kaplan and her archives class for last-minute photo research.

I've been hugely lucky to have the support of several formidable institutions over the course of this project. Thank you to the Leon Levy Center for Biography, where this work really began: to Kai Bird, Thad Ziolkowski, Shelby White, and my wonderful fellow fellows Nicholas Boggs, Miriam Horn, Susan Morrison and Lance Richardson, whose guidance and camaraderie has shaped this work from the earliest stages. A great boon of this fellowship was the intrepid research assistance of Michael Abolafia: thank you for finding the earliest portrait of Stein in the *San Francisco Chronicle*, and for helping untangle the Katz archive when it was still a mass of photos. Thank you to the New York Public Library and the writers' paradise that is the Dorothy and Lewis B. Cullman Center for Scholars and Writers: to Martha Hodes, Lauren Goldenberg, Paul Delaverdac, Catherine Nichols, Jean Strouse, and all at the

Berg and in the Manuscripts and Archives division and across the library who made my year there so special. It was a privilege and a joy to shape and share ideas in the company of Rozina Ali, Daphne A. Brooks, Colin Channer, Raghu Karnad, Margaret Kelleher, Claire Luchette, Neil Maher, Sarah Maza, Patrick Phillips, Daniel Saldaña Paris, Maurice Samuels, Brandon Taylor, Erin L. Thompson and C Pam Zhang. And thank you to all the staff and fellows at the Harvard Radcliffe Institute, which provided a wonderful setting to finish this book (where Stein began): especial thanks to Charlie Prodger, Saidiya Hartman, Jennifer Nelson, Rebecca Donner, Tiffany Florvil, Fushcia-Ann Hoover, Alia Farid, Joelle Abi-Rached, Jennie Stephens, Aida Hernandez Castillo, Diana Pardo, Oscar Lopez Gibson, Priya Sen, Matthieu Aikins, Peter Gray, Bill Dougherty, Maya Wilson, Maren Wong and Annika Khandelwal. Thank you to the Robert B. Silvers Foundation for a grant towards the writing of a piece on the Katz papers which evolved, eventually, into this book, and to Thea Lenarduzzi and all at the TLS for publishing it.

Thank you to so many archivists and librarians who have guided me through their collections, sent scans or advised me during visits. I'm grateful to all at the Denison Library of Scripps College, Claremont, where I greatly enjoyed perusing the Addison M. Metcalf Collection of Gertrude Steiniana, to Gabrielle Dean and Paul Espinosa at Johns Hopkins University Libraries for help exploring the Robert A. Wilson Collection of Gertrude Stein materials, to Tracey Schuster and all at the Getty Library for the Banyan Press and Claude Fredericks archives, to Jim Moske, Melissa Bowling, Lauren Rozati and Linzey Rice at the Metropolitan Museum of Art for papers relating to the Picasso portrait and for access to their collection of Stein photographs, to Rebecca Johnson Melvin and Valerie Stenner at the University of Delaware for the John Malcolm Brinnin Papers, to Matthew Mariner at UC Denver for the Donald Sutherland papers, to Monica Blank at the Rockefeller Archive Center for information relating to Leon Katz's Ford Foundation grant, to Gayle O'Hara at Butler University for the Allegra Stewart papers, to Katy Rawdon at Temple University for the Kate Buss papers, to the Lilly Library for the Harold and Virginia Knapik papers, to the Charles Deering McCormick Library of Special Collections for the Dick Higgins Archive, to the University of Iowa Libraries and the McFarlin Library at the University of Tulsa for their collections of Julian Sawyer papers, to the Chesney Archives of Johns Hopkins University and the Baltimore Museum of Art's Claribel and Etta Cone Collections for material relating to Stein's time as a medical student, to the Fales Library and Special Collections at NYU for the Judson Memorial Church Archive, to Columbia University Special Collections for the Random House records and the papers of Rosalind Miller, to the Princeton University Library Special Collections for the Charles William White Papers, to the Z. Smith Reynolds Library Special Collections and Archives for the Gertrude Stein and Conference Press Collection, to the Library of Congress for the Janet Flanner and Solita Solano papers, to the Bancroft Library for the Annette Rosenshine papers, to the UCLA Library Special Collections for the Gilbert Harrison Collection of Gertrude Stein materials, to the Harry Ransom Center for its Gertrude Stein Collection, and to the staff of the local history museum in Culoz. Thank you to Gitika Sanjay for research help at the Bancroft, and Maggie Mitts at the HRC.

I'm so grateful to all the Stein scholars who have shared their expertise over the course of this project. It was an enormous privilege to correspond with Edward Burns from the summer of 2020 until his death in November 2023: his encyclopaedic knowledge of Stein studies and personal experience of so many characters in this story provided a wealth of detail in emails I treasure. His papers, amassed since he began work on Stein in the 1960s, are now available at the Beinecke and I'm very glad to have been able to refer to them. He directed me to Sarah Kornfeld, who put me in touch with her father Larry: it was a huge pleasure to be able to interview him about his work on Stein with the Judson Poets' Theater, shortly before his death in August 2023. Thank you to Fred Katz, for memories of his father shared over a wonderful Sachertorte, to Ben Smith, Leon Katz's research assistant, for his memories of working with Katz on the notebooks, and to Cynthia Shane Smith for putting me in touch with Ben. Thank you to Marc Harrington for sharing excerpts of Claude Fredericks' journal as well as incredible photos of the 'Banyan Tots', to Martha Ullman West for letting me read her grandmother Alice Ullman's unpublished memoir of her years in Paris, to Carleen Gerber for her memories of her uncle Donald Gallup, to Linda Simon for sharing her correspondence with Max White and others, to Steven Watson for sharing his interviews with Virgil Thomson, Robert Bartlett Haas and others, to Glenn Johnston for alerting me to a trove of rare Stein volumes at Mercer Street Books, and to Emily Setina and Susannah Hollister for conversations and archival directions on the rich links between Stein and the New York School poets. Thank you to the late Gwendolyn Leick, granddaughter of Mabel Haynes, for sharing her memories and research, and for the gift of many of her own Stein books. Very special thanks to Catharine R. Stimpson and to Logan Esdale for invaluable comments on the manuscript and their much-appreciated support of this project.

A huge thank you to Caroline Dawnay, Sophie Scard and Kat Aitken at United Agents, to Kathryn Belden and Madison Thân at Scribner, and to everyone at Faber: Laura Hassan, Ella Griffiths, Sara Cheraghlou, Josh Smith, Jess Kim, Jo Stimfield, Kate Ward, Sam Matthews, Sophie Harris, Helen Bleck and Melanie Gee. I'm so grateful to all the friends, editors, scholars and fellow writers – in London, New York, New Haven and Cambridge – whose interest and enthusiasm have made this project such a joy from start to finish: to all who have shared their knowledge, suggested leads, sent photographs from libraries, listened to anguish over book structure, and invited me to write or think more deeply about Stein. Thank you to Nick During, who has lived this book with me and filled the years with happiness and fun. Thank you you most of all to Alison Wade, who's made possible everything I've done.

Gertrude Stein copyright material is quoted with permission from Stanford G. Gann, Jr, Literary Executor of the Estate of Gertrude Stein.

Quotations from *Ernest Hemingway, Selected Letters 1917–1961* edited by Carlos Baker, copyright © 1981 by Carlos Baker and The Ernest Hemingway Foundation, Inc. Reprinted with the permission of Scribner, an imprint of Simon & Schuster LLC. All rights reserved. Quotations from *A Moveable Feast* by Ernest Hemingway copyright © 1935 by Charles Scribner's Sons. Copyright renewed 1963 by Mary Hemingway. Reprinted with the permission of Scribner, an imprint of Simon & Schuster LLC. All rights reserved.

'Gertrude Stein' by Mina Loy quoted with permission from Roger Conover, Literary Executor of the Estate of Mina Loy.

Quotations from the Mabel Dodge Luhan Papers. Yale Collection of American Literature, Beinecke Rare Book and Manuscript Library © Yale University. All rights reserved.

Kenneth Koch's 'Stein Talk' is quoted with permission from Karen Koch.

Quotations from Donald Gallup's writings by permission of Carleen Gerber.

Quotations from *Letters by Virginia Woolf* published by Chatto & Windus, copyright © Quentin Bell and Angelica Garnett, 1910, 1917, 1919, 1920, 1924, 1975. Reprinted by permission of The Random House Group Limited.

Quotations from Richard Wright reprinted by permission of John Hawkins and Associates, Inc. Copyright © Richard Wright, 1945 and 1946.

Quotations from Leon Katz's writings by permission of Fred and Elia Katz.

INDEX

In this index, the following abbreviations are used: *AABT* – *The Autobiography of Alice B. Toklas*; ABT – Alice B. Toklas; GS – Gertrude Stein. Page references in italics are to illustrations.

Imbs, Bravig, 401
Izieu children's home, 175, 380

Jacot, Nellie, 295–6, 424
James, Henry, 39, 48, 90, 133, 146, 241, 242, 299, 412, 417
James, William, 21–2, 23, 24, 63, 70, 129
Jameson, Fredric, 361
Jessye, Eva, 137
Jewish identity: of GS, 16, 17, 54–5, 162, 174, 176, 187, 228, 306, 393, 394, 416; and blackness, 228, 416; *see also* antisemitism
Johns, Jasper, 432
Johns Hopkins Medical School, 24–7, *26*, 29, 228, 252, 253, 391, 396
Johnson, Ray, 432
Johnston, Jill, 433, 437
Jolas, Eugene, 116, 152
Jolas, Maria, 116, 152, 321
Joseph, Daniel, 339
Joyce, James: as rival to GS, 93–4, 95, 116, 197; *A Portrait of the Artist as a Young Man*, 93; *Ulysses*, 93, 94, 134, 152; T. S. Eliot on, 95; *Finnegans Wake*, 117, 188, 217; on GS, 117; Wyndham Lewis on, 117; biography by Herbert Gorman, 242; ABT on, 334; biography by Richard Ellmann, 334
Judson Poets' Theater, 355–6

Kahnweiler, Daniel-Henry, 80, 160, 161, 215, 281, 336, 400
Kaprow, Allan, 354
Katz, Leon, *292*; character, 246; early interest in GS, 246; adapts *Melanctha* for theatre, 246; transcribes and annotates GS's notebooks, 247–50, 254–8, 288, 357, 369–70; interviews Mabel Weeks, 251–2, 258–9; interviews Emma Lootz Erving, 252–3; interviews ABT, 9–10, 289–306, 307, 308–11, 370, 371–2; interviews Francis Rose, 307; interviews Bernard Berenson, 307; helps with ABT's cookbook, 309, 318; returns to America, 314; ABT misses after interviews, 314, 323; 'The First Making of *The Making of Americans*', 356–7; adapts *The Making of Americans* into libretto, 356; interviews Annette Rosenshine, 357–8; other work, 357; writes introduction to new edition of *Q.E.D.*, 359; playscripts about GS and ABT, 370–1; evades interview with Janet Malcolm, 372; completes study of notebooks, 9, 369, 436
Kenner, Hugh: *The Pound Era*, 334

Khokhlova, Olga, 111, 215
Knapik, Virginia, 346, 428
Knoblauch, May (née Bookstaver): family, 27; relationship with Mabel Haynes, 27–8, 31, 58–9; relationship with GS, 27–8, 58–9; feminist activism, 29, 265; GS's jealousy, 31, 252, 253; GS writes about relationship with, 34–5, 45, 121–3, 253; in GS's 'Diagram Book', 45, 253; marriage, 58–9, 258; finds publishers for GS's works, 59, 63–4, 258–9; ABT's jealousy, 123, 126, 225, 230, 259, 297–8, 340, 367–9, 371–2, 391; other literary ventures, 265; death, 265; Leon Katz's disclosure of GS's 'hopeless love affair' with, 357; *see also Q.E.D.* (GS)
Knowles, Alison, 377, 432–3
Koch, Kenneth, 376
Kooning, Willem de, 432
Kornfeld, Lawrence, 355, 356
Kostelanetz, Richard, 434
Kreymborg, Alfred, 78

Ladder, The (magazine), 359
Lane, John, 84
L=A=N=G=U=A=G=E (magazine), 358, 434
Larsen, Nella, 219, 220, 228
Laughlin, James, 404–5
Laurencin, Marie, 45, 150, 294
Laval, Pierre, 171, 181, 186
Lebender, Lena, 252
lectures: Oxbridge, 98–101; American tour, 139–50, *148*, 156, 209, 243–4, 298, 308, 318
Léger, Fernand: *Ballet mécanique*, 90
Lesbian Avengers, 360, *360*
Lescher, Robert, 329–30, 332
Levin, Calman A., 362
Levy, Harriet, 48, 49, 51–2, 56–7, 60–1, 294, 393, 394
Lewis, Wilmarth Sheldon, 157
Lewis, Wyndham, 116–17, 334
Library of America edition of GS's works, 361
Life (magazine), 89, *177*, 192–3
Little Review, The (magazine), 93–4, 231–2, 265
Liveright (publishers), 286
Living Theatre, 284–7, *285*, 354, 355, 423, 433
London: GS alone in, 30–1; GS and ABT's 'honeymoon' in, 79; Bloomsbury Group, 84; Grafton Galleries, 84; GS and ABT in before outbreak of First World War, 83–4; Edith Sitwell throws party for GS, 100; GS ballet premiere in, 157; Picasso retrospective, 336

298; *Doctor Faustus Lights the Lights*, 284–7, 285, 433; *Everybody's Autobiography*, 146, 159, 196, 206, 232, 317; *Fernhurst*, 359; 'Finally George', 114; Flaubert translation, 39, 40, 223; *Four in America*, 133, 140, 207, 208; *Four Saints in Three Acts* (opera libretto) *see* Four Saints in Three Acts; 'Gentle Julia', 85; *The Geographical History of America*, 155–6, 195, 419; *Geography and Plays*, 92–3; *G.M.P. (Matisse Picasso and Gertrude Stein)*, 120, 269, 355; *How to Write*, 120; *Ida*, 159–60, 407; *In Circles*, 356; *Ladies' Voices*, 423; *Last Operas and Plays*, 286; *Lectures in America*, 141, 146–8, 406; 'Let Us Be Easily Careful', 85; *Life* magazine report on Germany, 192–3; *Lifting Belly*, 87, 360, 361–2; *A Long Gay Book*, 60, 69, 120, 158; *Lucy Church Amiably*, 119, 120, 121, 355; 'A Lyrical Opera / Made by Two / To Be Sung', 105, 296; *The Making of Americans see* The Making of Americans; 'A Manoir', 368; *Many Many Women*, 120; 'Mildred's Thoughts', 159; 'Miss Furr and Miss Skeene', 315; 'The Modern Jew', 55; *The Mother of Us All* (opera libretto), 194–6, 284, 361; 'A Movie', 120; *Mrs Reynolds*, 166–7, 275, 373, 408; 'My Life with Dogs', 407; 'Natural Phenomena', 366; 'The New Hope in Our "Sad Young Men"', 194; 'No', 85; *A Novel of Thank You*, 208, 275, 332, 400; *Operas and Plays*, 120; 'Painted Lace', 85; *Painted Lace*, 323; *Paris France*, 162, 174, 190, 412; *Patriarchal Poetry*, 196, 327; 'Portrait of Constance Fletcher', 412; 'Portrait of Mabel Dodge at the Villa Curonia', 73– 4, 93; *Portraits and Prayers*, 141, 149; 'Preciosilla', 69, 106; 'Prothalemium for Bobolink and His Louisa', 408; *Q.E.D. see* Q.E.D.; 'Rue de Rennes', 303; 'Sacred Emily', 147–9; 'A Saint in Seven', 103; *Saints and Singing*, 433; *Saturday Evening Post* articles, 189–90; *Selected Writings*, 216, 261; 'Sentences and Paragraphs', 115, 232, 383, 384; 'She Bowed to Her Brother', 425–6; 'Short Sentences', 368; *A Sonatina Followed by Another*, 232–3; *Stanzas in Meditation*, 121, 208, 275, 367–9, 432; 'Superstitions', 407; *The Superstitions of Fred Anneday, Annday, Anday A Novel of Real Life*, 407; 'Susie Asado', 69, 72, 106; *Tender Buttons see* Tender

Buttons; 'They Must. Be Wedded. To Their Wife', 157; *Things as They Are* (originally *Q.E.D.*) *see* Q.E.D.; *Three Lives (The Good Anna, The Gentle Lena* and *Melanctha) see* Three Lives; *To Do: A Book of Alphabets and Birthdays*, 162; translation into Braille, 405; translation of Hugnet's poetry, 107, 120; translation of Pétain's speeches, 184–5, 186–7, 372, 410, 415; translations into French, 107, 140, 152, 174; translations into Italian, 418; translations into German, 401; 'Two: Gertrude Stein and Her Brother', 275; undergraduate essays and stories, 24, 55, 168, 407; *Useful Knowledge*, 119; 'A Valentine for Sherwood Anderson', 92; *Wars I Have Seen*, 178, 183–5, 187, 190, 193, 373; 'Water Pipe', 343; 'We Came A History', 434; 'We Eat: A Cookbook by Alice B. Toklas and Gertrude Stein', 316–17, 318; *What Happened*, 433; 'The Winner Loses', 164; *The World Is Round*, 244, 432; Yale Edition of the Unpublished Writings, 275–9, 282, 319, 323, 332, 362, 365, 368, 429; *Yes Is for a Very Young Man*, 191, 411

Stein, Michael (GS's brother): childhood and adolescence, 16–18, 273; in San Francisco, 19–20, 37, 43; ABT on, 20; manages GS's financial affairs, 20, 36, 37, 130; Paris apartment, 37, 48; jewellery designs, 393; patronage of Matisse, 38; purchases *Femme au Chapeau* from GS, 85; returns to California, 160; death, 178, 270

Stein, Rose Ellen (Julian Stein's wife), 142, 405

Stein, Roubina (GS's niece-in-law), 273–4, 319, 335–6, 429

Stein, Sarah (GS's sister-in-law), 28, 37, 38, 43, 48, 50, 178, 273, 349, 350; Matisse on, 392

Stein, Simon (GS's brother), 17, 18, 20, 270

Stein, Solomon (GS's uncle), 17, 271, 392

Stettheimer, Florine, 138

Steward, Samuel, 363–4; *Murder Is Murder*, 382–3; *Parisian Lives*, 426

Stewart, Allegra: *Gertrude Stein and the Present*, 435

Stieglitz, Alfred, 64, 258–9

Strachey, Lytton, 84

Stravinsky, Igor: *Rite of Spring*, 76, 287

Sutherland, Donald: GS and ABT meet, 244; scholarship, 244–5, 281; ABT on, 245; on Yale Edition advisory committee, 275; on ABT, 281–2, 315, 338, 427; correspondence with ABT, 291, 292, 293, 338; road trip with ABT, 325; supports ABT financially, 345

Sutton, William, 197

Tavernier, René, 174

Taylor, Father Edward, 324, 325, 428, 431

Taylor, Louise, 431

Tender Buttons (GS), 70–2, 76–8, 116, 358, 407, 433, 434–5

Tender Buttons Press, 435

Testimony Against Gertrude Stein, 152–3

Thomson, Virgil: on–off friendship with GS, 106–7, 114, 194–5; settings of GS's poetry, 106; operas (with GS) *see Four Saints in Three Acts*; *The Mother of Us All*; contributes to ABT's cookbook, 318; on GS/ABT relationship, 340; supports ABT financially, 345, 346; on importance of GS notebooks, 357; preface to Yale Edition volume, 417; mentors John Cage, 432

Three Lives (GS): *The Gentle Lena*, 40, 58–60, 252; *The Good Anna*, 40, 58–60, 223, 252; *Melanctha*, 40–2, 45, 58–60, 97, 140, 193–4, 220, 226, 227–9, 246, 252, 271, 416; publication, 58,

59, 85, 134, 258, 297; critical reception, 58, 59–60, 84, 97, 120, 134, 193, 219–20; French translation, 140; Etta Cone's involvement, 151–2; Leo Stein's opinions on, 302

Time (magazine), 128–9, 320, 340

Todd, Dorothy, 400

Toklas, Alice B.:

CHARACTER AND CHARACTERISTICS: attire, 8, 48, 56–7, 110, 192; smoking, 8, 47, 48, 113, 172, 177, 215, 291, 293, *300*, 314, 330, 337, 345, 383; hostility towards visitors, 8, 108–9, 298, 357; antipathy to Hemingway, 108, 150, 223, 291, 342–4; voice, 108, 337; moustache, 110; performative subservience, 110, 310; portrayal in *AABT*, 125–6, 215–16; 'Mama Woojums', 149; desire for privacy, 210, 230–2, 235–6, 242–3, 362–3, 364; in GS's notebooks, 248–9, 255–6, 309–10; 'old maid mermaid' personality type, 300, 341, 425; American identity, 306; 'St Thérèse' personality type, 309–10; inscrutability, 310; militancy, 315; taste for luxury, 330, 345, 346; handwriting, 345; obituary description, 347

LIFE: family, 47, 48, 210, 306, 308; childhood and early adulthood, 47, 241, 296, 306, 308, 310, 317; musical talents, 8, 310; friendships with women, 295–6; flirtations with men, 296, 424; goes to Paris, 48; in Italy, 56–7, 62, 336–7; inheritance income, 57, 85–6; moves into 27 rue de Fleurus, 61; 27 rue de Fleurus and 5 rue Christine apartments *see under* Paris; cooking, 8, 61, 192, 234, 293, 315, 316–17, 318–19, 330, 383; in Spain, 69; in London, 83–4, 100; in Wiltshire, 84–5; in Majorca, 86–7; war work, 87–9, *88*; godmother to Ernest Hemingway's child, 96; Bilignin home *see* Bilignin; dogs *see* Basket and Basket II, Pépé; gardening, 161, 264; remains in France during war, 160–3, 165–6, 170–6, 190; knitting and needlework, 164, 317, *350*, 351, 383, 425; in Germany, 192; grieves for GS, 205, 213–14, 215, 241, 266, 276–7; friendships, 205, 210, 213, 214, 215, 266, 280, 295–6, 299, 308, 313, 314–15, 317, 318, 324, 325, 339, 344–6, 347, 363–4, 428, 431; selective cooperation with GS scholars, 242–6, 291, 306, 321–2, 335, 417–18, 426; difficulties with Allan Stein, 273–4; financial hardship, 273–4, 291, 326–7, 344; funds Bernard Faÿ's prison escape, 281–2, 422; interviews with Leon Katz, 9–10, 289–306,

A ROSE IS A ROSE IS A ROSE.